THE WAR IN
EAST AFRICA
1939–1943

DESPATCHES FROM THE FRONT

The Commanding Officers' Reports from the Field and at Sea

THE WAR IN EAST AFRICA 1939–1943

From the Campaign Against Italy in British Somaliland to Operation Ironclad, the Invasion of Madagascar

Introduced and compiled by
John Grehan and Martin Mace
with additional research by
Sara Mitchell

Pen & Sword
MILITARY

First published in Great Britain in 2015 by
PEN & SWORD MILITARY
An imprint of
Pen & Sword Books Ltd
47 Church Street
Barnsley
South Yorkshire
S70 2AS

ISBN 978-1-78346-223-0

Typeset by Concept, Huddersfield, West Yorkshire HD4 5JL.
Printed and bound in England by CPI Group (UK) Ltd, Croydon CR0 4YY.

Pen & Sword Books Ltd incorporates the imprints of Pen & Sword Archaeology,
Atlas, Aviation, Battleground, Discovery, Family History, History, Maritime,
Military, Naval, Politics, Railways, Select, Social History, Transport, True Crime,
and Claymore Press, Frontline Books, Leo Cooper, Praetorian Press,
Remember When, Seaforth Publishing and Wharncliffe.

For a complete list of Pen & Sword titles please contact
PEN & SWORD BOOKS LIMITED
47 Church Street, Barnsley, South Yorkshire, S70 2AS, England
E-mail: enquiries@pen-and-sword.co.uk
Website: www.pen-and-sword.co.uk

Contents

List of Plates

A unit of the Somaliland Camel Corps on patrol in 1940.

Somaliland Camel Corps distinctive dress, based on the standard British Army khaki drill, but also included a knitted woollen pullover and drill patches on the shoulders. Shorts were worn.

Men of the Somaliland Camel Corps on patrol along the Somaliland-Abyssinian border in the summer of 1940.

A drawing depicting Captain Eric Charles Twelves Wilson in action during the so-called Battle of Tug Argan in August 1940.

A contemporary artist's depiction of Emperor Haile Selassie with two British Army officers.

Drawn by the artist William Timyn for the Ministry of Information during the war, this is a portrait of Field Marshal Viscount Archibald Wavell.

The vast panorama of Diego Suarez Bay as viewed from Fort d'Ankorike, a machine-gun emplacement in Antsirane.

The pillboxes, adjacent to the main Antsirane road.

The same pillboxes today.

Some of the fifty Royal Marines who were landed in the destroyer HMS *Anthony* at Diego Suarez.

A conference on board HMS *Ramillies* after the surrender of Diego-Suarez.

The pipes of the Royal Scots Fusiliers lead the victory parade through Antsirane after the French surrender.

The 25-pounders of the 56th East African Artillery firing at the French positions on the Andriamanalina Ridge.

The advance down Madagascar continues – a Ford 1-ton truck on the road heading southwards towards Antananarivo.

General Legentilhomme arrives at Tamatave to assume the post of High Commissioner, as the representative of the Free French National Committee.

The memorial erected by the Engineers of the Royal Scots Fusiliers to those Scots killed at Diego Suarez.

Introduction

The advantage in any fight is with the person who can land the first blow. In East Africa in 1940 that advantage lay with the Italians. Uncertain of Italian intentions, though aware of their Fascist sympathies, Britain strove to avoid any action that might provoke them into declaring war. Nevertheless, when General Sir Archibald Wavell's Middle East Command was given responsibility for the military forces in British Somaliland he urged the British Government to allow him to increase the Protectorate's garrison and prepare defensive positions. That was in January 1940. Until the reinforcement began, British Somaliland was held by the Camel Corps which consisted of only fourteen British officers, 400 African Askaris and 150 African reservists. A further seventeen officers and twenty Warrant and Non-Commissioned officers arrived from Southern Rhodesia in October 1939 to bring the total up 600 men to defend a country greater in size than England and Wales.

The War Office had considered the demilitarisation or complete evacuation of British Somaliland as such a small force could not possibly hope to stop any Italian moves against the Protectorate. Wavell, though, was reluctant to give up the country. The inland approaches to the capital of British Somaliland, Berbera, were through a crescent of rugged hills, crossed by just six roads capable of carrying motor vehicles, only two of which led to Berbera, the other four running to Djibouti, the capital of neighbouring French Somaliland.

As these two roads ran towards Berbera they travelled through difficult passes. One of these was very narrow and easily defended, whilst the other, the Tug Argan Gap, was some four miles wide. It was obvious which route the Italians would take if they invaded. This was where Wavell would build his defences and make a stand. All six of the roads passed through some form of defile and Wavell planned to defend these as well, to slow down the Italian advance and inflict casualties upon the enemy. The whole of this defensive plan would be conducted in conjunction with the French.

Just before war broke out with Italy, the 1st and 2nd battalions of the Northern Rhodesia Regiment of the King's African Rifles reached British Somaliland along with a battery of artillery and the 1st Battalion, 2nd Punjab Regiment, plus, at almost the last moment, the 2nd Battalion the Black Watch and 3/15 Punjab Regiment. Wavell's hopes were raised but then, on 17 June 1940, news reached the Middle East of the fall of France and the French Somaliland forces were withdrawn from the defence of the passes. The small British and Commonwealth force was alone.

When the Italians attacked it was, according to Wavell, with some twenty Colonial battalions, four Italian battalions, four groups of Pack Artillery, two groups of Medium Artillery, about thirty tanks, two sections of Armoured Cars and eleven groups of native irregulars – though research suggests that these numbers may have been somewhat inflated. The Italians also had strong air support.

The small British force could not hold out indefinitely but it did inflict heavy casualties upon the Italians before withdrawing. Eventually, the troops were evacuated and the Italians occupied the country. Wavell was criticised for failing to hold British Somaliland but he replied by claiming that the troops had conducted a textbook withdrawal in the face of superior numbers.

The second of Wavell's despatches in this volume includes reports from Lieutenant General W. Platt and Lieutenant General A. Cunningham, which describe the British operations which saw the conquest, or re-conquest, of most of East Africa from the Italians. Amounting to more than 74,000 words, this is a very comprehensive account of the period up to July 1941 and includes extensive appendices which detail the orders of battle of the East African forces at various times throughout this period and reveals the location and distribution of the supporting South African Air Force squadrons.

The area of operations was vast, extending over more than 500,000 square miles including Eritrea, Kenya, Ethiopia and Somaliland. Nevertheless, by May 1941 Italian resistance had practically ceased to exist.

Defeating the Italians was, in a sense, straightforward as the enemy was clear and obvious, but in French Somaliland the situation was far more complicated. As France was no longer involved in the war, French Somaliland was, theoretically, neutral. The Vichy French authorities refused to assist the British in any way and this was particularly the case with the Vichy Governor of Djibouti, who, according to Platt, was, "besides being fanatically anti-British", "reported to be self-opinionated, obstinate and proud to an extent which precluded all reasonable thinking. He had established himself as a complete dictator and used the death penalty ruthlessly against any who showed any pro-Free French leanings."

At first Britain allowed the passage of supplies into French Somaliland but, with the Governor still showing no signs of "reasonable thinking", a strict blockade, both on land and sea, was imposed. This, of course, further inflamed French animosity towards the UK – but it worked. After 101 days of blockade the Vichy French asked for negotiations to begin, which resulted in the occupation of the country by Free French forces.

On 15 September 1941, the East Africa Command was formed with Platt at its head. By this time the Italians had been defeated on almost every front and this was confirmed with their final surrender in January 1942. Platt's despatch on the period up to 8 January 1943 deals with, as he states, mainly with policing duties over the wide area under his command, including the Indian Ocean, which is the subject of the fourth despatch.

This despatch is the report on the capture of Diego Suarez by Rear-Admiral E.N. Syfret. The sudden and dramatic entry of Japan into the Second World War with its attacks on Pearl Harbor and Malaya, placed British territories in the Far East under immediate threat. Hong Kong and Singapore soon fell and Japanese forces drove into Burma.

So successful were the Japanese, it appeared that India, for so long the jewel in the crown of the British Empire, might soon be overrun. Only the most urgent reinforcement of the British forces in India could, it appeared, prevent disaster.

With the route through the Suez Canal denied to British shipping due to Axis control of the Mediterranean, the only way that reinforcements could be sent to India was around Africa. This shipping route, after rounding the Cape of Good Hope, travelled past the island of Madagascar. It was feared that if the Japanese could establish submarine and air bases on Madagascar they would be able to cut that vital shipping route. Consequently, Churchill agreed to send a large force to occupy Madagascar's main naval and military base of Diego Suarez. The only problem with this was that Madagascar was a French colony and it was held by pro-Vichy forces.

Knowing the difficulty that Britain had had with the Vichy authorities in French Somaliland there was little prospect of the regime in Madagascar agreeing to a take-over by either the Free French or the British. The place would have to be taken by force.

A large assault force, including three infantry brigades supported by tanks and artillery was despatched from the UK in March 1942 under conditions of the utmost secrecy to prevent the news reaching the ears of the Japanese who might seek to pre-empt the British move. Placed in charge of Operation *Ironclad* was Admiral Sir Edward Neville Syfret who commanded in addition to the land forces, the battleship *Ramillies*, the aircraft carriers HMS *Indomitable* and HMS *Illustrious* with eight squadrons of fighters and torpedo-bombers, and twenty-five other warships, plus landing ships. It would be the largest offensive operation undertaken by Britain since the Japanese had joined in the war.

Though leaflets were dropped shortly after the British attack upon Diego Suarez began on 5 May, inviting the French to surrender, the defenders opened fire on the Fleet Air Arm aircraft, clearly indicating that they were determined to oppose any British occupation. As it transpired, the French proved resilient opponents and for some time the operation hung in the balance as the British ground forces encountered well-prepared defences and stubborn resistance.

The deadlock was broken when a destroyer, HMS *Anthony*, braved the big guns of the coastal batteries and raced through Diego Suarez harbour at night to unload a party of Royal Marines in the enemy's rear.

The eventual capture of Diego Suarez came none too soon, as just three weeks later, Japanese submarines entered the harbour and crippled HMS *Ramillies*. Syfret's despatch on Operation *Ironclad* includes the report from the Army commander involved, Major-General R.G. 'Bob' Sturges, C.B., Royal Marines.

Despite their loss of Diego Suarez, so resolutely opposed to the British were the Vichy authorities, they refused to allow the remainder of the island to come under British administration. As there were suspicions that the French were permitting the Japanese to use the other ports on the island, the decision was taken in July 1942 to mount an operation to occupy the whole of Madagascar, the fourth largest island in the world.

Somewhat confusingly, the narrative of this operation, code-named *Stream-Line-Jane* is related in Platt's East Africa Command despatch and to follow the subsequent activities in Madagascar the reader will have to return to that despatch.

The operation began on 10 September 1942. Once again the French resisted. British and African forces landed at the ports of Majunga on the island's west coast and Tamatave, on the east. Through extremely difficult terrain and in torrential monsoon rain, the troops pushed southwards to the capital Tananarive (now called Antananarivo).

Even after Tananarive had been seized by the British forces, the French withdrew further south, refusing to capitulate. Finally, on 6 November 1942, Armand Léon Annet, hemmed-in on all sides by British and African troops, surrendered. After a short period of British control, Madagascar was handed over to the Free French.

*   *   *

The objective of this book is to reproduce the despatches of the likes of Wavell, Platt and Syfret as they first appeared to the general public some seventy years ago. They have not been modified or edited in any way and are therefore the original and unique words of the commanding officers as they saw things at the time.

The only change is the manner in which the footnotes are presented, in that they are shown at the end of each despatch rather than at the bottom of the relevant page as they appear in the original despatch. Any grammatical or spelling errors (such as Platt's spelling of the Ethiopian capital as Addis Abeba) have been left uncorrected to retain the authenticity of the documents.

Abbreviations

A/S	anti-submarine
A Tk.	Anti-tank
AA	Anti-aircraft
AC	Army Co-Operation
ADMS	Assistant Director Medical Services
ADOS	Assistant Director of Ordnance Services
AFC	Air Force Cross
AFV	Armoured Fighting Vehicle
ALC	Assault Landing Craft
AMC	Armed Merchant Cruisers
AMLO	Assistant Military Landing Officer
AOC	Air Officer Commanding
AOC-in-C	Air Officer Commanding-in-Chief
AQMG	Assistant Quartermaster General
Armd.	Armoured
B NCOs	British Non Commissioned Officers
BGS	Brigadier, General Staff
BLO	Bombardment Liaison Officer
Bn./Btn	Battalion
Bty.	Battery
C. in C.	Commander-in-Chief
CB	Companion of the Order of Bath
CBE	Commander of the Most Excellent Order of the British Empire
CD	Coastal Defence
Cdr	Commander
CMG	Companion of the Most Distinguished Order of Saint Michael and Saint George
CO	Commanding Officer
COS	Chief of Staff
CPO	Chief Political Officer
CRA	Commander Royal Artillery
CRE	Commander Royal Engineers
cwt.	centum weight (hundredweight)
DADOS	Deputy Assistant Director of Ordnance Services
DAPM	Deputy Assistant Provost Marshal

DCPO	District Chief Political Officer
DEOR	Duke of Edinburgh's Own Rifles
DF	Destroyer Force
DFC	Distinguished Flying Cross
Div.	Division
DMS	Director Medical Services
DR	Despatch Rider
DSC	Distinguished Service Cross
DSO	Distinguished Service Order
EA	East Africa/East African
FAA	Fleet Air Arm
FANY	First Aid Nursing Yeomanry
FF	Frontier Force
FOC	Flag Officer Commanding
FOO	Forward Observation Officer
ft.	foot/feet
GBE	Knight Grand Cross of the Most Excellent Order of the British Empire
GC	(Brigade) Gold Coast
GCB	Knight Grand Cross of the Most Honourable Order of the Bath
Gen.	General
GHQ	General Headquarters
GOC	General Officer Commanding
GSO1/2	General Staff Officer Grade 1/2
HE	High Explosive
HM	His Majesty
HMAS	His Majesty's Australian Ship
HMG	Heavy Machine Gun
HMNS	Her Majesty's Netherlands Ship
HMS	His Majesty's Ship
Hows.	Howitzer(s)
HQ	Headquarters
HRH	His Royal Highness
Inf. Bde.	Infantry Brigade
KAR	King's African Rifles
KBE	Knight Commander of the Most Excellent Order of the British Empire
KCB	Knight Commander of the Most Honourable Order of the Bath
KCMG	Knight Commander of The Most Distinguished Order of Saint Michael and Saint George
KCSI	Knight Commander of The Most Exalted Order of the Star of India

KCVO	Knight Commander of the Royal Victorian Order
L. of C.	Line(s) of Communication
LLD	Doctorate of Laws
LMG	Light Machine Gun
M/S	minesweeping
MBE	Member of the Most Excellent Order of the British Empire
MC	Military Cross
MD	Medicinae Doctor (Doctor of **Medicine)**
MM	Military Medal
MMG	Medium Machine Gun
MNBDO	Mobile Naval Base Defence Organisation
MRCP	Member of the Royal College of Physicians
MT	Motor Transport
Mtn.	Mountain
MV	Motor Vessel
MVO	Member of The Royal Victorian Order
NCSO	Naval Control Service Officer
NLO	Naval Liaison Officer
NMR	Natal Mounted Rifles
NOIC	Naval Officer in Charge
OBE	Officer of the Most Excellent Order of the British Empire
OC	Officer Commanding
OETA	Occupied Enemy Territory Administration
Ops.	Operations
OR	Other Rank(s)
para.	paragraph
pdr.	pounder
QMG	Quartermaster General
R/T	Receiver-Transmitter/Radio Transmitter
RA	Royal Artillery
RAF	Royal Air Force
RASC	Royal Army Service Corps
RDF	Radio Direction Finding (Radar)
RE	Royal Engineers
Regt.	Regiment
RFA	Royal Fleet Auxiliary
RIASC	Royal Indian Army Service Corps
RM	Royal Marines
RNC	Royal Natal Carbineers
RSF	Royal Scots Fusiliers
RWF	Royal Welsh Fusiliers
SA	South African
SAAF	South African Air Force
SAEC	South African Engineer Corps

SBG (bridges)	Small Box Girder (bridges)
SDF	Sudan Defence Force
SNO	Senior Naval Officer
SNOL	Senior Naval Officer Landing
SRAF	Southern Rhodesian Air Force
SS	Steam Ship
TS	Transvaal Scottish
UDF	Union Defence Force(s)
V/S	visual signal
VC	Victoria Cross
VD	Volunteer Officer's Decoration
VHF	Very High Frequency
W/T Sets	Wireless Telegraphy/Wireless
yds.	yards

1

GENERAL SIR ARCHIBALD P. WAVELL'S DESPATCH ON OPERATIONS IN SOMALILAND, SEPTEMBER 1939 TO AUGUST 1940

The War Office, May, 1946
OPERATIONS IN THE SOMALILAND PROTECTORATE, 1939–1940

PREFACE BY THE WAR OFFICE

1. The following despatch deals with the period from the outbreak of war with Germany in September, 1939, to the evacuation of British Forces from the Somaliland Protectorate in August, 1940, in the face of Italian invasion. It covers the preparatory stage before Italy's entry into the war on 11th June, 1940, and the brief period of operations from 5th to 18th August, during which the small British Garrison fought a fierce and skilful withdrawal action against overwhelming numbers.

2. This is the personal narrative of General Sir Archibald (now Field Marshal Lord) Wavell, Commander-in-Chief, British Land Forces in the Middle East. As such he was responsible for preparations over a vast area against the possible entry of Italy into the war on the side of Germany. When this occurred in June, 1940, he was faced with the problem of disposing pitifully small resources in manpower and material to meet enemy aggression in an area which included Egypt, Palestine, Transjordan, Sudan, Cyprus, Iraq, British Somaliland, the shores of the Persian Gulf and East Africa. The United Kingdom at the same time was facing a still more desperate situation caused by the fall of France and the apparent imminence of a German invasion.

3. No commander could have been satisfied with the inadequate resources available and it is understandable that the War Cabinet should have appeared to General Wavell to be preoccupied with the paramount task of the defence of the home country.

4. In retrospect it might appear that the policy of avoidance of any action which might give Italy cause for entering the war against the Allies was in some respects unjustified. On her eventual entry, all the disadvantages of such a policy became apparent, while the benefits which would have been gained by her continued neutrality tend to be forgotten. British Somaliland suffered particularly in lack of defence measures and intelligence of enemy dispositions owing to the original policy of complete evacuation in face of invasion. As a result of Anglo-French

Staff conversations just prior to the outbreak of war this policy was modified to the extent that the British Force was to withdraw to French Somaliland.

This policy was dictated by the general weakness of the position and by the inadvisability of expending resources on a Protectorate which had little or no strategic importance.

By December, 1939, the French had strengthened their garrisons in French Somaliland and a common defence plan and a more enterprising policy become possible. This plan was based on the defence of Jibuti and Zeilah by the French while the British defended Berbera, the capital and centre of British interests in British Somaliland.

5. The new defence policy required a change of administrative control of the forces in British Somaliland from the Colonial Office to the War Office. Owing to discussions between the War Office, Colonial Office and G.O.C.-in-C., Middle East, this change did not become effective until June, 1940, when the War Office finally assumed responsibility for the administrative control of the forces in the Protectorate.

6. Italian troops crossed the frontier on 5th August, 1940, and the small British Force, deprived of the expected support of the French garrison of Jibuti, was pressed back on the port of Berbera and successfully evacuated. Many of the troops so saved were re-deployed to return on the tide of British offensives six months later, when all lost territory was regained in the first stages of the destruction of the Italian Colonial Empire.

The following despatch was submitted to the Secretary of State for War on 12th September, 1940, by General Sir ARCHIBALD P. WAVELL, K.C.B., C.M.G., M.C., Commander-in-Chief in the Middle East.

I. – INTRODUCTION

1. For many years prior to the Italian occupation of Abyssinia in 1935–36 there had been no external threat to British Somaliland; and for the preceding 15 years the Protectorate had also been quiet internally. The military garrison had been progressively reduced until, after the financial crisis of 1931, it numbered only 14 British officers, 400 African Askaris and 150 African Reservists. This force, called the Somaliland Camel Corps, was the only military force for external or internal defence in a country of which the area was larger than that of England and Wales. In 1939 it comprised two Camel Companies, which included two Pony Troops, and one (Nyasaland) Rifle Company.

2. The Italian occupation of Abyssinia resulted in the Protectorate being faced by Italian territory throughout almost the whole length of its land frontier of over 750 miles. During the years 1936 to 1938 various proposals were considered on the defence policy to be adopted to meet this changed situation. In 1938 total de-militarisation of the Protectorate was considered as a solution, but it was eventually decided that in the event of war with Italy the role of the minute garrison

would be to impose such delay as was possible on the enemy's advance on Berbera.

3. In May, 1939, an Anglo-French conference was held at Aden, at which the defence of Jibuti and Berbera was considered. The northern coastal strip of Somaliland, at the east of which lies Berbera and at the west Jibuti, is closed in by a crescent of rugged hills through which only six motorable roads lead from the plateau of the interior. Four of these roads lead towards Jibuti and Zeilah and two towards Berbera. All six roads pass through some form of defile and it was agreed that the Allied plan should include the defence of these six defiles.

4. The two roads leading to Berbera, from Burao and Hargeisa respectively, pass through the belt of hills at the Sheikh Pass and the Tug Argan Gap. At the former the road runs through a steep and narrow pass, easily defended; but the Tug Argan Gap is some four miles wide, and was the obvious route by which the enemy would approach Berbera. In July, 1939, the sum of £900 was allotted for the defence of these two positions. Lieutenant-Colonel A.R. Chater, D.S.O., O.B.E., Royal Marines, who was O.C. Troops in Somaliland, at once began the work of organising the defence of these two passes. The money allotted was expended on the construction of concrete machine-gun posts, designed by regimental officers and constructed by the civil Public Works Department, and on providing these posts with water tanks. At the Sheikh Pass extensive demolitions of the road were prepared. Once the positions of Sheikh Pass or Tug Argan had been forced, there was no position on which a smaller force could for long delay an advance on Berbera, since the country was generally flat and open.

II. OUTBREAK OF WAR WITH GERMANY.

5. In July, 1939, approval was given for the embodiment of the Reserve; and the outbreak of war with Germany found the Somaliland Camel Corps (still at the strength given in paragraph I) disposed so that the towns of Burao and Hargeisa were covered by mounted units, while the Sheikh Pass and Tug Argan Gap were held by dismounted companies and machine-guns. In October a very valuable reinforcement of 17 officers and 20 Warrant and Non-Commissioned officers was received from Southern Rhodesia. No other reinforcements reached the Protectorate till 15th May, 1940.

The Governor's request to be allowed to enlist 50 additional men in the Camel Corps, made on 15th September, 1939, was not approved till the spring of 1940, some six months later. A recommendation submitted by myself to the War Office on 15th January, 1940, to mechanize two Camel Corps Companies was not approved until 19th May, 1940.[1]

6. I had taken over the Middle East Command at the beginning of August, 1939, and was responsible for military plans in Somaliland; but it was not until 13th January, 1940, as a result of the recent decision to defend the Protectorate, that the troops in British Somaliland came under my full operational control.

Administrative control remained under the Colonial Office till 1st June, 1940. The Camel Corps, on the outbreak of war with Germany, had been concentrated at the Sheikh Pass and Tug Argan positions, and the greater part of the Protectorate had been abandoned from a military point of view. It was obvious that the Camel Corps could not possibly hold the defences against any serious attack. It did not seem to me that this policy was consistent with our obligations towards our French Allies at Jibuti, where strong defences had been constructed, and that it would be fatal to our prestige to make so little attempt to defend the Protectorate. It did not at that time seem likely that the Italians, if they entered the war, would expend large forces in the occupation of a country which had little strategic value; and that small enemy forces might be held in check if the garrison received some reinforcement. I recommended accordingly that the Protectorate should be defended against Italian invasion.

7. On 19th December the Chiefs of Staff's Committee agreed that "the proposal to alter the defence policy of Somaliland to the defence of the territory, and in the last resort of Berbera, from the abandonment of the country in the face of any Italian invasion, is approved in principle." I was instructed to make the plans necessary to implement this policy, in collaboration with the French authorities at Jibuti. The proviso was made that no troops were to be moved into the Protectorate without the sanction of H.M. Government, "in order that the effect of such a movement on our relations with Italy can be studied and the necessary notification can be given to the Italian Government."

8. I visited French and British Somaliland from 9th to 13th January, 1940, to consider the plan of defence and the reinforcements necessary. I saw the defences at the Sheikh Pass and Tug Argan Gap and the defences of Jibuti; and discussed the defence of Somaliland with General Legentilhomme, the French military commander at Jibuti, and with Colonel Chater. By agreement with the French, General Legentilhomme had been placed under my orders.

9. I came to the conclusion that with a comparatively small reinforcement it would be possible to hold both British and French Somaliland against any probable Italian attack, and that it was most desirable to do so, both for reasons of prestige and because Jibuti and Berbera and the railway and roads leading thence into the interior formed the best line of invasion of Abyssinia. It was likely that if Italy entered the war we should eventually attack the Italian forces in Abyssinia, when sufficient troops became available. The loss of British Somaliland would increase the difficulties of such an invasion. I recommended that the garrison of British Somaliland should be increased by one battalion King's African Rifles at once, and by another battalion and a battery if relations with Italy deteriorated, that two mechanised companies should be formed in the Camel Corps, and that money should be allotted for the improvement of defences and roads. The money authorised by the Colonial Office had already been expended and the defences were still very incomplete. I emphasised that my recommendations represented a

minimum and might require to be increased. I also recommended that the passes at Dobo and Jirre, from which roads led down to Zeilah, should be occupied and defended by the French. This was a weak point in the Allied plans for the defence of Somaliland since the enemy by these passes could penetrate between Jibuti and Berbera and separate the French and British forces. General Legentilhomme had troops available to defend these passes, and was most anxious to do so, but had failed to obtain permission from the French Colonial Office. I decided in the event of war with Italy to place General Legentilhomme in command of both British and French Somaliland.

10. My recommendations were approved in principle by the War Office, but the French Colonial Office refused to allow General Legentilhomme to fortify Jirre, on the grounds that it was too far from Jibuti. General Legentilhomme placed a detachment at Jirre, but did not construct defences. Preparations were made to block the road through the Dobo defile by demolitions.

11. It was proposed to increase the garrison of Somaliland by the transfer of two battalions of the King's African Rifles and a battery from Kenya. These would hold the defensive positions, and release the Camel Corps to patrol the remainder of the Protectorate. But although the reinforcement of the garrison had been approved in principle in January, 1940, it was not till 9th March that authority was received to move one battalion, and owing to difficulty in providing the necessary shipping it was not till 15th May that the 1st Battalion Northern Rhodesia Regiment of the King's African Rifles, with certain administrative units, arrived at Berbera and began to disembark. Delay in giving authority for the move was apparently due to financial discussions between the War Office and the Colonial Office, and to Foreign Office apprehension that this move might be considered provocative by Italy. The move of the second battalion and the battery was approved "in principle" on 20th April, but permission for the move was only given on 6th June. There was a further delay owing to the slowness of the move of the West African troops which were to reinforce Kenya, before whose arrival more troops could not be taken from Kenya. The battalion and battery did not reach Somaliland till 12th July, 1940.

12. It was impossible for many months to obtain financial approval for the expenditure of any further money on defences or roads; and essential equipment, which had been ordered by Colonel Chater many months previously, was not supplied by the Colonial Office, which was still responsible for the administration of the troops. It was not till 1st June, 1940 that administrative control of Somaliland was taken over by Middle East. It seemed difficult to persuade the authorities to consider seriously the possibility of war with Italy; and even as late as April, I was still being refused permission, as the result of the Government policy of avoiding the provocation of Italy, to send any Intelligence agents over the frontier to obtain information of Italian dispositions, on the grounds that our relations with the Italians might thereby be impaired.

13. A further difficulty in dealing with British Somaliland was its distance of nearly 2,000 miles from Cairo. I had frequently asked for long-range aircraft for intercommunication in my wide-spread Command, but without success. It was difficult therefore for Commanders or Staff Officers to visit Somaliland at sufficiently frequent intervals. The A.O.C.-in-C. put an ordinary service machine at our disposal, whenever possible, but there simply were not sufficient aeroplanes for the many tasks in hand, and it was not often possible to spare one for intercommunication. There was no regular mail service and letters often required a month to reach Somaliland.

III. OUTBREAK OF WAR WITH ITALY.

14. At the outbreak of war with Italy on 11th June, 1940, the Northern Rhodesia Regiment, K.A.R., held the Tug Argan position, while the Somaliland Camel Corps held the Sheikh Pass, the Dobo defile, where certain demolitions were effected, and advanced positions at Hargeisa and Burao. There was also a force of Illalos (irregular native troops) which patrolled the frontier under the control of the District Officers.

15. Up till the end of July only minor military activities occurred. The Somaliland Camel Corps and the Illalos made a number of successful raids on the enemy's frontier posts. These raids were almost uniformly successful, in spite of the enemy's superior numbers, and reflect great credit on those who carried them out. There was a considerable enemy concentration in the Harar – Diredawa – Jijiga area but it remained inactive.

16. On 17th June news of the French armistice arrived. On 18th June Air Vice Marshal Reid visited Jibuti and was assured by General Legentilhomme that the French Forces there would fight on. Lieutenant-Colonel Chater received similar assurances from General Legentilhomme both on 18th June and on 3rd July. On 6th July I cabled to Colonel Chater that he should prepare a scheme for evacuation, as I considered that our position in Somaliland would be untenable, if the French at Jibuti ceased to fight. At this time there were in Somaliland one battalion K.A.R. (Northern Rhodesia Regiment) and one Indian battalion (1/2 Punjab Regiment), which had been sent from Aden a few days previously, besides the Camel Corps. Another battalion and a battery were on their way from Kenya, and I was considering diverting them to Aden if it was decided to evacuate Somaliland. Colonel Chater replied that when the additional battalion and battery arrived he did not consider his position untenable, even if Jibuti gave in. As General Legentilhomme continued to assure me of his determination to fight on, whatever happened, I allowed the battalion and battery to be landed at Berbera.

17. On 15th July General Germain, who had been sent by the French Government by plane to Italian East Africa to take over command from General Legentilhomme, arrived at the outposts of Jibuti. He was refused admittance by General Legentilhomme, who was still determined to continue the fight. On

22nd July, however, General Legentilhomme was overruled at a Council at which he announced his intention to the Civil authorities, and found himself unable to enforce his decision without bringing on an internal armed conflict. On 23rd July General Germain entered Jibuti and assumed office as Governor and Commander of the troops. On 27th July the French detachment which held the Pass of Jirre was withdrawn.

18. This collapse of French resistance released the whole of the Italian Eastern Army for operations against British Somaliland. This Italian force amounted to some twenty Colonial battalions, four Blackshirt battalions, four groups of Pack Artillery, two groups of Medium Artillery, about thirty tanks, two sections of Armoured Cars and eleven groups of Banda (native irregulars).

19. The garrison of British Somaliland now comprised the Camel Corps, the Northern Rhodesian Regiment, K.A.R., the 1st Battalion 2nd Punjab Regiment, the 2nd Battalion King's African Rifles and 1st East African Light Battery, which arrived from Kenya on 12th July. On 1st July the 2nd Battalion The Black Watch had been sent to Aden by cruiser, at the request of General Legentilhomme, who considered that the support of British troops might assist him to resist an attack on Jibuti, and that this assurance of British support would be a powerful factor in persuading the garrison of Jibuti to continue the struggle. This battalion was therefore also available to reinforce Somaliland.

20. When the French at Jibuti decided to accept the armistice, I had to decide whether to evacuate British Somaliland forthwith or to continue to hold it. After consultation by cable with Colonel Chater, who had now been appointed Brigadier, I decided that we should continue to defend the approaches to Berbera for as long as possible. Brigadier Chater reported that if the force was increased to five battalions he considered that there was a good prospect of holding his positions; also withdrawal without fighting at all would, I considered, be more damaging to our prestige than withdrawal after attack. The French had consistently reported that the morale of the Italian forces in the Harar area was low, and that they were unlikely to attack fortified positions with any vigour. Our patrol encounters on the frontier of the Protectorate seemed to confirm this estimate. I reported accordingly to the War Office, and ordered the 3/15 Punjab Regiment which was already under orders to proceed to Aden from India to go to Somaliland. Two 3-inch A.A. guns were sent from Aden to Berbera, where A.A. protection had always been sorely needed, but the great shortage of A.A. equipment in the Middle East had made provision impossible. Now with the increased force in Somaliland, it was essential to take risks elsewhere and these guns were sent from Aden, where they were replaced by guns from Port Sudan, which in its turn was reinforced from Port Said. Our general shortage and the movement of convoys made necessary this rather complicated shuffle.

21. On 1st August, 1940, the disposition of the forces in Somaliland was as follows:-

Covering Troops.
(a) Dobo area, one Company Somaliland Camel Corps less one Troop;
(b) Hargeisa area, Motor Company Somaliland Camel Corps less one Troop;
One Troop Somaliland Camel Corps; One Company Northern Rhodesia
Regiment, K.A.R.;
(c) Burao, one Company and one Motor Troop Somaliland Camel Corps.

An Officer's Patrol with wireless was on the coast road between Zeilah and
Berbera. A large number of Illalos were working in the forward areas, mostly
under the control of the District officers, to provide information of enemy
movement.

Tug Argan Position.
(a) Northern Rhodesia Regiment less one Company, Machine-Gun Company,
B Company Somaliland Camel Corps, and 1st East African Light Battery, held
the main position.
(b) The left flank of the Tug Argan position was covered by 2nd King's African
Rifles with Headquarters at Mandera.
(c) The 3/15 Punjab Regiment was concentrating at Laferug. On the arrival of
the 2nd Battalion, The Black Watch, on 7th August, the 3/15 Punjab Regiment extended the right flank of the Tug Argan position by holding the
approaches through the hills between the position and the Shell Gap defile on
the coast. The Black Watch became Force reserve at Laferug.

Other Positions.
The 1/2 Punjab Regiment held the Sheikh Pass, the Shell Gap (on the coast road
from Zeilah), the Bihendi Gap on the East of Berbera, and the Base at Berbera.

IV. ITALIAN ATTACK ON BRITISH SOMALILAND.

22. On 1st August, reports of an Italian concentration began to be received. On
5th August an Italian force of an estimated strength of two battalions with 30
motor vehicles entered Zeilah through the Jirre Pass. On the same day the Camel
Corps detachment at Dobo was forced to withdraw by a superior enemy force.

23. On 4th August the enemy began his advance on Hargeisa, and was engaged by
a motor company of the Somaliland Camel Corps, which inflicted considerable
loss. One enemy armoured car was set on fire and two others damaged by fire
from Boys rifles. Next day the enemy attacked our covering position at Hargeisa,
and after three hours' continuous fire by artillery, mortars and machine-guns,
attacked with 12 light tanks which overran the position and compelled a withdrawal. The enemy made no further advance on 6th or 7th August and was
apparently concentrating at Hargeisa.

24. The enemy resumed his advance from Hargeisa on 8th August. At 12.30 hours
on 9th August he encountered our forward delaying detachment, consisting of
one Company Northern Rhodesia Regiment with one machine-gun section of
the Somaliland Camel Corps. This position was quickly overrun by three tanks

which are reported to have been led round the mines, which had been placed in front of the position, by Somalis who knew their location. These tanks were reported as medium tanks, their type has not been definitely established, but they were certainly larger than light tanks. Since the force at this time possessed no weapon to deal with medium tanks, Captain Howden of H.M.A.S. Hobart sent a 3-pdr. naval gun with three ratings up to the battlefield where it was placed at Observation Hill in the Tug Argan position. On 13th August two Bofors guns also arrived at the front.

25. On 11th August the main attack on the Tug Argan position began. At 0730 hours a heavy, low altitude, air attack by bombs and machine-gunning was made on the 2nd battalion The Black Watch in reserve about Laferug. The battalion sustained no casualties and brought down one bomber by A.A. Bren fire. At 0840 hours an enemy bombardment opened on the Tug Argan position. The Tug Argan Gap, through which runs the main Hargeisa-Berbera road, is some 8,000 yards in width. It is flanked on the north-west by a succession of flat-topped hills with numerous deep sandy tugs ("tug" is the local name for wadi or ravine) separating them; and on the south-east by a range of hills varying from 600 to 1,500 feet above the floor of the gap. The country in the gap itself is fairly flat, sparsely covered with thorn bush and intersected with fairly numerous tugs of all sizes mostly running in a south to north direction. The Tug Argan itself is a large sandy river bed some 150 yards in width and running roughly south to north; it was on the southwest or enemy side of all our defended localities.

There were four forward defended localities named Black Hill, Knobbly Hill, Mill Hill and Observation Hill. These hills were from 1,000 to 2,000 yards apart and were held by three companies of the Northern Rhodesia Regiment and the Machine-gun Company of the Somaliland Camel Corps. There were two guns of the East Africa Light Battery on Knobbly Hill and two on Mill Hill. The comparatively short range of these guns necessitated their being put in these forward positions.

Behind these four forward posts was Castle Hill held by the remaining Company of the Northern Rhodesia Regiment. The posts themselves were reasonably strong but there was no depth in the position, nor did the ground lend itself to defence in depth, had more troops been available.

26. During the morning of 11th August the enemy made an infantry attack on the hill positions. The main localities held out successfully but some the enemy penetrated round the left flank, between the Northern Rhodesia Regiment and the 2nd K.A.R.

27. At 2000 hours on this date Major-General Godwin Austen arrived and assumed command. He had only completed handing over the command in Palestine on 8th August and was not available earlier. He was sent when it seemed likely the reinforcements ordered would increase the number of troops above that of a Brigadier's command.

28. On 12th August the enemy's attack developed in full force, each defended locality was attacked by large forces of infantry, supported by artillery. The enemy came on with great determination and undoubtedly suffered extremely heavy losses. Mill Hill position, which was the weakest of the four forward posts, since it had been the last constructed and its defences were still incomplete, fell at about 1600 hours. The section of 3.7 guns in this post was lost, but only 7 rounds of ammunition remained; the guns were rendered completely useless before withdrawal. The other posts all held out. The enemy succeeded in working round the left flank and reaching the high ground about Donkey Hill, which overlooks both Observation Hill and Castle Hill. Small detachments also penetrated to the Berbera road behind Castle Hill.

29. During the night of 12th-13th August the 2nd King's African Rifles, who were holding the hills on the left flank of the Tug Argan position, were driven from the Mirgo Pass; and the enemy thus threatened to cut the road between the Tug Argan position and Berbera. Measures were taken to restore the position in this area but were not completely successful.

30. Enemy action on 13th August was less determined. The garrison on Knobbly Hill broke up an enemy attack at daybreak and captured two pack guns; and further attacks on Black Hill and Castle Hill were also repulsed during the morning.

31. During the night of the 13th-14th August a convoy, consisting of one Company 2nd Black Watch with two carriers, was despatched to deliver water to Castle and Knobbly Hills and gun ammunition to Knobbly Hill. This convoy was ambushed near Castle Hill. One carrier fell into the ditch and could not be recovered and three lorries were abandoned by their Somali drivers. But the enemy then withdrew and the remainder of the column reached the posts, delivered ammunition and water, evacuated the wounded and returned before daylight on 14th August.

32. This incident showed Major-General Godwin Austen the danger of the line of retreat to Berbera being cut by continued enemy infiltration. It was also obvious that the enemy, with his great superiority in artillery and numbers, could concentrate on each post in turn and destroy it. There was only one battalion in reserve, and if this was used to counter-attack or to reinforce the forward positions there was a serious danger that the whole force might be surrounded and unable to retreat. In these circumstances Major-General Godwin Austen prepared a plan for evacuation, but decided to wait the issue of the next day's events.

33. On 14th August heavy enemy shelling began on Castle and Observation Hills at 0700 hours. Over 500 enemy shells fell on Castle Hill during the day. At 1600 hours a heavy infantry attack on Observation Hill was repulsed. Its garrison reported that many parts of the defences had been destroyed by gun fire, and that

it would be impossible to hold the post much longer. A message was sent to the post encouraging them to hold on, to which they responded.

34. Meanwhile a counter-attack had been made on the positions about Mirgo Pass which had been lost on 12th August. This was at first successful, but in the evening our troops were again driven back. Further east the Italians made an attempt to reach the Berbera road by the Jerato Pass, but were driven back.

35. The position early on 15th August was as follows. Observation Hill, which was vital to the defence of the whole position, was dominated by artillery from Round Hill at short range. Many of the defences had been destroyed; and the garrison, which had gallantly resisted for four days, was becoming tired. Attempts to dislodge the enemy from the Mirgo Pass and from the low ground south of Castle Hill had failed. There was also a threat from the enemy detachment advancing along the coast road from Zeilah, though this advance, which had been shelled by the Navy from the sea and bombed by the R.A.F., was not being pressed with any great energy. Enemy air attacks on troops and transport in the open had been constant. They were not very dangerous but had a considerable nuisance effect. In these circumstances General Godwin Austen came to the conclusion that a retreat on Berbera and evacuation was the only course to save the force from a dangerous defeat and possible annihilation. He accordingly telegraphed G.H.Q., Middle East, giving the two alternatives, immediate evacuation or continuation of the action with probable loss of a very large proportion of the force.

Lieutenant-General Sir H.M. Wilson, who was in temporary command of Middle East during any absence in the United Kingdom, decided in favour of evacuation. I have no doubt that both General Godwin-Austen's recommendation and General Wilson's decision were correct.

36. During the morning of 15th August the enemy remained inactive but during the afternoon he renewed his attacks. Black Hill was not directly attacked but the enemy infiltrated round this position and endeavoured to dig in a pack battery in a position behind the post. They were dispersed by gun fire and then shelled Black Hill heavily. Castle Hill was also shelled. The brunt of the enemy's effort was, however, made on Observation Hill which was subjected to a very heavy bombardment for two hours. This was followed by a fierce infantry attack at 1700 hours, under which the garrison at last gave way. I regret that the 3-pdr. gun of H.M.A.S. Hobart was here lost together with the detachment. Their presence and conduct had been of the utmost value to the morale of the garrison.

37. During the night of the 15/16th withdrawal from the Tug Argan position was carried out. It was covered by the 2nd Black Watch with two companies of the 2nd King's African Rifles in a position at Barkasan, five miles south-west of Laferug, some 35 miles from Berbera. It was intended that this position should be held for 48 hours, and that a further rearguard position should then be held at Nasiye, 15 miles from Berbera.

38. The movement to Berbera on the 16th was carried out without interference from the enemy; and embarkation began on the night of 16th/17th August. The Italians had lost two planes in an air raid on Berbera on 15th, and their air force was afterwards inactive over this area. During 16th August, the enemy occupied the Tug Argan position, but made no other forward move.

39. At 1040 hours on 17th August a report was received of an Italian column having entered Bulhar, 40 miles west of Berbera. H.M.S. Ceres, patrolling off this coast, engaged this column and stopped its advance. At 1050 hours on the same day the enemy began a series of attacks against the 2nd Black Watch and the two Companies 2nd K.A.R. at Barkasan, which lasted till dark. The attacking force consisted of at least a brigade of fresh troops with artillery and tanks, which had been brought forward in M.T. An attack on the left of the position was first repulsed; and then a battalion attacked the centre Company and in spite of heavy casualties began to surround the forward posts. The position was restored by the Company Commander, Captain D. MacN. C. Rose, who, with three carriers, led his Company Headquarters and reserve platoon in a bayonet charge which threw the enemy back some 500 yards. Later the enemy again attacked the left and centre with infantry supported by eight to ten tanks, of which at least two were larger than light tanks. This attack was also checked by the use of the reserve Company. At least one medium and two light tanks were destroyed by the fire of the Bofors. Towards evening a serious threat by another enemy battalion began to develop against the right flank, and there seemed a danger that the whole force might be cut off from its transport and line of retreat. A gradual withdrawal was therefore ordered. The rear parties of The Black Watch hung on to their posts until night fell and the whole force was able to reach its transport and embus without interference, the enemy failing to take advantage of his superior numbers or to press home his attack..

40. It had now been decided not to hold a further position at Nasiye, but to embark the whole force during the night of the 17/18th. By the morning of the 18th the whole of the force, with the exception of a few hundred men holding the outskirts of Berbera and a few stragglers, had been embarked. The wind, which frequently renders embarkation impossible at the port of Berbera for many hours at this time of year, had fortunately been favourable. The local Somalis of the Camel Corps were given the option of evacuation to Aden or disbandment. The great majority preferred to remain in the country. They were allowed to retain their arms.

41. During the 18th H.M.A.S. Hobart embarked the remaining personnel, including some small parties which continued to come in. During the evening the destruction of petrol, vehicles and other stores was continued by demolition parties. One raid by three aircraft was made in the evening, and bombs fell close to Hobart.

On 19th August H.M.A.S. Hobart finally sailed after destroying the principal Government buildings.

V. SUMMARY OF THE OPERATIONS.

42. Our total casualties were 8 British officers killed, 4 wounded, 4 missing; 8 British other ranks killed, 18 wounded, 17 missing; 22 Indian or African other ranks killed, 80 wounded, 99 missing: a total of 260, or little more than 5 per cent. of the force. Almost exactly half of these casualties were in the Northern Rhodesia Regiment of the King's African Rifles, who held the Tug Argan position. The great majority of the missing are believed to have been killed.

That the casualties were comparatively light was due to the fact that most of the troops who were heavily attacked were in strong defences; and that the withdrawals, which were skilfully carried out under cover of darkness, were not interfered with or followed up by the enemy, presumably owing to the heavy casualties he had suffered during the day.

43. Four 3.7 Howitzers, the only artillery with the force, were lost. These guns, owing to their comparatively short range, were placed in forward posts where they undoubtedly did great execution. Two were lost when the post on Mill Hill was overrun; and it was impossible to withdraw the other two when the main position was evacuated, as transport could not be brought up to the front line. All four guns were rendered useless before being abandoned.

The amount of equipment lost by the fighting troops was not abnormal, and was mostly incurred in the posts that were overrun by the enemy. A considerable proportion of the stores at the base and practically the whole of the transport of the forces was lost. This was due to the poor facilities of Berbera as a port. All embarkation and disembarkation had to be done by lighter, of which very few were available, or by ships' boats. Work is only possible at all for two hours each side of high tide. At the season of the year when the operations took place a strong wind, which blows for a number of hours during every twenty-four at irregular times, makes embarkation impossible. It was therefore rightly decided to concentrate on making certain of embarking all personnel. In daylight the ships would have formed a very vulnerable target for the enemy air force. As it happened, the enemy did not follow up to Berbera at once, but by the time that this was evident, the transport had been damaged to render it immobile. Its destruction was therefore completed by naval landing parties.

44. The conduct of the troops, as may be judged from the above account, was in every way excellent in very testing circumstances. They had to face greatly superior numbers, to endure continual heavy artillery fire, often at close range, and to withstand constant attacks from the air. The weather was hot and the climate of Somaliland induces extreme thirst. The steadiness and discipline of all units was very noticeable and there was no failure of resistance or premature retreat. The qualities of the African and Somali troops, on whom the brunt of the

fighting fell, are not usually best shown in static defence and they had not previous experience of shell-fire, yet they showed remarkable stubbornness and bravery. The Indian battalions fought with the skill and tenacity expected of them. The action of The Black Watch on 17th August was worthy of their best traditions.

45. The enemy attacked on many occasions with great dash and determination, and undoubtedly suffered very heavy casualties. After all allowance has been made for the tendency to exaggerate the losses suffered by the enemy, it seems certain that the enemy's casualties were not less than two thousand.

The enemy on several occasions failed to take advantage of his superior numbers and the favourable tactical positions he had obtained, and thus allowed our forces to escape from more than one very dangerous position.

46. An outstanding feature of this short campaign was the wholehearted co-operation afforded to the Army by the Royal Navy and the Royal Air Force. The work of the Royal Navy in disembarkation and embarkation of the force under the most difficult conditions was most remarkable and deserves the warmest thanks of the Army. I desire to express its appreciation to Rear-Admiral A.J.L. Murray, C.B., D.S.O., O.B.E., and to all those under him.

The Royal Air Force afforded the utmost possible assistance that their resources permitted, and took very considerable risks in doing so. The Army is deeply grateful to Air Vice Marshal G.R.M. Reid, D.S.O., M.C., and to the Royal Air Force at Aden. I attach as Appendix A a short report by Air Vice Marshal Reid on the work of the Royal Air Force.

47. The temporary loss of the Somaliland Protectorate was due to four main causes:

(a) Our insistence on running our Colonies on the cheap, especially in matters of defence.

(b) The slowness of the War Cabinet, in the first eight or nine months of the war, to allow proper precautions to be taken against the possibility of Italy joining the war against us. This resulted in long delays in the arrival of rein-forcements, the withholding of the money necessary for defences, the non-arrival of essential equipment, and a refusal to allow of measures to be taken to establish a proper Intelligence service for fear of impairing relations with Italy.

(c) The collapse of French resistance at Jibuti after a long period of uncer-tainty. It was this that allowed the full weight of the Italian concentration in the Harar area to be directed against British Somaliland.

(d) The almost complete lack of facilities in Berbera as a port. This was one of the chief reasons why it was impossible to send reinforcements rapidly. A full report of this had been made in 1936 by Colonel Hornby, but no steps were taken to carry out the recommendations made. It may be noted that it took a 3,000-ton ship ten days in normal conditions to unload at Berbera.

48. The reinforcement of Somaliland was piecemeal and hurried. The original delays in sending reinforcements have been explained in paragraph 11 above. That further reinforcements could not be sent earlier was due mainly to the meagre resources available in the Middle East to meet its very wide responsibilities. It was necessary to keep the commitment in British Somaliland to a minimum, hoping to the last that the French would continue the struggle at Jibuti, of which I had had repeated assurances from General Legentilhomme. The poverty of Berbera as a port made landing slow and difficult when reinforcements did arrive.

VI. APPRECIATION OF SERVICES.

49. I wish especially to bring to notice the work of Brigadier A.R. Chater, D.S.O., O.B.E. Throughout a most difficult and trying period his work and spirit have been admirable. His disposition of his slender resources has always been made with sound judgment; his appreciations of the situation have been well founded; and the way in which he has inspired and led the forces under his command has been admirable. I consider that his services in Somaliland deserve special recognition.

50. Major-General A.R. Godwin Austen showed great skill in his handling of operations during the short period he was in command. He took over while a battle was in progress, grasped the situation rapidly, and by his personal energy and spirit did much to inspire the resistance. It was due to his well thought out arrangements that the evacuation was carried out with so little loss.

APPENDIX "A"

Air Headquarters, Steamer Point, Aden.
22nd August, 1940.

THE SOMALILAND CAMPAIGN.

INTRODUCTION.

On 6th July, 1940, G.H.Q. Middle East asked O.C. Somaliforces whether, if the French at Jibuti accepted the terms of the armistice, he considered that British Somaliland was untenable and that troops should be gradually withdrawn. O.C. Somaliforces replied that with certain additional military forces he did not consider the position in Somaliland untenable provided he could rely on his Naval requirements and on air support from Aden.

2. In forwarding Somaliforce signal to G.H.Q., A.O.C. Aden stated that "a measure of air support could be provided but air forces here (in Aden) are small and have prior commitment with convoys and in defence of Aden."

3. The role of the air forces in Aden has been clearly defined:-

(a) Protection of convoys.
(b) Neutralisation of enemy air forces as far as possible to achieve (a) above and to protect shipping at Aden.

4. Permission was, however, obtained from H.Q. R.A.F. Middle East for a flight of aircraft to give close support in Somaliland to the best of their ability. It was never intended by Higher Command to use any more than this flight in close support of the Army except in the case of emergency.

OPERATIONS CARRIED OUT BY THE ROYAL AIR FORCE.
From outbreak of War with Italy up to Start of Advance on Somaliland.
5. Forty-four reconnaissances were carried out on the Somaliland – Abyssinian frontier.

These entailed thirteen detachments to Berbera each of about three days' duration. During this time our casualties were two officers wounded, one aircraft lost and one damaged.

From 5th August to 19th August.
6. The following was carried out:-

(a) Twelve separate reconnaissances.
(b) Nineteen bombing-reconnaissances employing thirty-two aircraft.
(c) Twenty-six bombing attacks on enemy troop concentrations, and transport employing seventy-two aircraft.
(d) Standing fighter patrols were maintained over Berbera for thirteen days employing 36 sorties.

In addition to the above, No. 223 Squadron carried out six long distance raids on enemy bases in the back areas, including Addis Abeba. The intention was to draw the enemy fighters away from British Somaliland. The total number of sorties for these operations was thirty-two.

7. During these operations approximately sixty tons of bombs were dropped and the total number of sorties was 184.

Casualties.
8. Our casualties were as follows:-

(a) Seven aircraft lost.
(b) Ten severely damaged and a number slightly damaged by enemy action.
(c) Twelve killed.
(d) Three wounded.

9. During the period under review the following enemy aircraft were shot down or damaged:-

(a) *By fighters* – One shot down and one heavily hit.
(b) *By bombers* – Two shot down in flames.

Achievements.
10. Long range fighters were used in standing patrols for the protection of Berbera against air attack during the evacuation. It will be noted that this port was reasonably immune from air bombardment during this critical period. Had this

not been so the evacuation might have been badly held up with unfortunate consequences.

11. In co-operation with the Royal Navy our air forces effectively delayed and finally stopped the Italian advance along the coast road from Zeilah to Berbera.

DIFFICULTIES UNDER WHICH THE ROYAL AIR FORCE WAS WORKING.

12. Although the maximum air effort possible was afforded in support of the Army in Somaliland it may not have appeared impressive from the ground. The difficulties under which we were working were as follows:-

(a) There was no protected aerodrome from which either our fighters or bombers could operate in Somaliland. The two aerodromes – one at Berbera and one at Laferug – were quickly made untenable by enemy bombardment which was practically unopposed by ground defences. Two of our fighters were destroyed in the initial stages on the ground owing to lack of protection normally afforded by the Army. Fighter aircraft therefore had to be withdrawn.

(b) In view of the above it was impossible to operate fighters at all and for this reason, and only this, the enemy had local air superiority.

(c) Because there was no aerodrome in Somaliland from which to work, our bombers were forced to operate from Aden which was a range of 200 miles over sea. At this range the air effort was greatly hampered and it was impossible to keep in close touch with the military situation.

(d) Since the enemy had local air superiority our bombers were continually being attacked by fighter aircraft while the crews were trying to concentrate their attention upon the ground to assist the Army and trying to get a grip of the fast changing military situation. This made our bombers extremely vulnerable.

(e) The aircraft with which we are equipped is a fast medium bomber which is excellent for its proper role but unsuitable for close army co-operation work, especially when not protected by fighters.

Conclusion.

13. In short the air effort expended in support of the Army in Somaliland was the maximum which could be given with the air forces available and with no protected aerodrome from which to work. It proved expensive in aircraft and crews but certain valuable results were obtained.

14. In conclusion the sincere thanks of the R.A.F. at Aden are due to the Military Authorities in Somaliland for their assistance, close co-operation and careful regard to our limitations in the circumstances.

Sgd. G.R.M. REID,
Air Vice Marshal,
Air Officer Commanding,
British Forces in Aden.

NOTE BY FORCE COMMANDER IN REFERENCE TO
PARA. 12(a) of REPORT BY A.O.C., BRITISH FORCES IN ADEN.

1. In normal circumstances A.A. Bofors guns would have been made available for the defence of aerodromes at Berbera and Laferug. None, however, existed with the force.

2. I would not like an impression to arise that no A.A. defence was provided by the Army at these two aerodromes. Each aerodrome was given ground and low altitude defences by a Platoon of Infantry with two A.A. V.B. guns; whilst at Berbera the A.A. layout of the two 3-inch A.A. guns included protection of the aerodrome as far as was possible, though the primary objective protected was the port area.

3. In actual fact, the platoon protecting the Berbera aerodrome brought down one enemy fighter.

Sgd. A.R. GODWIN-AUSTEN,
Major-General.

Note
1. *See* Preface para.

2

GENERAL SIR ARCHIBALD P. WAVELL'S DESPATCH ON OPERATIONS IN EAST AFRICA, NOVEMBER 1940 TO JULY 1941

The War Office, July, 1946
OPERATIONS IN EAST AFRICA, NOVEMBER, 1940–JULY, 1941
The following Despatch was submitted to the Secretary of State for War on the
21*st May,* 1942, *by General SIR ARCHIBALD P. WAVELL, G.C.B., C.M.G., M.C.,*
Commander-in-Chief in the Middle East.
(To COVER REPORTS BY LIEUT.-GENERAL W. PLATT AND
LIEUT.-GENERAL A.G. CUNNINGHAM.)

1. I forward herewith accounts of the operations in the Sudan from November 1940 to July 1941 by Lieut.-General W. Platt and of the operations from Kenya between November 1940 and August 1941 by Lieut.-General A. Cunningham. These two accounts between them describe the conquest of practically the whole of Italian East Africa between the dates given. This covering despatch is intended to give the strategical background of the operations and to explain the instructions I issued as Commander-in-Chief of the Middle East.

2. In a previous despatch dated 11th December, 1940, I described how East Africa was placed under my command on 3rd February, 1940. The very small force then in East Africa was reinforced by a South African brigade and South African Air Contingent in June and two West African brigades in July. The remainder of the 1st South African Division arrived during the autumn of 1940, so that by October 1940 there were three divisions in East Africa, the 1st South African Division, and the 11th and 12th African Divisions. None of these divisions was of normal composition; their organisation is given in the Appendices to Lieut.-General Cunningham's report.

3. During the autumn and winter of 1940–41, in deciding the operations to be conducted from East Africa, I had to take into account two conflicting policies which were urged on me from different quarters. I was being pressed by the Defence Minister at Home to move forces from East Africa to Egypt; he complained that there were large masses of troops and transport standing idle with no prospect of successful employment while there was great need for both further north in the Sudan and Egypt. During a visit I paid to London in August 1940 he had urged on me the policy of reducing troops to an absolute minimum in Kenya and he continued to suggest that a proportion of the troops in East Africa could

more usefully be employed elsewhere. On the other hand I was made well aware of the undoubted feeling of nervousness, not only in Kenya but also in Rhodesia and even in South Africa, that the forces in East Africa were not sufficient to prevent an Italian invasion of Kenya and of the countries further south; in particular there was fear of an enemy occupation of the port of Mombasa. General Smuts frequently impressed on me the danger of reducing the Forces in East Africa.

Furthermore, the South African Division had originally been provided on the understanding that it was not to be used north of the Equator, while it was very doubtful whether the African troops for climatic reasons and their low scale of equipment would be so suitable for operations in other theatres. I resisted, therefore, proposals to reduce the force in East Africa, at least until we had driven the enemy further back.

4. On 1st November Lieut.-General A. Cunningham took over command in East Africa from Lieut.-General D.P. Dickinson.

5. On the 2nd December, 1940, on the eve of the offensive against Marshal Graziani's forces in the Western Desert, I held a meeting at Cairo, at which the Commanders in the Sudan and East Africa were present, to consider the strategy to be adopted against Italian East Africa. I laid down the following general policy at this conference:-

In the Sudan:
(*a*) To prepare an operation for the recapture of Kassala, which had been occupied by the enemy soon after the outbreak of war with Italy, to be carried out early in 1941 if the necessary reinforcements could be made available from Egypt; this depended mainly on the success of the Desert offensive.
(*b*) To maintain pressure in the Gallabat area where a minor attack had been made early in November, but to undertake no large scale operations on that line.
(*c*) To further the rebellion in Abyssinia by all possible means.

In Kenya:
(*a*) In the south to advance to the frontier on the line Kolibio – Dif as soon as possible.
(*b*) On the northern frontier west of Moyale to maintain pressure on the enemy by means of small mobile columns.
(*c*) In May or June, after the rainy period, to advance on Kismayu; I had hoped for an advance on Kismayu before the rainy season but General Cunningham at this meeting informed me that after careful examination he did not consider it possible owing to water difficulties and lack of sufficient transport.
(*d*) In the spring and summer of 1941 to penetrate into south-west Abyssinia in conjunction with operations from the Boma area of the Sudan.

6. The ruling idea in my mind in the decisions taken at this conference was that the fomentation of the patriot movement in Abyssinia offered with the resources

available the best prospect of making the Italian position impossible and eventually reconquering the country. I did not intend at the time a large scale invasion either from Kassala towards Asmara and Massawa, or from Kismayu to the north. The two operations to Kassala and Kismayu were designed to secure our flanks and I intended that our main effort should be devoted to furthering and supporting the rebellion by irregular action. I intended after the capture of Kassala and Kismayu to withdraw as many troops as possible from the Sudan and East Africa for the theatres further north. I had carefully examined the possibilities of an invasion of Italian East Africa in force during the period before Italy entered the war. I had come to the conclusion that the only two lines of invasion which offered a good prospect of success for a regular force were from Jibuti on Addis Ababa or from Kassala on Massawa; and of these the advance from Jibuti offered the better prospect of success, since it seemed that the natural difficulties of the Kassala – Asmara route would require too great a force for the single road by which it would have to be supplied. The French collapse and the Italian occupation of British Somaliland in August 1940 ruled out the possibility of the Jibuti advance.

7. During a visit to the Sudan in November with the Secretary of State for War, Mr. Anthony Eden, I had discussed at length the requirements for the development of the rebellion in Abyssinia and had made arrangements to do everything possible to assist the patriots. I appointed Lieut.-Colonel O.C. Wingate as staff officer for patriot activities and his energy and initiative was an important factor in the means by which the patriot movement gained so great an impetus in the succeeding months. Towards the end of November he had flown into Abyssinia and met Brigadier Sandford who was already there with a small mission to prepare the way.

8. There were thus three separate lines of operation against Italian East Africa: in the north from the Sudan by Kassala into Eritrea, in the centre from the Sudan and later from East Africa into Abyssinia, and in the south from Kenya against Italian Somaliland.

9. The success of the offensive in the Western Desert of Egypt decided me to transfer the 4th Indian Division to the Sudan to enable the Kassala operation to be carried out. The decision for this transfer had to be made at very short notice, while the battle in the Western Desert was still in progress, since otherwise shipping would not have been available for some time and it would not have been possible to stage the attack on Kassala early in 1941 as I intended. Part of the 4th Indian Division was actually moved practically straight from the battlefield of Sidi Barrani to ships which conveyed them to the the Sudan, and they were in action again in the Sudan very shortly after their arrival.

The 4th Indian Division moved partly by sea to Port Sudan and partly by railway and boat up the Nile Valley. The whole division was due to complete its arrival in the Sudan about the middle of January. General Platt originally fixed the date for the advance early in March but I issued orders to him that he was to attack early in February at the latest. Eventually the date, 9th February was fixed for the operation. I had sent one squadron of infantry tanks to the Sudan for the operation; these were the only tanks I could spare in view of the operations in the Western Desert against Marshal Graziani's army.

10. Meanwhile the preparations for the rebellion in Abyssinia were pushed on with great energy. The chief objective was to place a sufficient quantity of food and stores into Abyssinia beyond the escarpment before the rain rendered further movement of transport impossible. A small force of one battalion of Sudanese and a number of specially selected British officers and N.C.Os. were also sent forward. The Emperor, Haille Selassie, himself crossed the frontier and entered his kingdom on 20th January. The subsequent operations of the small force which cleared the Gojjam of large Italian forces was a very remarkable achievement, due largely to the energy and initiative of Brigadier Sandford, head of 101 Mission, Colonel O.C. Wingate, who commanded the regular forces taking part, the British officers and N.C.Os. who assisted him, and the fine fighting qualities of the Sudanese battalion.

11. During the winter a small mobile force, known as Gazelle Force, under Brigadier Messervy, continually harassed the Italian communications with Kassala and caused them great inconvenience and considerable losses. Early in January there were indications of the enemy's intention to withdraw from Kassala; and while on a visit to Khartoum I instructed General Platt to be ready to advance his operation to prevent the enemy withdrawal. Before he could get his troops into action, however, the enemy had evacuated Kassala and commenced his retreat.

12. This enemy withdrawal and the rapid and effective pursuit which General Platt at once initiated caused me to review my original intention to confine the operation to the occupation of Kassala and a small part of Eritrea and to consider whether I should carry out a large scale operation into Eritrea with the intention of capturing Asmara. This would prevent my withdrawing troops from the Sudan for Egypt as early as I had intended, but operations were going very well in the Western Desert, there was no immediate need of additional troops in Egypt and there seemed a possibility that the enemy could be rushed over the mountain passes on to the Asmara plateau. I therefore instructed General Platt, during a visit I paid to the Sudan towards the end of January, to continue his pursuit and to press on towards Asmara. I also approved his proposal to use some Free French troops which were arriving at Port Sudan, together with the British and Indian troops already there, to advance along the Red Sea coast and into the hills towards Asmara.

13. I also visited Kenya at the end of January where General Cunningham informed me that in view of the success of the operations in the Western Desert, which was bound to have a considerable effect on Italian morale, and the fact that he had discovered additional supplies of water on the southern front, he was

prepared to make an attempt to capture Kismayu early in February instead of waiting till after the rains in May. I instructed him to proceed with his intention and told him that if the operation against Kismayu was successful he should endeavour at once to cut the Mogadiscio – Addis Ababa road by which the enemy drew a considerable proportion of his supplies.

14. On 12th February, after I had received the Cabinet decision to send all available troops from the Middle East to the assistance of Greece, I had to decide whether or not to continue operations against Italian East Africa or to withdraw troops from that theatre to replace those who had been ordered to Greece. In view of the complete defeat of the Italian forces in Cyrenaica, I decided to allow the operations against Italian East Africa to continue for the present at any rate. I issued instructions to General Platt to endeavour to capture Asmara and Massawa and to General Cunningham to continue his operations against Kismayu. I told General Platt that he was to confine his operations to the occupation of Eritrea and was not to advance south from Eritrea into Abyssinia and that I should withdraw two or three brigade groups from him as soon as possible after his capture of Eritrea. I told General Cunningham that if he was successful in capturing Kismayu, he should advance on Mogadiscio if possible, but I warned him that I should probably require the withdrawal of the 1st South African Division at an early date.

15. Early in 1941 the Union Government had offered a second South African division for service in East Africa. I considered however that I had at that time sufficient troops in East Africa and asked that the division might be reserved for use further north.

16. On 24th February, in view of the rapidity with which General Cunningham's operations had progressed and the apparently complete disorganisation of the Italian forces in the south, I instructed General Cunningham that after the capture of Mogadiscio he should if possible advance on Harrar to cut the communications between Addis Ababa and Jibuti, and told him that I proposed to initiate operations for the reoccupation of Berbera and British Somaliland, in order to open up a short line of supply to the forces which advanced on Harrar. General Cunningham pressed on his operations with the greatest vigour and was usually a little ahead of my proposals and intentions.

17. About the third week of March I had cause to reconsider the operations against Italian East Africa. At this time signs of an enemy counter-offensive in Cyrenaica were becoming apparent, practically the whole of of my trained reserves were in Greece or on their way there and my need of troops to form a fresh reserve in Egypt was urgent. The 4th and 5th Indian Divisions were held up in front of the strong Keren position which they had failed to carry in spite of very gallant efforts. I had to decide whether to make another effort to capture the Keren position and reach Asmara or to adopt a defensive attitude in Eritrea and begin withdrawing troops. The position we held opposite Keren was not well

situated for defence and the Italians, who were still in very superior numbers, might begin a counter-offensive if we accepted failure at Keren; and General Platt considered that a fresh attack might succeed. I therefore authorised him to continue his attempts to storm the Keren position, which he successfully accomplished on March 27th. The capture of this natural stronghold which the Italians had defended with such determination was a fitting climax to the great work in Eritrea of the 4th and 5th Indian Divisions, ably commanded by Major-General N.M. de la P. Beresford-Peirse and Major-General L.M. Heath respectively.

After the fall of Keren the Italians made little further effort to defend Eritrea, their oldest colony.

18. About the same time I had to decide whether to authorise General Cunningham to go on to Addis Ababa. I had originally intended to halt the operation after the capture of Diredawa and the reoccupation of British Somaliland, since I had urgent need of the 1st South African Division and some of the large quantities of transport which General Cunningham's operations were employing. Also it seemed to me that the occupation of Addis Ababa would confront us with an embarrassment of very large numbers of Italian civilians and would have no very great strategical object. I found, however, that General Cunningham was quite confident of capturing Addis Ababa and of dealing with the civilian problem and decided to allow him to continue his advance.

Addis Ababa was occupied on 6th April. In a remarkable campaign of two months General Cunningham's forces had captured over 50,000 prisoners and had occupied some 360,000 square miles at a cost of only 500 casualties, of whom under 150 were killed. His leaders in these operations were Major-General A.R. Godwin-Austen (12th African Division), Major-General H.E. de R. Wetherall (11th African Division) and Major-General G.E. Brink (1st South African Division).

19. Meanwhile a very skilfully conducted operation from Aden under the A.O.C., Air Vice-Marshal G.R.M. Reid, had resulted in the recapture of Berbera on 16th March. This was speedily followed by the reoccupation of the whole colony. The use of the port of Berbera and the road from thence to Harrar enabled General Cunningham greatly to shorten his line of communications.

20. The success of General Cunningham's operations involved us in some very difficult administrative and political problems, the administration of the conquered territory, the security and feeding of the very large Italian civilian population in Addis Ababa and its vicinity, and the question of French Somaliland with the port of Jibuti and the railway from there to Addis Ababa.

I had begun preparations for the administration of enemy-occupied territory in Italian East Africa as early as December 1940 and a nucleus organisation was in existence at the time the occupation began. So rapidly, however, did the advance proceed, especially in the south, that it was almost impossible for administration to keep pace. In the circumstances it reflects the greatest credit on Sir Philip

Mitchell, Brigadier Lush, Brigadier the Hon. F.R. Rodd and others that so much was accomplished and that there was no general breakdown of administration or of law and order.

21. The problem of the large Italian civilian populations in Asmara, capital of Eritrea, in Addis Ababa and elsewhere gave me anxiety both with respect to their safety and to the food problem. In the end our apprehensions were, however, largely relieved, the behaviour of the native population towards their former conquerors was in general tolerant and no revenge was sought, while the problem of food supply was of less difficulty than had been expected.

22. In connection with the feeding and possible evacuation of the population of Addis Ababa the position of the port at Jibuti and the railway was obviously of considerable importance. From the point of view of military administration the obvious policy was to come to an arrangement with the Vichy authorities for the use of the port and railway under certain terms in exchange for relaxation of the blockade to French Somaliland. It would probably have been possible to come to a satisfactory agreement and I proposed to open negotiations with the Governor of French Somaliland. The Free French were, however, anxious for political reasons to bring French Somaliland over to the Free French movement and were confident that this could be done by propaganda and by strict main-tenance of the blockade. H.M.G. decided that the Free French policy should be adopted. The problem remained unsettled up to the time that I left the Middle East; the Free French authorities failed to win over the colony to their movement and the blockade failed to have the effect of reducing its resistance.

23. After the occupation of Addis Ababa on 6th April, General Cunningham wished to employ his forces to the west and south-west in order to reduce the enemy centre at Gimma and to secure his line of communication in the Lakes area. I was, however, anxious to get as quickly as possible the South African divi-sion and a large quantity of transport to Egypt and ordered him to advance north to secure the main road from Addis Ababa to Asmara so that troops and transport from South Abyssinia could reach Egypt by embarkation at Massawa or Port Sudan or by the Nile Valley route. The 1st South African Brigade Group accord-ingly left Addis Ababa on 13th April and after capturing Dessie reached Amba Alagi on 8th May. The combined attack of the South Africans and the Sudan forces from the north resulted in the surrender of Amba Alagi on 17th May. The Duc D'Aosta, the Viceroy of Italian East Africa, surrendered at this place.

24. After the fall of Amba Alagi, the remaining centres of enemy resistance were in the Galla – Sidamo area in the south-west and in the Gondar area in the north-west. Some brilliant operations by the African divisions, assisted by a Belgian force from the Sudan, resulted in the complete liquidation of all Italian resistance in the south-west of Abyssinia, while the Italian outposts of the Gondar area were also cleared. The Gondar area itself was allowed to remain for the present as it could have no further influence on operations and I was anxious to transfer troops

back to the main theatre in Egypt as rapidly as possible. The 4th Indian Division had begun to return to Egypt immediately after the fall of Keren and the 5th Indian Division followed after the fall of Amba Alagi.

25. During the operations by regular troops in the south and in the north, the west centre of Abyssinia was being cleared by some daring operations of Colonel Wingate's small regular force of Sudanese troops and bands of Abyssinian patriots assisted by British officers and N.C.Os. The Emperor, with Brigadier Sandford, followed the operations of these troops, and the Emperor made a formal entry into his capital of Addis Ababa on 5th May.

26. The conquest of Italian East Africa had been accomplished in four months, from the end of January to the beginning of June. In this period a force of approximately 220,000 men had been practically destroyed with the whole of its equipment and an area of nearly a million square miles had been occupied. Some of the chief features of this remarkable campaign were the storming by British and Indian troops of the formidable mountain barriers at Keren and Amba Alagi, the boldness and skill with which the operations from East Africa were pressed over a distance of about 2,000 miles from the base, and the very skilful guerilla fighting in Western Abyssinia.

The ultimate pattern of the conquest was a pincer movement on the largest scale, through Eritrea and Somaliland converging on Amba Alagi, combined with a direct thrust through Western Abyssinia by the patriot forces. It looks Teutonic in conception and execution; but, as explained above, this result was not foreseen in the original plan but arose gradually through the development of events. It was in fact an improvisation after the British fashion of war rather than a set piece in the German manner.

27. As will be seen from the above, General Platt and General Cunningham acted on broad general instructions from me and I made no attempt to control their operations in detail. Success was due mainly to their boldness and skill in execution, the quality of their subordinate commanders and to the dash and endurance of the troops. Both South African and African troops greatly distinguished themselves.

28. The support of the R.A.F. and S.A.A.F., with comparatively small numbers and equipment far from modern, was altogether admirable; and the co-operation between army and air forces close and efficient.

29. The Royal Navy assisted with their usual efficiency and spirit at Kismayu, Mogadiscio, Berbera, Massawa and elsewhere.

30. I should like to add a special tribute to Field-Marshal Smuts for his unfailing support of the East African campaign; and to the generous response that the Union Government invariably made to any requests for assistance, either in personnel or material, during the whole period of my command in the Middle East.

REPORT BY LT. GEN. SIR WILLIAM PLATT, K.C.B., D.S.O., ON THE OPERATIONS IN ERITREA AND ABYSSINIA.
From 1st December, 1940, to 26th August, 1941.

H.Q. Tps., Khartoum.
11th September, 1941.

PART I (A)

The Planning for the Battle of Kassala.

On 2nd December, 1940, at a conference held at G.H.Q. Middle East, the C.-in-C. outlined the policy for the troops in the Sudan as follows:-

(*a*) To prepare to capture Kassala triangle in February.

(*b*) To maintain pressure in Gallabat area but to attempt no large-scale operations at present.

(*c*) To foster the rebellion in Abyssinia by all possible means.

The Enemy Situation.

By this time the enemy's chances of a successful major offensive against the Sudan had passed. Reinforcements consisting of 5th Indian Division, less one brigade group, much exaggerated by the enemy, were already in the country. We had fought the partially successful action at Gallabat. It was therefore probable that the Italian strategy would be:

(*a*) To remain on the defensive on the Kenya front.

(*b*) To prevent access from outside Ethiopia to the patriots, while concentrating inside to stamp out the revolt.

(*c*) To protect Asmara and Massawa and to remain on the active defensive in the Kassala and El Ghena areas.

Although the Italian main strategy would probably be defensive, an attack in force to recapture Gallabat seemed likely. If successful, this would do much to prevent the passage of men, arms and money into the patriot areas from the Sudan. Furthermore, a success in the Sudan was needed to offset the serious reverses the Italians had suffered in Albania and were then suffering in the Western Desert.

Enemy Strength.

At this time there were the equivalent of two Italian Divisions in the Kassala area, one in the area Kassala – Tessenei – Sabdarat and one in the general area Adardeb – Serobatib – Wachai – Baraka Valley. The defences of Kassala had been developed to such an extent that considerable forces would be needed if Kassala was to be attacked with any chance of success.

As a result of our recent offensive at Gallabat, the enemy had increased his forces in the neighbourhood of Metemma and along the Gondar – Metemma road, making it necessary for us to retain sufficient forces in this area to prevent a successful hostile offensive.

Preliminary Operations.

Additional to these plans to achieve surprise in the major action, certain complementary operations were to be staged:-

(*a*) In the Boma area, G.O.C. East Africa intended to operate about 15th January to capture Baco and Maji. The Equatorial Corps and Patriots were to cooperate.

(*b*) In the Upper Nile area, minor operations were to be carried out in January by 2/6 King's African Rifles and the Upper Nile Police Forces.

(*c*) In the Blue Nile area the company of the Frontier Battalion, which was already in the Belaya massif, was to be reinforced and the Emperor himself was to move into this area.

Forces Available for the Attack.
It was necessary, for purposes of defence, to maintain one brigade (7th Indian Infantry Brigade), less one battalion, in the areas Port Sudan – Gebeit and one complete Indian Infantry brigade group (9th Indian Infantry Brigade) to contain the enemy forces opposite Gallabat. That left 4th and 5th Indian Divisions with only two brigades each available for Kassala. Moreover, 5th Indian Division was short of 144 Field Regiment which was split between 9th Infantry Brigade at Gallabat and Gazelle Force. This was, to some extent, compensated for by the addition of one medium battery, 6-inch Hows., and two troops 3.7-inch Hows. Sudan Defence Force.

"B" Squadron 4 Royal Tank Regiment had arrived by sea some time previously and had been concealed near Port Sudan. Considerable difficulties of movement were caused by the wrong specification of weights and length of "I"[1] tanks being given to Sudan Railways. This resulted in the flats for moving this Squadron by rail being strengthened in the wrong way. When the real weights and lengths were discovered, hardly any time was left to modify the flats. It was never possible to move the whole squadron by rail at once. The first troop was moved forward 15th January and reached Sabdarat on night 23rd January.

Topography.
The country round Kassala can be compared with a sea studded with islands. The desert is the sea, the jebels the islands, rising steep and rocky from the desert plain. West of Kassala the jebels are few and unimportant. Eastwards they increase in numbers and size until the foothills are reached. North and South are scattered jebels of considerable tactical importance. The desert is, on the whole, good going for M.T. of all types. If the enemy held these jebels determinedly, it was an infantry task to drive him out. Previous experience in minor operations in this area had proved that the Italians did, in fact, hold these natural strong points even if surrounded by mechanized or motorised forces.

Concealment.
Such a country was unsuitable for the concentration of large forces if their presence was to remain undiscovered, quite apart from the difficulty of finding sufficient water. At the Butana Bridge, though water was plentiful, cover was scanty. For these reasons and to aid deception three brigade groups were initially concentrated at or near Gedaref.

Running North from Kassala is the Gash Delta, an area thickly covered by bush, containing ample water and intersected by numerous dusty tracks. This was capable of hiding a considerable force but it was too near the enemy in Kassala for it to be possible to conceal troops there for any length of time without their presence being discovered. The cover was sufficient to conceal the strength of troops located therein. 4th Indian Division, less two brigades, was eventually concentrated in the Gash, screened by Gazelle Force, which had been using this area as a harbour for some time.

Strength Needed to Capture the Kassala – Sabdarat – Tessenei Triangle.
To capture the Kassala – Sabdarat – Tessenei triangle, and confirm the victory, a force of four brigade groups supported by some medium artillery, tanks and aircraft, was necessary.

The Commander-in-Chief made a force known as "Force Emily" available for operations in the Sudan. This force was moved partly by sea and partly by the Nile Valley route. The first flight consisted of the 7th Indian Infantry Brigade Group plus 68 Medium Regiment, less one battery, and certain other units which arrived at Port Sudan on 30th December. This brigade was moved to the Port Sudan – Gebeit area. The remaining parts of the force were due to arrive by sea on 7th, 14th and 21st January. The part moved by Nile Valley route, consisting of the 5th Indian Infantry Brigade Group and the Divisional Cavalry Regiment, plus other units, was due to arrive at Wadi Halfa over a period of five weeks from about 30th December. For its success the attack needed a waning moon and 9th February was provisionally fixed. It will therefore be seen that there was very little time between the arrival of the last units of Force Emily and the attack. This was compensated for by the fact that the units of Force Emily were all seasoned troops and had had active service experience.

Arrival of Force Emily in the Sudan.
The arrival of Force Emily in the Sudan taxed the Sudan Staff and Railways to the utmost. At this time there were no L. of C. signals in the Sudan and the difficulty of getting instructions and orders to units as they arrived was very great. Although every effort was made to deliver to each unit as it disembarked at Port Sudan, or as it arrived at Wadi Halfa, a complete set of documents, code lists and instructions appertaining to the Sudan, this was not in every case successful. The Sudan railway is only single line and the circuit had been cut by the enemy at Kassala. Accurate timing was needed so that the necessary rolling stock and flats should always be available to meet units as they arrived into the Sudan. The shortness of time available made it impossible to keep stock waiting and it was for this reason that some units had to be sent forward to concentration areas without their transport. This meant that on arrival they were immobile and were unable either to move themselves away from the railway or even to draw rations. In spite of this, no very great discomfort was experienced by any of the units. In general, the concentration can be said to have been carried out successfully and that, with the exception of the unfortunate bombing of the train containing

3/14 Punjab Regiment, enemy action caused no delay or casualties. Credit is due to the Q Movement staff in Khartoum that this move was completed without a hitch.

Operations during the Concentration Period.
During December and January, all through the period of concentration of Force Emily, active patrolling was continued both in the Gallabat area and in the country around Kassala. Day and night patrols kept commanders well informed of the dispositions and strength of the enemy. In the Gallabat area our artillery cost the enemy much loss, and, although we were unable to occupy Metemma itself, it was made untenable by the enemy as any movements seen immediately drew our artillery fire. In the country round Kassala, frequent and daring patrols by day and night established such an ascendancy over the enemy that he never ventured out of his defended positions except in strength, and that only rarely. Gazelle Force and 2 M.M.G. Group, S.D.F. from Butana Bridge dominated all the country that was not actually inside the Italian wire and fortifications.

Patrols laid frequent ambushes on the roads leading east and south from Kassala, destroying enemy vehicles and keeping him continuously on the alert. The effect of these patrols was to give the personnel of Gazelle Force and 2 M.M.G. Group a feeling of confidence and superiority over the enemy which may account for the skill and dash with which they led the pursuit in later days. Documents subsequently captured prove that, so effective was the screen put up by our forces at this time that the enemy's intelligence was gravely at fault. His estimate of our strength was exaggerated. Throughout this period 203 Group, R.A.F., afforded support to ground troops. The Rhodesian Army Co-operation Squadron, operating with Gazelle, carried out several successful joint operations with ground troops, both by bombing and low-flying attack. Long distance raids were made from Khartoum as far as Gondar, Gura and Asmara, and into Ethiopia in support of Patriot activities.

Enemy Action.
On the other hand, this period was not without anxiety, for the enemy forces concentrating between Gondar and Metemma were considerable. Reports of the enemy strengthening his garrisons at Kurmuk in the Upper Blue Nile sector and of improving the motor road from Asosa to Kurmuk, were constant threats to the Nile L. of C. and the railway at Sennar.

Period before Italian Evacuation of Kassala.
From early January there were strong indications from all sources of intelligence that the enemy might be intending to evacuate Kassala. At first it was not possible to say definitely whether the moves which the enemy was making were a re-grouping of his forces to resist an expected attack by us, or were the preliminaries to complete evacuation. Our forces were far from concentrated and there was considerable risk that if a premature attack was launched against the Kassala – Sabdarat – Tessenei triangle, it might suffer a reverse from lack of sufficient

strength and delay the eventual advance unduly. So strong were the indications that the enemy really did intend to withdraw, probably to the line Aicota – Keru, that by 12th January, a conference was called of both Divisional Commanders in Khartoum to decide on the earliest possible date an advance could be made and what strength would be available.

On the evening of 12th January, an order was sent to 4th and 5th Indian Divisions ordering 11th Indian Infantry Brigade Group to concentrate forthwith in the Aroma area and warning them that the brigade might be required to seize the Jebel Mokram and Jebel Kawatab, large jebels on the north-east side of Kassala and approximately three miles from it, not earlier than the night 16/17th January. 5th Indian Division was warned that it might be required to seize the Jebel Ibrahim Tan not earlier than the same night. 5th Indian Division was given permission to move forward 29th Indian Infantry Brigade, 68 Medium Regiment, less a battery, and 28 Field Regiment. (These had been held back in Gedaref area for reasons of secrecy and deception.) Gazelle was ordered to be prepared to operate east of Sabdarat. Reliable information revealed that the enemy now intended to evacuate the Walkait (Tsegede) garrison. There were only mule-tracks from this area to Gondar and the L. of C. was to Tessenei. From this it was reasonable to suppose that these forces would retire on Barentu covered for the first part of their move by Umm Hagar garrison. This was confirmed next day by the Manager of the Italian Cotton Scheme south of Tessenei who gave himself up at the Butana Bridge and stated that the enemy intended to retire to the hills "on account of the superiority of our tanks." The date of the attack on Kassala was fixed for 19th January.

Advance Headquarters.
On 18th January, a small Advanced Headquarters was established at the Butana Bridge. Advanced Headquarters, 203 Group, R.A.F., were established at the same place and time.

Orders for Pursuit.
It now became clear that the enemy had escaped from Kassala. At 1940 hours, orders were issued for the pursuit to commence and 4th Indian Division were directed first on Sabdarat, second on Wachai, and third to exploit towards Keru up to the limit of administration. 5th Indian Division was directed first on Tessenei, second on Aicota, and third to be prepared to exploit either towards Barentu or Biscia. The "I" tanks were to follow 4th Indian Division as soon as they detrained at Aroma, although it was doubtful whether the country further east would be suitable for their employment.

Administrative Note.
A few words on the administrative difficulties are not out of place here. 4th Indian Division was extended from Sabdarat as far back as Derudeb, 165 miles to the north, with 5th Infantry Brigade moving from the Gedaref area, 150 miles to the south-west. The Central India Horse and some transport for 5th Infantry

Brigade were still on the Nile Valley route, 250 miles to the north-west in a straight line across the desert, and more than double that by rail. The situation of 5th Indian Division was, if anything, even more difficult as its rear H.Q. was still in Gedaref and it also had to maintain the force operating up the Setit River based on Showak. Signal communications were becoming stretched and later, particularly in the case of 4th Indian Division, reached breaking point.

The pursuit started on the northern road Sabdarat – Wachai – Keren with Gazelle Force leading 11th Indian Infantry Brigade and 4th Indian Division; 5th Infantry Brigade a long way behind and not reaching Kassala until 20th January. Gazelle had its first brush with the enemy near Wachai, where a rearguard of approximately one battalion was unable to impose any great delay on our advance. It was here that our troops had their first serious air attack, but luckily few casualties were inflicted and the troops were unshaken.

Simultaneously, 5th Indian Division led by 10th Infantry Brigade succeeded in crossing the Gash near Tessenei and pursued the enemy toward Aicota which was reported unoccupied on the morning of 21st January.

Kassala itself was found to be very little damaged. Railway water tanks were destroyed and some rails had been removed. Signal cable lines were left intact. On his entry into Tessenei Commander 5th Indian Division was given a letter from the late Italian Civil Governor pointing but that he had left the town practically undamaged and expressing the hope that throughout the campaign both sides would respect civilian property. The repair of the railway line was put in hand immediately and the first train arrived at Kassala, which became railhead, on 25th January.

Action at Keru.

On 21st January the first serious resistance was encountered by 4th Indian Division on the northern route at Keru, where the road passes through a long steep ridge of hills. The road runs through a very narrow gorge and was a bad road for M.T. even before the enemy demolitions had made it more difficult.

4th Indian Division attacked from the east, and at the same time a Mechanized Column consisting of No. 2 M.M.G. Group with 2 Highland Light Infantry under command (Commander El Miralai Orr Bey, D.S.O.), moved from Aicota via Biscia towards Daura Toat, thus getting behind the enemy forces at Keru. The reconnaissance of the Keru position revealed that the gorge was narrow with hills rising about 1,500 ft. on either side. The position was well prepared and held by five enemy battalions. It was an ideal rearguard position and it appeared that the enemy intended to hold this for some time. During the early morning, 21st January, the gun positions of 25 Field Regiment and H.Q. Gazelle Force were charged from the flank by a party of about sixty enemy cavalry. They pressed home their attack with gallantry, throwing bombs at our troops, and were only stopped 25 yards from the gun positions by the guns firing point-blank, and by fire from L.M.Gs., rifles, and even anti-tank rifles. An attack by an enemy battalion from Keru was repulsed by Skinner's Horse. Throughout the day there was considerable enemy air activity though no great damage was done. Signal communication was very difficult, the wireless being variable owing to the proximity of the hills, atmospherics and distortion. By the evening, 3/14 Punjab and 31 Field Regiment had arrived at Sabdarat. 5th Infantry Brigade, less 4/6 Rajputana Rifles, all its carriers and much of its M.T., had arrived at Kassala and was there joined by a detachment of four "I" tanks. 3/14 Punjab Regiment were unfortunate in being the only unit to suffer casualties from enemy air action during the concentration period. The train in which they were travelling was bombed south of Derudeb, one British Officer and 23 O.Rs. were killed, two British Officers and 20 O.Rs. wounded.

During the early hours of 22nd January, 4/11 Sikh Regiment, less one company, which was the motorised battalion operating with Gazelle, attacked the enemy positions on a hill to the south of the Keru gorge. This action was successful.

During the night 22nd /23rd January, the enemy retired eastwards from his strong positions, probably due to the arrival of 10th Indian Infantry Brigade across the road Aicota – Biscia east of Keru, but it was not until 1500 hours on 23rd January that Gazelle Force was able to get through the Keru gorge, due to the large number of mines and damage done to the road. Practically the whole of the enemy force, 41 Colonial Brigade, fell into the hands of the Mechanized Column and 10th Infantry Brigade, the enemy Brigade Commander and most of his staff with about 800 prisoners being captured.

With the unopposed occupation of Aicota on 21st January, and the forcing of the Keru gorge by 23rd January, the enemy had been forced off his first line of resistance. The way was now open for our forces to advance on Agordat and Barentu. 4th Indian Division, whose L. of C. had to remain on the line Kassala – Sabdarat – Wachai – Keru, was faced with considerable administrative difficulties and ever increasing length of signal communication. It was still encumbered by its "tail", consisting of 5th Indian Infantry Brigade, a large proportion of whose transport had not yet caught up. The road Kassala – Keru and beyond was little more than a track. It had to cross several khors and constant work was necessary to keep it passable. The evacuation of wounded over this long and rough track caused considerable hardship.

5th Indian Division, on the other hand, once they had passed Tessenei, were on to the main strada which runs all the way from Tessenei via Barentu, Agordat and Asmara to the sea at Massawa. This strada was a well made motor road, capable of taking two lines of traffic, and although it was not tarmac it had a good macadam surface.

10th Infantry Brigade and the mechanized column which had been sent from Aicota to cut off the Keru garrison, once 4th Indian Division had passed on towards Agordat, were collected about three miles south of Biscia. It could either be moved back through Aicota and thence east along the strada to assist 29th Indian Infantry Brigade advancing on Barentu from west; or, if a way could be found, directed south-east across country to cut the Barentu – Agordat road.

This would allow an attack to be developed against Barentu simultaneously from north and west. The only available maps gave no clue. A route was found starting approximately two miles east of Biscia railway station, which, after running across country in a south-easterly direction, struck the Barentu – Agordat road near Terchina, 25 kilos north of Barentu. During the period while this track was being made by the sappers, some of the transport of 10th Indian Infantry Brigade was lent to 4th Indian Division to assist, 11th Indian Infantry Brigade forward towards Agordat. 11th Indian Infantry Brigade was directed to cut across the Agordat – Barentu road south of Agordat as early as possible on 26th January.

In the meantime 29th Infantry Brigade had advanced along the strada from Aicota towards Barentu, and, having fought two successful small actions, first at Gogni, which they captured on 25th January, and secondly at Tauda on 29th January, was closing in on Barentu from the west.

The cross-country move of 10th Indian Infantry Brigade, which had one and a half field regiments and one troop of 6-inch howitzers under command, was carried out without interference from the enemy. Barentu was threatened from the north by 28th January as well as from the west.

While these advances were taking place, the force operating up the Setit River had been active, and by 26th January had occupied Umm Hagar. The enemy force in the Walkait, finding that their line of retreat through Barentu was likely to be cut, were directed across country on to Tole. Up to this time there was no information that a road or track practicable for M.T. existed, leading eastwards from Barentu towards the escarpment at Arresa, and it was not until late in the action against Barentu that ground reconnaissance behind the enemy position discovered this route, by which the enemy eventually attempted to escape.

Biscia is the terminus of the Italian narrow gauge railway. From Biscia towards Agordat the road is slightly better, and was in parts metalled. 4th Indian Division, led by Gazelle Force, moved rapidly on to Agordat and by the evening of 25th January, Skinner's Horse were in a position west of Agordat from which the town could be seen. The route had been blocked in various places by fallen tree-trunks and a few mines, but nothing serious was met, and it was clear that the enemy had been hurried in his retreat. On this side of Agordat, the road runs for some miles close to the Baraka River, which at that time was a broad, sandy, dry river bed – a considerable obstacle for M.T. without the use of Army track or other extemporised crossing material. Both banks are thickly overgrown with palm trees, impassable for M.T. except on the tracks. While 11th Indian Infantry Brigade was being pushed forward to place itself astride the Barentu – Agordat road, south of Agordat, Gazelle Force covered its left flank and secured the L. of C. of 4th Indian Division. The Commander 4th Indian Division took a risk by side-stepping his force from the west to the south of Agordat, and against a determined enemy capable of launching a counter attack his L. of C. would have been in jeopardy, but, throughout the advance from Kassala, the enemy had shown no very determined fighting spirit, and in the circumstances this risk was justifiable. By 27th January, 5th Indian Infantry Brigade had reached Biscia and was moving forward to join 11th Indian Infantry Brigade as quickly as it could be moved, bringing with it the "I" tanks. Such had been the speed of the move that 4th Indian Division Signals had now reached breaking point. Over 100 miles of cable had been used, and there had been no time to collect the cable which had been laid out in the Gash area before the advance had commenced. The cypher personnel were overworked, and were approximately 48 hours behind hand with their messages. Commander 4th Indian Division destroyed these messages and started afresh.

Agordat was the first town of any size met in Eritrea. It was a strong defensive position. To the north and west the Baraka Valley; south was the feature known as Laquatat – a large hilly feature, with concrete trenches, emplacements and O.Ps. East of the Laquatat feature and extending for about two miles is an open plain, intersected with dry stream beds, and defended by a series of field defences and anti-tank pits. This plain was bounded on the east by M. Cochen, a big, rocky feature rising 2,000 feet from the plain. At the foot of M. Cochen towards Laquatat is a low underfeature, a mere pile of rocks 100 feet high, forming a natural flank to the line of artificial defences across the plain. This feature was named Gibraltar by 4th Indian Division. The strada from Barentu approaches Agordat from a direction slightly west of south, and on entering the town turns sharply east and runs through a narrow gorge bounding M. Cochen on the north. From thence it runs through more open country until crossing the River Carabei at the Ponte Mussolini, a large modern bridge 18 kilos from Agordat.

The Course of the Battle.
The course of the battle was as follows.

Gazelle Force was first ordered to explore the possibility of encircling Agordat from the south, but found themselves entangled in the many khors and had to return. They next attempted to get round the north flank, but again difficulties of the Baraka River and the dom-palms were too great. Gazelle was then left watching the northern flank, whilst 11th Indian Infantry Brigade was moved across towards M. Cochen, 5th Indian Infantry Brigade stepping-up and taking its place on the left of 11th Indian Infantry Brigade, connecting 11th Indian Infantry Brigade and Gazelle Force. A night reconnaissance in force discovered that Laquatat was very strong. Commander 4th Indian Division therefore directed 11th Indian Infantry Brigade on to M. Cochen and two battalions supported by an Artillery O.P. Party succeeded in establishing themselves on the top of the mountain. They were strongly resisted by five battalions of the enemy and although severely counter-attacked, and on one occasion nearly driven off, a grip was maintained on the hill for 48 hours. A note-worthy incident of the fighting on this hill was the gallant bayonet charge by a party of Sappers and Miners led by an Indian Officer in aid of a hard-pressed party of 3/14 Punjabs. On the morning of 31st January, 2 Camerons attacked and stormed the rocky ridge known as Gibraltar. On this being secured, I Royal Fusiliers, supported by "I" tanks, launched a successful attack against the enemy positions in the plain between

Laquatat and M. Cochen. 2 Camerons exploited along the lower slopes west of M. Cochen, knocking-out enemy medium tanks with anti-tank rifles as they advanced. Shortly before mid-day three "I" tanks and the carriers of 2 Camerons carried out a raid along the west side of M. Cochen towards the main road. In this area they encountered enemy medium and light tanks and troops which were probably the enemy's counter-attacking force waiting in this area. Five medium and five light tanks were destroyed and large numbers of enemy troops, both Italian and Native, were killed. At 1430 hours 3/1 Punjabs, supported by two "I" tanks, passed through I Royal Fusiliers and secured some low hills just to the south-east of Agordat. These were captured just before nightfall, and the enemy's main L. of C. was cut. Artillery O.Ps. on M. Cochen had reported during the afternoon that they could see the enemy withdrawing from the Laquatat feature into the town, and the R.A.F. reported large bodies of enemy streaming through the gorge north of M. Cochen. Two "I" tanks under command of a Second-Lieutenant were sent into the gorge after dark in an attempt to create a panic. Next morning Agordat town was occupied by 5th Indian Infantry Brigade, and although the enemy and native population had indulged in a night of looting, destruction of property was not unduly great. A large quantity of war material and guns fell into our hands. A proportion of the enemy infantry escaped by rail and over the hills to the north of the main road.

Barentu Front.
In the meantime 5th Indian Division was attacking Barentu. By 27th January, 10th Indian Infantry Brigade advancing on Barentu from the north after their action east of Keru had reached a point about two miles north of the town. Here the road winds up a long and very steep gorge. The road itself works its way up the western side, and near the top the enemy had carried out a successful demolition, blowing hundreds of tons of rock down on to the road.

The country around Barentu is excellent for defence, consisting as it does of a number of low ridges, thickly covered by scrub. To a defender they offer a series of good rearguard positions. To an attacker they are difficult, as it is hard to point out an objective, and even harder for the attacking troops to know when they have reached an objective. Barentu itself is on a little knoll in the centre of a saucer of hills. The defence had the advantage of excellent covered lateral communications and although pressed from two sides, could deny artillery observation to us until the rim of the saucer was secured. It was through this type of rolling country that 29th Indian Infantry Brigade had to make its way ever since leaving Aicota. The advance of 29th Indian Infantry Brigade compared with that of the other brigades was slow. This was due to the rearguard actions fought, the enemy's use of mines, and the fact that this brigade could be given no troop-carrying transport. Only one demolition of any size was encountered by this brigade when on reaching a road bridge approximately 12 kilos west of Barentu they found it severely blown and an alternative route through the bushes heavily mined. This, however, did not impose any great delay, the artillery supporting 29th Indian Infantry Brigade being brought forward into action with praiseworthy energy and determination. On 1st February, No. 2 M.M.G. Group S.D.F., having worked its way across-country, carried out a successful raid on the road running east from Barentu where it inflicted heavy casualties on an enemy Colonial Battalion which was withdrawing eastwards. During the night 1/2nd February, the enemy evacuated Barentu, and, on the early morning of 2nd February, 10th and 29th Indian Infantry Brigades occupied the town. An immediate pursuit to the limit of endurance was ordered and taken up by No. 2 M.M.G. Group S.D.F. assisted by the R.A.F. The enemy suffered casualties all the way. He was intending to reach Arresa and the escarpment by way of an old track which had been allowed to become overgrown. This track ran through from Barentu via Scipitale Defile – Tole – and thence up the Torrenti Ambessa to Adi Raghebla. Some miles beyond Adi Raghebla the track descends steeply into the valley of the Mai Terageit and here the enemy finally abandoned the last of his vehicles and guns. Only one light car and possibly one motor cycle reached Arresa. The rest of the enemy force escaped as a weary and disorganised rabble.

PART I (B).

Gallabat Area.

Throughout the period of the pursuit, the 9th Indian Infantry Brigade had been containing the enemy at Gallabat, and, by active patrolling, had kept him fully occupied. On 25th January the advance towards Asmara had gone so well that the decision was made to make this the main thrust, and to be content with watching the route Gedaref – Gallabat – Gondar with a minimum force. Orders were issued cancelling the work already begun on the extension of the Sudan railway from Gedaref towards Gallabat. The railway from Kassala was to be extended as quickly as possible as far as Tessenei. This work was given priority over all other railway work in the Sudan. It was further decided that an all-weather road from Rashid to Gallabat was not now necessary, and that a well maintained dry-weather track would suffice.

The first indications that the enemy intended to withdraw from Gallabat came from Intelligence sources early in January, and there was every indication that this withdrawal would be co-ordinated with the withdrawal from Umm Hagar, Walkait and the Kassala – Sabdarat – Tessenei triangle. 9th Indian Infantry Brigade had kept up continuous patrol activity, but it was not until 30th January that the enemy's withdrawal became imminent. If this should happen 9th Indian Infantry Brigade were instructed to pursue with a mechanised column only. The main body of 9th Indian Infantry Brigade was ordered to remain in the Metemma area, so that they could be quickly switched to the main front. By 1st February the enemy was on the move, pursued by the mechanised column consisting of the carriers of 9th Indian Infantry Brigade and a Motorised Company of 3/12 Frontier Force Regiment, preceded by a detachment of 21 Field Company, Sappers and Miners. The enemy's retirement on this front was much less hurried than on the 4th and 5th Indian Divisional lines of advance and great delay was imposed by his lavish use of mines along the seventy miles from Metemma to Chelga. It was in clearing these mines that Second-Lieutenant Bhagat of 21 Field Company, Sappers and Miners, earned his V.C. for cool and conspicuous gallantry and endurance over a long period. After crossing the River Gandwa, where our mechanised column first made contact with the remnants of the Italian garrison of Karawa which was retreating in disorder harassed by the patriots, steady progress was made, and by 10th February, contact was made with the Abyssinian patriots in Wahni. By 13th February, 9th Indian Infantry Brigade, less 3/12 Frontier Force Regiment, was concentrated in Gedaref, leaving 3/12 Frontier Force Regiment supported by 144 Field Regiment, less one battery, 21 Field Company and one troop of "X" Light A.A. Battery, Sudan Regiment, in the areas Metemma – Gandwa – Wahni.

PART II.

Pursuit to Keren.

On 1st February, immediately after the battle of Agordat, Gazelle Force was directed to pursue the enemy towards Keren, but 18 kilos from Agordat it was held up until 1700 hours by the demolished Ponte Mussolini. The main girders of this bridge had been blown, and it was impossible to get M.T. over it. The Baraka at this point is about 150 yards wide, and at that time consisted of a strip of soft, deep sand over which vehicles could not pass without some form of temporary track. The construction of this track was made more difficult by the large number of mines which the enemy had laid around all the approaches to the bridge, and along the only alternative route. The enemy had covered this demolition and minefield by a pack gun and a few machine-guns. Accurate shooting by a section of field artillery succeeded in knocking these out quickly. By the evening of 2nd February, Gazelle with six "I" tanks and 11th Indian Infantry Brigade were only five miles from Keren.

Topography.

After crossing the Ponte Mussolini the strada runs in a general north-easterly direction over open, slightly rolling country. Ahead is the escarpment, a high, dark, solid wall barring the way into Eritrea. From this distance it appears to be a sheer cliff, stretching as far as the eye can see without a break. For the last few miles before Keren the road runs through a narrow valley, bounded on the left by the escarpment itself, and on the right by a great spur, whose highest peak rises to 6,000 feet.

In this valley and on the surrounding heights was fought the battle of Keren. Nowhere were the enemy O.Ps. less than 500 feet above the valley; in most cases they were 2,000 feet up.

Throughout the hours of daylight no movement of man, beast, or vehicle was possible unseen from at least one and usually many enemy view points. The valley was of sand and gravel, with sparse scrub and occasional tebeldi trees affording, in places, some cover from direct observation to men at rest and guns.

The valley varies in width from half-a-mile to a mile-and-a-half. The road runs along the south side until opposite M. Dologorodoc where it turns sharply north over a bridge, and, after climbing the lower slopes of this hill, enters the Dongolaas gorge. Up this narrow slit in the hills, nowhere more than 300 yards wide, the road climbs to the higher level of the plain of Keren.

Below Fort Dologorodoc and east of where the road crosses the valley is a wide amphitheatre known as the Happy Valley. The only entrance for wheeled-traffic is over the bridge at the corner where the road turns north. In the north wall of this cup is the Acqua gap, really only a lessening of height and steepness, down which the rain water from the plain of Keren makes its way. This gap is flanked on the east by M. Zelale, a high, rocky hill known from its shape as "The Sphinx".

Fort Dologorodoc, guarding the entrance of the Dongolaas gorge is itself overlooked on the east, north-east and north-west by Mts. Falestoh, Zeban and Sanchil. From all of these fire could be brought on to the Fort. Troops on M. Dologorodoc could never be out of sight of at least one of these.

North-westwards from M. Sanchil the series of features, Brigs Peak, Sugar Loaf, Saddle, Near Feature, Hogs Back, Flat Top Hill, Molehill, M. Samanna and North of Saddle, M. Amba, were all the scenes of serious fighting. These mountains are very steep. Their slopes are covered with large boulders and scrub. There were no paths up them when the troops first arrived. As an indication of their size and steepness, it was a good hour-and-a-quarter's walk to the gunner O.P. on Rajputana Ridge which is itself only half way up Brigs Peak. The railway from Agordat to Keren runs along the north side of the valley, and by the time it reaches Dongolaas gorge has climbed a third of the way up the lower slopes of M. Sanchil. A man standing in the valley sees the railway clinging, high up, to the hillsides above him. This railway was subsequently of great assistance to 4th Indian Division in maintaining the troops holding the heights.

At the time of the fall of Agordat the garrison of Keren was known to be one Colonial Brigade, and it was hoped that by moving rapidly, the town might be reached before reinforcements could arrive. By 2nd February it was discovered that one other Colonial Brigade and part of the Grenadier Division from Addis Ababa had been brought up. In the first rush Gazelle Force reached the road-block in the Dongolaas gorge. This was a formidable demolition covered by fire, and situated on the west side of Fort Dologorodoc. Once the enemy were in position it was difficult to get a view of this road-block from any point in the battlefield, except Cameron Ridge (a sub-feature of M. Sanchil). A detailed reconnaissance was, thereafter, only possible inside an "I" tank, 11th Indian Infantry Brigade was moving behind Gazelle with 2 Camerons embussed. On 3rd February the "I" tanks made a determined attack upon the road-block but were unable to get past. 2 Camerons went up the hill on the left towards Brigs Peak and secured Cameron Ridge. Skinner's Horse secured the right flank and a battalion was sent into Happy Valley to try and find a way round the right.

Factors Affecting the Decision to Fight at Keren.

The storming of the Keren position was no light task. Its natural strength, the difficulties of maintenance and the climatic conditions had to be faced. Every day the temperature was rising. A numerically superior enemy had chosen Keren as the ground on which to fight what might prove to be a decisive battle. The enemy had every advantage of observation and possessed a still strong and active air force. Gaining surprise was unlikely. The forcing of Keren was bound to mean hard fighting and casualties which would be difficult to replace.

The desirability of finding a way round was obvious. From almost the day of the first contact at Keren continuous and wide reconnaissances were made to north and south seeking an alternative way through the escarpment wall. 3 Central India Horse searched south for 60 miles until, making contact with No. 2 Motor Machine Gun Group S.D.F. which was facing Arresa. At Arresa was a possible gap, but the route had proved so difficult that the retreating Italians from Barentu had been forced to abandon all their vehicles. Now, not only were there the natural difficulties, but the way was blocked by enemy forces. No road capable of maintaining a force strong enough to fight its way through existed from Barentu, and the time it would take to build one would allow the enemy to make the Arresa position as formidable as Keren. A successful attack here would not return the same dividend as at Keren. Rain would bring M.T. moving between Barentu and Arresa to a stand-still. No way was found to the north either. It became clear that Keren is the only practicable approach to the higher levels of the escarpment for a force of any size.

First Attack on Acqua Gap.

By 6th February, as the situation in Agordat was quite calm, 5th Indian Infantry Brigade, less one battalion, was moved forward to the Keren area with the intention of attacking round the right flank through Happy Valley and Acqua gap. The difficulties of this operation will be appreciated when it is realised that throughout the entire battle the enemy had the high ground, and all movements, whether in M.T. or on foot, were clearly visible to his O.Ps. O.Ps. on Fort Dologorodoc and M. Sanchil have the road almost in enfilade for miles. O.Ps. on M. Samanna and M. Amba overlooked all administrative areas of the forward brigades. During the night 4/5th February, 3/14 Punjab Regiment went through 2 Camerons on Cameron Ridge and occupied Brigs Peak, but were driven off on the afternoon of the next day. 1/6 Rajputana Rifles occupied the extension of Cameron Ridge south of Brigs Peak, and although severely counter-attacked, held on. Throughout all this early period of the battle, the enemy was being rapidly reinforced, and was counter-attacking with skill and determination. At this time his troops were rather better at moving on the hill than were ours, and a certain amount of the lessons of Frontier Warfare had to be unlearnt due to the influence of artillery, mortars, L.M.Gs. and aircraft on mountain warfare. During the night 7/8th February, 5th Indian Infantry Brigade moved into the Happy Valley, and on the early morning of 8th February, 4/6 Rajputana Rifles attacked the Acqua Col. This was found to be wired and strongly held, and they were unable to reach their objective, eventually consolidating on a ridge below the col. 5th Indian Infantry Brigade remained in this valley some days, being subjected to fairly heavy attacks from the enemy airforce. Pressure against 11th Indian Infantry Brigade on Cameron Ridge and Rajputana Ridge features was severe, and a second attempt to secure Brigs Peak, which would relieve pressure on 11th Indian Infantry Brigade and give us artillery observation of Keren, was decided upon. This attack was carried out by 3/1 Punjab Regiment at 1500 hours in the afternoon of 10th February supported by a heavy concentration of artillery fire on Brigs Peak and M. Sanchil. The attack was successful and Brigs Peak was captured. Part of M. Sanchil was also captured, but had to be evacuated as the battalion was seriously reduced in numbers. During these operations our casualties in officers had been heavy. Lt.-Col. Whitehead, commanding 3/1 Punjab Regiment, Lt.-Col. Purvis, 4/11 Sikhs, Lt.-Col. Edwards, 1 Royal Fusiliers, Lt.-Col. Scott, Skinner's Horse, and Major Proctor, of 3/1 Punjab Regiment, were all seriously wounded.

Second Attack on Acqua Gap.

For the second attempt to force the Acqua Col., 29th Indian Infantry Brigade, which was garrisoning Barentu, was placed under command 4th Indian Division, with the limitation that it was only to be used to exploit complete success, and was under no circumstances to be employed as a reinforcement. The reason for attacking the Acqua Gap was that, in spite of the administrative difficulties of maintaining two brigades in the Happy Valley, this attack if successful, would cut across the enemy's line of communication at a most vulnerable spot, and offered the chance of cutting-off and capturing the greater part of his forces in Keren and on the hills to the West. The period between 10th and 12th February was very trying for the troops holding Brigs Peak and Cameron Ridge. The enemy counter-attacked continuously, and during the early hours of 11th February 3/1 Punjab Regiment were driven off Brigs Peak back on to Cameron Ridge.

The second attack on the Acqua Gap was carried out by 4/11 Sikhs on the right, directed on the Sphinx (M. Zalale) and the 4/6 Rajputana Rifles directed on a feature known as Hill 1565. Although attacking with great gallantry these battalions were unable to reach their objective, and owing to the shape of the ground and the length of telephone communications necessary, adequate artillery support was not forthcoming. Commander 4th Indian Division decided to terminate the operation. 29th Indian Infantry Brigade were withdrawn from the Valley, and returned to Barentu. During the night of 13/14th February the rest of our forces were also successfully withdrawn. Both of these brigades had to withdraw through the bottleneck described above, under observed and registered artillery fire from the enemy's guns on Fort Dologorodoc and surrounding features. In spite of this, and in spite of the activity of the enemy's artillery, the total casualties during withdrawal were two men slightly wounded. After the second unsuccessful attack on the Acqua Gap it was clear that any further assault on the Keren position would be a major operation. Shortage of transport made it impossible to maintain both divisions in the Keren area and at the same time build up sufficient reserves of ammunition, petrol and rations. It was decided that 29th Indian Infantry Brigade should remain in Barentu. The rest of 5th Indian Division was withdrawn to the area between Sabdarat and Tessenei where it could maintain itself from the railhead at Kassala with its own first-line transport. All second-line transport was put under control of H.Q. Troops in the Sudan. While it was in this area, 5th Indian Division carried out intensive training in mountain warfare for the purposes of studying tactics and making every man as physically fit as possible. For the purposes of deception, measures were taken to induce the enemy to believe that a thrust was intended from Barentu to Arresa and thence on to the plateau directed on Adi Ugri. During this period of patrol and administrative activity it was left to 4th Indian Division to hold the heights already secured opposite Keren and to make preparations for the reception at short notice of 5th Indian Division.

The Red Sea Coast.
As early as 21st January, Commander 7th Indian Infantry Brigade had reported that the enemy was withdrawing from the Karora area and asked permission to start a minor operation against the enemy garrison there. This permission was given. The idea of a thrust down the Red Sea Coast had been previously considered and at first it had been used to divert attention from Kassala. It was difficult to get accurate estimates of what water was available, but, after consultation with the Royal Navy, it was considered feasible to direct a force of approximately one brigade group from Port Sudan via Suakin – Karora – Nakfa – Cub Cub and on to Keren from the north.

The forces available were 7th Indian Infantry Brigade, less 4/11 Sikhs, which had previously been motorised and sent to join Gazelle Force. The battalion garrisoning Khartoum, 4/16 Punjab Regiment, was released. One battery, 25 pounders, No. 4 M.M.G. Company, S.D.F., 12 Field Company, Sappers and Miners, and 170 Light Field Ambulance were withdrawn from Keren front and sent to join 7th Infantry Brigade. Added weight was given to this force by the arrival in the Sudan of Free French Forces. These were 14 Battalion Etranger of the Foreign Legion, plus certain supporting troops, and Troisiéme Battalion de Marche (Tchad), known as Battalion Garby. The Foreign Legion, seasoned troops who had seen service in Norway, arrived by sea. Battalion Garby entered the Sudan by overland route from French Equatoria. These two units, under the command of Col. Monclar, were formed into a Demi-Brigade, known as the Brigade d'Orient. All French forces were placed under command of 7th Infantry Brigade.

To overcome the administrative difficulties of an advance down this coast, the plan was to use barges, dhows and small ships to move both troops and stores by sea first to Aqiq, and later to open a small port at Mersa Taclai. It was intended that if this force should be used later to threaten Massawa, Marsa Kuba would be opened as well. By 10th February, a column consisting of I Royal Sussex had occupied Mersa Taclai and by the 12th, after some minor engagements, was moving towards Nakfa and Cub Cub. 7th Indian Infantry Brigade Group gained wireless touch with 4th Indian Division on 17th February and from then on a nightly conversation in Pushtu took place between the G.S.O.I. of 4th Indian Division and the Brigade Major of 7th Indian Infantry Brigade. The first serious resistance encountered was at Cub Cub where the Battalion Garby distinguished itself. By 1st March, 7th Indian Infantry Brigade Group had cleared the Mescelit Pass, some 20 kilos north of Keren, and here the advance paused for a time to concentrate its scattered units and recast its plan for the advance on Keren.

Keren Front.

During this period 4th Indian Division endured a long and anxious time holding the hills on the north side of the road. The enemy extended his right flank further and further to the west, thus overlooking all the administrative areas of forward units and causing the 4th Indian Divisional Commander continual anxiety and a steady drain of casualties. The weather was hot and the strain imposed upon the troops considerable. During this period various expedients were used to get the railway working. Two diesel engines were sent from Atbara, which, after some delays, worked successfully. Owing to the gradients, the tonnage these diesels could move was small. Trollies and tracks pulled by 15 cwt. lorries were also used forward of railhead. Railhead was only shelled once. Throughout all this period the enemy's air was active but confined itself exclusively to attacks on the forward troops. The long columns of transport continually on the road between Keren and Kassala were never interfered with from the air. In order to build up sufficient reserves, R.A.S.C., R.I.A.S.C., and Cape Corps personnel were overworked and lorries were regularly doing a 48-hour turn-round between the dumping area and railhead. It is to the credit of the administrative staffs and services that, in spite of the large number of shells actually fired throughout the Keren battle, the gunners were never short and did, in fact, have a surplus. At this time troops in this area were suffering minor casualties from small cuts and scratches going septic. The administrative staffs managed to supply troops, even in the forward positions, with the oranges and fresh fruit necessary to maintain health. The forward dumping programme also needed considerable administrative skill and much hard work by the troops. Upwards from the railway, every article of necessity, including water, had to be carried by men and mules. Two Cypriot mule companies which had come into the Sudan about a month previously were moved up, and, after the mules and men had got used to moving at night on the steep, narrow, rocky tracks, proved themselves invaluable. 4th Indian Division, which was well equipped for desert warfare, had to adapt itself in battle to mountain warfare conditions. It was faced with both types of problem in the space of fifteen days.

On 17th February, the situation on the Keren front was as follows:-

5th Indian Infantry Brigade had relieved 11th Indian Infantry Brigade on the hills. 11th Indian Infantry Brigade was resting in reserve. The enemy had been reinforced by the majority of the Savoy Grenadier Division, in addition to the First Division, and was aggressive. He held the highest ground, and was continuing to extend his right round the northern flank of 5th Indian Infantry Brigade. On the other hand there was a steady flow of deserters at the rate of 150 a day. The enemy was known to have suffered heavily in the recent attacks. 7th Indian Infantry Brigade, from the north, was closing on Cub Cub, which, if taken, would allow this brigade to make its presence felt against Keren. The Foreign Legion, which had reached Suakin, was awaiting a ship to carry it forward to join 7th Indian Infantry Brigade. Administrative activity in building up the necessary reserves in the forward areas continued.

Reliefs.

The continued strain on 4th Indian Division was unavoidable. The relief of 4th Indian Division by 5th Indian Division would have delayed the administrative programme, as there was not enough transport to carry out this relief and continue dumping simultaneously. A suggestion that the forward troops of 4th Indian Division might withdraw to a position some miles further west out of the Keren Valley where they would not be so closely overlooked by the enemy on the high ground, though possibly tactically sound, would have had a depressing moral effect on our troops, and would have encouraged the enemy. 4th Indian Division was suffering 25 casualties a day. This flow of losses, a severe drain which the division could ill afford could only have been diminished by retiring between 10 and 12 kilos. For the sake of the bigger issues they had to be accepted. Withdrawal from the valley would have made the assault on Keren impracticable.

Plan and Concentration.

On 1st March the outline plan for what was hoped would be the final assault on Keren was formulated. The attack was to be by both divisions. 4th Indian Division was given objectives on the left of the road which included M. Sanchil, Brigs Peak, Hogs Back, Saddle, Flat Top Hill, Mole Hill and Samanna. The left flank having been thus secured, 5th Indian Division would attack right of the road. Exact objectives were not at this time defined, pending the results of further reconnaissances.

These attacks were to be consecutive and not simultaneous, so that each division could be supported by the maximum number of guns. Sufficient time was allowed between attacks for the necessary defensive fire on 4th Indian Division front and supporting concentrations on 5th Indian Division front to be arranged.

The date of the attack was fixed as 15th March. 5th Indian Division was not to come forward until the last possible moment. This was both to keep the enemy in the dark about the date of our intended attack, and to allow the forward dumping programme to continue unhindered. 5th Indian Division was to arrive in accordance with the following programme. Artillery – one gun per Battery and reconnaissance parties would arrive on 8th March; the remainder, 12th March. Infantry – the reconnaissance parties and one battalion from the leading infantry brigade on 10th March; balance of the leading infantry brigade on 11th March, and the second and third infantry brigades on the 13th and 15th March respectively. By this time 9th Indian Infantry Brigade Group from Gallabat, less one company of 3/12 Frontier Force Regiment and 21 Field Company, had rejoined 5th Indian Division from Gedaref. Certain Sappers and Miners companies were also sent forward in advance of 5th Indian Division for essential work in the forward area and the making of an advanced landing ground.

Administrative Arrangements.

Administrative layout was to remain on a divisional basis: 4th Indian Division's installations north of the road, 5th Indian Division's south of the road. An exception was made to this in the case of medical arrangements, in which 5th Indian Division was superimposed on 4th Indian Division, co-ordinated by A.D.M.S. 5th Indian Division.

By 8th March the 4th Indian Divisional plan was taking shape. It consisted of two attacks known as the right and left attacks. The right attack was to be carried out by 11th Indian Infantry Brigade, which had two additional battalions placed under its command. These were I Royal Fusiliers, borrowed from 5th Indian Infantry Brigade, and 2/5 Mahratta Light Infantry, which had been the L. of C. Battalion in the Sudan. The attack was to be on a three battalion front. Right – 2 Camerons on M. Sanchil and Brigs Peak; centre – 1/6 Rajputana Rifles on to Saddle and Hogs Back; on the left 2/5 Mahratta Light Infantry on Flat Top Hill. I Royal Fusiliers and 4/6 Rajputana Rifles were to hold a firm base on Cameron Ridge and Rajputana Ridge. The role of these two battalions was in reality a reserve under the Divisional Commander for exploiting from M. Sanchil to Keren in conformity with the success gained by 5th Indian Division.

In the left attack 5th Indian Infantry Brigade, less I Royal Fusiliers plus 51 Commando, was to secure the left flank of 11th Indian Infantry Brigade from counter-attacks from the M. Amba direction by taking the three ring contours, known as left, centre and right bumps, of M. Samanna.

Artillery.

The artillery programme for 4th Indian Division was almost ready, and involved dumping 300 rounds per gun at the gun positions, with another 450 rounds per gun readily available behind. The provisional estimate for the 5th Indian Division attack was 600 rounds a gun.

5th Indian Division's Plan.

After reconnaissance 5th Indian Division was directed to capture M. Zeban by way of Fort Dologorodoc. This objective, though most formidable, had certain advantages. The attack was to be in close co-operation with 4th Indian Division; each division could effectively help the other. The time-lag between the two attacks could be reduced to a minimum as the gunner problem of switching from support of 4th Indian Division to support of 5th Indian Division was comparatively simple. These objectives were within range of almost all the artillery of both divisions without guns having to be moved. The reduction of the time between the attacks automatically relieved the strain on 4th Indian Division which was bound to be counter-attacked strongly shortly after reaching its objectives.

The alternative was to attempt once again to force the Acqua Gap. Success in this area offered the chance of cutting-off and capturing the greater part of the Keren garrison. Its disadvantages were that the two divisions could not effectively support each other; the artillery problem was intensified and 5th Indian Division would not get the benefit of all the 4th Indian Division's guns; maintenance of a division through the bottleneck between Fort Dologorodoc and the bridge would be liable to enemy interference; there was no chance of getting the tanks and carriers up the Acqua Gap; against a numerically superior enemy there was a chance that both attacks would fail from lack of weight. Although a drive through the Dongolaas Gorge would not succeed in cutting-off so many of the enemy forces, it offered a better chance of opening the road to Asmara.

The task of assaulting Fort Dologorodoc was given to 9th Indian Infantry Brigade, and 2 Highland Light Infantry from 10th Indian Infantry Brigade was placed under its command. 29th Indian Infantry Brigade was initially concentrated close behind 9th Indian Infantry Brigade, and was to be prepared to go through and capture M. Zeban, and thence onwards to M. Canabai. Exploitation eastwards over Falestoh Col between M. Falestoh and M. Zeban was to be limited to point 1565.

Effect on 4th Indian Division Plan.
The decision to attack Fort Dologorodoc enabled Commander 4th Indian Division to place the two battalions holding Cameron Ridge and Rajputana Ridge at the disposal of Commander 11th Indian Infantry Brigade, to give the assault on M. Sanchil and Brigs Peak a greater chance of success. Should M. Sanchil not be captured, enemy fire from there would have a serious effect on 9th Indian Infantry Brigade on Fort Dologorodoc.

R.A.F.
In support of these operations, one squadron and one flight of Army Co-operation aircraft were available, based on the main landing ground at Agordat, and using the advanced landing ground at Force Headquarters to keep in the closest touch with the tactical situation. Three bomber and one fighter squadrons and a fighter flight were kept under direct control of the Air Officer Commanding. These formations were warned that detachments of bombers and fighters might be called for in close support of ground troops. For the day of the attack, six sorties were placed at the disposal of C.R.A's, and six sorties were retained for tactical reconnaissance.

Operations on 15th March.
Zero hour for the 4th Indian Divisional attack was timed for 0700 hours 15th March. Sunrise was about 0630 hours. The sun rose straight over the opposite ridge, shining down the valley, blinding artillery O.Ps. and the attacking

troops. It was not until 0700 hours that the sun was sufficiently high to see clearly eastwards. The Italians "stood to" at dawn and usually went back behind the slopes for breakfast shortly after. The artillery concentrations would make it hard for them to get their men up again. Zero at 0700 hours would allow the attacking troops to have breakfast and start the day reasonably administered. During the early hours of the morning 9th and 29th Indian Infantry Brigades had concentrated behind the lower slopes of Cameron Ridge. The assault on Fort Dologorodoc was to be carried out by 2 Highland Light Infantry, which was to approach its objective from a south-westerly direction. This attack was not to go in until M. Sanchil and Brigs Peak had been secured. It was calculated that these hills would be in our hands by 0900 hours. The exact time of the attack depended on when the artillery supporting 4th Indian Division could be spared to support 5th Indian Division. By 0945 hours the situation on the 4th Indian Division front appeared to be sufficiently satisfactory for the order to be given to 5th Indian Division to attack. At this time it was not confirmed that Brigs Peak and M. Sanchil had been captured, but progress appeared to be satisfactory, and there was every prospect that both M. Sanchil and Brigs Peak would be secured shortly.

The attack of 2 Highland Light Infantry was stopped within 200 yards of the starting line by severe flank fire by machine-guns in enfilade, located on the lower eastern slopes of M. Sanchil. By 1300 hours it was clear that 2 Highland Light Infantry could make no further progress from this direction, and it was decide that they should be side-stepped to their right to approach Fort Dologorodoc from the south instead of the south-west. This new attack was timed for 1530 hours.

Capture of Fort Dologorodoc.
The weather on 15th and 16th March was extremely hot, with cloud and a heavy, oppressive atmosphere. The heat and radiation from the rocks for troops awaiting in the bottom of the valley was very trying. The lack of success of 2 Highland Light Infantry was as much attributable to physical exhaustion as to enemy action, although this was severe. It was also clear that Fort Dologorodoc was far too big an objective for one battalion. Commander 9th Indian Infantry Brigade planned to assault Fort Dologorodoc at dusk from the south with two battalions: right – 3/12 Frontier Force Regiment; left – 3/5 Mahrattas. These two attacks were successful in capturing two sub-features of Fort Dologorodoc, known as Pimple and Pinnacle, by midnight. Touch with these two battalions was lost, but Commander 9th Indian Infantry Brigade ordered 2 West Yorks on to the col between Pimple and Pinnacle where they arrived shortly after midnight. Before first light the enemy from the Fort itself counter-attacked strongly, but met the whole of the 9th Indian Infantry Brigade in line. The plan had been for 2 West Yorks to go through 3/12 Frontier Force and 3/5 Mahrattas and assault the Fort under cover of a timed artillery programme. In the confusion of the counter-attack, communications broke down, and it was impossible to stop the artillery concentration which came down on the Fort as planned. This, in fact, was most

fortunate, as the enemy's counter-attacking forces found themselves between the small arms fire of 9th Indian Infantry Brigade and the artillery fire falling on their own fort behind. They broke and were pursued into the Fort by 9th Indian Infantry Brigade, 2 West Yorks reaching there at 0600 hours, immediately exploiting 800 yards beyond.

Situation on 4th Indian Division Front.
By this time the true facts of the 4th Indian Division right attack became clear. 2 Camerons had reached their objectives but had suffered such heavy casualties that they had not sufficient remaining strength to clear the enemy off M. Sanchil and Brigs Peak. The 1 Royal Fusiliers, sent forward to reinforce 2 Camerons, also reached the objective, but could not clear the enemy off, and by nightfall, confused fighting was still in progress. 1/6 Rajputana Rifles secured the Hogs Back, losing 50 per cent. of their strength, but succeeded in maintaining their grip, and repulsing the enemy counter-attacks with heavy loss. Two companies 4/6 Rajputana Rifles were sent forward to reinforce 1/6 Rajputana Rifles. 2/5 Mahratta Light Infantry gallantly carried Flat Top Hill, and succeeded in consolidating, but this battalion was also so reduced in numbers that it could not exploit to Mole Hill. It was decided that no useful purpose would now be served in doing so.

In the 4th Divisional left attack, 4/11 Sikhs captured the left bump of M. Samanna, but although making repeated attempts failed to gain the centre bump, which was held by a battalion of Alpini. On 16th March 4/6 Rajputana Rifles less two Companies attacked Brigs Peak, but was unable to make any progress beyond that already achieved. Confused fighting continued throughout the day, the enemy, who consisted of Bersaglieri and the Savoy Grenadiers, fighting determinedly, were holding positions under the rocks which were practically immune from shell fire. During the evening, a report was received that Brigs Peak was captured, and that only a few enemy remained on M. Sanchil. On receipt of this information, 10th Indian Infantry Brigade, which was being held as force reserve, was put under command 4th Indian Division and sent to Cameron Ridge in order to move over the col separating M. Sanchil and Brigs Peak; and exploit into the plain west of Keren. Unfortunately this report was premature. The leading battalions of this brigade were committed during the night to attacks on M. Sanchil and Brigs Peak. 3/18 Garhwal Rifles in particular suffered heavy loss. The Commanding Officer and all other British officers except one became casualties. The enemy still held ground from which he could direct effective machine-gun and mortar fire against advancing troops.

Withdrawal from M. Sanchil and Brigs Peak.
By the evening of 17th March it was clear that the much reduced forward elements still on M. Sanchil and Brigs Peak could not be maintained. They were suffering heavy casualties. The intervention of the only remaining battalion of 10th Indian Infantry Brigade, the weak 2 Highland Light Infantry, would be unlikely to produce the required results. A further assault would probably cause

the destruction of 10th Indian Infantry Brigade, the only available force reserve. 3/18 Garhwal and 4/10 Baluch were withdrawn during the night 17th/18th March to the valley. 2 Highland Light Infantry were left on Cameron Ridge until night 18th/19th March, when they also were withdrawn and 10th Indian Infantry Brigade was concentrated as Force Reserve. M. Sanchil and Brigs Peak were thereafter subjected to heavy shelling by 6-inch Hows. Flat Top Hill and Hogs Back were firmly held.

Effect on 5th Indian Division.
On the 5th Divisional front, the capture of Fort Dologorodoc was only half way to the Divisional objective. The plan was for 29th Indian Infantry Brigade to go through 9th Indian Infantry Brigade and capture M. Zeban. Until M. Sanchil was secured it was not considered wise to launch 29th Indian Infantry Brigade. The direction given was to hold the Fort throughout the 16th, while the 10th Indian Infantry Brigade assisted 4th Indian Division to secure M. Sanchil. The enemy counter-attached determinedly. These attacks were broken up by artillery and the dogged resistance of 9th Indian Infantry Brigade, helped, throughout the day by close support from the R.A.F.

Attack Resumed by 5th Indian Division.
Shortly after midday, orders were issued for the advance to be resumed during the night 16th/17th March. 5th Indian Division was to start from the Fort at approximately 2200 hours. Unavoidable delays, caused by difficulties of com-munications, the delay in making a mule track up to the Fort, and unexpectedly serious casualties in the administrative staff of I Worcesters, compelled zero hour to be postponed until 0030 hours 17th March. This delay, though unavoidable, caused great anxiety, as it was expected that the thrust by 5th Indian Division would relieve the severe pressure on the tired and much reduced battalions of 11th Indian Infantry Brigade.

Progress of 29th Indian Infantry Brigade.
In their advance from the Fort 29th Indian Infantry Brigade encountered strong opposition, and were unable to reach their objective, I Worcesters becoming pinned half-way up Falestoh Col. The enemy's fire was severe. Communications were broken. Supply became difficult, and during the 17th both food and ammu-nition were dropped on I Worcesters by the R.A.F., using one Wellesley and one Vincent. Eventually it was found impossible to get on, and 29th Indian Infantry Brigade consolidated positions already held between six and eight hundred yards beyond the Fort. By 1530 hours on 17th March, the Commander of 29th Indian Infantry Brigade appreciated that administrative difficulties and the great heat of the day had broken the impetus of his attack. 10th Indian Infantry Brigade having been committed on M. Sanchil, there was nothing left with which to make a further advance without a period of reorganisation. Carriers of 10th Indian Infantry Brigade and some "I" tanks were in the Happy Valley to secure the right flank of 5th Indian Division and prevent any debouchment by the enemy from the

Acqua Gap. There then ensued a period of holding what had been gained, with daily counter-attacks by the enemy, who fought most determinedly to recapture Fort Dologorodoc.

Arresa Area.
Before the main attack on Keren on 15th March, subsidiary operations had been started by No. 2 M.M.G. Group, reinforced by Skinner's Horse and two Mounted Infantry Companies S.D.F. against Arresa. Although operations here were unable to make ground, they did succeed in delaying the move of enemy forces.

Co-operation by 7th Indian Infantry Brigade.
The operations of 7th Indian Infantry Brigade were co-ordinated with 5th Indian Division attack on the 15th. These operations were successful in containing a large part of the enemy's forces although they were unable to make very much ground. The enemy was holding M. Engiahat, a large square hill of the same type as those around Keren. The road from the north winds through narrow passes and along the edge of river beds, where in places it hangs above the river on a ledge 50 or 60 feet above the river bed. Commander 7th Indian Infantry Brigade had hoped to be able to send a column across-country east of M. Engiahat to cut the Keren-Asmara road east of Keren. At this time a practicable route had not been found. The enemy were still holding positions east of Engiahat which blocked any advance in this direction. The effort of 7th Indian Infantry Brigade was of assistance to the main battle in that it did contain forces which the enemy commander badly needed at Fort Dologorodoc.

Death of Gen. Lorenzini.
On 19th March General Lorenzini was killed. This officer was held in high repute by his own troops. He was personally gallant and had had much experience of fighting in the Middle East. His death was a severe blow to the enemy.

Offensive resumed 25th March.
After a week, during which the enemy launched no less than eight counter-attacks against Fort Dologorodoc, the Commander, 5th Indian Division, was in a position to resume the offensive. His object was to open the road to Keren for the passage of mechanised forces.

The enemy positions covering the road.
M. Sanchil throws off a spur to the northeast. Along the east side of M. Sanchil, round this spur, and then in a westerly direction, runs the railway. At the level of the railway the spur flattens out and its surface is much broken. This area was aptly named "Railway Bumps". The Railway Bumps spur ends at a junction of two dry stream beds. The main one is the khor which comes down the Dongolaas gorge parallel with the road. The subsidiary comes in from a north-westerly direction and where it joints the main khor, its banks are steep, the right bank being the Railway Bumps, the left bank Railway Ridge. Machine-guns in position on Railway Bumps and Railway Ridge commanded the Dongolaas gorge, the east

side of M. Sanchil, the west side of Fort Dologorodoc and the road-block. As long as they were in position it was impossible for the sappers to open the road. The capture of Railway Bumps and Railway Ridge was the 5th Indian Divisional objective.

This task was given to 10th Indian Infantry Brigade supported by all available artillery. On their left 4th Indian Division was to contain the enemy and attract his attention, but otherwise was given a passive role. On their right, 9th Indian Infantry Brigade was to advance and secure the sub-features known as Hillock A, Hillock B and Red Hill which lie between Fort Dologorodoc and M. Zeban. After these objectives had been reached and when the road-block had been cleared, a mechanised column consisting of "I" tanks, of which there were still fourteen in action, and a force of carriers collected from several battalions was to secure Keren and then move west into the Mogareh valley to engage any mechanised forces or troops found there. 29th Indian Infantry Brigade was to advance through 9th Indian Infantry Brigade, capture M. Zeban and exploit to M. Canabai commanding the road east of Keren. In this attack also, 7th Indian Infantry Brigade from the north was to co-operate to the full.

The Attack.

10th Indian Infantry Brigade attack went in at 0415 hours on 25th March and made rapid progress in securing all its objectives. By about 1000 hours the sappers were able to start work on the road-block. They were still under mortar and artillery fire. 10th Indian Infantry Brigade succeeded in consolidating its objectives and, throughout the 26th, work on the road-block continued. On this day the Italians made one of their last air-attacks against our troops. The R.A.F. with their variety of machines from Hurricanes to Vincents had gained air superiority. By a continuous forward policy they had driven their opponents from the air and destroyed their machines on the ground. The army was indeed grateful for the immunity from hostile air-attack thus gained. The advance of the mechanised column and 29th Indian Infantry Brigade was timed for 0530 hours on the morning of 27th March. During the early hours of 27th March there were indications that the enemy might be withdrawing. 29th Indian Infantry Brigade advance went with great speed and it became clear that the enemy's resistance was broken. By 1000 hours the mechanised force had established itself in Keren. Throughout the morning white flags appeared on M. Sanchil, Brigs Peak, M. Zemanna and M. Amba. The battle of Keren was won. It had been won by the tenacity and determination of commanders and troops, by whole-hearted co-operation of all ranks, whether forward or back, of whatever race or creed, and by the continuous support given to infantry by the Royal Artillery, who, between 15th and 27th March, fired over 110,000 shells borne by 1,000 lorries from railhead over 150 miles away.

This time the Foreign Legion succeeded in making its way across-country and by 28th March had reached the road, unfortunately too late to cut off the retreating enemy, but taking 800 prisoners on the way.

5th Indian Division took up the pursuit, led by the mechanised column, and by 2030 hours that night had reached Kilo 56 at the bottom of the hill up to Ad Teclesan. 4th Indian Division, less 7th Indian Infantry Brigade, took no further part in operations, being under orders to return to Middle East.

Casualties.

Casualties amounted to 500 killed and 3,000 wounded with a high proportion of slight cases. These were regrettably high figures, but they were only five per cent. of the eventual losses of the enemy in killed, wounded, and prisoners of war.

Ground at Ad Teclesan.

Asmara is in the centre of a plateau about 7,000 feet high. The road from Asmara to Keren falls steeply from Ad Teclesan down to the level of Keren, a drop of over 2,000 feet.

The natural difficulties facing 29th Indian Infantry Brigade when they reached Kilo 56 on the evening of 27th March appeared even more difficult than those at Keren. Though the road winds upwards following the contours, and is throughout its length well graded, its general trend is a slope from left to right, across the face of the escarpment of the Asmara Plateau. As at Keren, the road ascent ran almost parallel to the enemy positions crowning the heights. Between Kilo 56 and Ad Teclesan, the country consists of big, rounded hills, less rocky than those at Keren, and on the whole not so steep. There is more vegetation and the country is greener.

From an operational point of view, the main difficulty is that there is no flat ground. The road is carved out of the sides of the hills. During the greater part of the action, at Ad Teclesan, movement, except on foot, was confined to the road. Transport could not be parked off it. It was impossible to deploy more than a few guns and even they were at an undesirably long range.

The railway takes a different route, south of the road, but even along the railway there are few, if any, places where it was possible to deploy wheeled-vehicles off the railway track itself.

The enemy's withdrawal from Keren had been cleverly carried out. He had been able to remove about 60 per cent. of his artillery, which was now in position at Ad Teclesan. All his anti-aircraft artillery had likewise been withdrawn. He had managed to get back some of his infantry units, but all had been severely handled. Their morale was low, as was evidenced by the quantity of rifles and war material of all kinds abandoned by the road side and the numbers who surrendered as prisoners of war. Had the enemy not been so soundly beaten at Keren, the task confronting 5th Indian Division at Ad Teclesan would have been one of extreme difficulty.

Situation on 28th March.

By 0900 hours 28th March, the enemy was being pursued by the tanks and carriers known as Fletcher Force, which had reached the first road-block and demolition at Kilo 56 on the evening before. 29th Indian Infantry Brigade

Group, with two of its battalions in lorries, 3 Central India Horse, No. 1 M.M.G. Group, S.D.F., and 20 Field Company, Sappers and Miners, under command, was close behind. Every effort was being made to get 68 Medium Regiment over the road-block at Fort Dologorodoc. It was the intention that they might hit the retreating enemy at the earliest possible moment. The enemy's distaste for this weapon was known.

The difficulties at the road-block were still considerable. It needed good driving and excellent traffic control if serious delays were to be avoided.

7th Indian Infantry Brigade Group had been ordered to clear mines from the road leading into Keren from the north and to make touch with 5th Indian Division, but only to employ the minimum of troops for this task. The remainder of the brigade was to concentrate back at Chelamet preparatory to operating along the Red Sea littoral against Massawa. The French troops who had come over the hills and cut the road east of Keren, arrived without rations or water, and very tired. They were collected in M.T. and taken back to Chelamet.

Arresa Front.

There was no longer any need to keep mobile forces tied up, attempting to break through to Arresa. Two mounted Infantry Companies S.D.F. were left in that area with instructions to make their way through to Adi Ugri and cut the Gondar road south of Asmara. Skinner's Horse and No. 2 M.M.G. Group S.D.F. were withdrawn via Barentu and Agordat to Keren so that they would be ready to take up the pursuit as soon as the enemy was forced from the Ad Teclesan area.

Action at Ad Teclesan.

The enemy had made three effective road-blocks on the road below Ad Teclesan. Each of these was covered by machine-gun and artillery fire. Out-flanking tactics were necessary; these took time. The mules used at Keren had not caught up. Maintenance of troops operating off the road was difficult. 29th Indian Infantry Brigade succeeded in forcing their way past the first two road-blocks and nearly to the top. Simultaneously, two companies of 10th Indian Infantry Brigade, with a detachment of Skinner's Horse and one M.M.G. company S.D.F., moved along the railway threatening the enemy's flank. Finally 9th Indian Infantry Brigade moved forward through 29th Indian Infantry Brigade, and, after hard fighting, cleared the last road-block on the early morning of 1st April. At 0630 hours on the same morning, the leading troops of 5th Indian Division were met by emissaries of the enemy, who stated that they had been ordered to cease resistance and asked that Asmara should be treated as an open town.

Our leading troops entered Asmara at 1315 hours.

Though troops in Asmara itself had been ordered to cease resistance, there was no indication that resistance would cease in other areas. Air reports confirmed that the enemy were withdrawing troops and guns to the south of Asmara. These columns were successfully attacked by the air. By 0655 hours on 1st April, orders had already gone out directing that the operations by the 7th Indian Infantry Brigade and the Free French against Massawa should commence. Special instructions were given to these forces to prevent sabotage of the port of Massawa.

Immediately after the fall of Asmara, the main object became the capture of Massawa, if possible undamaged, and with the shipping known to be there intact. The plan was for 7th Indian Infantry Brigade Group to move eastwards from Chelamet over an unknown track, which proved to be extremely difficult. The troops had to work hard in a high temperature to get their vehicles over bad going, varying from boulder-strewn tracks to soft desert sand. Preparations were made to open a port at Mersa Cuba for the supply of this force when it reached the sea.

Further Pursuit by 5th Indian Division.
At the same time pursuit of the enemy was organised along both the main roads leading south from Asmara. The limits of pursuit were defined as the River Tacazze on the way to Gondar, and on the eastern route, the position which the enemy were known to be preparing at Amba Alagi. 5th Indian Division was directed to send one brigade group from Asmara down the main Asmara-Massawa road to co-operate with 7th Indian Infantry Brigade in the capture of Massawa. A road-block was encountered between Asmara and Nefasit, but it was not covered by enemy fire, and imposed no great delay. Later 144 Field Regiment and 68 Medium Regiment, less one battery, reinforced 10th Indian Infantry Brigade.

Dealings with Italian Civil Authorities.
On 2nd April it was made clear to the civil authorities that the future welfare of the civil population depended to a large extent on the degree of co-operation afforded by them. As communications to the Sudan were long and difficult, transport of all kinds was limited, and the needs of the fighting forces necessarily came first, it was to their own interests not only to prevent sabotage, but to repair the railway, roads and teleferica at the earliest possible moment. It was most strongly stressed that unless the port and port facilities at Massawa were surrendered intact, together with the shipping lying in the harbour, the British authorities could not guarantee to feed the civil population of whom so many were women and children. The civil authorities agreed to assist in reopening communications and in keeping order in the city, but said they could not answer for the military authorities in Massawa.

Situation in Asmara.
The population of Asmara at the time was approximately 40,000 Italians and 40,000 natives. The problem of administering this large mixed population, mostly armed, with limited staff to deal with civil problems, no police and no surplus of troops, was one which taxed all resources severely. Natives, particularly units still in existence as such, had to be disarmed before the Italian population.

Surprisingly little difficulty was encountered. There was some shooting by natives, but no major disorders occurred, nor were there any serious attempts at sabotage.

Communications with Italian Commander, Massawa.

Telephonic communication with Massawa was still open on one line. By this the Italian commander at Massawa was warned that the British would accept no responsibility for the feeding of the Italian population of Eritrea and Abyssinia if any of the ships in the harbour were scuttled, or of the harbour or its facilities were damaged. On 2nd April, the Italian commander of Massawa opened communications with Commander 10th Indian Infantry Brigade through his Chief Staff Officer. The warning about destruction of the port was given to him in writing, and he was informed that this warning had also been communicated to the Duke of Aosta.

At 0830 hours on 3rd April, 7th Indian Infantry Brigade, advancing south, was only 25 miles from Massawa. By that evening it had made contact with the enemy forces. 7th Indian Infantry Brigade Group was placed under command 5th Indian Division in order to co-ordinate the attack on Massawa.

On the other fronts the Mounted Infantry from Arresa had reached Adi Ugri, releasing all British and Imperial officers and men who had been taken as prisoners of war by the Italians. Mobile forces had occupied Adowa and Adigrat over 100 miles from Asmara.

At Adigrat natives were found looting mattresses on which their wounded, compatriot soldiers lay. Beyond Adowa native children, some not more than two years of age, were found brutally and horribly mutilated.

In the meantime, 4th Indian Division, less 7th Indian Infantry Brigade, were clearing Keren battlefield, preparatory to moving back to Middle East. On 29th March, orders were issued for the first brigade group of 4th Indian Division to move to Port Sudan for embarkation.

On 5th April, further demands for troops were received from Middle East, and practically all of the remainder of 4th Indian Division, less 7th Indian Infantry Brigade, was released. It was sad to part with this Division, which had rendered such distinguished service under Major-General Sir Noel Beresford-Peirse, K.B.E., D.S.O.

Terms of Surrender of Massawa.

That evening, the Admiral commanding the Italian Forces in Massawa sent in a flag of truce, and asked for our terms for the surrender of Massawa. These were dictated over the telephone to Commander 5th Indian Division, who passed them on to the Italian envoys. A truce until 1100 hours 6th April was imposed, but the terms were refused and hostilities were resumed at 1300 hours.

Capture of Massawa.

Massawa was now attacked from the north and west, and after some fighting, the enemy surrendered. Commander 5th Indian Division entered Massawa, receiving the surrender of the Admiral Commanding at 1410 hours on 8th April. It was then found that considerable destruction to the town had been carried out, many ships scuttled in the harbour, and the port facilities badly damaged. Prisoners included over 450 Officers and 10,000 Other Ranks, both Italian and Native.

Many enemy units were represented from the forces that had been broken at Keren and Ad Teclesan, and had made their way to Massawa.

PART III.

Operations leading up to the Battle of Amba Alagi.

After the capture of Massawa, the two main enemy centres of resistance in Northern Ethiopia were Amba Alagi and Gondar. The remnants of the Italian armies from Eritrea had retreated along the two main roads from Asmara to these areas, and for some time previously the enemy had been preparing a defensive position to hold the Toselli Pass where the road goes over the first big range of hills leading into central Ethiopia. Gondar had always been a big military station, the centre of the Italian military organisation in the country North and West of Lake Tana. At this time, commitments elsewhere made it imperative for the C.-in-C. to withdraw as many forces as possible from Eritrea. The policy laid down by him was that no major operations should be undertaken in Eritrea and Northern Ethiopia which would interfere with the withdrawal of troops to the Middle East. Though the enemy forces which had withdrawn southwards were no longer a menace to the Sudan and though they had little chance of staging a counter-offensive to recapture Eritrea, their continued presence in the country was a source of possible future trouble and disturbance. It was desirable that they should be eliminated.

Forces available.

The forces which remained and were available for operations against Amba Alagi and Gondar and for internal security for the whole of Eritrea were:-

5th Indian Division.
Two M.M.G. Groups S.D.F.
One Commando.
One Battery 68 Medium Regt, R.A.
Two Companies Mounted Infantry, S.D.F.

Commitments.

One brigade, at least, was needed to garrison Asmara.

One brigade could easily have been expended on guarding important centres and dumps of captured stores in other parts of Eritrea and the Tigre. At the time of the fall of Massawa, only light mobile forces had pursued the enemy southwards along the two roads from Asmara. Central India Horse was in the area of Mai Mescic. They were soon withdrawn on relief by Skinner's Horse. No. 1 M.M.G. Group had reached the river Tacazze at Mai Timchet on the way to Gondar. No. 2 M.M.G. Group was carrying out a reconnaissance down the Red Sea coast as far as Zula.

The task of attacking the Amba Alagi position was entrusted to 5th Indian Division. Amba Alagi is 235 miles south of Asmara. Transport was very limited. Reconnaissance revealed that the Amba Alagi position was naturally strong. The administrative problem of staging a battle in this area was considerable and involved a dumping programme which necessarily took time. At first only the minimum troops were kept forward in the area Mai Mescic, Quiha and Macalle. Their task was reconnaissance and to act as a screen to protect the dumping programme and the concentration of other troops at the last possible minute. Sufficient troops were not available for operations to be undertaken in strength against Gondar and Amba Alagi simultaneously. It was decided to engage Amba Alagi first as success here would open the road to Addis Ababa, allowing the move of South African forces to be routed through Massawa to Middle East.

Topography – The Amba Alagi Position.
Amba Alagi is a mountain over 10,000 feet above sea level. The road into Ethiopia crosses a spur of this mountain at the Toselli Pass which is defended by a fort. The approach from the north is steep and winding and for some miles the road works its way through a narrow valley overlooked on both sides by commanding heights. The general run of the high ground which culminates at Amba Alagi is north-west to south-east. North-west of Amba Alagi itself is a long range. Little Alagi, Middle Hill, Elephant, Pinnacle and Sandy Ridge are prominent features of this ridge, all of which had tactical importance. South-west from Amba Alagi runs the narrow Castle ridge, culminating in Castle Hill. Almost due North of Amba Alagi and Little Alagi is Bald Hill, a high flat-topped feature with precipitous sides. South-east of Amba Alagi and the other side of the pass, two prominent hills, Triangle and Gumsa, intervene between Toselli and Falaga Passes. The road over the Toselli Pass is a good all-weather, graded main road. The road to the Falaga Pass takes off from the east side of the main road some 35 kilos north of Amba Alagi. This road was found to be bad but just practicable for one-way M.T. for some distance beyond Debub. This was the route that the Italians themselves had used in the final stages of the Abyssinian war. Opposite where the Falaga road leaves the main road, another track strikes off to the south-west through the hills as far as Socota. With difficulty this was practicable for M.T. but there was no road or track from Socota eastwards to rejoin the main road. As an indication of the size and steepness of the country, it was a four hours' walk from the main road to Sandy Hill, where H.Q. 29th Indian Infantry Brigade were later established.

The Plan of Attack.
There were three possible ways of attacking the enemy forces at Amba Alagi. To the east by way of the Falaga Pass; astride the road directly at the enemy position; from the right along the ridge which leads from Sandy Hill to Amba Alagi. At this time accurate estimates of the enemy strength were not available but his force was known to be a collection of bits and pieces from many units with a large number of guns, including anti-aircraft. Many of these latter were sited on the tops of the hills. There was a road-block beyond the village of Enda Medani Alem overlooked and covered by fire from Bald Hill. The enemy, as at Keren, had the high ground and the observation. As at Keren the problem was one of attacking an

enemy holding a naturally strong position of his own choosing. The plan was based on a double bluff. First, a force was to move against the Falaga Pass playing upon the enemy's fears. As the Italians themselves had used this route in the Abyssinian war, it was reasonable to suppose that they were nervous of this flank as they would consider this the most probable line of advance. The second bluff was to make the enemy think that we intended to advance astride the road. At Barentu, Agordat, Keren and Massawa, our advances had been astride road approaches. It was hoped that he would be deceived by movements indicating that we intended to follow custom. The real attack was to be carried out along the ridge to the west of the road. At first sight the country here appeared to be unsuitable and it was for this reason that it was calculated that the enemy's defences would not be so strong on this side.

Preparations.

In order to stage an attack along the ridge, very careful preparations were necessary. Everything, once it left the road, had to be carried either by men or mules and at this time there were no mule units with 5th Indian Division. Scarcity of lorries had made it impossible to ferry forward either of the Cypriot Mule Companies which had done so well at Keren. 5th Indian Division were forced to collect mules from the countryside and to detail mule-leading parties from each unit, thus further reducing fighting strength. Sandy Hill and Sandy Ridge, which were the starting areas of the attack, were in view from Amba Alagi. Precautions were taken to deceive the enemy. No. M.T. was allowed beyond truck-head some miles away but in full view of the enemy; movement of formed bodies was forbidden west of the main road; maximum use was made of all available cover; reconnaissance parties of all kinds were kept to a minimum and their movements rigidly controlled. Movements of units were carried out at night or in the twilight. No movement, unusual noises or smoke fires were permitted in the forward bivouac areas. These precautions continued throughout the 72 hours taken to move 29th Indian Infantry Brigade, its supplies and ammunition, up the mountain to its battle positions. Despite patrol encounters the enemy failed to discover the presence of this brigade.

Disposition of Forces.

Commander, 5th Indian Division, divided his forces as follows.

On the left operating against Falaga Pass was a formation known as Fletcher Force. This consisted of:-

Skinner's Horse.
51 Commando.
One Company 3/12 Frontier Force Regiment.
One M.M.G. Company S.D.F.
Troop 25 Pounders.
Troop 6-inch Hows.
Troop 3.7-inch Hows., and
One Section of a Field Company Sappers and Miners.

This force was to demonstrate against the Falaga Pass, timing its operations to produce their maximum effect on the night before the main attack. In the centre 3/18 Garhwal Rifles, with a detachment of Sappers and Miners, were to stage a demonstration up the main road on the evening before the main attack, maintaining this deception by a bold action throughout the night with the object of simulating the beginnings of a brigade attack. The main attack was entrusted to 29th Indian Infantry Brigade.

Course of the Operations.
The maps in possession of 5th Indian Division were bad and inaccurate. Operations had necessarily to be conducted step by step as it was not possible to deduce accurately from the map what type of country was likely to be met. It was also necessary to fight both to gain observation for our own artillery and deny it to the enemy.

4th May was fixed for the attack. For a week before this Fletcher Force fought its way forward towards Falaga Pass. Their operations were successful and resulted in the capture of many prisoners as well as securing Commando Hill from which good observation was obtained. On the night of the 3/4th May, Skinner's Horse and 51 Commando attacked strongly but met with stiff resistance and had to withdraw about midnight. Though this attack may have appeared to Fletcher Force to have been a failure, it did in fact achieve its object and the enemy was convinced, until too late, that our attack was coming from the direction of the Falaga Pass.

Feint by 3/18 Garhwal Rifles.
On the afternoon of 3rd May the carriers of 3/18 Garhwal Rifles debouched in the Enda Medani Alem valley, occupying it by 1730 hours as if anxious to make as much ground as possible before dark. The rifle companies occupied in succession the hills to the west of the village, so timing their movements that the last thing the enemy saw before dark was a steady advance towards his position. After dark vigorous patrolling was carried out and one patrol succeeded in scaling the precipitous Bald Hill. This bluff was successful. The enemy believed he had repulsed a strong attack. Behind 3/18 Garhwal Rifles noise, activity and the display of lights, all carefully controlled, gave added realism to the deception. The enemy was deceived by these manoeuvres, and placed his forces to repel an attack astride the road and from the direction of Falaga Pass.

The Attack of 29th Indian Infantry Brigade.
At 0415 hours on 4th May, 29th Indian Infantry Brigade moved forward to the attack supported by all available artillery. The attack went with great dash and speed, capturing Pinacle and Elephant Hill. Beyond this the ridge narrows and is devoid of cover, all approaches being commanded by machine-guns from Bald Hill, and other prominent features. The maps had given no indication of the exceeding steepness and narrowness of the ridge beyond Elephant. Further advance in daylight was impossible. At 0415 hours on 5th May, the attack was resumed and Middle Hill was captured. Between Middle Hill and Little Alagi

the ridge again narrows to a razor-back about 150 yds. wide, wired, flanked by precipices and under machine-gun fire. I Worcesters reached, and at one place went through, the wire, but became pinned and could not move in daylight. Middle Hill was consolidated and the Worcesters were withdrawn to this area on the night 5/6th May. 29th Indian Infantry Brigade was now definitely checked.

Operations by Patriots and South African Forces.

In other areas Allied forces were closing in on Amba Alagi. A strong force of patriots under Ras Seyoum and accompanied by a small force of S.D.F. had advanced over the hills to Socota, 50 miles south-west of Amba Alagi. Here they had captured the Italian garrison and destroyed the fort. Proceeding eastwards across-country, they struck the main road about Quoram and Alomata on 2nd May and then advanced on Mai Ceu which they summoned to surrender on 6th May. Elsewhere patriot forces had been directed to cut the roads Debarech – Gondar – Chelga, Gondar – Dessie, Dessie – Assab and communications round Dessie itself.

South African Forces.

A detachment of 1st South African Brigade, which had captured Dessie, was sent forward from Dessie on 30th April. Advancing rapidly, in spite of road-blocks, by 5th May their advanced forces had reached Alomata, where they were delayed by a serious road-block. Their advance moved so successfully that the rest of the 1st South African Brigade Group, less one battalion, was ordered to join their leading troops and operate against Amba Alagi. G.O.C. East Africa signalled that he proposed to place this brigade group under command Troops in the Sudan on its arrival at Alomata. This offer was gratefully accepted. On 8th May 1st South African Brigade came under command 5th Indian Division. Difficulties of communication were considerable. Wireless was not working very satisfactorily in the mountains. Touch was made with the South African Brigade by liaison officers. Later the Commander 5th Indian Division flew to meet Commander 1st South African Brigade. From now on the enemy forces at Amba Alagi were closely beleaguered.

Re-adjustment.

Since 29th Indian Infantry Brigade was now held up, it became clear that more weight was necessary on the left flank and that Fletcher Force needed infantry. The advance so far had made the L. of C. much more secure and 3/12 Frontier Force Regiment could now be spared from L. of C. work. This battalion was sent to join Fletcher Force. 3/18 Garhwal Rifles, having accomplished their job of deceiving the enemy in the centre, were relieved by Skinner's Horse and also joined Fletcher Force, which became 9th Indian Infantry Brigade (less one battalion).

Attack on 8/9th May.

On 29th Indian Infantry Brigade front an out-flanking movement further to the south was carried out. 6/13 Frontier Force Rifles, with one company 1 Worcesters under command, descended by night some 2,000 feet into a narrow valley from which they climbed up to within assaulting distance of Castle Ridge. This was attacked silently at 0410 hours on 8th May, artillery concentrations being put down to simulate a dawn attack on Little Alagi and Bald Hill. All objectives except a small portion of Castle Hill were quickly captured. On the north end of Castle Hill a white flag was displayed but when 6/13 Frontier Force Rifles advanced to take over the position, they were greeted by a shower of bombs and suffered severely. A thick mist then came down on the hill-tops, under cover of which the Italians were able to assemble for a counter-attack. This was successful and Castle Hill was recaptured by the enemy. Owing to the need for achieving surprise and complicated by the mist, our artillery had not ranged on Castle Ridge and could not consequently give effective support to 6/13 Frontier Force Rifles.

In the centre demonstrations were kept up to play upon the enemy's nerves and keep him watching this sector. These demonstrations drew a most impressive amount of enemy fire.

Operations of 9th Indian Infantry Brigade.
During the night of 7/8th May 9th Indian Infantry Brigade had made ground towards the Falaga Pass, capturing many prisoners and much material. On the following night they secured the pass but found that the M.T. track ended. From there they were directed across country, capturing Gumsa ridge which gave direct observations on to Toselli Fort. 5th Indian Division now held the centre hill on Castle Ridge, Middle Hill and Gumsa, thus closely investing the enemy position on three sides. Throughout all this period our artillery had been obtaining better and better observation until by this time they were making life very difficult for the enemy.

In the meantime, 1st South African Brigade had been making good progress, and, by 13th May, were in close touch with the Amba Alagi position from the south. The problem of command was difficult, particularly in regard to artillery support, while the South Africans were advancing from the south side of the hill. Throughout 14th May the South African Brigade advanced towards Triangle, the big feature overlooking the pass from the south-east.

Assisted by the Patriots, who, in this area, did excellent work, the Triangle was captured by 0800 hours on 15th May, finally closing the circle. This made further resistance by the enemy merely useless waste of life, and, on 16th May, an armistice was asked for and granted. Subsequent negotiations resulted in the unconditional surrender of the Italian garrison who were granted the honours of war.

PART IV.
Operations leading to the capture of Debra Tabor.
After the surrender of the Italian garrison at Amba Alagi it was essential for political and operational reasons to capture Debra Tabor as a preliminary move against Gondar. G.O.C. East Africa had no troops available but ordered Com-

mander 101 Mission to move against Debra Tabor. He, however, became involved in the battle near Addis Dera, where the Italian forces under Maraventano were defeated after a three days' battle.

Situation at Debra Tabor.

Debra Tabor lies on the road between Dessie and Gondar, over 150 miles from Dessie. It is naturally strong and was defended by field-works and wire. The road is in parts an unmade track, which, in wet weather, becomes impassable for all wheeled traffic. The Italian garrison was estimated as about 2,500. This proved to be an under-estimate.

At this time Debra Tabor was being watched by a force of patriots known as Begemeder Force, who were unable to make headway against its defences. The detachment of the Frontier Battalion S.D.F., which had been co-operating with them, had been withdrawn to Dessie. The following force was collected and ordered to make its way to Debra Tabor where it was to act in co-operation with the patriots. One squadron, Skinner's Horse, less the carrier troop, plus one troop. One company, 3/2 Punjab Regiment, plus a mortar detachment of three 81mm. Italian mortars. One section 20 Field Company, Sappers and Miners, and a detachment of M.T. Section 20 Field Company was later relieved by a section of 8 Army Troops Company, Sappers and Miners.

The Rains.

The timing of this operation was made difficult on account of the increasing rains. There was a distinct chance that the whole force, or at least all the vehicles of the force, might get completely bogged and have to be abandoned until after the rains ceased some time in September. On the other hand it was important to strike at the Italian forces quickly before the effect of the surrender by the Viceroy at Amba Alagi had time to wear off.

By 7th June the road Dessie-Gondar was cleared as far as Kilo. 154, but beyond this there were still road-blocks and land-slides which took time to repair. It was not until 14th June that the road was sufficiently repaired for the column to start from Dessie, reaching Debra Tabor on 16th June where contact was made with the patriot forces.

Situation on 16th June.

On 16th June the garrison of Debra Tabor, though not surrounded, was completely cut-off, patriot forces being astride the road both east and west of the town. The total number of patriots was about 8,000. Reports that the enemy in Debra Tabor were only waiting for the arrival of a British force before surrendering proved incorrect. There was much jealousy between the patriot forces who were making no serious attempt to capture the town. After reconnaissances, plans were made to attack in co-operation with the patriots but on no less than five separate occasions, after all plans and arrangements had been made, the patriots failed to co-operate. The total strength of our column was only 250 men, too weak to stage a successful attack without patriot co-operation. The difficulties of co-operating with patriots are exemplified by the fact that on every occasion our commander was assured that "the attack would really go in this time."

Parley with the Enemy.

On 25th June the enemy opened negotiations under a flag of truce asking for terms of surrender. These were substantially the same as at Amba Alagi and were handed to the Italian envoys. An armistice was agreed on until 1600 hours, 27th June. No satisfactory answer being received, operations recommenced.

Operations 27th June–22nd July.

No further confidence could be placed in patriot co-operation so the column commenced harassing tactics with light machine-guns and mortars. These continued until, on 1st July, a letter was received from the Italian Commander asking for a meeting which was fixed for 1100 hours on 2nd July. At this meeting terms of surrender were discussed and settled. Our troops entered Debra Tabor on 3rd July and took over all important installations. The enemy garrison marched out on 6th July, and, after receiving the honours of war, laid down their arms. Patriots occupied the forts and native quarters. Prisoners captured were 2,400 Italians, 2,000 natives and a miscellaneous collection of M.T., sufficient to lift 1,200 men. Six guns and a quantity of ammunition were also taken. The surrender of Debra Tabor was strange, considering the Italian Commander at Gondar intended to relieve this garrison on 15th July.

Weather.

The weather throughout these operations had been bad and was getting worse. The ground was sodden, movement of M.T. difficult. Nights were cold and usually wet. Bivouacking on sodden ground in soaked blankets was a daily occurrence and the troops suffered much discomfort.

Subsequent Operations.

The next problems were first to evacuate the prisoners and to protect them from patriot attentions during their move to Dessie, and secondly to reconnoitre towards Gondar and make contact with the commander of a party of patriots known to be some miles further to the west. One troop, Skinner's Horse, and a section of Sappers and Miners, moved off from Debra Tabor and by 8th July had reached a point 42 miles to the west having surmounted considerable difficulties of bad and blocked roads. The whole force was successfully concentrated back in Dessie by 14th July, Debra Tabor being left in charge of officers of 101 Mission and the patriots.

PART V.

Advance against Gondar from Gallabat.

Own troops.

On 3rd March 3/12 Frontier Force Regiment, less one company, was withdrawn to Gedaref to join 9th Indian Infantry Brigade, before moving to Keren. One company 3/12 Frontier Force Regiment and 21 Field Company, Sappers and

Miners, was left to continue the pursuit along the Gallabat-Gondar road. This force patrolled forward until finally stopped by the enemy holding the escarpment a few miles west of Chelga. On 5th April they were joined by 3 Ethiopian Battalion and C Troop Light Artillery Battery, S.D.F. By 15th April, the company 3/12 Frontier Force Regiment and 21 Field Company, Sappers and Miners, were withdrawn to rejoin 5th Indian Division and a force known as Kerforce, comprising 3 Ethiopian Battalion and a Composite Battalion made up of companies from various S.D.F. units, took over operations on this sector.

Enemy positions.
Opposite the Composite Battalion the enemy was holding the western edge of the escarpment. His forward line of defended localities was some eight to ten miles west of the escarpment, and was held in strength. The escarpment itself is between five and ten miles west of Chelga. A flanking movement was the only possible way of striking at Chelga or the communications behind.

Administration.
Administrative difficulties were considerable. The road Metemma-Gondar is only a dry-weather track, and becomes impassable by wheels during the rains. It is seriously interrupted some 25 miles east of Gallabat by the unbridged Gandwa River. Movement by M.T. off the road in the Chelga area is not practicable. The country had been burnt. There was not sufficient grass for camels, nor could they have been used in the steep hills in that area. Mules and horses belonging to the Composite Battalion were below strength and in poor condition as a result of previous strenuous campaigning. Rain began to fall by 15th April.

Neither time nor resources admitted the construction of an all-weather road. The decision was made to operate against Chelga for as long as possible, and if success had not been achieved to withdraw this force to the Sudan when rain made its further maintenance impossible. The Composite Battalion was assisted by various bands of patriots. On 22nd April an action took place near Tankal, a village on the edge of the escarpment, eight miles south of Chelga. The enemy attempted to drive off our forces, consisting of one company and some patriots. They were unsuccessful and Tankal was held. Enemy casualties were eighty dead.

This thrust against Gondar from the west contained a force of enemy greater than itself, and kept it watching in both directions during the time of the operations against Debra Tabor.

Operations on 18th and 19th May.
On 18th May the Composite Battalion worked its way round on to the plateau, establishing itself on a ridge 1,000 yards north-east of Chelga Fort. In getting there they captured five officers and 300 other ranks.

On 19th May the enemy, strongly reinforced, attacked the Composite Battalion inflicting fairly severe casualties. Rain and the impassability of the tracks prevented further operations north of Chelga, and, on 22nd May the Composite Battalion returned to Amanit, on the road west of Chelga. Except for harassing tactics and a minor offensive by two companies to cover the withdrawal, no further operations took place on this front. By 30th June the Composite Battalion was concentrating at Gallabat, with forward posts on the Gandwa. As a result of this withdrawal, the enemy was able to move forces from the Chelga area across to the south-east of Gondar, where they were established some 36 miles south-east of Gondar covering the road to Debra Tabor.

PART VI.

Operations against the Wolchefit Pass.

By 12th April No. 1 M.M.G. Group, S.D.F., pursuing the enemy retreating towards Gondar, crossed the Tacazze River with little opposition. By 13th April it had reached the Wolchefit Pass, but, in attempting to patrol up it, two vehicles were ambushed and destroyed.

Topography – The Wolchefit Pass.

The Wolchefit Pass is not in the true sense of the word a Pass. It is an ascent from a lower level on to a plateau 4,000 feet higher. The road from Debivar zigzags up the face of Green Hill. Before it reaches the top of Green Hill it turns sharply, being carved out of the sheer cliff face along the western side. To construct this portion of the road, the Italians had been forced to suspend men by ropes over the top of the cliff. The top of Green Hill itself is a ledge still a considerable distance below the level of the plateau proper. The road from half way up Green Hill is covered by machine-gun and mortar fire. The original garrison on the top of the Wolchefit was estimated as 3,000 white and 2,000 native troops, with thirty guns, machine-guns and mortars. There were also reported to be a few light tanks but these have never been confirmed. The natural strength of the Wolchefit is twice that of Amba Alagi and five times that of Keren. Exhaustive reconnaissances have proved that there is no feature in the area of Debivar from which any observation could be got on to the top of the plateau. The enemy has command of movement in the valley. His guns and mortars are placed out of range of anything smaller than 25 pounders. The country round Debivar is such that Battery positions for field artillery, within effective range and under cover from enemy fire, are difficult to find. One battery of 25 pounders is about the limit that can be fitted in.

The only other way on to the escarpment so far discovered is by a mule track which winds eighteen miles through the hills and comes up on to the plateau at Bosa, fifteen miles west of Debarech. This track is only fit for mules, and at times in the rains is impassable even by them. The plateau itself reaches 10,000 feet. Conditions on the top in the rainy season are uncomfortable and cold. The country on top is rolling. As far as is known, no great physical difficulties exist between Wolchefit and Gondar. The road Wolchefit – Gondar is an all-weather M.T. road. Up the pass it is mined and blocked by demolitions. The exact extent of these demolitions are not yet known but it is believed that they are not unduly serious and that a Sappers and Miners Company with power tools could probably clear a way in a few days uninterrupted work.

Operations.

Up to date it has been impossible to force a way up the Wolchefit Pass. Operations have been confined to assisting patriot forces already on the plateau. These consist of a force operating from Bosa, commanded by Major Ringrose with one company of 3 Ethiopian Battalion under command. Nearer Gondar a party of patriots under el Bimbashi Sheppard came across from the Chelga direction and occupied Amba Giyorgis on the road Wolchefit – Gondar. The third party are the patriots who assisted in the capture of Debra Tabor under Major Douglas. These three parties, all of which vary daily in numbers, have been the only forces directly threatening Gondar since the fall of Debra Tabor and the withdrawal from Chelga.

Capture of Debarech.

By 28th May el Bimbashi Sheppard was occupying Amba Giyorgis and the whole road from inclusive Amba Giyorgis to exclusive Debarech was in patriot hands. Between 28th and 31st May severe fighting in the Debarech area resulted in the capture of Debarech. The enemy suffered more than 400 killed and over 150 deserters. Three small forts to the west of Debarech were also captured and the enemy was penned into the tongue of land immediately round the Wolchefit forts.

Night Attack 17th June.

Nothing further was undertaken until 17th June when Major Ringrose made a successful night attack on one of the forts at the Wolchefit. His troops were allowed to enter by unsuspecting sentries and the Italians were caught sleeping. The enemy casualties were over 100, several places were burnt and mines laid. Our casualties were three slightly wounded.

Loss of Debarech.

On 23rd June the enemy counter-attacked strongly against Ringrose's patriots who were dispersed and defeated. Ras Ayalu and his son, who had loyally supported Ringrose, were captured. Major Ringrose himself was slightly wounded and barely escaped with a small bodyguard and his two British wireless operators. The enemy recaptured Debarech and advanced some distance westwards towards Bosa.

Formation of Necol.

On 27th June one battery 28 Field Regiment was sent down to the Wolchefit and "Necol" was formed consisting of 28 Field Regiment less one battery, No. 2 M.M.G. Group, S.D.F. less one company, 51 Commando and 20 Field Company, Sappers and Miners. This force was ordered to assist the patriots by every means in their power with the object of securing a bridgehead on the top of the pass, and thus allow the road-blocks to be cleared for an advance on Gondar. On 6th July a plan was made to attack the Wolchefit Pass with regular troops, the patriots co-operating. In outline the plan was as follows:-

Plan to attack Wolchefit.
3/14 Punjab Regiment was to start from Zarema, the village where the mule track to Bosa leaves the main road, and march to Bosa. From there a reconnaissance was to be made, it being left to the discretion of the Officer Commanding 3/14 Punjab Regiment to decide whether or not the operation was feasible. He alone could decide, after having seen the country. A gunner O.P. with a wireless set accompanied 3/14 Punjab Regiment. The supply of regular troops on the top of this pass was a matter of difficulty, and the success or failure of the operation depended upon very close timing and the maintenance of wireless communication with the troops on the plateau. The R.A.F. guaranteed 30 sorties by Wellesley aircraft for the purpose of dropping ammunition and supplies. It was realised that a full scale of rations for Indian troops could not be maintained until the road was opened. Major Ringrose was confident that sufficient fresh meat and vegetables could be obtained locally, and would be supplied by the patriots to ensure that this battalion had enough to eat. There was no organised mule transport but patriot volunteers were plentiful, though, in the event, proved themselves extremely unreliable.

Course of the Operation.
3/14 Punjab Regiment arrived at Bosa on 13th July. On 14th July a reconnaissance in strength was made. The enemy had been fully informed of these operations and launched an immediate counter-attack against the leading companies of 3/14 Punjab Regiment. The gunner O.P. was over-run within 15 minutes of being established. A cloud, descended, making observation difficult. Patriot forces had become mixed with the enemy native troops, and it was impossible to distinguish friend from foe. There were undoubted cases of treachery. Patriots supposed to be friendly were seen firing on our officers and men. Commander 3/14 Punjab Regiment was killed. Surprise was lost, and, there being no further chance of renewing the operation, 3/14 Punjab withdrew.

In these operations time again was the limiting factor, not only on account of supplying 3/14 Punjab Regiment but also because 28 Field Regiment was under orders to sail for the Middle East, and could not be retained in the forward area later than 19th July.

R.A.F.
Since this operation, the pressure on Gondar and the Wolchefit Pass has been maintained mainly by the R.A.F. and S.A.A.F. On completion of their operations in the Galla Sidamo, the S.A.A.F. was placed at the disposal of 203 Group R.A.F.

Patriot Activity.
Since 15th July patriot activity has died down. The weather is bad and the patriots are anxious about the cultivation of their crops. It is unlikely that they will produce any major effort until their crops are harvested. Major Ringrose, his bodyguard, and one company of 3 Ethiopian Battalion attacked the enemy positions at Cianch between Wolchefit and Bosa on 26th August capturing 108 Italians,

8 natives and some mortars and machine-guns. The patriot forces under Major Douglas have moved closer to Gondar and supported by the S.A.A.F., are increasing their pressure on Gondar from this direction. Communications at the moment are bad, and news is only coming through by runner, taking in some cases five or six days to reach Asmara.

PART VII.

Operations in the Blue Nile Frontier Area and Baro Salient.

Along their western frontier, the Italians had maintained garrisons covering the entrances into Ethiopia. During the summer and autumn of 1940, the strength of the Sudan Defence Force had not allowed more than defensive patrolling by Police and "Armed Friendlies." Many of these patrols were led by Political Officers of the Sudan Civil Service, who were not professional soldiers, but who displayed commendable skill and courage in this frontier patrol work. The efforts of these small parties were assisted by the R.A.F. who effectively bombed enemy garrisons and carried on a leaflet and propaganda war, mainly directed against his native troops, whenever aircraft could be made available.

It was not until January 1941 that sufficient reinforcements in the form of 2/6 King's African Rifles and the Belgian Contingent in the Sudan allowed of more active operations being undertaken in the frontier area.

It was important that the enemy's frontier posts in the neighbourhood of the Blue Nile should be removed so that the camel routes into Ethiopia could be opened for the supply and maintenance of the rebellion, which could not have flourished without a steady flow of arms, money and material from the Sudan. The removal of the enemy forces from this area automatically lessened the threat against the Nile L. of C. and the Sudan Railway, which, if cut about the Sennar Dam, would have left the troops operating in the Butana Bridge and Gallabat areas isolated from Khartoum.

On 9th January our patrols entered Guba, the Italian frontier post covering the north bank of the Blue Nile. The post was found deserted, and a considerable quantity of war material was discovered. This post had been induced to evacuate by air action, and the action of armed friendlies.

On 20th January 5 Patrol Company, Frontier Battalion, encountered a force of the enemy at the Shogali crossing of the Blue Nile. A sharp action ensued, the enemy withdrawing towards Asosa. On 12th February Kurmuk was captured by detachments 2/6 K.A.R. and Sudan Frontier Police. This cleared the last Italians out of the Sudan. Operations continued with the object of attacking Asosa.

Topography.

The Sudan, east of the White Nile, is mainly flat grass country. As the frontier is approached, the country rises into foothills of considerable size, and, about Asosa and Afodu, is mountainous, Afodu itself being on top of an escarpment.

At this time 2/6 K.A.R. were spread from Kurmuk to the Baro Salient, a distance of over 200 miles. The Belgian Contingent was disposed behind the

K.A.R. protecting the White Nile. Advancing from the north based on Roseires, the Eastern Arab Corps, Sudan Defence Force, with 5 Patrol Company, Frontier Battalion, and C Troop Light Artillery Battery, S.D.F., under command were co-operating with the northern detachment 2/6 K.A.R. Between 14th February and 9th March Qeissan and Belad Deroz were captured by the Sudan Defence Force, and, on 9th March, after heavy fighting, the escarpment at Afodu was stormed by the Eastern Arab Corps with two companies 2/6 K.A.R. under command. Guns and stores, and some M.T. fell into their hands. The advance was immediately pressed on towards Asosa.

In the meantime a detachment of the Belgians had moved forward, and was in a position facing Asosa from the south. Unfortunately the Belgian Contingent, which had been ordered to cut the road east of Asosa, was too late, and a con-siderable body of the enemy escaped. After the fall of Asosa the whole of the Blue Nile frontier was cleared and open for the passage of camel caravans to the Gojjam. Units of the Eastern Arab Corps were moved to the area east of Gallabat, as has been previously described.

Operations against Gambela.

The next important centre of enemy resistance was in the area Gambela – Dembi Dollo. A detachment of 2/6 K.A.R. which had been operating at Asosa now marched south-east, encountering strong enemy positions on the Dabus River based on Mendi. By 20th March the remainder of 2/6 K.A.R. had been concen-trated, and was about three miles west of Gambela. Here they were subjected to heavy attacks by enemy aircraft. On 23rd March the Belgian Battalion from the Asosa area was also moved south to operate against Gambela, and from now on the whole of the Belgian Contingent, later brought up to three battalions and one field battery, operated in this area. On 22nd March 2/6 K.A.R. with that portion of the Belgian Contingent which had been moved forward, attacked Gambela and, after severe fighting, captured it on the 23rd. Here again the enemy escaped.

From Gambela the Belgian Contingent patrolled towards Dembi Dollo, while 2/6 K.A.R. moved north to the Dabus River and Ghidame. The enemy's position at Dembi Dollo was found to be strong. Throughout April there was consider-able fighting here, with patrol actions along the Dabus River. On 21st April 2/6 K.A.R. were ordered to operate south and south-east towards Mendi and Ghimbi in co-operation with one Belgian battalion which, after the capture of Dembi Dollo, was directed on Yubdo. Thereafter 2/6 K.A.R. was to continue eastwards to Lekempti, and the Belgians towards Gore, as far as the administra-tive situation permitted. Patrol activity continued in this area, and various small actions were fought, but the enemy positions at Dembi Dollo were too strong for the Belgians to take. The enemy had air superiority in this area, the majority of our Air Force being engaged in Northern Ethiopia. At the end of April the Belgians had six companies spread out from the Bortai River to Gambela. Throughout the month of May, 2/6 K.A.R. and the Belgian Contingent were thrown on the defensive. Initiative had passed to the enemy who threatened to retake Asosa and Afodu with his considerable garrison in the Mendi area. This necessitated the disposition of 2/6 K.A.R. to cover the approaches from Mendi over the River Dabus, and the temporary evacuation of Ghidame. The weakness of our forces must now have been apparent to the enemy.

The Belgians were subjected to regular air bombing. There was a considerable amount of sickness amongst them. Until the westward drive from Addis Ababa and the Lakes diverted the enemy's threat to Asosa, it was not safe to move 2/6 K.A.R. southwards from the Dabus River to co-operate with the Belgians.

In June 2/6 K.A.R. moved south to Ghidame, operating from there south-eastwards to cut the road Dembi Dollow – Yubdo. The road was attacked on 3rd July, and by the 4th July good progress was being made. On 2nd July the Belgian Contingent forced the River Bortai, attacking towards Dembi Dollo on the 3rd. At 0200 hours on 4th July General Gazzera asked for terms and surrendered the remnants of his army to the Belgians.

PART VIII.

Operations in the Boma.

During the early stages of the war operations on the Boma Plateau had been confined to patrol activity only. It was not until forces operating from Kenya along the west side of Lake Rudolph were ready, that the Equatorial Corps could undertake an advance into southwest Ethiopia. Maji was the centre of the Italian resistance in this area. The natives were friendly neither to the Italians nor the British and even before the war had been a constant source of trouble. Sudan forces in this area consisted of four companies of the Equatorial Corps and a nebulous force of patriots who, in this area, achieved very little. Time and resources did not allow the making of an all-weather road across the Boma Plateau towards the frontier. It was therefore not possible to maintain regular forces in active operations during the rains, which, in this area, begin early in the year. On 17th February these decisions were conveyed to the O.C. Equatorial Corps. He was instructed to take steps immediately to dump forward sufficient supplies to maintain at least one company of the Equatorial Corps and the patriots, who numbered about 500, during the rains.

The general outline of the plan was for companies of the Equatorial Corps to move on Maji via Zilmanu in co-operation with 25th East African Brigade. On 19th February No. 2 Company of the Equatorial Corps encountered a battalion of 18th Colonial Brigade. An action ensued in which the enemy left 150 dead, our casualties being 5 killed and 9 wounded including one British officer. The enemy battalion was driven off.

On 2nd April Maji was reported strongly held by the enemy and there was a considerable number of anti-British natives with a stiffening of regulars in the Zilmanu and Beru areas. Between these posts the country was in a state of semi-civil war. On 8th April a message was received from G.O.C. East Africa that Maji had been evacuated and expressing the opinion that the Merille tribe would not submit unless Maji was occupied by regular troops. He also stated that 25th East

African Brigade would only be able to garrison Maji for a limited time as it was wanted for further operations. He asked if the Equatorial Corps could take over the garrisoning of Maji. This was agreed to and the Equatorial Corps moved forward to occupy Maji. The rains had already started and the state of the tracks was appalling. The country is covered with tropical jungle. Progress was slow and difficult. By 25th April the Equatorial Corps was still ten miles from Maji, having been held up by road conditions and flooded rivers. It was not until early in May that Maji was occupied. The only practicable route into Maji came from the north, and O.C. Equatorial Corps found it necessary to establish a garrison at Masci, nine miles north of Maji, where contact was made with 2/4 K.A.R.

On 13th May, O.C. Equatorial Corps reported that he was confident of being able to occupy Maji indefinitely but it was essential that one company should occupy Masci to cover the only practicable route which came into Maji from the enemy's direction. Owing to the rains his L. of C. was precarious. He had reached the limit of M.T. Beyond garrisoning Masci and Maji, only defensive patrols could be undertaken. At this time the whole Boma area was under heavy, continuous rain. The many rivers were rapidly rising and some were now twelve feet deep.

By 1st June, Advanced Headquarters of the Equatorial Corps was fully established in Maji. Irregular activities were directed from there, mainly in the direction of Shoa Gimira. During June the country was gradually cleared of enemy.

PART IX.

The Patriot Campaign – 1940.
The month of November 1940, when a forward policy in Gojjam was decided upon, found the enemy and ourselves disposed as follows in the area of potential revolt:

Gojjam.
The enemy had three Colonial Brigades (sixteen battalions) concentrated on the three main strongholds, Dangila, Burye and Debra Markos, with four Blackshirt battalions in support. We had Mission 101, consisting of Colonel D.A. Sandford, D.S.O., two other British Officers and three N.C.Os., accompanied by the Emperor's representative Azajh Kabada and protected by the patriot leaders, Dedjasmatches Mangasha and Nagash, who had received about 1,000 rifles from us.

Armacheho – Begemeder.
Excluding the forces gathered at Metemma to meet our offensive there, the enemy had one Colonial Brigade, twelve Blackshirt battalions and two Cavalry Groups in the area.

We had Major Arthur Bentinck of Mission 101, accompanied by the Emperor's representative, Tsahafi Taezaz Haile, as a result of whose efforts only one chief, Gerasmatch Redda of Chelga, took armed action against the Italians. In addition Captain Foley, R.E., was operating on the Gondar-Metemma road with a small band and supply of explosives.

Walkait.

The enemy had three Colonial battalions and one Blackshirt battalion in the area. We had no representative but had armed two chiefs, Dedjasmatch Adane and Fitaurari Misfin, who caused the Italians a certain amount of trouble.

Shoa and Wollo.

We had no communication with these areas, which contained some important patriot leaders, Ras Ababa Aragai, Fitauraris Gerasu Duke and Shakka Bakale.

The Plan.

One convoy had reached Mission 101 in the Gojjam since its departure from the Sudan in August, 1940. The R.A.F. based on the Sudan had begun deep raiding on Dangila, Bahrdar Giyorgis and Enjabara. This had stirred the patriots to some activity of a minor nature, and the Italians to counter-activity, raids and cross-country marches. Some of the irregular Banda leaders on the escarpment of Gojjam were thinking of transferring their allegiance to the Emperor. The Italian command, anxious about the potential threat in Gojjam, appointed their most distinguished colonial commander, General Nasi, to the new Western Command, which included the three first zones mentioned above. They further agreed (on a financial consideration) with the hereditary leader of Gojjam, Ras Hailu Tekla Haimanot, that he should return to the province, and by their concentrations at Metemma and in Beni Shangul were clearly hoping to forbid our arms traffic into Gojjam, limited though that was by the lack of animal transport and the poverty of our own resources.

In November, following the visit of the Secretary of State for War (Mr. Anthony Eden), a new G(R) staff for the rebellion was appointed in Khartoum. Major O.C. Wingate, D.S.O., took charge of operations. They were given considerable resources in finance and weapons, and the first step in the forward policy now initiated was a flight on 20th November by Major Wingate to Colonel Sandford's Headquarters in central Gojjam, where the principles of the forthcoming offensive were discussed.

At this and later conferences the following plan of action was evolved.

The Emperor Haile Selassie, with his bodyguard, was to enter Ethiopia as soon as possible and to make his first camp on the massif of Belaya, a patriot area detached from the escarpment and lying 90 miles north-west of Burye.

For this purpose, one company of the recently formed Sudan Frontier Battalion was to occupy Belaya, and later was to be followed by three of the remaining companies.

1 Ethiopian Battalion, which had just begun its training in Khartoum, was to be distributed into Operational Centres under British Officers and N.C.Os., and these were to march into Gojjam via Belaya and attach themselves to various patriot chiefs.

2 Ethiopian Battalion and 4 Eritrean Battalion were to be brought from Kenya to form the nucleus of the Emperor's Bodyguard, which would, however, have a fighting role.

Further members of the Bodyguard were to be found by Colonel Sandford in Gojjam and sent to Belaya for training.

Up to 25,000 camels were to be raised in the Sudan to transport the necessities for a nine months' campaign as far as the escarpment.

Colonel Sandford was to raise up to 3,000 mules in Gojjam for the escarpment haul.

The supply of arms and ammunition to the quarrelsome and ineffective chiefs north of Gojjam was to cease, but the section of Mission 101 was to remain there to keep the population sweet with money and food.

The ultimate object of this plan was to seize an Italian stronghold in Gojjam, preferably Dangila, instal the Emperor nearby, and from this centre to widen the area of revolt and desertion.

For the rest of 1940 and until 20th January, 1941, work to put the plan into operation went steadily ahead. 2 Ethiopian Battalion arrived in the Sudan from Kenya and began its training, though 4 Eritrean Battalion arrived too late to participate in warlike activity. Three Operational Centres were formed and by 20th January, one had already gone forward. By the same date four companies of the Sudan Frontier Battalion, who were to be the spearhead of the movement, reached or were marching for Belaya, at whose foot an aerodrome was nearing completion. Thousands of camels with volunteer drivers had been collected from all over the Sudan, and were on the move to Belaya. Difficulties, however, were experienced in getting the Abyssinian end of the scheme to keep pace with the Sudanese. It was found that the patriot chiefs did not take kindly to the idea of releasing men from their own forces and so weakening themselves in order to increase the Imperial Bodyguard. They were also very slow in collecting mules. In the end it was found necessary to drive the camel transport up the escarpment into Gojjam, and this, in combination with the arduous approach over lava soil to Belaya, was responsible for the large animal mortality (12,000 out of 15,000 camels) of the Gojjam campaign. First attempts to break a route for M.T. to Belaya failed.

Meanwhile the R.A.F. continued to drop bombs and propaganda on the Gojjam strongholds, and included Burye and the main frontier Banda posts of Guba and Wanbera in their programme. Exploiting the rout of Colonel Rolle's Banda in October, we armed the negroid Gumz people near Guba, and this, associated with the intensification of our propaganda and a series of heavy air attacks, led to the panic abandonment of Guba in the first days of January. This constituted the first Italian territorial loss in the campaign, and, by removing the threat to our lines of communication from the south, greatly simplified our penetration of Gojjam.

The Advance.
On 20th January 1941 the Emperor Haile Salassie crossed the frontier from the Sudan into Ethiopia at a point near Umm Idla, escorted by 2 Ethiopian Battalion. A special security route had been chosen for him running east-south-east by

compass-bearing to the north-western slopes of Belaya, but this proved too difficult for M.T. and he eventually reached Belaya by horse on 6th February. In the meantime Colonel O.C. Wingate had been appointed commander of the forces in Gojjam, and Brigadier D.S. Sandford became Political and Military Adviser to the Emperor.

The appearance of this mixed Sudanese and Ethiopian force, enlarged by rumour, at Belaya, and the arrival of the Emperor, had the desired effect on the Italians and their dependents. The system of guarding the entries to the escarpment by territorial Banda broke down entirely. The chiefs of Tumha, the important district on the scarp-edge west of Dangila, who were brothers of Fitaurari Tafere Zalleka, the patriot chief of Belaya, had already come over; and now Fitaurari Zalleka Birru who commanded the local bands both in Matakal (the key to Enjabara and Burye) and in the Wanbera district, proclaimed his submission to the Emperor.

This crumbling of their first line of defence, coming after the failure of their last efforts to crush the central Gojjam patriot chiefs, Dedjasmatches Mangasha and Nagash, and coming also at a time when they were in sore need of reinforcements for the Eritrean and Somalia fronts, seems to have decided the Italians to abandon, at a convenient time, western Gojjam and the Brigade H.Qs. of Dangila and Burye, and to fall back in the north on Bahrdar Giyorgis and in the south on the line of the Temcha river south of Dambacha.

The first step in this retreat was taken before our regular forces could intervene. On 16th February, when one company of the Frontier Battalion was approaching his area, Colonel Torelli, commanding the nine battalions in Dangila, withdrew to Piccolo Abbai, and thence after a short rest at Meshenti, to Bahrdar Giyorgis. He lost several hundred deserters en route and was harried by patriots and by a Bimbashi of the S.D.F. with one mortar and 20 regular troops, but his casualties to fire were not large. In the following weeks he was able to withdraw all the outlying garrisons of Alefa and Achefer, Zeghie, Debra Mai and Addiet, without great loss, to Bahrdar, where he was invested by "Beghemder Force" consisting of one company of the Frontier Battalion and an Operational Centre of 180 men acting under the G.S.O.2 of Mission 101. The role of this small force, which it successfully accomplished, was to prevent Torelli from breaking back and attacking the rear of the Frontier Battalion and 2 Ethiopian Battalion once the Italian Commander understood the midget from which he had run. Dangila had meanwhile been looted by the patriots.

With the danger from the north sealed off, the remainder of the Frontier Battalion (less 5 Company), 2 Ethiopian Battalion, No. I Operational Centre, a platoon of four mortars and a Field Propaganda Unit were formed into "Gideon Force" under the command of Colonel Wingate and assembled in the former Italian Fort of Enjabara on the axial road of Gojjam on 23rd February. One week previously Colonel Natale, commanding the Italian Brigade Group in Burye, had withdrawn the garrisons of two Colonial battalions from Enjabara on to Burye. This column had again been harassed, somewhat more vigorously, by the patriots of Dedjasmatch Nagash but had nevertheless been able to reach Burye. The timely arrival of our troops in Enjabara stopped looting and saved a month's supply of Italian rations for the entire force. From now on it was discovered that it was possible for Gideon Force to live on the country and on captured food.

It was now necessary to operate rapidly if the garrison of Burye was not also to escape, without damage, to a defensible line preparatory to the next step in Italian policy, which was to hand over the government of the Gojjam to Ras Hailu and trust to the jealousy between the Imperial and the Gojjam dynasty to divide Gojjam and smother the revolt. The British Gojjam command therefore decided to march south by night on 25th February in order to bypass Burye to the north and occupy the road south of Burye leading to Debra Markos, where, with the aid of a rebellious countryside, they might hope to ambush Natale's column.

The Italian commander at this moment played into our hands by his indecision. Believing that too much prestige had already been lost by the precipitate withdrawals from Dangila and Enjabara (and in the first case the Italians had been obliged to abandon all their M.T.), fearing that further withdrawals would increase the rate of desertions and, supposing that, for the time being, he was safe in Burye, Natale decided not to withdraw for the present. If the Italians had withdrawn at this moment after destroying their copious stores in Burye, with their M.T. and their forces intact, they might have confronted Gideon Force with great difficulties of administration and have checked its advance.

As things were, Natale does not seem to have been aware of the approach of Gideon Force until it was on the outskirts of Burye. By that time, the column, four miles long as it marched at night with its 700 camels and 200 mules, had been exaggerated past recognition by local report and propaganda. 600 men had been multiplied by ten, with the result that when Natale left, he left in a disorderly hurry, and his retreat was harried by troops of a fighting quality and a persistence many times superior to those of the irregular patriot forces with whom he had skirmished in the past.

The Road Battles.

In the new plan, 2 Ethiopian Battalion, supported by patriot irregulars, were to attack the forts of Jigga and Dambacha on the Gojjam road, while the Frontier Battalion and mortars were to threaten the outer forts of Burye and the fort of Mankusa a few miles to the south of Burye. These operations were successfully carried out in the period 27th February-4th March, while the main forts of Burye were effectively attacked by the R.A.F. After a smart action in daylight (the only such action deliberately undertaken by Gideon Force during the campaign) on Burye southern fort on 27th February, followed by harassing fire on the fort throughout the night, attention was switched to Mankusa fort on the enemy's line of retreat. Mankusa was harassed and set ablaze by mortar and Vickers fire and by the cries and conjurations of the propaganda unit. Considerable desertions were suffered by the Italians, morale was at a low ebb, and this final threat to his only communications persuaded Natale to break out to the south on 4th March, screened by low-flying Italian aircraft.

The retreat was followed up and skilfully harassed in camp at night with light machine-gun fire from two companies of the Frontier Battalion, who inflicted losses on the enemy later reported as four lorry-loads of wounded. The enemy was thus pushed through Jigga fort, and, on 6th March fell into an ambush laid by the 2 Ethiopian Battalion (some 400 men) in a river-bed west of Dambacha. Here some 1,000 casualties, including 180 killed, were inflicted on the enemy column and two of his armoured cars were captured before he had been able to smother 2 Ethiopian Battalion by sheer weight of numbers. The losses of this Ethiopian Battalion were surprisingly light – one British Officer, 90 men and the whole of the battalion camel transport – but the disorganisation that they suffered in this gallant action was such as to render them practically valueless for the rest of the campaign. Attacked at the same time from the rear by companies of the Frontier Battalion and on the flank by patriot bands, which were always more active when he was on the move, the enemy was thoroughly scared. On 8th March he evacuated Dambacha, and, on the 10th, burned down and abandoned Fort Emanuel east of the river Tamcha, thus giving up his original plan of defence of Eastern Gojjam. The commander of Gideon Force and the Frontier Battalion pressed hard on his heels, and on 13th March were in contact with him on the Gulit Hill position just west of Debra Markos. He had concentrated here all the remaining forces of Gojjam except for the garrison of Bahrdar Giyorgis, and a battalion at Mota. Ras Hailu was also called in with his Banda to help in the defence of the town.

Operations round Debra Markos.
As the enemy withdrew deeper into Gojjam his forces naturally increased and the British and Ethiopian regular forces diminished, since it was necessary, if only for the protection of valuable stores, to garrison positions such as Emanuel and Dambacha, to reform 2 Ethiopian Battalion, and to protect the L. of C. used by the few lorries captured at Burye, on which supply now depended. At Debra Markos the disparity of the forces opposed had reached something fantastic; 12,000 Italians and Colonial troops were contained by two companies of the Frontier Battalion, supported by the mortar platoon (four mortars) of 2 Ethiopian Battalion, totalling 300 men. The enemy's illusions as to our regular strength were at last beginning to be dispelled; Natale was disgraced by General Nasi and replaced by Colonel Maraventano, and the enemy broke back on 17th March and re-occupied Fort Emanuel with some 1,500 troops.

In this predicament, which synchonised with a heavy enemy counter-attack for Bahrdar Giyorgis, the commander of Gideon Force had to decide whether to withdraw to the Tamcha river and take up a position defending the Emperor's Headquarters, which were now outside Burye, or to advance boldly and by continuous manoeuvre pin the bulk of the enemy's forces to the perimeter forts of Debra Markos. The latter course was rightly taken, and after a small Ethiopian regular force, accompanied by a British engineer, had been detached to interrupt the road between Debra Markos and the Blue Nile and to contact the chief Lij Belai Zelleka, whose help, it was thought, might be useful in that area, a series of new attacks was launched on the enemy defences north and north-west of Debra Markos.

In view of our great poverty in numbers, a new technique had to be thought out for these attacks, which were strikingly successful in inflicting casualties upon the enemy and in lowering his morale. The country was well covered, and our forces were thus able to lie up in the day-time, only a few miles from the enemy's positions without detection by his air or his native cavalry. Action was taken only at night, when approach marches reconnoitred during the day were carried out by parties which rarely exceeded a hundred men for a single operation, and usually numbered forty to fifty. The alternative methods used were to lay light machine-guns from close range on the enemy's camp fires when they were still burning, or (more commonly, for the enemy soon adjusted himself to this ruse) to approach, armed simply with bomb, rifle and bayonet, bomb his positions from ten yards range, carry them with the bayonet, beat off counter-attack, and withdraw before dawn. The hour chosen for these attacks was usually when the enemy was sleepiest, and his customary reaction was to continue firing with machine-guns and artillery until dawn, thus waging a war of nerves upon himself. Naturally the most absolute discipline of silence, fire-control and sense of direction was demanded of the troops who took part in these attacks, and it was here that the natural fighting qualities of the Sudanese and the training of the Frontier Battalion and its officers were demonstrated. Between 19th March and 3rd April, when the Ethiopian flag was raised by Ras Hailu over the citadel of Debra Markos and the last Italian troops had abandoned the town, attacks of this kind were made with success on Abima Fort, Addis Fort, and all the Gulit positions. The most impressive of these took place on Gulit on the night of 24th March, when four of the main positions were entered by our men. The effect of these guerilla methods could be judged by the stream of desertions coming at the rate of over a hundred men a day from the enemy's forces in Debra Markos. On 1st April the enemy abandoned Gulit and the evacuation of Debra Markos began.

A small force of three platoons and the mortar section was detached to support the troops that had already joined Lij Belai Zelleka on the line of the enemy's retreat to the Blue Nile. They were accompanied by the irregulars of Azaj Kabada, the Emperor's representative. If it had not been for the treachery of Lij Belai, who abandoned the ambush by agreement with Ras Hailu (into whose noble family, he, a commoner, wished to marry), it is possible that the Maraventano column which was already shedding thousands of deserters, would have surrendered north of the Blue Nile crossing. As it was, twenty-eight enemy lorries and two armoured cars were ambushed and destroyed by the forces left in the lurch by Lij Belai, and a large number of Italian Colonial troops were killed. Azaj Kabada's men co-operated creditably in this action, which, apart from one bomb raid on the Debra Markos forts, was the first in which Ethiopian irregular patriot forces had played a prominent part since the entry of Gideon Force into Gojjam. From now on a striking characteristic of the patriot irregulars came into evidence. Unwilling to sacrifice themselves when the issue of the war was in doubt and providing nothing more concrete than a camouflage to the small number of our forces, from henceforward to the fall of Addis Ababa they risked themselves more and more in open battle and were largely responsible for the eventual surrender of the Maraventano column at Agibar east of the Blue Nile on 22nd May. Operations carried out beyond the Blue Nile were under the direction of Lt.-General Cunningham, G.O.C. East Africa, and therefore are not described in this report. It is sufficient to say that Maraventano surrendered 7,000 men, with 7 guns and nearly 200 automatics, heavy and light, to 140 Sudanese and Ethiopian regulars and 2,000 patriots under Ras Kassa, after a three-day battle in which the Sudanese showed their customary address, discipline and coolness and the Ethiopians a new reckless courage. This quality may partly be attributed to a desire for loot and partly to the removal of the haunting fear of Italian reprisals on their families and villages.

The Emperor entered the citadel at Debra Markos on 6th April. As Ras Hailu (believed to be in communication with the enemy) remained in the town with 6,000 Banda, and as relations between him and the Emperor were frigid, the bulk of Gideon Force was kept in Debra Markos until 28th April, when they accompanied the Emperor across the Blue Nile to Addis Ababa. By this time some of the Frontier Battalion M.T. had been skilfully driven across the difficult country of Belaya and hauled by rope and manpower up the escarpment, and the pontoon bridge across the Nile at Shafartak had been repaired. The last remaining Italian force in eastern Gojjam, 69 Colonial Battalion at Mota, had also been reduced by the usual combination of deception and harassing force, after a strenuous march by the Sudanese plainsmen of the Frontier Battalion in their cotton uniforms through a blizzard in the 14,000 foot Chokey Pass. At Mota 400 Italian Colonial troops surrendered to sixty Sudanese and stores and ammunition were captured. Similarly big stores of foodstuffs had been saved from looting at Debra Markos.

Thus in a campaign which lasted for six weeks and in which the sole regular force had been 50 British officers, 20 B.O.R.'s, 800 Sudanese and 800 Ethiopian troops, with four 3-inch mortars and without air support after the Italian evacuation of Burye (when the Sudan's limited resources of aircraft had to be concentrated on Keren) the whole of Gojjam had been cleared of sixteen Colonial battalions, two regular Banda groups and four Blackshirt Battalions, with pack artillery appropriate to three Colonial brigades (six batteries) and with considerable aircraft. Half of this force was eventually captured by the regular troops described above, the other half was evacuated across Lake Tana to the neighbourhood of Gondar. This remarkable achievement in guerilla warfare was due to the far-sighted and determined organisation of transport from the Sudan base, to the skill of the Frontier Battalion, the drive of the command and the patient preparation of the Gojjam countryside by Mission 101 and the Emperor's representative. Gideon Force was broken up at the end of April 1941, but elements of the Frontier and two Ethiopian Battalions formed the guard of the Emperor when he re-entered Addis Ababa on 5th May.

Operations at Bahrdar Giyorgis and in Beghemder.
Major A.C. Simonds, M.B.E., G.S.O.2 to Mission 101, had been appointed to the command of "Beghemder Force" in February, with the special role of investing the Italian Force under Colonel Torelli in Bahrdar Giyorgis and later marching across the Blue Nile into Beghemder where he was ordered to cut communications between Gondar – Debra Tabor – Dessie and to force the evacuation of all small enemy forts in the province. The forces under his command were 3 Company Frontier Battalion, No. 2 Operational Centre (180 Ethiopians) and Fitaurari Birru, the Imperial nominee as Governor of Beghemder, who arrived with 500 Beghemder peasants at Bahrdar Giyorgis and lost 450 of these to desertion the following day.

Bahrdar was closely and successfully invested by this small force, whose main role of securing the rear of Gideon Force was thus achieved. On two occasions, on 19th March and 26th April, Torelli made determined sorties to the south from Bahrdar Giyorgis with greatly superior forces, but failed with loss to break through. On the first occasion he came out with five Colonial battalions, pack artillery and mortars against 250 Sudanese and 75 patriots but was stopped after losing 175 men. On the second occasion he lost 150 killed and wounded, our losses being two killed and three wounded. As usual the Sudanese soldier set a high example of coolness and discipline. Torelli was himself wounded, and on 2nd May he evacuated Bahrdar Giyorgis, which was occupied by 3 Company Frontier Battalion. Meanwhile the commander of Beghemder Force, with No. 2 Operational Centre and the stores of No. 3 Operational Centre, Fitaurari Birru and 74 Ethiopians, was ordered to cross the Blue Nile into Beghemder. The province was entered on 28th March.

In Beghemder two patriot chiefs, Dedjasmatches Danyo and Bellai, with 7,000 men, exercised a nominal control over about a quarter of the province. Another quarter was found to be neutral and the rest actively hostile. Immediate action was taken on the Gondar – Debra Tabor – Dessie road which was blocked and mined. A sharp engagement was fought against an enemy force some 300–400 strong on 13th April by No. 2 Centre and Dedjasmatch Danyo, who blew up four enemy lorries and killed 52 Italians including the commander of the column as well as about 100 Banda. Reinforcements were sent in about 90 M.T. from Gondar but the new column was halted and a relieving force of one battalion, sent out from Debra Tabor, was also ambushed and forced to retire. Another relieving column from Debra Tabor succeeded in extricating the Italians at the cost of six ammunition lorries, 80 killed and 200 Italians wounded. The patriots fought gallantly, and, from this time onward, the enemy made no more attempts to reach Debra Tabor with M.T. from the north, with consequent far reaching effects on local morale. Whole sections of the province declared themselves for the Emperor, including the large districts of Gaint and Dera, and the Italians evacuated all outlying posts in Beghemder on Gondar, Debra Tabor, Hag and Taragadam. Debra Tabor was in effect isolated, for mining and sabotage operations to the south had cut it also off from Dessie, and, in conjunction with the operations of Imperial forces at Amba Alagi, rendered retreat impossible for the garrison of Dessie when 1st South African Brigade broke through the defences of that town.

On 3rd May, the day after the capture of Bahrdar Giyorgis, the commander of Frontier Battalion moved 3 Company across the Blue Nile into Beghemder, leaving 4 Company at Bahrdar Giyorgis with orders to collect animal transport and follow to Debra Tabor. H.Q. Frontier Battalion reached the outskirts of Debra Tabor on 7th May and from then until arrival of 4 Company on 16th May, in spite of continual rain, inadequate clothing and cover, and much lameness caused by jigger sores, they maintained systematic nightly bombing attacks on the Debra Tabor garrison, which consisted of two Blackshirt and two Colonial battalions and a regular Banda group. 4 Company continued the work with mortar support until 20th May, when the battalion was ordered to Dessie, much to the regret of the commander, who, after an exchange of correspondence with Colonel Angelini, commanding the Debra Tabor garrison, believed, that in spite of his instructions to hold out to the last man, Angelini would have surrendered with a little more pushing. Major Simonds was withdrawn at the same time. Debra Tabor did not fall until the beginning of July 1941, but it remained isolated throughout the intervening period as a result of the work of Beghemder Force and the Frontier Battalion.

Operations North and West of Gondar.
As stated above, an early decision was taken to stop the supply of arms and ammunition to the quarrelsome patriot chiefs of Armacheho, among whom, hampered at the same time by the incompetence of the Emperor's representative, Major Count Arthur Bentinck had now to keep the peace. The withdrawal, with the loss of all their M.T., of the Italian garrison from Walkait and northern Tsegede, however, gave a fillip to patriot activity at the beginning of February, and Major Bentinck was able, without the support of an operational centre or a single British officer or other rank to occupy Colle Chek a few miles north-west of Gondar, and so to draw off part of the enemy's reserves during the battle of Keren.

Meanwhile the various patriot and former pro-Italian chiefs in Walkait and Tsegede assembled in conference, and, under the influence of Major Ringrose, who was later to lead the patriots in this area, and of an able Abyssinian priest Abba Qirqos, at length resolved their differences and decided to go to war. Part of them, without a British representative, went east to the main crossing of the Tacazze on the Gondar-Adowa road; but although they captured two Italian posts there and caused some anxiety to the Italian command, which is reflected in the war diaries for March of General Frusci, G.O.C. Northern Command, they were unable to stop the flow of reinforcements from Gondar to Keren and Asmara at a crucial moment of the Keren battle. Major Ringrose meanwhile marched south with the rest of the chiefs and eventually occupied Dabat and Debarech and a large part of the road between Gondar and the main Italian defence position on the Wolchefit Pass. Though later driven out of Debarech by a break-back of the beleaguered Wolchefit garrison, with loss of his transport and wounds to himself, his forces still threaten the road joining Gondar to its outlying northern forts and have recently carried the position at Cianch.

Part of the Eastern Arab Corps and the whole of 3 Ethiopian Battalion had meanwhile destroyed 27 Colonial Battalion on the hills near Chelga, but the despatch of a reserve Colonial Brigade by the Gondar Command and the flood-ing of the communications at the Gandwa crossing obliged this force to withdraw to the Sudan along its only L. of C., the earth road from Gondar to Metemma.

FIRST REPORT BY LIEUT. GEN. SIR ALAN CUNNINGHAM, K.C.B., D.S.O., M.C., ON EAST AFRICA FORCE OPERATIONS COVERING THE PERIOD FROM 1ST NOVEMBER 1940 TO THE FALL OF ADDIS ABEBA, ON 5TH APRIL, 1941.

PART I. – INTRODUCTION

When I took over command of East Africa Force on 1st November 1940 the military policy, which of necessity had had to be one of passive defence, was assuming a more offensive character. Owing to the few troops which had been in existence in Kenya when the Italians came into the war, to the fall of Moyale, and to the evacuation of British Somaliland, the morale of the civilian population was at a low ebb, and schemes had even been worked out for the evacuation of women and children from Nairobi. The recent arrival of 1st S.A. Brigade, which pre-ceded the remainder of 1st S.A. Division, marked the turn of the tide for the local morale.

2. At the beginning of November 1940 the force consisted of 11th and 12th (African) Divisions each containing one East African and one West African Brigade. 1st S.A. Brigade had been attached temporarily to 12 (A) Division. The force was on a two divisional front with 11th (A) Division on the right holding a line from Malindi, thence to Bura on the river Tana and along the river to Garissa. The right of 12th (A) Division was at Wajir whence, westwards, Marsabit and Lokitaung were held. The military boundary between the Sudan forces and the E.A. forces was the political boundary between the Sudan and Kenya, a fact which was made necessary for administrative reasons, but was not really satisfactory from the military point of view because any general advance would entail both E.A. and Sudan forces operating in the same area. The distance from Malindi to Lokitaung was 650 miles as the crow flies. It will be appreciated therefore that the defence of Kenya had to be carried out by holding isolated localities where water existed, on the tracks leading out of Kenya into Italian territory. Most of these localities have been mentioned in the description of the line held above. The policy for defence was to provide the localities with the strongest physical forms of defence possible, e.g., wire, mines, tank traps, etc., but that they should be

lightly held. The main defence depended on the provision of highly mobile reserves kept outside and behind the localities for immediate counter-attack.

3. My predecessor had been able to establish energetic patrol superiority over the large area of desert which separated the two forces, but owing to shortages of various sorts, chiefly M.T., was unable to do more.

An important part in establishing control over No Man's Land was played by the Irregular Companies. The first two Somali Irregular Companies were formed in September 1940 with the object of countering the activities of Italian Banda in the Northern Frontier District of Kenya. Italian Banda consisted of Colonial troops specially enlisted and normally operating in the vicinity of the areas from which they were recruited. They were well led by specially selected Italian officers who "lived native" and with their knowledge of the country, and independence of communications, not only had a serious nuisance value but also provided the enemy with much valuable information about our troop movements.

The two Somali Irregular Companies each about 125 strong under British officers selected for their local knowledge, proved a valuable counter to Italian Banda in the Northern Frontier District. Backed up by offensive patrols of regular troops, they operated from one water hole to another, and although always inferior in numbers to the Italians very soon forced the enemy to adopt a much more defensive attitude in the vast No Man's Land which then separated our leading troops from those of the enemy.

At a later stage Irregular Companies were similarly organised from Abyssinian refugees and deserters, and later still from Turkana tribesmen in the area west of Lake Rudolf. During the operations in this area, and in the operational area of the 1st S.A. Division, Irregular Companies were frequently employed to cooperate with regular troops. Their principle role was the protection of exposed flanks, and movements directed against the enemy's L. of C. in cooperation with attacks carried out by regular troops.

4. With the arrival of the 2nd S.A. Brigade and later of the 5th S.A. Brigade the 1st S.A. Division was established under command of Major General G.E. Brink, C.B., D.S.O. I was then able to place the force on a three division front, 11th (A) Division on the right, 12th (A) Division in the centre, and 1st (S.A.) Division on the left. The length of the front to be held seldom permitted me to form a force reserve, though from time to time I depended on formations out resting in the Highlands or units under training. The Order of Battle of E.A. Force on 1st January 1941 is given in Appendix "A", and the Air Forces stationed in Kenya in Appendix "B".

5. In view of the mixed composition of E.A. Force, e.g. all the artillery less the light batteries was South African, I felt I must be in a position to move South African formations and units from one Division to another as the situation demanded. I appreciated that the desire on the part of the South Africans to keep 1st (S.A.) Division complete would very naturally be strong. I was able to take

advantage of Field-Marshal Smuts' visit to Kenya in the first week of November to put this point before him. Field-Marshal Smuts most helpfully gave me a free hand in the matter, with the exception that he did not wish me to break the Brigade Group organisation. I was able to give this undertaking readily. As a result one S.A. Brigade was continuously employed under one or the other of the African Divisions, and other South African units were changed about as required. This gave an elasticity to the force which was of the very greatest value to me and enabled me to use the splendid South African troops to the best advantage. I am most grateful to Field-Marshal Smuts, and to the South African Commanders and troops who accepted this decision so loyally, and co-operated so well with the Imperial Commanders on the occasions when it became necessary to place them under African formations.

6. Although everywhere except at Marsabit itself our troops were in desert country, the characteristics of the terrain on the east of the forward line held were quite different to that on the west. The 400 miles of country from the sea to just short of Marsabit was all waterless, flat bush. The actual density of the bush varied considerably, but there were very few places where the light tanks could not push their way through. Movement of armoured cars off the tracks was restricted in parts of this area, but large portions of it were by no means impassable to these vehicles. Except in the rains, the surface of the soil permitted movement by M.T. anywhere, where the bush was thin enough to let it through. During the rains the many large patches of black cotton soil became impassable for days at a time.

Round Marsabit and west of it was quite a different picture. The Chalbi desert and the lava escarpment which surrounded Marsabit hill were completely open. The lava belts were impassable to M.T. without preparation, but in dry weather the sandy portions of the Chalbi desert could be driven over anywhere. Further west, north and west of Lake Rudolf, was stony country with some very thin bush, and hills from which observation was possible over great distances. Furthermore armoured cars could drive over it anywhere, albeit slowly.

To the east the bush country extended unbroken to the foot hills of British Somaliland and the Arussi Hills. In the west, on the northern side of the Chalbi desert, the country facing 1st (S.A.) Division was firstly similar to that north of Lake Rudolf already described, and then consisted of low hills covered with bush of varying density.

7. I had been instructed by General Wavell at the Khartoum Conference at the end of October to examine, immediately on my arrival, the possibility of carrying out an operation for the capture of Chisimaio before the rains broke in March. I came to the conclusion that the forces required for such an operation at that time, would be six brigade groups, one of which should preferably be an armoured brigade. I very reluctantly decided that the operation would not be possible until after the rains were over in May. The morale of the Italian troops was obviously good; many of them had fought in British Somaliland, and in the small local brushes we had with them they were fighting very well. On the other

hand many of my own troops were untrained in field-work and movement by M.T.; some battalions had not even completed their musketry. Furthermore, there was not sufficient M.T. in the country to motorise fully the six brigades I felt were necessary, to carry supplies over the long L. of C., nor to provide the water echelon required to transport the water over the stretch of country between Tana and the Giuba, which my information at that time gave as being completely waterless. Also the shortage of supporting arms caused me some concern. It was not then apparent that the enemy would fail to put up a determined resistance, and his positions were strongly wired, entrenched, mined, and provided with tank traps. In February when the main advance took place the total supporting arms in E.A. Force for all fronts, outside the infantry units, was as given below. Furthermore my battalions had no Bren carriers:-

Artillery-
　36 field guns, 18pdrs. and 4·5 hows. (Equal to 1½ modern regiments.)
　24 3·7 hows.
　4 60pdrs.
　4 6in. hows.
Tanks-
　12 Light Mk. 1.

8. I decided therefore to occupy the period before the rains broke in reducing the distances everywhere between my own forces and the Italians preparatory to a major offensive after the rains, to make every effort to find and develop water in the waterless belts, to construct routes forward through the bush suitable for two lines of M.T., and to establish large forward dumps. I may say here that the 280 miles of bush between the Tana and the Giuba was traversed only by narrow, winding bush tracks originally made by game and widened later merely by occasional human use.

Further, it was my intention to make use of this period to obtain moral ascendancy over the Italians by every means possible, such as by vigorous offensive patrolling, and by cutting out isolated posts. Initially I ordered the forward move in the south to the boundary of Italian Somaliland, and in the north as far as Hobok, these advances to commence on 15th January. Nevertheless I later instructed my Divisional Commanders that the extent to which they did in fact move forward was only to be limited by administrative possibilities.

9. It will be readily appreciated that the administration and maintenance of the forces in the type of terrain over which the operations were to be carried out presented problems of considerable difficulty. For instance, before any advance was undertaken all forward troops were already being maintained by road hundreds of miles in front of railhead. The troops on the Tana were 230 miles in front of railhead, at Wajir 300 miles, at Dukana 390 miles, at Lokitaung 317 miles. The greater portion of the roads were liable to be impassable in wet weather. The resultant commitment in transport, particularly as these distances were increased

by our forward moves, was extremely heavy, but by the establishment of large dumps as far forward as I could get them I was able to reduce the transport requirements for the first phase of the campaign. In spite of the large amount of transport I was able to obtain through the good offices of the Union of South Africa, at no time had I too much, and during subsequent operations my plans had invariably to be based on the availability of transport as one of the main factors in deciding my moves.

10. Even before operations began the 1,300 miles of road which had to be maintained under military arrangements was a heavy enough commitment; but our subsequent advance throughout the whole campaign increased this out of all proportion.

11. Another important aspect of the operations from the point of view of administration was the provision of water. This problem had received special previous study in conjunction with the Quartermaster General of the Union Defence Forces, Brigadier General J. Mitchell Baker, C.B., D.S.O., A.O.C.

M.T. convoys for the carriage of water were organised, and special vehicles and equipment provided by the Union Government. A very valuable supplement to the water convoys was furnished by the work of the 36 Water Supply Company, S.A.E.C. which, aided by geophysical experts, developed boreholes, and a limited supply of water in the vast track of hitherto waterless bush between the Tana and Giuba rivers. The existence of this waterless area had been regarded as one of the most formidable obstacles to an advance on the Giuba position. The fact that at no time were the troops without the daily allowance of one gallon per man and half a gallon per radiator does credit to those who organised the supply.

12. The first of the cutting-out operations, directed against El Wak, some 110 miles from our forward positions at Wajir, took place between 16th and 18th December 1940. This raid was most successfully carried out by 12th (A) Division. In order to gain maximum experience of moving large M.T. columns over long distances at night, both the 1st S.A. and the 24th Gold Coast Brigades were used, although the forces in El Wak were known to consist of only one battalion and 16 guns and some Banda. A large proportion of the enemy battalion escaped into the bush, but all the guns, a quantity of stores, and a number of prisoners were captured at a very small loss to our troops, and considerable loss in killed and wounded to the enemy.

I cannot speak too highly of the way in which Major General A.R. Godwin Austen, C.B., O.B.E., M.C., planned the operation, nor of the dashing manner in which it was carried out by both brigades This action marked the start of the ascendancy of the morale of E.A. Force over that of the Italians.

13. Shortly after this raid the whole military aspect in Africa was altered by the successes in the Western Desert, and the enemy withdrawal in Eritrea. About the 1st February 1941 I came to the conclusion that an operation on a reduced scale against Chisimaio would have a reasonable chance of success owing to the

lowered morale of the Italians. I calculated I had sufficient transport for a force of four brigades, as the finding of a limited supply of water by boring on both possible routes forward had reduced to a certain extent the amount of water transport required. In view of the short time before the rains, and the necessity for a full moon, so that the initial moves could be carried out at night, I decided to commence the operation on 11th February, i.e., 10 days time. No written orders were issued, and only a minimum number of individuals were informed.

The original orders covered the capture of Chisimaio and a bridgehead at Giumbo only, but I informed my Commanders that if the enemy resistance on the Giuba broke, the line I would aim for would be Mogadiscio – Iscia Baidoa – Lugh Ferrandi.

14. Meanwhile on the northern front the 1st S.A. Division, which then consisted of 2nd and 5th S.A. Brigades and the 25th E.A. Brigade, had been ordered to make good the triangle El Yibo, Gorai and Hobok, and to capture Kalam.

The object of these operations was to open up the patriot country in the Galla Sidamo and gain touch with the patriot chiefs. At the Cairo Conference I had been specially instructed to employ South African troops for this purpose, as General Wavell considered their organisation and training rendered them more suitable for it. At the time 1st S.A. Division was sent up to this front, I was of the opinion that operations on the other fronts before the rains would have to be limited and hence hoped I had cast the South African Division for the more active role. I always had in mind the possibility of turning from the west the strong enemy position on the Moyale – Mega escarpment.

15. When I assumed command the struggle for air supremacy was in its early stages, and the enemy's preponderance in bombers and fighters was very pronounced.

Our Air Forces then comprised one A.C. Squadron of the S.R.A.F. (which was transferred to Sudan in the first week in November) and one A.C. Squadron of the S.A.A.F., the latter in embryo. A further A.C. Squadron of the S.A.A.F. was formed and took the field in the middle of December. In addition there were two bomber squadrons and two fighter squadrons of the S.A.A.F. Of the latter, one was equipped with Hurricanes and the other with ancient Furies.

Owing to the direct threat to Mombasa, the gateway of Kenya and of our L. of C., the Hurricanes had to be concentrated there and in Nairobi for purely defensive purposes, leaving the defence of the whole of our troops, aerodromes and such important places as Nanyuki, to the Furies.

For some inexplicable reason the Italians utterly failed to make use of the golden opportunity at this time to take the offensive in the air, though our troops behind the River Tana and our outlying communications were open to heavy bombing attacks by them.

As soon as the Italians' lack of enterprise was realised, some of the Hurricanes were dispersed over the front with the result that the course of the air operations changed rapidly, and by the beginning of February our Air Forces had established air superiority.

At Appendix "B" is shown the Order of Battle of Air Forces in Kenya on 1st January 1941, and the estimated number of Italian aircraft within reach of our bases, and in Appendix "J" is shown how the Army Co-operation Squadrons were allocated to divisions during the operations.

PART II – OPERATIONS.
A. Operations of 1st S.A. Division.
(1st January to 5th April, 1941).

16. As already explained, I had allotted the 1st S.A. Division, consisting of the 2nd and 5th S.A. Brigades and 25th E.A. Brigade, to the northern front, with the object of penetrating the Galla Sidamo country to stir up the chiefs there to rebellion and if possible to turn the enemy out of his strong position on the Moyale – Mega escarpment.

Facing me on this front the enemy had approximately three Italian divisions (21, 22 and 24) in considerable depth, of which two (21 and 24) were east of Lake Rudolf with some artillery in the Moyale – Mega – Iavello area, while the Hobok – Gorai – El Yibo triangle was held by approximately 1,600 Banda under European officers and N.C.O.'s.

17. By the end of December the S.A. Division had taken over this sector, with the 2nd and 5th S.A. Brigades, which had arrived in Kenya in October and November respectively, at Marsabit, and the 25th E.A. Brigade at Lokitaung.

The Order of Battle of 1st S.A. Division on 1st January 1941 is given in Appendix "A."

18. Operations on this part of the front are really divided into two parts, those to the west of Lake Rudolf being entirely separated from those on the east, the only road communication being round the south of the lake.

19. The 2nd and 5th S.A. Brigades were employed on the east of Lake Rudolf. Marsabit, where the brigades started from, is separated from Southern Abyssinia by a waterless stretch of country about 120 miles wide, across which there were at the time only two possible ways into enemy territory. The first was the road from Marsabit to Moyale, which wound up the steep escarpment through country favourable to the defender. The enemy position on the escarpment was known to be strong, and a direct advance against it over this road offered little chance of success. The road was not only in a very bad condition but also likely to become impassable during the wet weather. The second was the road across the Chalbi desert, via North Horr, to Dukana. This road was also in very bad condition and, moreover, it was said that during the rains even animals were unable to move across the Chalbi desert. But in spite of these disadvantages the road did present a route into Abyssinia around the Moyale – Mega escarpment.

20. With the object of stirring up rebel activity Intelligence officers had been operating in this area for some time, supplying arms and ammunition to patriots who went back to operate behind the enemy lines. There were considerable hopes, which unfortunately were not realised, that a Shifta rebellion thus encouraged would break out in the Galla Sidamo area.

21. At this time the rebels in the Tertale area were beginning to harass the enemy and my information was that active support of this uprising might possibly spread the rebellion throughout Southern Abyssinia.

22. On this front the Irregular companies had already paved the way for an advance by capturing Dukana, an important water-point north of the Chalbi desert, and they further proved their worth by the assistance they gave to the S.A. Division both in securing the Hobok – Gorai – El Yibo area, and in subsequent operations.

23. On 16th–18th January El Yibo and El Sardu were taken by 1st N.M.R. (2nd S.A. Inf Bde) and the enemy pushed over the border. 2nd Regt. Botha of 5th S.A. Inf Bde were sent to Turbi near the foot of the escarpment to prevent the enemy moving on to Marsabit. It remained there until Moyale fell.

24. On 31st January 1st S.A. Division, which had completed its concentration at Dukana, moved 2nd and 5th S.A. Infantry Brigades up to the frontier in preparation for an attack on Gorai, El Gumu and Hobok the following day. The move was made in M.T., armoured cars being used for a distance of 25 miles to break a way through the bush for the troop carriers after the road finished. The two brigade groups, with 2nd S.A. Brigade on the right, each moved in several parallel columns towards El Gumu. When 2nd S.A. Brigade struck the road El Gumu – Gorai it swung right-handed and moved against Gorai from the north, whilst 5th S.A. Brigade moved straight across country against El Gumu.

Gorai was strongly defended by the enemy, who had well-prepared positions, but after a sharp engagement the fort was occupied at 1645 hours by the 2nd F.F. Battalion. The thick bush in the area unfortunately prevented one company of this battalion, which had worked round N.E. of the fort, from cutting off the retreating enemy. The enemy did not abandon their positions until the armoured cars had smashed down the barbed wire entanglements round the fort and the infantry had gone in with the bayonet across 400 yards of open country. Our casualties were slight. In the meantime 5th S.A. Infantry Brigade had captured El Gumu with the loss of only one O.R. killed.

The resolute action of the armoured cars undoubtedly saved us many casualties at both Gorai and El Gumu, but the bush prevented pursuit.

25. On 2nd February 5th S.A. Infantry Brigade moved against Hobok along the road El Gumu – Hobok. Attempts to cut off the enemy's line of withdrawal to the north, along the Lac Bulal, failed owing to a bush fire which the enemy had started to cover his withdrawal. Once the brigade had worked round the bush fire,

armoured cars made two more attempts to reach the Lac Bulal north of Hobok, but the country was so broken that the attempt had to be abandoned. After the enemy post had been heavily shelled by our artillery, and also bombed and machine gunned by aircraft, armoured cars crashed through the wire at 1715 hours, but found that the enemy had withdrawn leaving a considerable quantity of equipment behind.

26. In furtherance of the object of helping the rebellion another advance was made and on 7th February Ganciaro was occupied without opposition while on 9th February the 1st S.A. Irish (5th S.A. Inf Bde) with one company of 1st F.F. Bn occupied Banno after a sharp engagement with the garrison of two Colonial Infantry Battalions, which withdrew into the mountains to the north. Four days later the enemy brought some guns and shelled our positions at Banno in order to cover the removal of a large dump of stores in the mountains immediately to the North of the fort. The fact that the enemy were able to do this showed the amount of trust which could be placed on the Shifta.

27. General Brink now asked whether, in order to secure his right flank and ensure a more reliable and shorter L. of C., he could not carry out operations against the Moyale – Mega escarpment. This was an operation which I always had had in mind, and now that the Shifta had turned out to be nothing more than groups which merely harrassed Italians and looted wherever they could, I gave the necessary permission.

28. The plan adopted was for the 5th S.A. Infantry Brigade to move direct from Ganciaro on to Mega. The 2nd S.A. Infantry Brigade was to make an enveloping movement round the north of the town to get astride the Mega – Moyale road where they would be able to prevent the escape of the Mega garrison on that route, or its reinforcement from Moyale. The brigade was then to carry out an attack from the east on Mega, in conjunction with that being carried out by 5th Infantry Brigade from the west.

29. On the 14th February the 2nd S.A. Brigade, leaving 1st N.M.R. in divisional reserve, broke off from the Ganciaro – Mega road due east across country to El Sod. The first part of the cross-country route took some time to traverse as the column had to wind about among the trees, through sand which was deep in places. After crossing the Mega – Iavello road the going became much better. One company of the 2nd F.F. Battalion was left on this road to prevent enemy movement along it in either direction. This company was attacked from the direction of Iavello by a strong enemy force of 15 tanks and motorised infantry which was evidently attempting to reinforce the Mega garrison. After a sharp encounter in which both sides suffered casualties, the enemy withdrew hurriedly towards Iavello. There is no doubt that the action of this company in preventing the arrival of these reinforcements had a material effect on subsequent operations at Mega.

On the morning of the 15th there were indications that the enemy were attempting to reinforce Mega from Neghelli, but they were dispersed by 2nd Infantry Brigade by artillery fire from El Sod. 2nd Infantry Brigade then recommenced their march on Mega, encountering very thick bush and sticky black cotton soil. The original intention for them to attack Mega directly from the east was found to be out of the question as the country was entirely open and exposed to the enemy artillery. Brigadier F.L.A. Buchanan, M.C., therefore continued with all his forces round to the south of the town but found the defile, through which the road in went, was very heavily mined and guarded by machine-gun nests.

Meanwhile the 5th S.A. Brigade had approached from the west, and on the 16th February attacked the high ground dominating the approaches to Mega from that side. They came under considerable artillery fire but fortunately it was ineffective owing to the high percentage of blinds. In the afternoon very heavy rain fell over the whole area and continued throughout the rest of the day. The black cotton soil became sodden and prevented the transport with water and supplies from reaching the troops, the 2nd Brigade not receiving any until after the fall of Mega. On the 17th, while the 2nd S.A. Brigade were searching for a way in through the hills south and south-east of the town, the 5th S.A. Brigade attacked, and consolidated their position within two miles of Mega, with troops on their left flank overlooking the town. Eventually on the 18th Lieut-Colonel C.L. Engelbrecht leading one company of the 2nd F.F. Battalion from the 2nd S.A. Brigade scaled a precipitous cliff on the south-east of the town, although a native guide had reported this route to be completely impracticable, and captured the enemy's main gun positions.

Meanwhile, the two battalions of the 5th Brigade had attacked again in the rain and mist, working forward from feature to feature, till eventually at 1745 hours they were about to launch their final assault. The enemy however, who had just lost his guns, realised his position to be hopeless and surrendered.

Besides 26 officers, 598 Italians and 374 natives, our captures at Mega included four medium and three field guns and a large stock of machine-guns, rifles and ammunition.

30. In the evening of 22nd February a patrol of Irregulars who had been sent forward by 2nd S.A. Brigade to contact friendly natives, entered Moyale without opposition, the garrison having hurriedly withdrawn to Neghelli on the day Mega fell. 2nd S.A. Infantry Brigade following up the Irregulars occupied the town the next day and found that the enemy had abandoned a large quantity of war material, including one field and four medium guns.

31. Both the brigades patrolled actively from Mega and Moyale towards Iavello, Neghelli and Mandera, and plans were being made for the capture of Iavello, but the heavy rains which then began made all the roads impassable at periods and movement and maintenance became increasingly difficult.

32. During this period 25th E.A. Brigade, which had only two newly-formed battalions, carried out the operations to the west of Lake Rudolf. I had given instructions that this brigade was to move forward with the eventual object of capturing Kalam. The initial advance proceeded with no difficulty and Todengang and Namuruputh were occupied on 9th February. The subsequent advance towards Kalam proved a different matter. The country to the north of Lake Rudolf, in the Omo Valley, was occupied by wild Merille tribesmen whose traditional enmity towards the Turkana had been fostered by the Italians so that it included us. A large number of these tribesmen concentrated to stop the advance of the 2/4th K.A.R. who were very soon in difficulties, as they were not able to reach the water-holes which the tribesmen were guarding and their transport was unable to get up to them owing to the badness of the track. The Battalion was eventually extricated by the dispersal of Merille concentrations by air action and by sending forward water trucks escorted by armoured cars. This was not done, however, before considerable suffering from thirst had occurred.

33. I decided it would be unprofitable at this stage of the campaign to try to carry out operations against the Merille, so I ordered General Brink to take up a defensive position in the area Namuruputh – Todengang on this part of his front.

34. A meeting was arranged on the 19th February between Brigadier W. Owen, M.B.E., M.C., commanding 25th E.A. Brigade, and the Merille chiefs, which at first appeared successful. But it was soon apparent that they would only come to heel when the enemy was evicted from the Omo delta and we occupied Kalam which, it was reported, was held only by Merille and some of the Donyiro tribe.

Owing, however, to administrative difficulties and the state of the road it was not until 24th March that we were able to capture Kalam and push patrols further up to the north.

35. The problem of settling this area is a difficult one as the tribes are hereditary enemies of each other. It is impossible, therefore, to persuade one tribe to disarm unless the next tribe does so simultaneously. This obviously cannot be done until all the country to the north is in our hands.

36. After the capture of Mega and Moyale I was considering employing the 1st SA Division for the advance from Mogadiscio into Abyssinia as not only did I think that their greater fire power and superior equipment would be needed in the Abyssinian Highlands where the conditions would be strange and difficult for African troops, but also because I wished, for political reasons, to give the South African Division a more prominent part in the campaign, and it appeared doubtful whether operations north of Mega and Moyale would be possible in the approaching rains. I therefore issued orders for the 21st EA Brigade to move from Wajir to relieve the 2nd and 5th SA Brigades on the escarpment where there was a danger of their being marooned in the rains, and for these brigades to move back where they would be suitably placed should I decide to move the 1st SA Division over for the advance into Abyssinia from Italian Somaliland.

During the period 5th-10th March the changeover was completed, but only with great difficulty owing to the state of the roads. Divisional Headquarters, Divisional troops and 5th SA Infantry Brigade went to Wajir and 2nd SA Infantry Brigade to Isiolo. At this time I was continually receiving reports which indicated that the rains would be early and had in fact set in in some parts of the Northern Frontier District. Since the move across to the eastern front was only practicable if the roads, or rather tracks, were dry, and as I found I was able to continue the advance north into Abyssinia with troops already in Italian Somaliland very much earlier than was at first estimated, I was very regretfully forced to abandon the project of using the South African Division on the other front and therefore gave orders for it to concentrate in Kenya.

37. It had recently been decided that as soon as I could spare the 1st SA Division it should be transferred to Egypt. I therefore notified C-in-C Middle East that the 1st SA Division Headquarters and 5th S.A. Brigade could now be spared, but that I required 2nd S.A. Brigade for operations in British Somaliland to back up the forces which Aden were landing to take Berbera. This Brigade, less one battalion which went by road with the first line transport, embarked at Mombasa on 16th March and arrived at Berbera on 23rd March.

38. Meanwhile, on the northern front, 21st E.A. Brigade occupied Iavello which patrols had discovered to have been evacuated by the enemy.

On 31st March, 21st E.A. Infantry Brigade, after a short, well-conceived and skilfully carried out operation, drove the enemy out of Soroppa, capturing the commander of the 18th Colonial Inf. Bde., 27 Italians and 360 natives, as well as five field guns and a number of machine guns.

39. On 6th April, 12th (A) Division assumed command of the 21st and 25th E.A. Infantry Brigades and the area for which, 1st S.A. Division had hitherto been responsible.

40. At the beginning of these operations to the east of Lake Rudolf the 2nd and 5th S.A. Brigades had to endure appalling conditions of heat and dust from the hot lava bed of which the country up to Gorai is composed. What made it worse was that there was no shade whatsoever. Although in subsequent operations the heat was not so great, the men always had to be on short rations of water, as until they captured Mega, it had to be carried up 200 miles from the rear. Until the fall of Moyale opened up the shorter L. of C., the difficulties of supply were always great, as the roads were either so rough that considerable driving ability was required in crossing them or so thick in powdered dust that even a little rain made them impassable.

41. I wish to place on record my appreciation of the sound judgment and determination in face of great difficulties of terrain, shown by Major-General G.E. Brink, C.B., D.S.O., Commander 1st S.A. Division, in bringing these operations to a successful conclusion.

B. Operations of 11th and 12th (A) Divisions,
(11th February to 25th February, 1941.)

42. After the raid at El Wak, and while our forward policy was developing, the enemy decided to withdraw practically the whole of his Colonial Forces to the Giuba, leaving west of the river only a screen of Banda, and one battalion and some guns at Afmadu in a strongly wired position.

At the commencement of the operations I estimated that his forces were disposed as under:

Lower Giuba and Chisimaio (i.e., south and inclusive of Gelib), 102nd Division (Four Brigades and Div. troops, three Banda groups and Chisimaio command.)

Upper Giuba (north of Gelib exclusive), 101st Division (Two Brigades and Div. troops, and three Banda groups.)

Against this force I employed four brigade groups fully motorised. The Order of Battle of 11th and 12th (A) Divisions at the commencement of these operations is given at Appendix "C."

43. It will be recalled that although patrolling was being carried out many miles forward of them, the actual forward localities occupied by my troops were along the River Tana to Garissa, thence to Wajir, joining up with the 1st S.A. Division at Marsabit. The defended localities at Bura, Garissa and Wajir were initially the bases of the various advancing columns.

44. My plan for the capture of Chisimaio directed 12th (A) Division (1st S.A., 22nd E.A., and 24th Gold Coast Brigades) from the Garissa – Wajir area on to Afmadu. From there one column (1st S.A. Brigade) was to move south, capture Gobuen, and form a bridgehead at Giumbo, while another column (24th G.C. Brigade) was to capture Bulo Erillo, and move on to Allessandra and threaten Gelib. I did not expect, in view of the strong positions held by the enemy in this area, that this brigade by itself would be able to capture Gelib, and gave instructions that provided sufficient threat was developed to draw the enemy reinforcements at Margherita northwards, or at least to prevent them moving south, I would be satisfied until greater strength was available. The timing was so arranged that this threat was to be produced before Gobuen was attacked. In view of the importance of Gobuen the bulk of the artillery and the tanks went to the 12th (A) Division.

11th (A) Division (23rd Nigerian Brigade) from the Bura area, proceeding by Lac Badana, was to attack and capture Chisimaio. As I wished first to make sure of the key position of Gobuen, and to conceal the advance of the southern column against Chisimaio as long as possible, the move forward of the 11th (A) Division was ordered to take place on 15th February, viz., after the attack had developed on Gobuen.

45. The Royal Navy, "Force T" under Capt. J.H.H. Edelsten, R.N., and consisting of H.M.S. Shropshire, H.M.S. Hawkins, H.M.S. Hermes, H.M.S. Capetown,

H.M.S. Ceres, H.M.S. Kandahar, were co-operating by bombarding Brava and movement on the coastal road in the early stages of the operation so as to assist the deception that the attack was to take place farther north, and a plan was prepared for the bombardment of Chisimaio in support of the attack of 11th (A) Division. Arrangements were also made to sail a convoy into Chisimaio as soon as practicable, and if Gobuen and not Chisimaio were captured an attempt was to be made to land stores on the beach near Gobuen, so as to enable operations to continue.

46. Previous to the operation the S.A.A.F. had carried out a most successful fighter attack on Afmadu, Dif and Gobuen accounting for 10 enemy aircraft.

Highly effective bombing of Afmadu and Gelib was also undertaken on the afternoon of the day preceding the attack.

Arrangements were made whereby fighters and A.C. aircraft should land on Afmadu and Gobuen aerodromes as soon as they were captured.

47. In order to lead the enemy to believe that another column was advancing via El Wak a feint was made on this sector. From subsequent information received it is believed that the Italian Commander of the sector opposite Wajir claimed that his troops had stopped the advance of an enemy division, this "division" consisting in fact of little more than two platoons and a few armoured cars.

48. Food and water were taken with the forces engaged to last up to 21st February. If Chisimaio had not been captured by then, or the Navy had been unable to land those commodities on the beach near Gobuen, it would have been necessary for our forces to return to the Italian Somaliland border as I would have been unable to maintain them forward.

49. Under the policy laid down before I decided to attack the Giuba, the initial forward moves to the frontier of Italian Somaliland commenced on 15th January, and by 11th February the forward troops of 11th (A) Division were at Badada, and those of the 12th (A) Division had attacked and taken Beles Gugani. The 22nd Infantry Brigade and attached troops carried out the advance on 12th (A) Division front to Beles Gugani with speed and determination, and their rapid advance over tracks which quickly became dust pans, was in all probability instrumental in causing the Italians to make the decision, which became known later, to evacuate Chisimaio without fighting.

50. On 11th February 22nd Brigade Group, 12th (A) Division, attacked Afmadu which was in our hands by 0700 hours, the bulk of the enemy garrison having withdrawn during the night. 24th Gold Coast Brigade Group were passed through Afmadu that night directed on Bulo Erillo and Gobuen respectively. At this period it was thought advisable to carry out all moves at night, both to conceal our lines of advance, and to avoid air action against our columns.

On the morning of 13th February 24th Gold Coast Brigade Group attacked Bulo Erillo. This attack met with considerable resistance on the part of the enemy, who was entrenched behind strong wire, and used armoured cars. After severe fighting the enemy was driven out leaving a number of prisoners, 5 armoured cars and some artillery and other weapons in our hands. The attack was led by the 2nd Gold Coast Regiment, with great gallantry. Although the leading troops of this Battalion had practically all their white personnel killed or wounded, the attack was pressed home with unabated vigour and courage.

51. On the evening of this day (13th) information reached me which indicated that some or all of the enemy were evacuating Chisimaio. Although every effort was made to accelerate the advance of 1st S.A. Brigade and cut off the with-drawing enemy, they succeeded in eluding our advance. On the following morning (14th) 1st S.A. Brigade attacked Gobuen supported by 12 Light Tanks. The village was held by weak enemy rear guards which were rapidly driven in, retreating across the river Giuba and burning the bridge behind them. During this action the enemy developed considerable shell fire from Giumbo on the far bank of the river against our forward troops. Consequently the crossing of the river was not accomplished at once as I had hoped.

Meanwhile I received information that Chisimaio harbour in front of the oil tanks was covered with oil; that aircraft flying low drew no fire, and that Com-mander "Force T" had gone in with H.M.S. Shropshire to bombard the forts at point blank range and had drawn no reply. I was therefore convinced that Chisimaio had been wholly evacuated. In consequence I ordered 12th (A) Divi-sion to send 22nd Brigade from Afmadu to occupy Chisimaio immediately as, in accordance with my original plan, 11th (A) Division were too far back for the purpose. This was safely accomplished by 1700 hours 14th February, and the forts in Chisimaio Island were occupied by 1900 hours. All the white population had been evacuated and considerable demolition done. That the evacuation was hurried, however, was proved by the fact that we were able eventually to put into commission three of the eight 4·9 C.D. guns, and ten of the sixteen 77mm A.A. guns. Quantities of stores and ammunition were abandoned by the enemy.

The capture of Chisimaio was completed six days before the date I had given in the time table for the operation.

52. A remarkable feature of the operation up to this period was the almost complete lack of enemy interference from the air. The fighter ground attacks at Gobuen and Afmadu aerodromes, and in the air, preceding the opening of the campaign had resulted in driving the enemy out of the air practically altogether. At this stage enemy aircraft were seldom seen by day and he confined himself to bombing on moonlight nights. I was therefore able to remove all restrictions on daylight movement and henceforth our columns moved almost entirely by day.

53. At that time it became apparent that there was considerable apprehension and disorganisation amongst the enemy forces. It was clear therefore no time was to be lost in forcing a crossing over the river, a fact which I impressed on the Commander of 12th (A) Division. The river was 580 feet broad at Gobuen, and

tidal for 14 miles, but narrowed and became shallower northwards. At Gelib, and in some places north of this point, it could be waded. On both banks was a belt of tropical growth of varying thickness, north of Gelib continuous, south of Gelib sometimes broken by cultivation. The enemy had disposed the greater part of his forces along the river bank defending all the more obvious crossing places, but my information was that he had one fully motorised brigade (15th) in reserve behind Gelib.

54. I realised that it was quite impossible for the enemy to defend the whole river and that to effect a crossing could only be a matter of time, the only danger being immediate counter-attacks delivered from the rear. I urged the Commander of 12th (A) Division to tap in all along and seize possible bridgeheads, and it was my intention, had he not been successful in doing so with his own resources, to bring up the 11th (A) Division and place the force on a two-divisional front so as to increase the chances of finding a suitable crossing place quickly. On the night of 17th/18th February however, the 1st S.A. Brigade managed to effect a crossing at Ionte. During that night they were counter-attacked by a force of the enemy from Giumbo; the counter-attack was successfully beaten off with great loss to the enemy. On 19th February the Gold Coast Brigade also succeeded in forcing a crossing at Mabungo. This crossing entailed cutting a track for three miles through the tropical jungle belt mentioned above, which work was successfully and rapidly carried out.

To cover the movement to Mabungo and to delude the enemy into thinking that a frontal attack was intended, a concentration of field and light guns was directed against the defences covering Gelib. In addition enemy communications in Gelib itself were kept under fire by 60pdrs. This ruse was entirely successful. Many casualties were inflicted by this bombardment and the enemy had to change his L. of C. in this area.

By the morning of the 20th pontoon bridges of improvised bridging material had been established both at Ionte and at Mabungo and I was in a position to bring up the 11th (A) Division, and place them close up behind the bridgehead at Mabungo preparatory to advancing on Mogadiscio should the attack across the river be successful. Before this advance could take place it was essential that Gelib should be taken, and I instructed the Commander of the 12th (A) Division to carry out an operation with this in view. Meanwhile the 1st S.A. Brigade had crossed the river at Ionte and were directed to cut off Giumbo. This operation was carried out with considerable skill, and entailed an arduous march across the peninsula to the sea. Practically the whole of the garrison at Giumbo capitulated, those that did not proceeded on foot along the sea coast towards Modun, and were taken prisoner later.

55. The plan of the Commander of the 12th (A) Division for the capture of Gelib was as follows. The 22nd Brigade Group was ordered to proceed from Mabungo along a track which was marked on the map, but of the condition of which nothing was known, to cut the road to Mogadiscio some 18 miles east of Gelib.

Meanwhile the Gold Coast Brigade Group was to advance south from Mabungo, and the 1st S.A. Brigade Group north from Ionte. This operation was carried out with complete success on 22nd February. All three brigades completed their tasks in an exemplary manner, but I must particularly mention the march, practically across country, of the 22nd Brigade Group, which called for the greatest endurance and skill, and also the rapid manner in which 1st S.A. Brigade was able to fight its way north in the face of opposition, and be the first to enter Gelib at 1000 hours on the 22nd February.

56. I wish to commend Major-General Godwin Austen for the skilful plan which he made for the crossing of the river, and the careful instructions he gave for its implementation. The battle of the Giuba undoubtedly dealt the enemy a blow from which he never recovered, and laid the foundation for subsequent successes.

57. During this day enemy forces from Bardera counter-attacked the bridgehead at Mabungo which was held by the 2nd Nigeria Regiment of 11th (A) Division. The counter-attack was not pressed home, was easily beaten off, and did not interfere with my plans of passing the 11th (A) Division across the bridge.

58. At this time I became aware that the enemy had committed practically the whole of the forces facing me to the defence of the river, and very little was left between the river and Mogadiscio. Some thousands of prisoners had been taken; it was known that whole units were dispersing into the bush, and the orders and counter-orders given by the enemy were indicative of extreme confusion. I felt sure, therefore, that in view of the disorganised state of the enemy, I would have little difficulty operating northwards to Harrar after Mogadiscio had been captured. Although the distance by road from Mogadiscio to Harrar was 804 miles, I found that by denuding the troops left on the Kenya front of transport, I would just be able to use a force of three brigades against Harrar. I therefore cabled on 22nd February to the Commander-in-Chief, Middle East, pointing out that as the rains in this area arrived later than in Kenya, I would be able to continue operations, and that I thought I could capture Harrar by the end of the first week in April. Permission to continue was duly received.

59. At 0600 hours on the 23rd February the 11th (A) Division with the 23rd Nigerian Brigade and the 22nd E.A. Brigade under command, began their advance from Mabungo to Mogadiscio, and that evening after a sharp fight, elements of the 22nd Brigade occupied Modun, and the next morning Brava. The 1st S.A. Brigade was placed in Force reserve and directed to Brava, and it was my intention that the 12th (A) Division should move northwards via Bardera and Iscia Baidoa. Unfortunately owing to administrative difficulties connected with the amount of supplies which could be landed at Chisimaio, I was not able to advance in this direction till a few days afterwards. The revised Order of Battle is shown in Appendix "D."

60. On 24th February the Nigerian Brigade Group which was destined to lead 11th (A) Division passed through 22nd E.A. Brigade at Modun and Brava. Merca

was captured on 25th February after encountering some opposition. That same evening some light forces of the 11th (A) Division entered Mogadiscio, having been unopposed for the final 20 miles.

The distance covered by the Nigerian Brigade Group between 0600 hours 23rd February and 1700 hours 25th was 275 miles.

61. H.M.S. Shropshire carried out a most effective bombardment of enemy camps and dispositions near Modun cross roads on the day previous to its capture. Observation for the bombardment was undertaken by an S.A.A.F. Glen Martin aircraft, the observer of which had fortunately been previously instructed in spotting for naval gun fire. That a large number of casualties were caused during this bombardment was confirmed subsequently on the capture of Modun.

62. About this time all indications showed that the enemy had left Bardera and that 101st Division was withdrawing northwards. I was still not able to operate strong forces from 12th (A) Division, but ordered the Commander to move light forces to Bardera, Dolo and Lugh Ferrandi. These operations were undertaken quickly. Bardera was occupied on 26th February, Iscia Baidoa on 28th February, Lugh Ferrandi on 3rd March, Dolo on 5th March. A further number of prisoners were taken including the commander and staff of 20th Colonial Brigade. It transpired that the whole of the African personnel of this brigade, some 3,000 men, had dispersed into the bush.

63. The policy of breaking the crust and then motoring straight on, regardless of what was happening in rear, was fully justified in the result, though in face of a more determined enemy, counter-attacks against our rear and communications would doubtless have been troublesome.

Shortage of water and difficulties of supply in the hot bush country over which our advance took place worked their effect on the Italian units which had been left behind, the personnel of which eventually surrendered in great numbers or dispersed into the bush.

64. The rapid advance beyond the Giuba of some 300 miles was met by bringing the port of Chisimaio into use as an advanced base. Stores and supplies were brought by sea from Mombasa. Difficulty encountered at the port due to damage and destruction carried out by the Italians was overcome through the excellent work of the staff attached to the port both ashore and afloat which enabled the main requirements of the Force to be landed. Even so, it was necessary to maintain the 300 miles of road L of C in addition.

65. At a conservative estimate the number of the enemy made non-effective by operations up to the fall of Mogadiscio by killing, prisoners or dispersion was 31,000. This accounted for the whole 102nd enemy division and more than half 101st.

Great quantities of war material, so much that it had not been assessed at the time of writing, was captured, and in Afgoi and Mogadiscio main ammunition dumps, engineer and ordnance stores, etc., were found complete. The amount of war material and military supplies captured did not support the theory that the enemy were short of essential stores, and later captures also confirmed that he still had considerable military means.

Although we were informed in Mogadiscio that no petrol had been left, the offer of rewards resulted in the disclosure of 350,000 gallons of motor spirit and 80,000 gallons of aviation. This enabled the advance to be continued with light forces before the ports of Mogadiscio or Merca were opened.

C. Operations of 11th (A) Division from fall of Mogadiscio to fall of Addis Abeba.
(26th February to 5th April, 1941.)

66. When I asked the C.-in-C. Middle East for permission to advance to Harrar, I also asked him if the port of Berbera could be re-opened, to enable me to transfer my L. of C. using that port as a base. From Mogadiscio to Giggiga is 744 miles by road while from Berbera to Giggiga is only 204 miles; hence this transfer would effect a reduction of the road L. of. C. of 540 miles. Consequently A.O.C. Aden was ordered by C.-in-C. Middle East to prepare a plan for the re-taking of Berbera by sea in co-operation with the advance of my forces north-wards.

67. Some difficulty occurred at this time in regard to the opening of the port of Mogadiscio. On 2nd February magnetic mines had been laid by Naval aircraft in the entrance of the harbour. Apparatus for successfully sweeping these mines was not immediately available. Consequently I decided to establish temporarily a base port at Merca using lighters and tugs which had been found at Mogadiscio. Some 200 officers and crews of the British Mercantile Marine had been discovered as prisoners on capturing that port. My thanks are due to a number of these who, in spite of having suffered the privations and hardships of 6 months of prison life, with great self-sacrifice volunteered to assist in the reconditioning of the damaged tugs and the opening of Merca as a port.

As soon as Mogadiscio was declared safe ships were diverted there and it was brought into use as the Advanced Base. Damage to cranes, jetties and decauville railways had been done by the Italians and lighters had been sunk. In a very short period of time, however, thanks mainly to the good work of the S.A. Harbour Construction Company and the 24th Workshop Park Company, over 500 tons were being unloaded daily, and, as excellent storage sheds existed, Depots were soon established.

68. As no shipping for M.T. was available, the road L. of C. from Kenya – now some 800 miles in length – had still to be kept open for use by M.T. convoys; a large portion of it had broken up into dust pans and this journey was becoming increasingly difficult.

69. The administrative arrangements of the advance from the Tana River had been based upon the previous establishment of dumps of supplies, petrol and

ammunition as far forward as possible. This avoided heavy daily convoys from railhead, and had the effect of reducing the length of the L. of C.

For the advance north from Mogadiscio no such facilities were available. There was no respite for the accumulation of reserves, for the re-organisation of transport units, by now much dispersed and in need of servicing, nor for the regrouping of staffs to establish new depots. Improvisation and individual initiative followed by much hard work on the part of lorry drivers, depot staffs, and others too numerous to mention, alone made it possible for the flow of supplies to keep pace with the advance. The line of supply to the 11th (A) Division increased at a rate of 40 miles a day to a distance of 750 miles from Mogadiscio and that to the 12th (A) Division to over 450 miles.

With the sole exception of the 70 miles narrow gauge railway from Mogadiscio to Villagio d'Abruzzi which the 38th S.A. Railway Construction Company very soon had working, maintenance over these distances had to be effected entirely by M.T. convoys over roads which could at best be said to be good only in parts.

70. After the fall of Mogadiscio my information was to the effect that the remnants of the Italian Giuba forces were withdrawing on Giggiga and, except for these, no other serious enemy forces existed south of this place. The enemy in the northern area consisted of three fresh brigades between Giggiga and Harrar and one in British Somaliland.

71. After a pause of only three days, thanks to the petrol captured from the enemy and the possibility of using the port of Merca, the 11th (A) Division was in a position on 1st March to resume the advance on Giggiga with a mobile column from the Nigerian Brigade.

The strength of this column varied with the ability to supply it. Thus Dagabur, 590 miles north of Mogadiscio, was attacked on 10th March by a column consisting only of some armoured cars and two companies of the 2nd Nigeria Regiment, with the remainder of the battalion 100 miles behind. I consider the courageous advance of this column under the command of Lieut.-Colonel J.A.S. Hopkins, unsupported for many miles back, is worthy of special mention. At Dagabur a small Italian rear guard was surprised on the point of withdrawing in lorries, and Lieut.-Colonel Hopkins was able to cut off the retreat of the rear lorries with some loss to the enemy in killed, prisoners and transport.

The average distance covered daily by the leading troops after leaving Mogadiscio was 65 miles. The Order of Battle of 11th (A) Division on 11th March is given in Appendix "E."

72. Information was now in the hands of the Air Force that the enemy were using almost exclusively Dire Daua aerodrome and its two satellites close by. Another fighter ground attack was organised and took place between 13th–15th March. This operation resulted in the loss to the enemy of 20 aircraft, 6 destroyed in the air, 9 on the ground and 5 damaged. Our losses were two Hurricanes. The value at this particular period of these heavy losses to the enemy was very great. Our

further advance was over mountain roads through many narrow defiles and passes, where our columns would have been extremely vulnerable to air attack. Although they were bombed sporadically the attacks were not pushed home and little damage resulted. Our columns were still able to advance by day.

73. On 19th March supply arrangements permitted 11th (A) Division to continue the advance from Dagabur with the whole of the Nigerian Brigade.

The remaining two brigades which had been placed under the orders of 11th (A) Division, namely, 1st S.A. Brigade and 22nd E.A. Brigade, were not able to operate forward of Dagabur till 21st and 26th March respectively owing to administrative restrictions.

Giggiga was attacked on 17th March and occupied by advanced forces of the 23rd Nigerian Brigade with only slight opposition, the enemy retiring to a position covering the Marda Pass.

74. Meanwhile, A.O.C. Aden, taking advantage of the threat to Giggiga, through which ran the only easily passable road from British Somaliland into Abyssinia, successfully attacked Berbera on the 16th March from the sea, with two Indian Battalions and attached troops.

The plan for the capture and opening of the port, the provision of the port personnel and the landing of the stores necessary for the further advance of my troops, were all in his hands.

I would like to place on record my appreciation of the great ability shown by Air Vice-Marshal G.R.M. Reid, D.S.O., M.C., in carrying out the operation, and the fine spirit of co-operation and helpfulness displayed by both Air Vice-Marshal Reid and his staff in the establishment of the port. Colonel A.H. Pollock, M.C., who commanded the troops which carried out the landing, and who subsequently became Area Commander Berbera, was responsible, with the assistance of the Royal Navy from Aden, for the handling of the supplies from Aden destined for my troops. I wish also to commend the efficiency shown by the Royal Navy and Colonel Pollock in this work. Although short-handed and with poor facilities, great energy and determination resulted in landing sufficient stores to enable my advance beyond Harrar to proceed without a pause, a state of affairs which at one time I did not think would be possible.

75. As our advance was proceeding northwards from Mogadiscio the enemy in British Somaliland had issued orders for the withdrawal of their forces. The rapid advance on to Giggiga, however, cut their normal route for retirement and the 70th Colonial Brigade under General Bertello attempted to escape by Borama and Dire Daua. The subsequent adventures of this column are obscure. It became known that General Bertello had passed through Dire Daua mounted on a mule shortly before we captured that place. Furthermore, large parties of prisoners in British Somaliland and just south of the border were captured at various subsequent dates. It is assumed therefore that 70th Brigade melted away.

On the 20th March a small column of Nigerians occupied Tug Wajale on the British Somaliland border, and two armoured cars, led by the Chief Engineer E.A. Force, motored through Hargeisa to Berbera and established contact with Aden Force.

76. The occupation of Giggiga marked the end of the fighting in the flat bush country, and the commencement of a period of hill fighting in the Abyssinian highlands. Up to the present our tactics had almost invariably been the same, the reconnaissance to find the flanks of the enemy position by armoured cars, its rapid envelopment by armoured cars and embossed infantry if the going permitted, or infantry on foot if it did not. It was seldom during the period up to Giggiga that some form of mechanised column could not be placed behind the enemy position. It was our experience that as soon as the Italian Colonial Infantry realised there was something behind them their resistance gave way.

With the entry into the hills it was clear that A.F.Vs. could no longer be depended upon to the same extent as heretofore, and that the Infantry would have to revert to true infantry fighting on their feet. In anticipation of such a situation arising I had formed a small transport company of 600 mules in Kenya, and had arranged to portee one 3·7 in. How. Battery, mules and guns complete. Owing, however, to the extreme difficulty of getting them over the long distance from Kenya, I was not able to get them up in time for the operations covered by this report.

77. The Marda Pass appeared to be held strongly by the enemy, and viewed towering above the extensive flat plains of Giggiga, looked indeed a formidable proposition. Nothing could move on the Giggiga plain without being seen, and the aerodrome was in full view of the hills 9,000 yards away. The enemy appeared to be holding a broad front and therefore Commander 11th (A) Division decided he would await the arrival of 1st S.A. Brigade and attack the pass with two brigades on 23rd March. Patrol activity by the Nigerian Brigade during this period resulted in a claim by the enemy that heavy attacks had been carried out, all of which had been repulsed with great loss. On 20th March I received definite indications that the enemy was planning a further withdrawal and it was decided to attack with the Nigerian Brigade only, next day. After stiff fighting 1st Nigeria Regiment were able to take a height overlooking the pass on its northern side by 2000 hours on the evening of the 21st. The enemy evacuated the pass that night. It transpired that the position was in fact 4 miles in breadth. It was heavily wired, had gun positions tunnelled into the hills, extensive tank traps and mine fields. It had however no depth, and there is little doubt that, the occupation of the height captured by our troops had made it untenable.

78. After the action at the Marda Pass it became possible to transfer the L of C of the 11th (A) Division to the line Berbera – Hargeisa.

The Force at this time was, therefore, maintained from two advanced bases, Berbera and Mogadiscio, with L of C from the former 250 miles and from the latter 800 miles. It was, moreover, necessary simultaneously to maintain from the port of Chisimaio some 4,000 L of C troops and, in addition, to keep the whole of the 1,600 miles of road L of C to Kenya open for the passage of motorised units and M.T. convoys, since facilities for handling M.T. at the ports did not exist.

79. Two more enemy prepared positions remained in front of Harrar, the first at the Babile Pass, the second above the Bisidimo River. In order to force the first of these the Commander 11th (A) Division planned to move by two roads, send-ing the Nigerian Brigade by the southern route, while the Royal Natal Carbineers took the old road to the north. The Babile position looked even more formidable than the Marda Pass. High broken hills, steep-sided and formed of granite blocks, flanked the roads on both sides. The southern road had been blocked by crater-ing and a cliff fall. Some considerable resistance was met by the Nigerians, who owing to better going reached the position first. The Royal Natal Carbineers found the old disused road extremely difficult going; by dint however of energetic perseverance, they were able to make their presence felt. The Italians had not expected the old road to be used, and feeling the weakness of their left flank, were forced off the position on the evening of 24th March, and the Nigerian Brigade continued their advance on the 25th.

80. On the morning of the 25th an announcement was picked up on the wireless that Harrar had declared itself an open town. Having had no official com-munication to this effect, I had a message dropped on the town informing the authorities that operations would go on, and unless all troops were withdrawn to the west of the town, it could not be considered open. Notwithstanding this, the Nigerian Brigade met with opposition at the Bisidimo position during the morning of the 25th, coming under fire at first light from Medium and Field guns based on the high ground covering Harrar.

Two batteries of the 7th S.A. Field Brigade were brought into action in the only possible position which was entirely open except for a little cover from observa-tion by scrub and bushes. Although they came under intense fire while deploying, they succeeded by 1200 hours in establishing a superiority of fire over the enemy guns which they eventually silenced. At the same time they gave supporting fire which enabled the 1st and 2nd battalions of the Nigeria Regiment to advance.

With the arrival of a section of six inch Hows. the enemy abandoned his guns and withdrew.

81. As soon as the enemy had withdrawn an Italian Civil Official appeared with a white flag, and was met by Major-General H.E. de R. Wetherall, C.B., D.S.O., O.B.E., M.C., Commander 11th (A) Division. This official attempted to insist that the message which had been dropped in the morning meant that the Italian forces should be given time to withdraw west of the town, and said they would have done so by 0700 hours the following morning. Major-General Wetherall however, left him no illusions on this point, and sent him forward with the armoured cars to occupy the town. The occupation took place without incident

on the evening of the 25th; the Italian troops encountered laying down their arms. Amongst other war material captured were two batteries of 105mm. guns, weapons which had not before been met.

82. In the period covering the advance from Mogadiscio to Harrar a further 19,000 of the Italian armed forces were accounted for, killed, prisoners, or by desertion, bringing the total up to that time to 50,000.

83. I would here bring to notice the achievement of the Nigerian Brigade and attached troops, under the command of Brigadier G.R. Smallwood, M.C., who commenced their advance from the Giuba on 23rd February and were in the van of 11th (A) Division until the capture of Harrar on 25th March. Thus in 30 days they had covered 1,054 miles, an average of 35 miles a day. The final 65 miles into Harrar entailed an advance through most difficult country in face of opposition from three strong positions, yet the distance was covered in three-and-half days. The Nigerian soldier, unaccustomed to cold and damp, fought his way from the hot and dusty bush to the wet and cold highlands of Abyssinia, where he maintained his cheerfulness and courage in spite of strange conditions and the strenuous climbing operations made necessary by the terrain.

84. On 21st March I had received a telegram from the Commander-in-Chief Middle East to the effect that he saw no military advantage in going beyond Dire Daua unless it was likely to end the campaign, and pointing out the dangers of becoming too deeply committed. I was told that the C-in-C did not wish to hamper my action, and was asked for my views.

I replied that my information showed that there were only two brigades between my forces and Addis Abeba; furthermore that there were no signs of reinforcements being moved up to the Auasc River which would be the enemy's last line of defence before Addis Abeba; that the morale of the Colonial troops in front of me was very low, and they had little fighting value. Under these conditions the capture of Addis Abetoa seemed quite possible. Although I was not prepared to say that this would result in the capitulation of the enemy, yet if Eritrea went as well, I thought they would give in.

85. It should be mentioned that it was at this time that the German threat from Tripoli was developing. I had been informed that 1st S.A. Division was to proceed to Egypt as soon as my operations were finished, and that as much transport and as many other units as possible, were to be sent up as they became available. I therefore informed C-in-C that on account of the Jibuti railway there would be no new transport commitment in an advance from Dire Daua to Addis Abeba. Furthermore I stated that I could release 1st S.A. Division Headquarters and 5th S.A. Brigade then in Kenya, at once. I received permission to proceed with the advance on Addis Abeba.

86. On 27th March the 1st S.A. Brigade took the lead and advanced from Harrar on Dire Daua. Two routes were available to the Auasc River and it had been the

intention of Commander 11th (A) Division to move 1st S.A. Brigade through Dire Daua westwards by the northern route over the low ground, and to send a column from the Nigerian Brigade by the southern road over the Mountains. The enemy however, had carried out extensive demolitions, more particularly on the mountain pass leading down to Dire Daua where in five separate places the road was blown on the steepest slopes. The crater in one of these demolitions was 70 yards long. An initial estimate for the filling up of these craters was given as eight days. Some of the Nigerian Brigade were moved up to assist in the re-establishing of the road. In the event, the road was open in 36 hours, an achievement which gives great credit to the 1st S.A. and 54th E.A. Field Companies and 1st Nigeria Regiment who worked continuously until the demolitions were cleared.

Meanwhile two companies of the 1st Transvaal Scottish were sent off on foot to capture Dire Daua which was entered unopposed on 29th March. The retreating Italians had left the town some time before our troops, delayed by demolitions, entered. It was found that 7 Italians had been murdered and mutilated by armed deserters from the Italian Colonial Infantry. Order was quickly restored by our troops.

Owing to the demolitions Commander 11th (A) Division was not able to adhere to his original plan, namely to advance a Nigerian column by the southern road, but had to send 1st D.E.O.R. from 1st S.A. Brigade by this route instead. He did, however, maintain his original intention to send the greatest weight by the northern road.

87. During the advance an enemy map had been captured, marked with successive delaying lines, which it was thought had been worked out some time before against the threat of an advance from French Somaliland. It appeared also as if demolitions and defences had been partly prepared a considerable time previously, as from this point to the Auasc very extensive cratering was met on both roads. It was a matter of some amazement that during this period in only a few cases did the enemy cover his demolitions by fire, and even then at the first sign of an enveloping movement by our troops he either surrendered or withdrew. From this time to the Auasc very little resistance was made, though considerable toil was required to overcome the demolitions.

It was expected that the enemy would put up a fight on the line Miesso – Asbar Littorio, and it eventually became known that he intended to do so. He placed the weight of his troops, however, covering the southern road, as he over-estimated the time it would take us to clear the Dire Daua road. He was therefore taken by surprise when he found our heaviest attack developing on the northern route, and he withdrew, one column retiring behind the Auasc, the other column by the southern road through Sire towards Cofole.

On 1st April 1st S.A. Brigade occupied Miesso and 22nd E.A. Brigade were passed through towards the Auasc.

Air operations at this period were mainly directed towards the enemy columns retreating by both rail and road. The railway system from Dire Daua to Addis Abeba was the main target and several direct hits by bombs on trains were registered. The attacks added still further to the confusion amongst the enemy.

88. At this stage, in view of the low morale of the enemy facing me, a condition which had now spread to the Blackshirt Battalions and other white units, I had no doubt whatever that my troops would cross the Auasc without difficulty, and that the fall of Addis Abeba was imminent. Addis Abeba had to my knowledge a white civilian population of some 20,000 and a native population of about 100,000. The protection of the white population in Abyssinia under circumstances such as were now coming about, had always been a matter of some concern to me. I was most anxious to avoid any form of pillage or more serious incidents in that dangerous excitable period, which always exists in a town between the withdrawal of the enemy and the first entry of our troops. I was well aware of the significance of any untoward incident in the eyes of the United States and the rest of the civilised world.

89. On 30th March I therefore telegraphed General Wavell placing these views before him and suggesting that the time had come for a direct approach either by himself or by myself to H.R.H. The Duke of Aosta in Supreme Command of the troops in Italian East Africa, on the question of the protection of the population of the town. On 31st March I received the following message from the C-in-C for H.R.H. The Duke of Aosta.

> "I am anxious to avoid any possibility that Italian women and children should be endangered in the course of military operations. Your Royal Highness must realise that your present military situation may make their protection in certain areas a difficult matter. I am prepared to offer co-operation in ensuring their safety so far as is consistent with my military duty of continuing action against your forces still in arms. I have therefore authorised General Cunningham to get in touch with Your Royal Highness by means which he will suggest and to report to me any proposals which may mutually ensure the safety of women and children in zone of operations."

This message was duly dropped on Addis Abeba from the air with a message from me to say that an envoy could be sent by air during certain hours, to land behind our lines with safety. On 2nd April an Italian aeroplane dropped a message for me from H.R.H. acknowledging the receipt of the C-in-C's message and saying that his envoy would land next day on the aerodrome specified. I telegraphed General Wavell at once giving him a summary of the conditions I proposed handing to the Italians.

Next morning, just before the envoy arrived, I received a further wire from the C-in-C which was so badly mutilated that I was unable to make much sense from it. As by this time my troops were across the Auasc, and might have been fighting near Addis Abeba that evening, I felt there was no time for further reference and I would have to act on my own initiative.

It should be noted that the envoy was only authorised to speak about the particular position in Addis Abeba. A copy of the conditions handed to him is given in Appendix "F" together with the Italian reply I received next day. This was merely acknowledged without comment.

90. On 4th April I received from Troopers direct a wire to say that the Defence Committee did not endorse the conditions put forward by General Wavell and that no offer to assume responsibility for feeding and protecting enemy civil population should be made without mentioning the unconditional surrender of Italian armed forces. Terms should be included also that ships in Massawa harbour were to be handed over to us intact for the evacuation and feeding of the Italian civilian community. It appeared to me that it was not clear to the Defence Committee that the conditions were to cover Addis Abeba only, a town which was necessary to me for the continuance of military operations, being the junction of all the main roads in Abyssinia.

If I had made demands as outlined above, in the event of refusal, the only action I could have taken was to stop short of Addis Abeba. In fact, I had nothing to bargain with. There was no direct threat to Addis Abeba, with which the Italians were not in a position to deal, by any forces other than my own. Nevertheless, as the Italian Military Command in their reply had not accepted the terms I had laid down in full, I cabled C.-in-C. Middle East offering to delay my advance and reopen negotiations.

As I had no reply in 24 hours I removed all restrictions and allowed the troops to continue their advance.

91. While these negotiations were taking place the advance of 22nd Brigade on to the Auasc was continuing, and our troops were in contact on the river on 2nd April. Both the road and railway bridges were found to be blown. The enemy put up some resistance to frontal attacks, but about half a mile from his main position a place was found where the river could be waded, and as soon as he discovered his flank was being turned he withdrew. A new road bridge was built and the advance was continued next day, 3rd April. The 22nd E.A. Brigade reached Adama that day, and were instructed to try to cross the river Auasc at Ponte Malcasa, and attempt to cut off the enemy column which was known to be withdrawing by Sire. The bridge had been destroyed and the enemy offered considerable resistance. A large part of the enemy column therefore escaped, though the capture of the road junction south of Ponte Malcasa some days later resulted in the cutting off of some units.

92. On 4th–5th April a series of combined bomber and fighter attacks were carried out by the Air Force on Addis Abeba aerodrome. The results of these attacks were the most successful yet attained. It was estimated that the enemy lost 32 aircraft, 3 destroyed in the air, 17 on the ground, and 12 damaged. The

shambles on Addis Abeba aerodrome was apparent to our troops after entering the town, and further increased their confidence in the efficiency of the Air Force in aiding their advance.

93. During this time the 1st S.A. Brigade was being moved up to occupy Addis Abeba, which was entered by a mixed force officially at 10.30 hours 6th April.

On the evening before, while at Adama, the 22nd Brigade had received a request from the Italian officials in Addis Abeba to send some troops in to prevent looting. A few armoured cars and infantry were duly despatched.

During the period between the commencement of the advance from Harrar and the entry into Addis Abeba a further 15,000 of the enemy were calculated to have become non-effective. Millions of pounds worth of war material of all sorts was found in the city and captured on the way there.

94. It is interesting to note that although during the whole period of the advance from the Giuba 11th (A) Division consisted of three brigades, only on one occasion, namely, at the Babile Pass engagement, was it found necessary to use more than one at a time. At the Babile Pass only one extra battalion was employed. I consider the greatest credit is due to Major-General Wetherall, Commander 11th (A) Division, for his cool-headed judgment, drive and daring acceptance of risks throughout the advance.

95. It was not found possible immediately to use the railway line from Dire Daua to Addis Abeba, as the Italians had not only removed all the serviceable engines and the spare parts and machinery from Dire Daua to Addis Abeba, but had also completely destroyed the railway bridge over the Auasc River.

Eventually with the assistance of some Greek mechanics, one engine at Dire Daua was made sufficiently serviceable to go out along the line and bring in others from which one engine was then made available for drawing a train. This train conveyed 100 tons of supplies and stores to Auasc on 9th April, only three days after the occupation of Addis Abeba.

D. Operations in British Somaliland
(16th March to 5th April, 1941.)

96. As already referred to, a force from Aden was landed in British Somaliland and captured Berbera on 16th March. By previous arrangement with Aden, it was my responsibility to relieve one of the two Indian battalions sent over from there, and to take over command of Berbera and administration of British Somaliland as soon as possible after the landing.

In view of the importance of my L. of C., of the presence of formed but isolated groups of the enemy still in that area, and the necessity for a senior military commander on the spot, I decided to move the personnel of the H.Q. and two battalions 2nd S.A. Infantry Brigade by sea from Kenya to Berbera, the remaining battalion and all the transport proceeding by march route.

Brigade H.Q. and 2nd F.F. Battalion and 1st Natal Mounted Rifles duly arrived at Berbera on 23rd March. The transport proceeding by road did not arrive until 5th April. In spite of this, by the use of twenty 30-cwt. lorries sent over from Aden, and some hired transport procured through the offices of Lieut.-Colonel R.H. Smith the Senior Political Officer, Brigadier F.L.A. Buchanan, M.C., V.D., commanding 2nd S.A. Brigade was able to do valuable work in cleaning up isolated pockets of the enemy and establishing political control over the country.

97. On 8th April Brigadier A.R. Chater, C.B., D.S.O., O.B.E., who had been appointed Military Governor British Somaliland under my general direction took over from Brigadier Buchanan.

Immediate steps were taken to re-raise the Somaliland Camel Corps, the Illalos and the police force, many of the personnel of which were left in British Somaliland when the evacuation took place.

The troops left under my command by A.O.C. Aden are given in Appendix "G."

E. Operations of 12th (A) Division
(26th February to 5th April, 1941.)

98. On 25th February 12th (A) Division consisted of the 21st E.A. Infantry Brigade at Wajir and the 24th G.C. Brigade which was at Gelib. The 22nd E.A. Brigade had been put under 11th (A) Division for the advance on Mogadiscio, and 1st S.A. Brigade had come into Force Reserve. 12th (A) Division had been instructed on 24th February to reconnoitre towards Bardera and, if it was found unoccupied, to make demonstrations towards Iscia Baidoa.

On 26th February I met the Commander 12th (A) Division at Gelib and explained the scope of future operations and emphasised the limitations imposed by the existing supply situation. Commander 12th (A) Division anticipated that if Bardera was occupied he could capture it by 2nd March and Iscia Baidoa by 5th March. To assist in the capture of Bardera and subsequently to garrison that place it was arranged that one battalion of 21st E.A. Brigade from Wajir should move there direct. Considerable apprehension was felt at the time about troops getting caught by the rains in Bardera and Iscia Baidoa with insufficient supplies. The same day a report was received that a patrol of the 24th G.C. Brigade had entered Bardera which was found to be unoccupied. Reports were also received that Iscia Baidoa and Dinsor had already been evacuated as a result of a message from the Duce ordering the evacuation of Italian Somaliland for Abyssinia. This was confirmed by patrols which occupied Iscia Baidoa on 27th February and captured 200 native troops and large quantities of ammunition, supplies and petrol.

99. At this period 12th (A) Division was given a call on 1st S.A. and 22nd E.A. Brigades to assist in pacifying the large area of country for which it was responsible. The right boundary of this Division was brought right up to the Mogadiscio – Belet Uen road so as to free 11th (A) Division of pacification tasks.

100. On 3rd March patrols reported Lugh Ferrandi, unoccupied except for a few civilians whom they collected. H.Q. 24th G.C. Brigade moved to Iscia Baidoa

and further patrols were sent to Dolo and Oddur. The patrol to Dolo found it unoccupied. The Oddur patrol reported Uegit evacuated and looted, and then proceeded on 4th March to occupy Oddur which was also found deserted.

On 6th March a patrol was despatched from Dolo to Mandera on receipt of information that Mandera had been evacuated and that the nearest enemy were at Neghelli. This patrol reported Mandera deserted, on 15th March. A further patrol was despatched from Iscia Baidoa along the road Belet – Uen and found this route to be impassable in wet weather.

101. In anticipation of the projected transfer of 1st S.A. Division to the eastern sector to take Harrar, 12th (A) Division H.Q. moved on 7th March to Bulo Erillo so that it would be more conveniently placed to move into 1st S.A. Division area. When this project was abandoned owing to early rains hampering movement, 12th (A) Division H.Q. opened on 11th March three miles north of Giumbo to facilitate the supply of Division H.Q. and Divisional troops from Chisimaio.

102. During the whole of this period both the 1st S.A. Infantry Brigade and the 22nd E.A. Infantry Brigade which, for reasons of supply were located at Brava and Merca, had been rounding up a considerable number of prisoners left over from the Giuba battle and locating large quantities of ammunition, supplies and petrol in the area Bur Acaba – Afgoi – Modun. Active patrolling by these brigades resulted in hundreds of Italians, Colonial Infantry and Banda surrendering with their arms and equipment, and much was done to restore order in this area. Patrols of 2nd Gold Coast Regiment from Iscia Baidoa to Bur Acaba collected further prisoners.

As a result of desertions, armed bands in considerable numbers were engaged in banditry and looting all over the occupied territory. From this time onwards troops were in constant demand by the Political authorities for the restoration of order and this state of affairs still exists.

103. On 11th March 22nd E.A. Brigade reverted to command 11th (A) Division and 1st S.A. Brigade together with the 22nd Mountain Battery, 4th S.A. Field Brigade, and 2nd S.A. A.Tk. Battery were also placed under command 11th (A) Division.

104. A column consisting of 3rd G.C. Regiment, 51st G.C. Light Battery and a troop of armoured cars left Dolo at 0630 hours on 17th March to reconnoitre to Neghelli. Progress was slow owing to minefields and road-blocks. Four miles east of Neghelli opposition was met and overcome, and Neghelli itself was occupied at 0830 hours on 21st March. No administrative arrangements could be made at that time to maintain troops in Neghelli, so the column returned to Dolo on 26th March. On 23rd March the Commander 12th (A) Division had been ordered by me to do what he could to keep the enemy forces north of Neghelli engaged. By making a show of force in this area it was hoped to delay the withdrawal of enemy forces on the route Neghelli – Addis Abeba and thus to contribute to the success of operations being undertaken by 11th (A) Division in the

Harrar – Auasc River area. Unfortunately this message was delayed and before receipt the Neghelli columns, which had never been intended to stay, had been withdrawn. Accordingly, re-occupation was decided upon provided the necessary administrative arrangements could be overcome. A column of 3rd G.C. Regiment less two companies, one troop of E.A.A.C. Regiment and a section of 51st G.C. Light Battery left Dolo early on 30th March and reached Neghelli on 1st April. In the meantime, however a patrol of 1/2nd K.A.R. from the 21st E.A. Infantry Brigade at Iavello had already re-occupied Neghelli on 30th March. The 3rd G.C. Regiment remained in Neghelli and the 1/2nd K.A.R. patrol returned to Iavello. No enemy were reported near Neghelli but local riots were taking place between Boran and Somali tribesmen and punitive patrols had to be sent out to round up offenders. The enemy were believed to be holding a position in the area Uaddara and a patrol was accordingly sent out to investigate. The patrol returned on 5th April and confirmed that the enemy were holding a strong position in the area of Uaddara.

105. On 6th April 12th (A) Division H.Q. moved to Neghelli and took over from 1st S.A. Division, the 21st and 25th E.A. Infantry Brigades and all Divisional troops not proceeding to Middle East. The 24th G.C. Brigade less 3rd G.C. Regiment at Neghelli remained under command of Force in the area Lugh Ferrandi – Oddur – Iscia Baidoa with the task of clearing up and patrolling the area.

The Order of Battle of 12th (A) Division at this time is given in Appendix "H".

PART III. – GENERAL.

106. *Control and Headquarters.*

The problem of control of the operations was intricate. Although originally Force H.Q. was based on a Corps Staff Establishment, it was found necessary owing to the many local problems of supply, personnel, finance, &c., to expand it into a minor G.H.Q. whose dealings were very largely concerned with South Africa, the Government of Kenya and the Governors' Conference. A large portion of my staff, and strictly speaking myself also, had firm roots in Nairobi and many major responsibilities in that place.

In the campaign which has been described it will be remembered that the main advance in the south was, in the initial stages, carried out by two divisions at one time, and it was quite clear to me that it would be necessary either to improvise a Corps H.Q. and place one of the Major-Generals in command, or to go forward and control the battle myself. It was quite impossible for me to give a general directive to 1st S.A. Division in the north and to rely on General Brink to carry it out, but in view of the interplay between the 11th and 12th (A) Divisions which was bound to happen when they reached the Giuba, I was convinced I could not follow this procedure in their case. I did not like the idea of forming an improvised Corps H.Q. as neither the Commander nor the staff would have time to get to know each other. I therefore decided to form an Advanced H.Q. and go forward and fight the battle myself.

107. On 9th February, therefore, Force H.Q. was divided into two, with Rear Force H.Q. at Nairobi and Advanced Force H.Q. at Garissa. Advanced Force H.Q. consisted of the majority of the General Staff and representatives of the branches, while the Rear H.Q. continued to operate with the remaining personnel. As operations progressed, Advanced Force H.Q. moved forward. Moves were carried out in three echelons. The main operational group was air-borne. It was preceded by an advance signal centre and a portion of Advanced H.Q., which went by road two or three days ahead to establish communications. After the departure of the air party the rear echelon of Advanced Force H.Q. followed by road. Owing to the distances involved in the moves and the state of the roads, it was usually a week after the departure of the Advance Party before the Rear Party arrived, and Advanced Force H.Q. was complete again.

The following moves were carried out by Advanced H.Q.:-

10th February. Nairobi – Garissa.
18th February. Garissa – Chisimaio.
27th February. Chisimaio – Mogadiscio.
20th March. Mogadiscio – Gabredarre.
27th March. Gabredarre – Giggiga.
1st April. Giggiga – Harrar.

108. Although the arrangements for Advanced H.Q. worked reasonably satisfactorily, things were not so happy at Nairobi. Many important matters were either neglected or left in the hands of junior officers who had not the experience to deal with them. Heads of services had no one to go to for guidance and control, and, moreover, were out of touch with what was going on in front. I was only once able to go back to Nairobi myself.

Before serious operations began I had always felt that the best solution would have been to add a floating Corps H.Q. to the Force which could have taken charge of any front where two divisions were being employed; my experience during operations confirmed this view.

As Advanced H.Q. got further and further away from Nairobi I asked for a Major-General with the idea of making Nairobi a base area under his command. Before sanction had been obtained, however, Addis Abeba had fallen and a new situation presented itself.

109. I should call attention here to the necessity for rapid, accurate and efficient staff work in all branches which the speed and nature of the operations demanded. Both at my Advanced and Rear H.Q. and in all formations the staffs and subordinate personnel were not found wanting. I wish to mention particularly the work of Brigadier J.K. Edwards, M.C., my B.G.S., as being of outstanding merit. In his cool-headed yet rapid and clear interpretation of my directions he showed himself a staff officer on whom complete reliance could be placed.

Administration was the key-note of the operations, the burden of which fell mainly on the shoulders of the A.Q.M.G.s Colonel A.C. Duff, O.B.E., M.C., and

Colonel Sir Brian H. Robertson, Bt., D.S.O., M.C., one of whom was always with me forward and the other at Rear H.Q. I found them undaunted by the magnitude of the demands made on them. That, through all the vicissitudes of bad roads, and ports without appliances, ample supplies were able to keep up with the troops, must be accounted a fine achievement by these two officers and all who worked to the same purpose.

110. It would not have been possible to split the H.Q. into two unless large numbers of male clerks, signallers, cipher personnel and M.T. Drivers had been replaced in Rear H.Q. by women.

Great credit is due to Lady Sidney Farrar for raising a F.A.N.Y. unit from local resources and for the tireless efficiency shown in training and organising it. The work of these ladies was invaluable, and in spite of long and arduous hours always remained excellent.

111. *Intelligence.*

By the end of January, 1941, the small Intelligence Section, which had been formed in September, 1939, had been expanded into a G.H.Q. Section complete, with a total strength of 75 officers and 110 O.Rs. All these, except two officers, were found from South African, East African and West African resources.

Information about the enemy was obtained from many sources. Until Italy declared war, reasons of policy had prevented employment of agents in Italian territory, but after June, 1940, Galla and Somali tribesmen were employed. Although they were not skilful agents they produced useful information.

All information received in Nairobi was quickly sifted and signalled on by the quickest means to the small Intelligence Branch which worked at Advanced Force H.Q. This information often proved of inestimable value.

Intelligence Officers worked in the field and employing agents were often joined by so many volunteers that they became leaders of bands of Patriot scouts, and as such played an active part in the operations.

112. The question of security had necessarily to receive close attention in view of the Italian civil population which remained in the various towns which were captured. Security personnel were moved immediately in rear of the leading troops and as soon as a town was entered they established security control. In addition, they often had to carry out various administrative and political duties until the arrival of the appropriate staffs. To maintain wireless security it was necessary to have a regular system of changing code names and stencil ciphers. The organisation of these changes over such a wide front which lacked normal means of communication required careful preparation.

As the situation demanded, Censorship offices were opened to deal not only with letters from the troops and communications to the Press but also to censor enemy civilian and Prisoners of War correspondence.

I consider that one of the main reasons why our intelligence was better than the enemy's was because of our better security organisation.

113. Particular attention was paid to propaganda which, though under the general direction of Cairo, had necessarily to be evolved locally to a great extent on account of the delay in communications. Great use was made of locally-prepared pamphlets dropped on enemy troops. My policy in these pamphlets was to ensure that all enemy troops knew what was happening in the operations in Italian East Africa, to encourage the Somali and Eritrean troops to desert and return to their homes before they were taken as prisoners of war, and to incite Abyssinians to throw off the yoke of the Italian. Considerable success was achieved; many desertions and several surrenders were directly due to the pamphlets, while reports showed that the Italians were always very concerned about our activities in this direction in lowering the morale of their troops.

News for the troops was not neglected, news sheets being prepared and issued regularly, while in Mogadiscio and Addis Abeba Italian and vernacular newspapers were started to keep the local population informed of world news.

114. *Engineers.*
Until January, 1941, the Engineer troops were employed on defensive positions, principally on the Tana arid at Wajir; on construction or improving and maintaining the roads or tracks running fanwise from Nairobi to Lokitaung, Marsabit, Wajir, Garissa and Bura; and providing water supplies in the base areas and along the Lines of Communication, by deep-well boring.

During the period immediately preceding the advance to the Giuba four floating bridges were built over the Tana, two at Garissa and two at Bura.

115. From the crossing of the Giuba onwards the L. of C. lengthened so rapidly that very little transport could be spared for engineer materials from the carriage of rations, petrol and ammunition. Consequently most of the engineer work depended upon finding materials on the line of advance and fortunately, the enemy usually left ample materials to repair his demolitions.

Italian engineer stores at Mogadiscio and at Addis Abeba in particular saved invaluable time and transport. Near Mogadiscio three road bridges and one railway bridge over the 200ft. wide Uebi Scebeli were destroyed by the enemy and rebuilt from materials left in his engineer park at Afgoi; which provided also an excellent bridge, portable in light parts, which was later used to replace the demolished road bridge over the Auasc River. At Addis Abeba also sufficient of this equipment was found to provide a 220ft. bridge at Ponte Malcasa and a considerable reserve for future needs.

116. Engineer work on the advance from Mogadiscio to Addis Abeba consisted mainly of the clearing of minefields and road blocks, and making deviation causeways across streams where bridges had been demolished, followed by bridge construction.

Apart from the pontoon bridges over the Tana and the Giuba, upwards of 70 bridges from 25' to 220' in length, in single or multiple spans, were built, almost all of captured Italian material. This process is still going on.

unit of the Somaliland Camel Corps on patrol in 1940. (*Historic Military Press*)

The men of the Somaliland Camel Corps had a distinctive dress which was based on the standard British Army khaki drill but also included a knitted woollen pullover and drill patches on the shoulders. Shorts were worn.
(*Historic Military Press*)

Men of the Somaliland Camel Corps on patrol along the Somaliland-Abyssinian border in the summer of 1940. At the beginning of the East African Campaign in the Second World War, the SCC numbered some 1,475 men.
(*Historic Military Press*)

A drawing depicting Captain Eric Charles Twelves Wilson during the so-called Battle of Tug Argan in August 1940, part of the actions for which he was awarded the Victoria Cross. (*Historic Military Press*)

(*Left*) A contemporary artist's depiction of Emperor Haile Selassie with two British Army officers. (*Right*) Drawn by the artist William Timyn for the Ministry of Information during the war, this is a portrait of Field Marshal Viscount Archibald Wavell, who authored two of the despatches in this volume. (*The National Archives*)

The vast panorama of Diego Suarez Bay as viewed from Fort d'Ankorike. Antsirane is in the middle distance, and in the far distance the range of heights, which includes that named Windsor Castle, can just be distinguished. (*Courtesy of John Grehan*)

The pillboxes, adjacent to the main Antsirane road, which formed the centre of the French defences. (*IWM; A8888*)

The same pillboxes adjacent to the main Antsirane road today. (*Courtesy of John Grehan*)

Some of the fifty Royal Marines who were landed in the destroyer HMS *Anthony* at Diego Suarez. They climbed the cliffs and captured the French Artillery HQ and the French Naval HQ where they freed four Fleet Air Arm pilots and sixty soldiers who had been captured. (*IWM; A8865*)

A conference on board HMS *Ramillies* after the surrender of Diego-Suarez between (from left to right) Brigadier T.W. Festing, Rear Admiral Syfret, Major General Sturgess, and Captain Howson RM, who was Syfret's Chief of Staff. *(IWM; A8995)*

The pipes of the Royal Scots Fusiliers lead the victory parade through Antsirane after the French surrender. *(Courtesy of A. Lowe)*

The 25-pounders of the 56th East African Artillery firing at the French positions on the Andriamanalina Ridge. (*IWM; MAD 122*)

The advance down Madagascar continues – a Ford 1-ton truck on the road heading southwards towards Antananarivo. (*Courtesy of A. Lowe*)

Sovereignty restored. General Legentilhomme arrives at Tamatave to assume the post of High Commissioner, as the representative of the Free French National Committee.
(*Courtesy of A. Lowe*)

The memorial erected by the Engineers of the Royal Scots Fusiliers to those Scots killed at Diego Suarez. Many veterans can recall the two words at the top of the plague – DINNA FORGET.
(*Courtesy of A. Lowe*)

117. The most notable engineer task in the operations northwards from Marsabit, and probably of the whole campaign, was the construction of a new road 180 miles long from Marsabit via Kalacha and east of the Huri Hills to Mega climbing 4,000 feet in the last 20 miles. This new road made a vital all weather link to replace the track across the Chalbi Desert to North Horr, Dukana and Ganciaro over which the advance of the 1st S.A. Division had been made, but which is impassable after rain. The new road was built in six weeks under most trying conditions across lava debris thrown out by the numerous volcanoes in the region. The heat of the sun and reflected heat from the hard basalt boulders made work extremely arduous in the daytime, and heat radiated from the rock allowed little relief for several hours after sunset.

118. In the south during the preparatory period Road Construction companies, covered only by very light forces, drove broad roads through the bush 70 miles forward from both Garissa and Bura on our front line, the River Tana, and water-boring units were also at work right forward at this stage. In quite a number of the preliminary operations auto-patrols from the Road Construction companies moved forward just behind the most advanced troops. This plan proved of the greatest assistance in maintaining the speed of the advance.

119. No service pattern bridging equipment arrived from the United Kingdom in time to be used in this operation.

This was not unexpected in view of shipping difficulties. Locally designed pontoon bridging, assault boats and S.B.G. bridges were therefore made in Kenya and South Africa and a "Bridge Coy" was improvised from lorry chassis for their carriage to the Giuba. Because of a shortage of steel plates of suitable thickness the pontoons were heavy, and a complete lack of high tensile steel made it necessary to use timber (necessarily "green" as there was no seasoned stock), for the superstructure, and mild steel for the S.B.G.

The improvised equipment was therefore clumsy, and the timber parts warped in the sun, making assembly difficult; but it served its purpose.

120. The four native African Field Companies, one East African, two Gold Coast and one Nigerian, have done remarkably good work in spite of having been ill equipped and sixty per cent. under strength in British N.C.O.s.

The main engineer effort was supplied by South Africa which provided well trained and well equipped units for every purpose. I cannot mention all the units who have earned it, but their comrades in other units will not grudge particular attention being called to the Road Construction and Maintenance Companies and the Water Company. The vital work of these units has been carried out with great skill and perseverance under the most arduous conditions.

I must draw attention to the work of Brigadier A. Minnis, C.B.E., who, before the operation took place, by his initiative and foresight had made R.E. provision, to a large extent locally improvised, which enabled the advance to proceed without serious check.

121. *Survey.*

Until the establishment of a Survey Directorate at the end of October, 1940, the only maps available for the operations were the out-of-date 1/1,000,000 series. Organised mapping of the probable area of operations on the 1/500,000 scale was then started, the data for the maps being collected from many sources, chiefly from Italian maps. As fresh data became available new editions were issued, while road strips of the more important roads were compiled from air photographs, and the details incorporated in the maps.

By the day operations began maps were ready as far as Mogadiscio. Artillery maps on the 1/25,000 scale had also been prepared from air photographs for the River Giuba position from its mouth to just north of Mabungo, together with large scale maps of Chisimaio and Mogadiscio.

As the advance proceeded, maps were prepared and issued well in time, information being mostly collected from captured Italian maps and from air photographs along the routes. Artillery maps of the Marda Pass and the Auasc position were also prepared. In view of the speed of the advance this must be considered a very successful achievement.

The satisfactory position in East Africa Force with regard to maps was mainly due to the careful preparation and detailed organisation made in the few months preceding the start of operations, under the direction of Colonel M. Hotine whose special knowledge and ability and untiring drive were outstanding.

122. *Signals.*

From the time Advanced Force H.Q. left Nairobi on 10th February, 1941, communications had to be maintained almost entirely by W/T. This was due to the tremendous distances separating Advanced Force H.Q. from the Divisions, Divisions from their Brigades, and sometimes Brigades from their battalions. At one period Advanced Force H.Q. was as much as 746, 570 and 250 miles away from the three Divisions.

The daily average of messages dealt with at Advanced Force H.Q. including D.R. messages and re-routing was over 1,000, while that of the Divisional H.Qs. was about 250.

123. Under the best conditions communications in these circumstances would not have been easy, but as it was, the Signals had to compete with three grave disabilities, lack of powerful wireless sets, a large percentage of partially-trained personnel, and the complete blackouts or heavy fading which constantly ocurred owing to the atmospheric and terrestrial conditions in the Northern Frontier District of Kenya and Italian Somaliland.

124. 25 (A) Corps Signals and reinforcements for the skeleton 11th and 12th (A) Divisional Signals only arrived in this country from England as operations were beginning. The men in these units, owing to various circumstances, had received little training before embarkation, a fact fully realised by the War Office, who I understand, sent a certificate with them to this effect. Had the other two

disabilities not been present, the partially-trained operators would more easily have been able to deal with the volume of traffic, but as it was, the lack of skilled operators capable of working sets under adverse circumstances proved a considerable hindrance to the free flow of orders and messages necessary to control operations over such large areas.

After approximately 2½ months spent on board ship all the officers and men experienced severe physical exhaustion during the marches and long spells of duty. Life suddenly maintained on bully beef, biscuit, and a small supply of water did not help to improve physical or mental fitness. This strain was further increased by the high percentage of sickness due to lack of acclimatisation which was unavoidable, since many of the men went direct from the boat to the field.

125. The limited resources in trained personnel had continually to be split owing to the necessity of sending forward advanced signal centres whenever Headquarters moved. Force H.Q. moved six times, the shortest distance being 200 miles in a straight line, and the greatest over 300 miles. This meant it was generally a week between the Advance Signal Centre leaving for a new H.Q. and the Rear Signal Centre arriving there. The 11th (A) Division moved its H.Q. 21 times, the average distance covered being 77 miles; the movements of the H.Q. of 12th (A) Division were similar, while those of the 1st S.A. Division were also abnormal.

126. 15-cwt. Ford trucks were issued in lieu of a proportion of motor-cycles as the latter were found unsuitable in the bush. These trucks proved invaluable for D.R. and D.R.L.S. work. The D.Rs. themselves worked heroically for very long hours, covering enormous distances over the bad roads and tracks.

127. The fact that reliance had to be placed almost entirely on W/T communication meant considerable strain on the cipher personnel, the shortage of which was further aggravated by having to detach men for the new sub areas made necessary by the advance. Extra men who were withdrawn from units to fill gaps only received their cipher training as operations proceeded. This involved a great strain on all the trained cipher personnel who worked tirelessly for very long hours under difficult conditions throughout the operations.

128. The fact that communications functioned even as well as they did is a tribute not only to the endless work of the experienced officers and N.C.Os. but also to all ranks, who worked hard during real and active operations to bring themselves up to the standard which they eventually reached.

129. *Medical.*
A remarkable feature of the campaign was the very low incidence of sickness of both white and native personnel, having regard to the terrain over which the operations took place. In the pre-war Kenya Military Report the following passage occurs:-

Chapter VI., para, I (4th Sub-para.).
Active Service Conditions.

"One of the outstanding lessons of the last campaign in East Africa was the unsuitability of other than native troops for employment on active service in East Africa. British, South African and Indian troops alike had a very high sick rate and were generally unable to adapt themselves to local conditions."

Yet one South African Brigade, many other South African technical units, and Imperial white personnel were continuously in the hot, low-lying Northern Frontier District of Kenya from August, through the "little" rains, until the advance started, and fought on throughout it. Their sick rate was never abnormal.

130. The following figures are given as an indication of the health of the force, up to 5th April, 1941:-

(*a*) Admission rate all diseases. 500 per thousand per annum. (This figure was 2,200 per thousand in the 1916–1918 E.A. Campaign.)

(*b*) Death rate from, all diseases. Per thousand per annum: Europeans 1·8, Non-Europeans 3·8. From malaria only ·28 and ·26. (The similar figure for E.A. Campaign 1916–1918 was 42 per thousand per annum.)

No one measure adopted to protect the health of the troops can be given pride of place. It was appreciated that under active service conditions a high degree of efficiency is not attainable by any one means; reliance was therefore placed not so much on perfecting any single means as on bringing to bear as many protective measures as could be reasonably applied.

131. The lessons of the E.A. Campaign 1916–1918 on both sides showed the necessity of ample and balanced diet during operations of long duration. Although, therefore, except on the few occasions when there was time to buy and butcher fresh meat, during the advance the staple bully beef and biscuit formed the basis of the ration, yet throughout the whole period the hard scale was supplemented by other items both more appetising and health producing.

The usual anti-malarial and anti-dysentery protective measures, and the necessity of disease prevention generally, were stressed. Credit must be given to the various medical officers, on the staff and with units, in that they were able to bring home to individuals the importance of preventive measures, and the C.Os. for their efficient co-operation in seeing that they were adopted.

132. The evacuation of sick and wounded from a force continuously advancing with great rapidity is in any country a source of difficulty. In country such as East Africa it is not only a source of difficulty, but one of great anxiety, since apart from geographical conditions, climatic conditions have also to be contended with.

In the first stages, evacuation was only possible by air for a limited number of the more serious cases. The remainder had to go by Motor Ambulance Convoys for hundreds of miles. Later evacuation by Motor Ambulance Convoys was only necessary as far as the ports of Chisimaio, Mogadiscio and Berbera, whence it was effected by Hospital Ship.

Throughout the operations there was no hitch in the attention to, and the care and evacuation of, the sick and wounded.

It will be clear that at all stages of the operations, for most casualties long and trying evacuation by bad tracks was unavoidable. I had continually stressed the need of air ambulances for this particular campaign, but the demand on production for fighting aircraft precluded their supply. Had the casualties, not been low, the lack of air ambulances would have caused great suffering.

133. I wish to bring to notice the high standard of work and unfailing devotion to duty of all the Medical staff and personnel of the force, and I feel that the very satisfactory medical situation owed much to the great experience and practical knowledge of Brigadier A.J. Orenstein, C.M.G., L.L.D., M.D., M.R.C.P. the D.M.S. of East Africa Force.

134. *Transport.*
Right up to the time of the occupation of Addis Abeba it was necessary to keep open the whole length of the 1,900 mile road L of C to the base at Nairobi for use by motorised units and M.T. convoys who bad to move on all or any part of it.

It will be apparent that with the enormous distance of road L of C involved, an immense amount of work was demanded from the M.T. Companies of the Force. Long and continuous driving over indifferent roads and sand tracks in high temperatures must have been a considerable strain. It was borne by South African, East African and West African drivers alike with a willing and cheerful devotion to duty that is beyond praise.

135. To the mobile and static workshops that repaired and kept the M.T. vehicles on the road, praise is no less due. Their work was never ending and often had to be carried out under very trying conditions.

PART IV. – CONCLUSION.

136. The campaign up to the capture of Addis Abeba resulted in the occupation or reoccupation of 360,000 square miles of territory, the freeing of British Somaliland, and the capture of the enemy's capital. Forty thousand prisoners were left in our hands, and many more are still coming in. Reliable information showed that including desertion and other causes, at least 75,000 of the enemy's armed forces had been rendered non-effective. For this result I must pay tribute to the Commanders and Staffs for their skilful planning and speedy initiative, to the troops for their relentless persistence in advancing under the varied arduous conditions which they met; in the Northern Frontier District, in heat and dust, and long periods on only a gallon of water per man; in the Abyssinian hills in wet and cold, and undertaking operations calling for the highest degree of physical fitness and resistance to fatigue. Although food was always plentiful the staple "Bully Beef" was seldom replaced by fresh meat, and most of the white personnel had no bread for the whole period of two months. Owing to the speed of the advance and the distances covered, it was impossible to maintain a regular service

of mails, a matter of considerable concern to many of the men. All these discomforts were met by both white and native troops with the imperturbable cheerfulness which has long been the characteristic of the British soldier.

137. Our total casualties during the period 11th February to 5th April were:-

Killed	135
Wounded	310
Prisoners	4
Missing	52
	501

It might appear from this figure that there was in fact very little serious fighting. This is by no means the case. Nearly always when our troops met the enemy they were heavily fired on, and the number of automatics and heavy machine-guns captured testified to the fire power the enemy could develop. I attribute the reasons for the low number of casualties firstly to the superior mobility of our forces which enabled them quickly to find the "soft spot," secondly to the cover provided by the bush, and thirdly to lack of marksmanship of the Italian Colonial Infantryman who when pressed was inclined to shoot high.

138. I wish to express my grateful thanks to Vice-Admiral R. Leatham, C.B., R.N., Commander-in-Chief East Indies, and all ranks and ratings concerned, for the invaluable help rendered by the Royal Navy throughout the operations, commencing with the efficient support given by "Force T" in the bombardment of the coast before the capture of Chisimaio, and later during the forcing of the Giuba. The successive opening of the ports of Chisimaio, Merca, Mogadiscio and Berbera enabled my operations to proceed without a pause. In every case facilities for unloading were poor or non-existent, but the difficulties were surmounted with the efficiency and drive we have come to expect from our sister service.

139. I cannot speak too highly of the part played by the Air Forces in this campaign. The Air Officer Commanding remained with me throughout the operation, thus facilitating the requests for immediate air assistance. From the commencement of the campaign our Air Forces, under Air Commodore W. Sowrey, D.F.C., A.F.C., ably assisted by Brigadier H. Daniel, M.C., A.F.C., S.A.A.F., established complete air superiority, with the result that the advance of the troops was little interfered with by enemy air activity, and after the crossing of the Giuba we moved wholly by day. Bombing and "ground strafing" by the enemy was sporadic and normally ineffective. During the later stages of the campaign a support group consisting of bombers, fighters, and A.C. machines was formed, and its Air Force Commander with his own communications advanced with the Commander of the leading troops. The value of this arrangement from the army point of view cannot be overstressed. Air support for the forward troops of the nature called for by the situation, was "on tap," and engendered the greatest confidence amongst both commanders and men.

140. To the pilots of the S.A.A.F. fighters, who destroyed such a number of enemy machines on the ground, and to the S.A.A.F. bombers which created such havoc amongst the retreating enemy, must be ascribed their great share of the credit for the successes gained. The invaluable work of the S.A.A.F. Army Co-operation Squadrons was carried out with daring and efficiency. Without the continuous employment of the Communication Flight, R.A.F., control of the operations spread over such a large area of country would have been impossible. I would like to mention the ground staff which, in spite of lack of spares and facilities generally, by dint of unceasing toil kept the maximum number of machines in the air.

The number of enemy aircraft destroyed during the period was 57 against our own losses of 8.

141. Here I must express my great appreciation of the assistance given so freely in every way possible to the Army by His Excellency the Governor of Kenya, Their Excellencies the Governors of Tanganyika, Nyasaland, Northern Rhodesia and Uganda through the East African Governors' Conference, the Government of Southern Rhodesia, and various civil authorities and institutions. All requests that I have had to make from time to time met with immediate response.

142. It is not too much to say that the willing co-operation given to the Army at all times by the Kenya and Uganda Railways and Harbours Administration played a large part in furthering the operations. In particular, their invaluable assistance in the construction and repair of large quantities of military material of various types must be mentioned. To Brigadier General the Hon. Sir Godfrey Rhodes, C.B.E., D.S.O., and the officers and employees of the Administration the Army owes its gratitude.

In addition to this practical help the Kenya and Uganda Railways and Harbours has as part of the common war effort assisted His Majesty's Government by large remissions of financial charges that would normally be due to them for military traffic.

143. A great deal of voluntary work for the benefit of the Army has been undertaken. Subscriptions have been made towards the welfare of, and gifts for, the troops. Ambulances and mobile canteens have been presented, and my Welfare Officers have been greatly assisted by provision of accommodation for officers and other ranks for periods of leave.

144. The Force owes a great debt to Lady Moore who, in addition to many other activities, organised and managed the voluntary Kenya Women's Emergency Organisation which ran the badly-needed canteens in Nairobi, and provided vegetables and other comforts for the forward troops when possible.

145. It would be idle to close this report without reference to the assistance given by the Union of South Africa, without which the campaign could not have been undertaken.

Apart from the fighting troops, I was indebted to the Union for much of the mechanical transport which made the supply of troops over such great distances in front of the railheads and ports possible, and to them also I owed the provision of a large number of special technical units without which operations in the type of terrain covered could not have taken place. It was with remarkable forethought that these units had been formed before the war and furnished with the most modern equipment.

Through the personal interest of Field Marshal Smuts I was at the start able to knit the Force into a whole, and all the many resources which the Union placed at my disposal were pooled for the common good of the whole force. I knew that no appeal to them would go unanswered if it was humanly possible to meet it. The spirit of co-operation extended right down to the lowest ranks, giving me the greatest confidence in the South African troops, a confidence which was fully justified by the achievements of the South African Division and all other South African troops during the campaign.

(Sgd.) A.G. CUNNINGHAM,
Lieutenant General,
General Officer Commanding,
East Africa Force.

6 June 1941

SECOND REPORT ON EAST AFRICA FORCE OPERATIONS COVERING THE PERIOD FROM OCCUPATION OF ADDIS ABEBA ON 6TH APRIL, 1941, TO THE CESSATION OF HOSTILITIES IN THE AREA FOR WHICH EAST AFRICA FORCE WAS RESPONSIBLE. ON 11TH JULY, 1941.

PART I. – INTRODUCTION.

My previous report dealt with the operations carried out by E.A. Force up to the entry of the troops into Addis Abeba on 6th April, 1941.

After this date my immediate responsibilities were both operational and political. It was most desirable to deal the enemy a knock-out blow as soon as possible, but at the same time it was imperative to release as many units and as much transport as possible for Egypt. On the political side it was necessary to place the administration of Ethiopia on a firm base, to re-establish the Emperor, and to lay the foundations of an Ethiopian administration so that full use of Ethiopian military resources could be made after the shortest time, with the eventual object of releasing more of my troops. The pacification of the occupied territories and particularly of the eastern border of British Somaliland where there had been considerable looting of cattle and rape was also imperative.

2. After the fall of Addis Abeba, Asmara and Massawa, the enemy withdrew into three centres or "ridotti" and into the province of Galla-Sidamo. The centres were Dessie, Amba Alagi and Gondar, whereas in the Galla-Sidamo his main forces of approximately 40,000 infantry and militia with about 200 guns, were in

three groups covering an area of about 400 by 300 miles, one group in the Uaddara – Alghe – Sciasciamanna – Soddu area, one in the Gimma area and one in the Lechemti area. The Civil Government had gone to Gimma, but the Viceroy himself went to Dessie.

3. The situation of my own troops was as follows: (H.Q.) 1st S.A. Division and 5th S.A. Infantry Brigade were in process of being transported to Egypt. 2nd S.A. Infantry Brigade had also been offered to Middle East and were at or near Berbera waiting for ships to take them north.

11th (A) Division, consisting of 1st S.A. Brigade, 22nd E.A. Brigade (less one battalion on the L. of C.) and 23rd Nigerian Brigade, were at Adama and Addis Abeba.

12th (A) Division were attacking northwards, from Iavello with 21st E.A. Brigade. One Battalion 24th G.C. Brigade was garrisoning Neghelli and the remainder of the Brigade were employed in restoring order in southern Italian Somaliland. 25th E.A. Brigade, also under this division, was advancing towards Maji.

4. After the fall of Addis Abeba I felt my best chance of a speedy liquidation of the enemy in the south was to advance on Gimma, the seat of Government for Iea, and I commenced operations to this end. Before these had developed I received a message from the C.-in-C. to the effect that it was essential that the road from Addis Abeba north to Asmara should be opened as soon as possible so as to allow passage of troops to Egypt via Massawa, or Port Sudan, and he wished me to attack Dessie which, was 250 miles north of Addis Abeba. I therefore instructed Commander 11th (A) Division to undertake this task with, 1st S.A. Brigade Group with the idea that they should fight their way northwards and eventually embark from Massawa or Port Sudan, for Egypt. This Brigade Group commenced their advance from Addis Abeba on 13th April. I informed C.-in-C. Middle East that I felt I could not clear the road northwards of Dessie with my own resources, and asked that the Sudan forces should attack Amba Alagi which was the only important remaining defended position on the road. In due course I received notification that the Sudan Forces would carry out this attack but not until 3rd May.

5. It was now apparent to me that I had not enough troops to carry out my first intention of both advancing on Gimma and, by pressure from both divisions advancing north and south, clearing the enemy out of the area of the Great Lakes south of Addis Abeba. I considered that of the two objectives, if only one were to be carried out, the latter was the more important.

The troops at Sciasciamanna were a constant threat to my L. of C. at Moggio and Adama, and it would be a great advantage to me also to have a through road via Neghelli from Kenya. I therefore ordered 11th (A) Division to concentrate on attacking Sciasciamanna, and 12th (A) Division to advance on Dalle and Hula.

For this latter purpose I relieved the Commander and two battalions of 24th G.C. Brigade, who were restoring order in Italian Somaliland, by garrison battalions, and on 16th April sent them to 12th (A) Division.

The account of the action of 1st S.A. Brigade on Dessie and the operations of 11th and 12th (A) Divisions are given in paras. 54 to 62.

6. During the whole period after passing Harrar my commanders were receiving continual requests from civilians in outlying districts all round Addis Abeba and along the lines of communication to rescue them from the threats, either real or imaginary, of attack by Ethiopians. The answering of these calls for assistance was hampering the real effort of the fighting troops, and I felt the time had come to make another approach to H.R.H. Duc D'Aosta and to tell him that I could no longer be responsible for any civilians not in our hands. Therefore on 9th April I telegraphed to General Wavell asking him if I could make an approach on these lines, and received permission from him to do so by return.

I thereupon had the following message dropped from the air at both Gimma and Dessie.

"To His Royal Highness Amedeo of Savoia, Viceroy of Ethiopia, Duke of Aosta or to his representative of the Supreme Command, from General Cunningham, Commanding British Forces in East Africa.

"In view of present military situation have further communication to make to Supreme Command on the subject of the safety of Italian women and children in Ethiopia which is now precarious. If in the interests of Italian civilians the Supreme Command wishes to receive this communication arrangements will be made as before for a representative to land by aeroplane on Chinile aerodrome between the hours of 9 and 10 returning betwen 2 and 3 on the 14th or 15th April."

7. In due course an Italian aeroplane landed at Diredaua satellite aerodrome between 0900 and 1000 hours on 15th April. I met the envoy myself and explained the situation to him verbally, namely that all the Rases who had worked with the Italians had submitted to the Emperor and Ethiopians everywhere were flocking to his standard; moreover the whole country was swarming with armed deserters from the Italian army who were turning into marauding bands, which were attacking Italian civilians and property; if I were to answer all requests for protection which I was getting, military operations would be hampered, and that neither myself nor my Commanders would be fulfilling our military duty of waging war against the Italians to the utmost degree; only on one condition could we accept any responsibility for civilians not in our hands and that was the unconditional laying down of arms, when we would be in a position to undertake the protection, feeding and evacuation of Italian nationals. The envoy asked me to confirm that we would look after the civilians already in our hands. I said I would to the best of my power, but took the opportunity of impressing upon him that incidents such as shooting of Abyssinians in Addis Abeba by Italian police

made my task extremely difficult. I gave the envoy until 1000 hours on 17th April to reply. On that day an aeroplane again landed at the same aerodrome with a message to the effect that, in view of the importance of the proposals and the grave responsibilities they carried, they would have to be referred to Rome. Furthermore they were required in writing. I thereupon sent the following message

"In the interests of humanity, and in view of the perilous military situation in which the Italians in Ethiopia are now placed, I am authorised by the Commander-in-Chief, Middle East, to send the following message:-

"Unless the Italian troops in Italian East Africa lay down their arms, no responsibility for protecting and succouring Italian nationals can be accepted except in places already occupied by forces under British Military command.

"It is the duty of the British Military Commanders, with all the forces at their disposal, to prosecute the war against the Italian army with the utmost vigour, and nothing will be allowed to interfere with this object as long as fighting continues.

"A reply may be sent on 9700 K/cs British call YNC, Italian call YNI, between the hours of 0515 and 0815 GMT, and 1215 and 1515 hours GMT up to inclusive 20th April."

That very morning the BBC made an announcement to the effect that H.R.H. Duc D'Aosta had sent an envoy over to ask for peace terms. It was quite clear to me that such a premature announcement, which was in fact an iniquitous mis-representation of the real facts, could only result in prejudicing any chance there was of getting the Duc D'Aosta to agree to the terms. Up to that time his attitude, as shown through his envoys, had been courteous and displayed a willingness to listen. The announcement could only have the effect of stiffening him, more particularly as it would prejudice him in the eyes of the Fascist Chiefs with whom he was reported already to be on bad terms.

On 20th April I received the reply given in full below.

"With reference to your letter do not take into consideration your proposals of military character Stop The responsibility concerning white population passes on to you when your troops or natives armed ordered by your officers or whoever under your orders occupy the places in which the white population is.
di Savoia."

8. In order to understand the background against which operations by my troops were being undertaken, it is necessary here to explain the activities of the Ethiopian patriots. The Emperor, by his presence in the Gojjam, had rallied most of the leaders in that province to his cause. The notable exception was Ras Hailu, who had been working in co-operation with the Italian forces in Debra Marcos. When forces under the Kaid occupied this place and the submission of Ras Hailu to the Emperor had been obtained, the Patriot movement grew in momentum

and it became possible to direct forces to specific tasks under instructions from the Emperor.

On the arrival of the Emperor at Addis Abeba on 5th May he re-established personal contact with the leaders from other provinces and fresh impetus was given to the movement in different parts of the country.

On the same day, all irregular troops which had entered Ethiopia from the Sudan came under my command, except for certain Sudanese units, which were gradually being withdrawn to the North.

9. In the Gojjam it had been found that the formation of "operational centres" was a good method of enlisting and directing patriot activities. The "Operational centre" consisted of a British Officer and four or more B N.C.Os., who formed the nucleus, and to which were attached up to 70 selected Ethiopians. They were well armed, carried explosives and money, and, when possible, W/T sets.

Owing to the rapidity of the enemy withdrawal in the Gojjam, and commitments in connection with the raising of units for the Emperor's entry into Addis Abeba, only a few centres had been formed. The general policy decided upon, therefore, was for each Division to direct Patriot activities in their own areas, a special Staff Officer being attached to each Division for that purpose, and I arranged with the Emperor that he would instruct selected Ethiopian leaders to provide the desired numbers of Ethiopian soldiery. Officers to lead the Patriots were found from various sources as, by experience, it had been found that patriot activities proved most successful under the general direction, and in some cases, the personal leadership, of selected British Officers, though the men remained under the immediate control of their own leaders. With the progress of the campaign, certain patriot leaders displayed, more than once, powers of leadership which may well be employed in the future Ethiopian army.

This policy proved successful in the north and central Abyssinia, but was not so satisfactory in the area north of Neghelli and Iavello owing to the generally disturbed state of this district, the Amhara – Galla problem, and the lack of outstanding leaders.

10. The Patriots proved most successful in harassing enemy lines of communication and in besieging isolated enemy garrisons. By carrying out these tasks, these Ethiopian forces caused the Italians considerable alarm and anxiety and lowered their morale. By this means they contained large numbers of the enemy away from the main scene of the operations.

Patriots have also excelled in following up an enemy withdrawal. This was very evident in the final phase after the crossing of the Omo, when Patriot forces operated ahead of our regular forces. In this respect their familiarity with, and speed across, country was used to the best advantage.

It was found that Patriots would fight with great courage and take great risks in certain circumstances, especially when following up a beaten enemy, but, as a rule, they were unsuccessful in direct attacks on fortified positions and disliked such actions. They were apt to be unreliable and difficult to control at night, and it was best to leave it to them to conduct such operations themselves. Finally, it was never safe to assume that a force of Patriots would take the field on two consecutive days at the same strength owing to food difficulties internal feuds and rivalries.

Administration.

11. Up to the capture of Addis Abeba the troops in the northern sector were being maintained by road from Berbera, a distance of 550 miles, and in the southern sector from Mogadiscio. The roads in the south were however rapidly deteriorating by reason of the rain, and the bridges at Dolo and Lugh Ferrandi were precarious on account of floods. It was therefore decided to maintain the western portion of the Southern Sector from a railhead at Nanyuki in Kenya, in spite of the very long road L of C.

All the roads north from Mogadiscio were in a very bad way through wash-outs and mud, but it was still just possible to get a few wheeled vehicles through from Kenya.

12. In the Northern Sector every effort was made to get the railway from Diredaua into action. There were plenty of rolling stock and engines in Addis Abeba, but with the blowing of the Auasc Bridge these were cut off from the Diredaua section. The Auasc Railway Bridge had been of special girder construction borne on high piers, the track being 120 ft. above the water. Its replacement was impossible for a very long time. Work on a low level diversion was commenced though it was not expected to be ready until 10th July. Between Addis Abeba and Diredaua there were no other major demolitions on the railway. Six engines had been left in Diredaua but all had parts taken away or some other form of demolition carried out on them. Furthermore the machinery in the well fitted machine-shops had been treated in the same way. Nothing daunted, 38 Railway Construction Company set to work, and on 7th April had the first train running from Diredaua to the Auasc with 100 tons of supplies and stores. By getting spares from Addis Abeba and making others, by the end of May they had all six engines running at Diredaua and were able to run two trains a day to the Auasc. Here a road link had to be introduced to transport the stores to the other side of the river.

13. The disabilities of Berbera as a port were a cause of constant concern, and it was not before the end of May that a start could be made to build up a reserve. Up to that time the forces in the Northern Sector had been living hand to mouth. Meanwhile their ration strength had been steadily increasing, as had their petrol consumption. The latter had risen by the end of June to 45,000 gallons a day.

14. By the beginning of July some 30,000 prisoners had been evacuated, a matter of considerable intricacy in view of the slender transportation resources.

This evacuation entailed the formation of four staging camps between Addis Abeba and Berbera whence they were evacuated by sea to Mombasa as shipping became available.

In this connection the AOC at Aden rendered great assistance by forming a camp for 2,500 prisoners there. This camp was kept filled from Berbera and emptied by sea to Mombasa as shipping became available at Aden.

This enabled the camp at Berbera periodically to receive additional prisoners and permitted continuous evacuation to take place from the forward areas.

PART II. – OPERATIONS.
A. Operations of 11*th and* 12*th (A) Divisions (6th April – 3rd July,* 1941).
(The Order of Battle of 11th and 12th (A) Divisions at this time is
in Appendix "A".)

15. At the commencement of this period 11th (A) Division had 1st SA Brigade in Addis Abeba, 22nd EA Infantry Brigade with two battalions at Ponte Malcasa south of the Auasc River, and 23rd Nigerian Brigade back at Diredaua.

12th (A) Division had head of 21st EA Brigade at about Soroppa advancing north with great difficulty on account of the rains, 3rd GC Regiment were patrolling north from Neghelli to Uaddara, and also experiencing difficulty due to the weather but not to such a great extent. The 24th GC Brigade less 3rd GC Regiment were clearing up in Italian Somaliland. The important bridges at Dolo, Lugh Ferrandi and Melka Guba were being continually broken by the floods, the latter being the only one by which troops could be sent from one line of advance to the other, i.e., from the Iavello road to the Neghelli road and vice-versa. This was a great handicap as it eventually proved very difficult to send supporting arms from one Brigade Group to the other, a procedure which the shortage of guns etc. made very necessary.

25th EA Brigade (12th (A) Division) were undertaking operations against Maji with the object of handing it over to the Equatorial Corps in the Sudan when captured. It was thought that the capture of Maji would have a stabilising influence on the turbulent tribes of the Ilembe triangle.

16. The enemy Order of Battle south and west of Addis Abeba was as follows:-

Uaddara front	24th Division
Giabassire front	21st Division
Sciasciamanna	25th Division
Gardulla-Soddu	101st Division
Gimma-Bonga	22nd Division
Lechemti} front	{26th Division
Ghimbi }	{23rd Division

It should however be remembered that many of the units had been heavily engaged, and no reinforcements were available. The divisions were therefore considerably below strength. Nevertheless they were strong in guns (about 200 exclusive of AA), possessed armoured cars, and between 20 and 30 medium and light tanks.

17. My instructions to Commander 11th (A) Division were to attack Gimma as early as possible and to operate southwards from Ponte Malcasa against the tail of the column retreating south through Aselle under General de Simone, who had been commanding the Italian troops since the Giuba. I impressed on Major General Wetherall the importance of ensuring proper protection of Adama and Moggio on his L or C, which would have been very vulnerable to attack by a determined enemy.

A battalion of 1st SA Brigade with supporting arms was immediately despatched down the Gimma road, and steps were taken to move up 23rd Nigerian Brigade to relieve the remainder of 1st SA Brigade so that they could carry out the attack on Gimma.

18. On 11th April I received a cable from C-in-C, which has already been mentioned, to the effect that he considered it imperative for me to attack Dessie and open up the road north to the Sudan. I therefore countermanded the orders for the attack on Gimma and directed 1st SA Brigade Group on Dessie.

23rd Nigerian Brigade relieved 1st SA Brigade who had two battalions in Addis Abeba, and one on the Omo River where the Gimma road crossed it. The bridge at this point had been blown by the enemy.

1st SA Brigade commenced their march on Dessie on 13th April. The account of the operations carried out by the Brigade Group is given later.

19. It was now apparent that with only two brigades in the Adama – Addis Abeba area I could not expect to accomplish any great success against the enemy in Gallo-Sidamo from the north. It was known that a considerable force of the enemy in the Quoziam area on the Blue Nile had been cut off by our occupation of Addis Abeba, and west of that town, at Lechemti and Ghimbi, strong forces existed. Although the presence of the large number of Italian civilians in Addis Abeba was a cogent form of protection in itself, I could not leave the Fiche and Lechemti roads entirely open. It was therefore necessary for both local defence and internal security reasons to keep two battalions in Addis Abeba. 11th (A) Division was left therefore with only three battalions for operations southwards. One of these battalions, 3rd Nigerian Regiment, was located on the Omo with instructions to rouse local patriots and direct them against the rear of the Abalti position on the other side of the Omo River. 22nd EA Brigade with the remaining two battalions advanced southwards from Ponte Malcasa on Aselle and Cofole with the object of maintaining maximum pressure on Sciasciamanna in conjunction with the advance of 12th (A) Division northwards. My object at this time was to effect a junction of the two divisions on the Addis Abeba – Dalle road.

On 16th April the 22nd Brigade Group advanced successfully to Bocoggi taking some prisoners on the way, but here found that the road ceased to exist. As rain had already commenced falling it was decided to abandon the Aselle road and transfer the 22nd Brigade effort to the Moggo – Adamitullo road where it was hoped the going was better. Steps were taken to repair the bridges blown by the enemy on that road, and by 24th April 22nd Brigade were advancing south of Ponte Machi.

20. About this time I received information that a mechanised enemy column of a brigade group with tanks, armoured cars and six batteries, was assembling near Sciasciamanna under General Bertello with the avowed intention of attacking the L. of C. at Noggio. Considerable M.T. movement at night with headlights had been seen on the roads, and heavy A.A. fire was encountered by our aeroplanes whenever they approached the woods north of Sciasciamanna. These woods were bombed by the Air Force with what was known afterwards as considerable effect. It was considered advisable until the situation was cleared up to arrest the southward movement and be ready to occupy a defensive position between the Lakes Lagana and Algato. Nevertheless a small column operating west of Lake Algato towards an enemy position at Ficche continued with its attack, captured the position, and took 8 guns and 100 prisoners. It seems probable that this small attack upset the enemy's plans for counterattack as the only northward movement of the enemy appeared to be carried out by a few tanks which advanced up the road from Sciasciamanna as far as the Auada River and then returned; no counter-attack materialised.

21. Meanwhile 12th (A) Division had concentrated the whole Gold Coast Brigade on the Neghelli road and both this Brigade and 21st Brigade on the Iavello road were advancing slowly northwards. Two positions on these roads at Uaddara and Giabassire respectively had been responsible for holding up the Italians in the Abyssinian war for nearly a year. Both these positions had been prepared by the Italians a long time previously and were strongly held and fortified.

22. 24th Gold Coast Brigade commenced their initial moves for the attack on the Uaddara position on 19th April and finally captured it on 10th May. The country in that area is precipitous, intersected with deep ravines and covered with impenetrable forest. During the period up to 2nd May extensive patrolling was carried out in the thick bush to determine the enemy's strength and to locate his flanks. The enemy's position was found to extend to a depth of 5 miles on either side of the road. The nature of the country almost entirely precluded the use of A.F.V.s. The position was held mainly by Eritreans who, as it proved, had apparently not been shaken as were the other Colonial troops. The conditions of wet and mud were appalling and the Gold Coast troops were feeling the cold. In spite of all these difficulties the attack was begun on 3rd May when the 2nd Gold Coast Regiment made a wide flanking march cutting their way through the belts of thick forest with their pangas. On 4th May 1st Gold Coast Regiment supported by artillery attacked two prominent hills which were strongly held by the enemy. A.F.V.s were sent up an old Abyssinian track to support the flank attack by 2nd Gold Coast Regiment but could make little progress. Later in the afternoon 2nd Gold Coast Regiment came in on the enemy's left rear and by 5th May had cut the road behind the position. The enemy however still held his main

positions and it was not until 10th May that he was finally driven from them on the two hills. In capturing this very formidable position the determination shown by the Gold Coast troops sustained the fighting reputation which they had gained in the first phase of the campaign.

23. During this period 21st E.A. Brigade on the Iavallo road was advancing towards Giabassire. On 5th and 6th May they attacked with success the forward position at Budagamo and continued their march under almost impossible road conditions.

It must be remembered that the whole of the operations of 12th (A) Division round Neghelli and Iavello were being carried out during the period of the heavy rains of which the peak period in that area is the month of April. As the advance of 12th (A) Division proceeded the rains proceeded with them; the peak period in the Addis Abeba area is August, and month by month the volume of rain in this area was increasing while decreasing in the south. I had been told before leaving Kenya that no operations could be carried out in Southern Abyssinia after March. Yet operations were in fact undertaken right up to the present time (July). It would be idle to pretend that the rains were not the greatest hindrance, but the conditions were conquered by grit and determination, and in this connection I particularly wish to mention the march of 21st E.A. Brigade over practically non-existent roads. Brigadier A. McD. Ritchie, D.S.O., was never daunted and his cheerful tenacity was echoed right through his Brigade. To the columns in the north I had added caterpillar tractors, which had been captured, carried in lorries, to salvage vehicles which got stuck, but I was unable at that period to get them round to 12th (A) Division.

24. About this time I received a wire from the C.-in-C. suggesting that operations should now cease against the Italians left in Italian East Africa as there appeared little chance of liquidating them before the heavy rains. I was asked for minimum garrisons on the defensive, and told to be prepared to release everything else for Egypt. I replied to the effect that I was extremely anxious to clear the Neghelli – Addis Abeba road of the enemy so as to remove all threat to Moggio and Adama, which I considered very vulnerable points on my L. of C., and to get a through road to Kenya. That if General Wavell wished it I would put a term to the operations. The C.-in-C. wired back I could have until the end of May.

25. For the whole of this period 2nd S.A. Brigade had been waiting for shipping and I had very regretfully been unable to use these troops. I now pressed Middle East to give me the earliest date by which shipping could arrive, to which question 3rd June was given in reply. On 21st and 29th April respectively I therefore decided to place 1st Natal Mounted Rifles and 1st Field Force Battalion from this brigade under General Wetherall with instructions that they would have to be released on 27th May.

26. Meanwhile 12th (A) Division had captured Alghe and the Uaddara position, and Bertello's threat had not materialised, so I instructed General Wetherall to

continue his advance southwards, capture Sciasciamanna, and join forces with the 12th (A) Division. If this attack was successful there appeared every prospect that the considerable enemy forces on the two roads leading south from Dalle would be trapped.

His plan was to advance with one battalion west of the lakes, by a track running through Bubissa to cut the Sciasciamanna – Soddu road, while another column of two battalions advanced direct on Sciasciamanna across the Auada and Dadaba Rivers.

27. The Air Force had nullified the enemy air opposition after attacks on Dessie aerodrome on 6th April and on Gimma aerodrome on 10th April, and as the aircraft were therefore available I arranged with Air Headquarters for the formation of a close support group in order to give the divisional Commanders additional air support for their operations. During the advance of the 1st S.A. Brigade towards Dessie 4 Hartbees and 4 Gladiator aircraft had been put under the operational command of the Brigade Commander and the value of their close support had been proved. Accordingly a Close Support Group consisting of two flights of Battle bombers, one flight of Gladiator fighters and two flights of Hartbees co-operation aircraft, was formed on 20th May and put under command of 11th (A) Division.

This arrangement worked with considerable success as the close support group could be stationed on an advanced landing ground in close proximity to the advanced divisional headquarters. Considerable time saving was effected by having the bombers and fighters standing by ready to take-off to attack targets located by the army co-operation aircraft. With the remnants of the Italian divisions attempting to escape across country the quick results thereby achieved were invaluable, especially in the way in which offensive action could be taken against any enemy A.F.V.s located either from the air or by the ground troops.

The heavy bombers and Hurricanes were stationed in Addis Abeba during the whole period of these operations and in spite of very bad flying conditions they were used extensively to attack targets farther afield and to drop pamphlets.

28. On 11th May the 5th K.A.R. advancing west of the lakes captured Bubissa, taking some prisoners and guns, but were counter-attacked by six medium and three light tanks and a Banda group. The C.O. decided that he would be unable to hold the position and conducted an orderly withdrawal behind the Gidu. The armoured cars covered the withdrawal and acted as a decoy to the enemy tanks. Unfortunately three armoured cars got bogged following the infantry over soft ground and had to be abandoned after all weapons, etc., had been removed. (In point of fact all these armoured cars were eventually recaptured.) Meanwhile on 13th May 1 N.M.R. attacked the positions covering Sciasciamanna. This energetic attack was completely successful and resulted in the capture of 800 prisoners, two batteries of artillery and nine tanks. The advance was continued to Sciasciamanna which was entered on 14th May, and to Dalle which was occupied

on 17th May. A further 650 prisoners, some guns and armoured cars were captured.

29. The enemy now appeared to be in a state of great confusion. Their 21st Colonial Division was on the road between Alghe and Dilla, and the 24th Colonial Division between Afrara and Hula, and it seemed that with the occupation of Dalle these two divisions were completely cut off. Our patrols from 12th (A) Division operating northwards towards the very strong Giabassire position north of Alghe found it abandoned, with wounded and heavy guns left behind.

30. I therefore arranged to meet Commanders of 11th and 12th (A) Divisions at the former's Headquarters near Alatu on 17th May to concert further plans.

At this time I was of opinion that if I occupied Gimma very little more resistance would be made in the Galla Sidamo. Amba Alagi had fallen and the Viceroy was captured. The Supreme Command had been taken over by General Gazzera who had his Headquarters at Gimma which was also the seat of Government. The women and children there, amounting to 2,000, would no doubt be an added embarrassment but were not a very great addition to the large numbers already in our hands. It appeared to me that the great military and political advantages to be gained from the final liquidation of the enemy in Italian East Africa far outweighed any embarrassment the added civilians and prisoners would give us. Finally there appeared every likelihood of cutting off or destroying four of the six enemy divisions left in the Galla Sidamo by the occupation of Soddu, and therefore Gimma could not be very strongly defended. I placed this point of view before the C.-in-C. concurred.

It was my plan therefore to stage an attack towards Gimma as soon as possible. In order, however, to make the Neghelli – Addis Abeba road absolutely secure, and to complete the cutting off of the enemy 21st, 24th and 101st Divisions, I considered that Soddu should be my immediate objective. This place stood at important road junctions which would preclude any enemy movement either north or east against my forces except from Gimma itself.

I had hoped to carry out this attack with a formation of 12th (A) Division and to transfer the pressure of 11th (A) Division from the Sciasciamanna area to the all-weather Addis Abeba – Gimma road where 3rd Nigeria Regiment was holding the left bank of the River Omo, so that Gimma could be attacked from two directions. 12th (A) Division had however been experiencing very heavy rain all over their L. of C., and the advances they had been making against very strong positions had of necessity been slow. I could not count on getting them up quickly. The enemy were clearly straining every nerve to form a defensive front east of Soddu, and I considered therefore that I must attack them as soon as possible and not give them time to do so. I therefore ordered 11th (A) Division to advance on Soddu as soon as possible. I told General Godwin Austen, however, that he was to make every effort to concentrate one of his brigades as soon as possible with the object of relieving 11th (A) Division, either at Soddu if it was captured, or to continue the attack against it if it were not. It was my intention only to leave one brigade of 12th (A) Division and all the supporting arms in the north and to withdraw the remainder to the Kenya frontier so as to ease the supply situation, and release more transport for Egypt.

31. The enemy 21st and 24th Divisions were still continuing their weary march northwards to Dalle which, it will be recalled, was in our hands. The only road by which withdrawal in M.T. could take place branched left from the Uondo – Sciasciamanna road some 10 miles north of Dalle. If this road could not be opened up the only alternative was for these divisions to abandon their equipment and take to mule tracks. Contact had been made with the rear of 24th Division by the 1st Gold Coast Regiment which was leading the eastern column of 12th (A) Division, and the Brigade Commander and the greater part of the rear Brigade was captured at Hula. The 21st E.A. Brigade had now reached a stage where it was impossible to advance further with M.T. owing to the state of the roads. 1/2 K.A.R. was therefore placed on an improvised pack basis and continued the advance northwards on foot with the object of driving 21st Division into the hands of the South Africans at Dalle. The remaining two battalions of 21st Brigade returned to Iavello.

32. General Gazzera was issuing a constant flow of orders to 21st and 24th Divisions to attack our forces at Dalle who, he thought, were in very small numbers. He was obviously quite out of the picture as to the real state of affairs. Desertions of Colonial troops were becoming wholesale, and it was only a short time after this that, having become aware of the true state of affairs, Gazzera issued an order that only nationals were to continue the retreat, and all Colonial troops were to be abandoned. I cannot say I was enamoured of the internal security prospect with which I was almost certainly to be faced in the future as the result of this order.

33. 11th (A) Division had now available the 22nd E.A. Brigade in which 1/1 K.A.R. (who were still on L. of C. duties north of Mogadiscio) were replaced by 2nd Nigeria Regiment from Addis Abeba. 1 N.M.R. and 1 F.F. Battalion were directly under command of the division.

The Commander 11th (A) Division therefore decided to form a defensive flank in the Dalle area with the two South African battalions, and to use the 22nd E.A. Brigade to carry out the attack on Soddu. The enemy were known to be organising a defensive position west of the River Billate, which was crossed by the Soddu road at Colito.

34. On 19th May Colito was captured by the 2nd Nigeria Regiment and a bridgehead established by 1/6 K.A.R. The bridge was not completed until 21st May but the attack on the main position was carried out by 1/6 K.A.R. on 19th May. This action was distinguished by the way in which an enemy counter-attack, which was supported by M.II medium and light tanks and armoured cars, was broken up before it properly materialised. In spite of having no anti-tank guns and only anti-tank rifles on a very reduced scale, the native troops destroyed the counter-attack

with great loss to the enemy, and as a result of a most dashing charge, captured a number of prisoners and tanks. One medium tank was captured single-handed by a British N.C.O. who climbed on to the back of the tank, opened the top of the turret and killed all the crew with his revolver. The other tanks then turned tail, presumably because, as it was afterwards discovered, their commander was killed in the captured tank.

35. As a result of this action the defence of Soddu crumbled and with only slight opposition the town was occupied on 22nd May. The delay in occupation was due to the time taken in repairing the demolitions left behind by the enemy.

Between the capture of Soddu and the start of the Battle of the Omo, by the actions of Ficche and Sciasciamanna, 12,852 prisoners, 42 guns, 23 A.F.Vs, including 5 Medium Tanks, were captured, including the Divisional Commanders and the greater part of 21st, 25th and 101st Divisions. General Pralormo, with the remnants of 24th Division, took to the bush, having abandoned most of his equipment.

36. It was now necessary for me to make a plan for further operations towards Gimma, and I ordered the Commanders of 11th and 12th (A) Divisions to meet me at Alatu on 24th May. Here Commander 12th (A) Division reported to me the very great difficulties he was encountering due to the rain and the roads. It was quite apparent that I would be unable to use either of his formations to attack towards Gimma from the south as I had hoped to do. I found at the most that the 24th G. C. Brigade of the 12th (A) Division could concentrate in the Dalle – Soddu area soon and could relieve 11th (A) Division of all garrison duties, and protect its rear. This would release the two South African battalions to proceed to Berbera for embarkation, and would free the whole of 22nd E.A. Brigade for the further advance. In order to enable an advance also to be made on the Addis Abeba – Gimma road, where the enemy were holding a position at Abalti southwest of the Omo, I arranged to transfer the Nigerian Brigade to this front. To do this I relieved the 1st Nigeria Regiment in Addis Abeba by garrison troops and moved up 1/1 K.A.R. which had in the meantime been similarly relieved. As time was all important so that the enemy could not strengthen his defences on the unexpected line of attack from the south, I was unable to sort out the battalions and return 2nd Nigerian Regiment which was with 22nd E.A. Brigade, back to the Nigerian Brigade. I therefore sent 1/1 K.A.R. to the Nigerian Brigade who were to attack Abalti.

37. It should be noted here that administrative limitations in connection with transport and the port of Berbera, precluded the use of more than two brigades for operations beyond Addis Abeba. The L. of C. from Kenya through Iavello and Neghelli was in a most precarious condition due to rain, and I could not hope for any easing of the administrative problem from this direction.

38. I impressed on General Wetherall the necessity for speed and that the time factor must take precedence of all other considerations. The period of heavy rains

was getting nearer and I was most anxious to liquidate the enemy in the Galla Sidamo before they took place.

The new line of advance towards Gimma opened by the capture of Soddu crossed the River Omo near Sciola. This river was a considerable obstacle, 450 feet wide, and required special bridging equipment. Provision had been made for this equipment for the crossing at Abalti on the Addis Abeba – Gimma road but there was insufficient available forward of Berbera for the second crossing at Sciola. It should be remembered that due to the long road link on the L. of C. from Berbera to Diredaua, priorities for stores and material had to be worked out very carefully so that the most efficient use could be made of the limited transport available. Two crossings of the Omo had not been foreseen and therefore the transport to move more bridging forward had not been made available. This fact unfortunately caused some delay in attacking the enemy position on the Omo south of Gimma. The number of bridges which had been constructed up to this time was 70 and captured or locally made material was beginning to run short.

39. My intention now was for whichever of the two brigades could get across the Omo first to advance and attack the enemy facing the other brigade in the rear. E.g. if 22nd E.A. Brigade succeeded in reaching the Gimma – Addis Abeba road first they were to turn right towards Addis Abeba and not left on Gimma.

At this time, most unfortunately, the Omo came down in flood. Although it was a wide river, in normal times it could be waded in many places, but with the floods it was 6 feet deep with a 6 knot current. This again delayed matters considerably.

So both the Nigerian Brigade at Abalti in the north, and the 22nd Brigade south of Gimma were faced with a considerable problem. In the south the enemy were holding, on both banks, the foot-bridge which crossed the river where the road met it. A gallant attempt was made to rush this foot bridge but was repulsed with some loss of life. The Brigadier therefore decided on crossing with the few assault boats available, some three miles south of the footbridge.

On 2nd June three platoons of 5th K.A.R. were able to get across, and to establish a precarious bridgehead. In spite of heavy shelling and the fact that no means existed for rapid reinforcement, this party held on for three days during the whole slow process of getting 5th K.A.R. across the river in the few assault boats available. During this period a platoon of 1/3 K.A.R. (MGs) succeeded in working their way forward and in bringing the enemy 105 mm. gun batteries under M.G. fire. Great difficulties were being experienced in the construction of pontoon ferries and no vehicles had been got over.

In spite of this and the fact that they were out of range of artillery support, 5th K.A.R. executed a wide turning movement northwards, and succeeded, though greatly exhausted, in reaching the road north of the foot-bridge. The enemy Blackshirts counter-attacked several times during this operation, but were beaten off with great loss.

To attack with one battalion without A.F.Vs. or transport, with the river at its back and no means of rapid reinforcement or artillery support, was without doubt taking a considerable risk. Brigadier Fowkes had, however, already been delayed by demolitions and mud and, recognising the need for speed, gladly and justifiably took the risk and met with great success.

40. In the north at the Abalti crossing it had been intended to cross on the night of 1st June. Our troops had been on this position for some time, much reconnaissance had been carried out and thought given to the plans for crossing the river. Even without the flooded river the operation was difficult. All possible places where bridging could be carried out were under direct observation of the enemy from the ground rising up to the Abalti escarpment 9,000 yards back, as were the roads leading up to it. Off the roads the country was broken and steep and could only be covered on foot.

It was planned to cross the river at a point facing the broken and very steep ground south of the road as all information was to the effect that the enemy did not consider this was feasible and had no important defences in that area. A few nights previously a rope was put across the river, and on the night of 30/31st May the 3rd Nigeria Regiment moved into concealment in the bush near where the rope was in position. Here again it would not be possible to put vehicles across for some time and all troops going over had to be self-contained until a ferry could be built. It was estimated that the bridge would take six days to build. (It eventually took 18 days.)

The first attempt to cross was made on the night of 31st May/1st June but unfortunately the current at the place chosen was found to be too swift and the attempt proved abortive. After further reconnaissance another spot was chosen and the attempt made again on the night of 4/5th June. On this occasion the attack was completely successful. 3rd Nigeria Regiment advanced on foot some 2,000 yards and then swung right cutting off the enemy's defences on the river. 1/1 K.A.R., crossing at the same place, advanced straight on and were able to reach the spot where the road climbed the escarpment cliff 9,000 yards back, located the wires for two major demolitions, cut them, and proceeded to take Abalti. The enemy, sure of our inability to cross the river, were completely taken by surprise. A F.O.O. was captured asleep in his O.P. and staff cars containing officers from Gimma coming forward to ascertain the situation, motored unwittingly into the middle of our troops. In the two crossings of the Omo 3,900 prisoners and 20 guns were taken.

41. It was now apparent that the enemy forces east and south of Gimma had been totally defeated and that Gimma could be taken at any time. The defeated enemy were withdrawing north of Gimma. South-west of Gimma at Bonga was still the 22nd Division although I had information that this Division was withdrawing to Bedelle across country. North of Gimma the 23rd and 26th Divisions were in the Lechemti – Ghimbi area under De Simone. The Lechemti area had been considerably harassed by patriots and there were indications that De Simone thought

he was too strung-out and was contemplating withdrawal behind the Didessa at Ghimbi and Bedelle. There was a good motorable road from Addis Abeba to Lechemti. Furthermore the occupation of Gimma at this stage would cause me some embarrassment in view of the large number of civilians there. I therefore decided to transfer the main weight of attack as soon as possible along the Lechemti road, with the object of once more cutting the enemy forces in two and dealing with each portion separately. It was essential to get 22nd Brigade on to a good line of supply as soon as possible. The road through Sciasciamanna and Soddu was in an execrable state and with the increasing rain it was feared might become impassable altogether. Moreover permanent bridging of the Omo on this road would have been extremely difficult. 22nd E.A. Brigade was therefore directed on to the Gimma – Addis Abeba road to the point where it crossed the Little Ghibbie so that its line of supply could be down this road, and 23rd Brigade was ordered to send light forces forward from Abalti to clear the road as far as this point and establish contact with the 22nd E.A. Brigade. Meanwhile the process of transferring 23rd Nigerian Brigade and the bulk of the artillery to the Lechemti Road was begun, and by the evening of 9th June 3rd Nigeria Regiment had arrived at Ambo being followed by the remainder of the brigade and the artillery.

42. I had been quite certain that as soon as we came within measurable distance of Gimma the enemy would make an attempt to hand the town over to us and was equally certain I would not take it over unless and until I required it for the continuance of operations against the enemy forces. I therefore prepared a message for General Gazzera, and held it ready either to drop from the air or hand over to any white flag which might appear. Sure enough, on 9th June Gimma wireless station broadcast a request for us to listen in, and sent over a message declaring Gimma an open town and saying that the town would be handed over to us and representatives would be sent out to meet our forces on the Little Ghibbie. I merely replied that I would hand the representative a message. This was done on 10th June when the following message was handed over.

"To His Excellency General Gazzera.
From Lieut. General Sir Alan Cunningham,
General Officer Commanding East Africa Force.
I have to inform you that until all Italian Forces within reach of my troops lay down their arms, none of the British troops under my command will enter Gimma unless I order them to do so to continue the fight against the Italian armed forces.

In accordance with my previous warning to His Royal Highness di Savoia, I am quite unable to accept any responsibility for the safety of your nationals in Gimma."

Furthermore I instructed 11th (A) Division that until it became an operational necessity, Gimma should only be entered if it appeared that the women and children were in real danger from lawless native elements.

43. Another broadcast message was received from Gimma which is so indicative of the anxious state of mind of the enemy that it is given here in full.

"Italian column commanded by General Pralormo near Kindo on the river Bottego is in desparate condition because attacked by rebels. We beg the English H.Q. to help that column. We will be grateful. Commander of the city of Gimma General Bisson Milio."

General Pralormo was the commander of 24th Division, the elements of which took to the bush after being cut off at Dalle. He had been contacted on the Omo south of Soddu by a few of our armoured cars and called on to surrender. This he had refused to do as he stated we had insufficient forces. He had subsequently failed to cross the river Omo and was repeatedly attacked by patriots. The Gold Coast Brigade brought him in to Soddu with the remnants of his forces on 17th June.

44. Meanwhile General Bisson who had been left by Gazzera in charge of the Gimma area was in constant touch with Brigadier Fowkes of 22nd E.A. Brigade at the Little Ghibbie. On 14th June I received an answer from Gazzera to my message, in which he stated at considerable length that he had left General Bisson to negotiate and that outrages against the civil population would be the responsibility of the British. To this I replied curtly that there was no military or political advantage to me in the occupation of Gimma for the present, and I accepted no responsibility for the safety of the city. I also told Brigadier Fowkes that I would be satisfied with the surrender of all troops south of Mendi, which was in fact the whole of the Italian Southern Command.

45. Previous to the advance towards Gimma, patriots under the Chief Gerasu Duke with British Officers had been instructed to invest the city. This they had done with great success, but in the process the patriot forces had been swelled to some 12,000, not by true patriots but by many lawless elements who had attached themselves to the force in the hope of loot when the city fell. On 15th June it appeared that Gerasu Duke was not in a position to control this force and Brigadier Fowkes told me he was concerned lest the city should be overrun, which he stated could happen in a few hours, before he could get forces into it to keep order. I therefore asked the Emperor to send down his representatives to divert the patriots to fighting the Italian forces, leaving only sufficient to maintain the pressure on Gimma. On 17th June the Emperor's representatives arrived on the spot, but it was reported to me that they had failed in their task. I now received information that Gazzera, who had proceeded to Bedelle some time previously, had washed his hands of Gimma and was even resenting Bisson's references to him. Furthermore, the advance of the Nigerian Brigade along the Lechemti road was progressing, the enemy rear-guard left east of the Didessa amounting to some 400 white troops had been all either killed or captured, and the attack on the Didessa position would be carried out in a few days time. Also all indications showed that the enemy had given up hope of holding the Didessa and

intended to withdraw all their troops to the Dembidollo – Gore area. I therefore decided that no further advantage was to be gained by remaining outside Gimma, more particularly as it was now necessary to commence an advance northwards through Gimma in conjunction with the operations being carried out against Ghimbi, to prevent, as far as possible, the withdrawal of the enemy forces on the Bedelle – Dembi front. I therefore ordered the occupation of Gimma as part of a general advance northwards through that town. It was occupied without incident by 22nd E.A. Brigade on 21st June.

The total number of prisoners taken in the Gimma area was 12,000 Italians and 3,000 Africans. Generals Scala, Tissi, Bisson and Maynardi and eight Brigade Commanders were among the captured.

46. The enemy situation at this time was that 22nd Division which had been at Bonga and had had orders to go to Dembi on foot, were now diverted to Gore. The 23rd Division was being withdrawn from Mendi to move southwards to the Dembidollo area, and 26th Division had some elements behind the Didessa at Ghimbi and some at Bedelle, but were about to withdraw into the Iubdo area.

47. The situation which now confronted us was that the rains were increasing in intensity and the tracks leading on from the Didessa were extremely unreliable and narrow. On the Lechemti, or main front, one-way traffic had to be instituted for many miles.

48. On the other hand the enemy were gradually being reduced in numbers. A very successful action by the patriots under Fitaurari Misfin resulted in the occupation of Bedelle on 20th June yielding a considerable number of prisoners and much equipment.

49. On 27th June 1/1 K.A.R. attacked Dembi and captured General Nam and 700 prisoners.

West of Gimma General Bertello with a small force gave himself up to 22nd E.A. Brigade on 28th June thus closing his long flight from British Somaliland.

50. There could therefore only remain to General Gazzera some 2,000 nationals and 4,000 Colonial troops. The latter, however, were now so unreliable that there was no need to consider them.

By the end of June it became apparent that the enemy had given up all hope of holding out anywhere except in the Dembidollo area. Gore and Bure were occupied by patriots and Pialorsi with 22nd Division was therefore cut off.

In view of the very few enemy left and the scattered nature of his forces retiring on Dembidollo, I impressed on the Emperor that the greatest chance of reaching a speedy conclusion on the Galla Sidamo front lay with the patriots, and urged him to spur them to greater efforts. As far as my troops were concerned I was sure, if only they could come up to the enemy, no further fighting would be required to cause the enemy to give in.

I was convinced that the forces in Galla Sidamo were on their last legs, my only fear being that they might maroon themselves in the mud and make it impossible for our troops to reach them. My information was to the effect that movement anywhere off the permanent roads, which ended at Lechemti and Gimma, was impossible after the middle of July when it was said that even the villagers shut themselves up in their villages and were unable to move out until September when the heavy rains finished.

51. On 3rd July, however, my anxiety on this score was ended, as General Gazzera broadcast a message to Addis Abeba that he was sending a car-load of delegates down the Dembidollo – Gambela road to negotiate the surrender of all troops in the Galla Sidamo.

52. The only Italians now left in the area for which I was responsible were the very inconsiderable party under Raugei, 600 Italians and some Banda, marooned on the northern borders of French Somaliland. The fiery Danakhils, who inhabited that area and who had hitherto been friendly to him, had turned against him and were attacking him. He was in desperate straits for supplies and eventually surrendered in two parties on 8th and 11th July.

53. The surrender of the Supreme Commander, General Gazzera, the whole of the province of Galla Sidamo and Raugei's column west of Assab, marked the elimination of all Italian troops in the area for which I was responsible and the conclusion of the campaign waged by East Africa Force which had started on 11th February.

It seems worth mentioning, in view of the many enemy claims that they were overwhelmed by superior numbers, that at no time were more than three brigade groups plus two battalions engaged in operations against the 40,000 enemy infantry and militia in the Galla Sidamo, where as at the commencement of these operations the enemy had five times as many guns as we had. After the fall of Sciasciamanna only two brigade groups were used.

B. Operations of 1st S.A. Brigade.
(13th April – 8th May, 1941.)
(Order of Battle as in Appendix "A".)

54. On 13th April 1st S.A. Brigade Group left Addis Abeba and in spite of extensive demolitions one mile beyond the Mussolini tunnel some 100 miles north of Addis Abeba, were able to occupy Debre' Sina with 1st D.E.O.R. on 14th April. This was done after slight enemy opposition had been overcome, while work on the road demolitions continued. On 16th April the advance continued from Debre' Sina and after encountering minor road blocks the leading troops on the 17th reached the southern approaches of the Combolcia Pass, where they came under enemy shell-fire.

55. It was soon apparent that the brigade was in contact with a strong enemy position well supported by artillery and sited in most difficult country. The

enemy shelling was heavy and accurate, and in addition to a number of casualties two of our 18 pdr. guns were damaged.

The road to Combolcia which ran over a series of saddles with steep mountainous country on either side, could be seen to be deliberately blocked by a mass of enemy vehicles. To the west of the road the ground was open and marshy and impassable to vehicles, but on the eastern side where there was a parallel valley a mile or two away, there was promise of a possible covered approach. The leading companies of the 1st D.E.O.R. were therefore ordered to seize commanding features on that side.

The battle then resolved itself into three phases, which altogether occupied five days, along and difficult approach, the attack, and the hurried flight of the enemy.

56. On 18th April the 1st Duke of Edinburgh's Own Rifles were ordered to move along the high ground to the east of the road with 1st Transvaal Scottish operating on the lower slopes and 1st Royal Natal Carbineers in reserve. Patriots under Lieut. A.G.S. Campbell were directed round both flanks of the enemy's position to locate the extent of his position and to harry his rear, and if possible to get astride his L. of C. Enemy artillery interfered considerably with these movements. On the afternoon of the 19th April the Italians launched a strong counter-attack on the right flank of 1st D.E.O.R. which was beaten off with heavy loss to the enemy.

Progress continued to be slow in the mountainous country where all weapons, supplies and water had to be carried by hand, and where signal communications were very difficult. On the night of 20/21st April 1st R.N.C. relieved 1st D.E.O.R. who had then been four days and nights in the mountains.

The steady pressure of our advance had caused a continual thin stream of prisoners and deserters, which undoubtedly lowered the enemy's morale, but all reports showed that his main position was held by at least 2,000 Europeans, apart from African troops.

Meanwhile Campbell's scouts had been doing valuable work in occupying outlying features and harrying the enemy's flanks, and our artillery had moved into more concealed positions and gradually established a superiority of fire.

57. On 22nd April the assault was made by 1st R.N.C. who seized the main enemy position, while the 1st T.S. swept up enemy opposition on the lower slopes down the road. About 1430 hours the enemy were in flight, but road-blocks and the difficulties of the country, no less than the physical strain on the infantry of the preceding days prevented any effective pursuit. A large number of prisoners and material were taken including 8 medium, 12 naval, 4 field, 3 light and 4 A.A. guns.

58. On 23rd April the extensive road-blocks were cleared except for a small one which was covered by accurate enemy artillery fire. The artillery was brought forward into action and the D.E.O.R. who were then once more in the van, moved

forward across country, finally occupying on the morning of 26th April features which overlooked Combolcia.

The road-block having been removed under cover of darkness during the night 25/26th April, 1st T.S. moved straight on to Combolcia where a considerable number of prisoners and material were captured.

59. 1st T.S. then continued the advance on to Dessie and found 46 lorries and 6 medium guns abandoned on the road; these evidently having been cut off by enemy demolitions which had been blown prematurely.

While work on the demolitions was proceeding, enemy artillery fire opened from Dessie. Our own artillery was brought into action and the infantry were deployed into the hills to engage enemy infantry now appearing on the mountain tops.

60. However, soon after our medium artillery opened fire, a deputation came from Dessie to discuss terms. Unconditional surrender was demanded and given, and 1st T.S. moved forward into the town in enemy transport, as its own transport was stopped by a destroyed bridge, the passage over which was not made good until 30th April.

The garrison of Dessie consisted of 5,000 Italians and 3,000 native troops; the area was full of guns, M.G., ammunition and war material of all sorts. Altogether in the Combolcia – Dessie engagement 52 guns were captured.

The battle of the Combolcia Pass and the capture of Dessie was a considerable victory. It was evident from the defensive positions and the number of guns captured that the Italians were determined to make a strong resistance. At Combolcia the positions were well dug and heavily wired, and Dessie itself was prepared for all round defence, there being seventeen localities, supported by seven forts and numerous strong points.

61. On 30th April 1st R.N.C. with supporting arms continued the advance to the north, while the remainder of the brigade continued to clear up Dessie and patrol along the roads to Gondar and Assab. On 1st May 1st R.N.C. occupied Waldia taking 200 prisoners, but a demolished tunnel on the road held up further advance for three days. In the meantime Campbell's scouts were directed forward on to Alomata and Quoram. On 5th May Alomata was occupied and some prisoners including two Brigade Commanders were captured; but road blocks 8 miles to the north prevented a further advance until 7th May.

62. On 7th May the remainder of 1st S.A. Brigade Group, less one company of 1st D.E.O.R. and some armoured cars, which were left to garrison Dessie, moved forward, and on arrival at Alomata on 8th May I placed them under command of Kaid for operations against Amba Alagi from the south, which place was then being attacked by him from the north.

C. Operations against Maraventano's Column.
(4th April – 22nd May, 1941.)

63. On the 4th April the Italians evacuated Debra Marcos. The garrison of Debra Marcos had apparently received orders to withdraw to Dessie, but the occupation of Addis Abeba by our troops on 6th April deprived them of the use of the only known motorable road between Debra Marcos and Dessie. A column of some 14,000 including 700 civilians, under the command of Colonel Maraventano withdrew across the Blue Nile at Safartak and was pursued by one weak company of the Frontier Battalion, Sudan Defence Force, as far as Cuiu near Ficche. On the 8th April this column was located at Quoziam when they were effectively bombed and machine-gunned by our aircraft. After further bombing on 23rd April Maraventano abandoned his M.T. and took to the hills. The Frontier Battalion Company which had now been reinforced by portions of two Operational Centres and a platoon of the 2nd Ethiopian Battalion (a total strength of 150 all ranks) again took up the pursuit. Maraventano's column, although reduced by desertions to about 8,000 combatants, made towards Addis Dera presumably with the object of eventually reaching Dessie.

Dessie, however, fell on 26th April to the 1st S.A. Brigade and it then appeared likely that Maraventano would surrender, but in spite of being harassed by his pursuers, hampered by the lack of transport and food, and burdened with many sick and wounded, he stubbornly continued his arduous trek towards Uorro Ilu where he apparently decided to remain as he considered the country suitable for defence and shelter, and food was available. On 14th May, however, there were indications that Maraventano was again on the move, this time in the direction of Debre Sina (Agibar). A small force was sent off at speed to take and hold the fort at Uoghidi which commanded the enemy line of retreat. This fort was successfully occupied and its Banda garrison joined our forces. On 17th May our main force had followed up and gained contact with the enemy rearguard travelling over extremely difficult country.

64. On 18th May the enemy column having deployed on a plateau, Colonel O.C. Wingate, D.S.O., Commander of the Sudan and patriot forces, decided to attack wherever possible, and proceeded to do so. These attacks were continued on the 19th and on the 20th, when the Italians were seen to be withdrawing. Once more a general advance of the patriot forces was ordered. A running fight ensued, the patriots fighting with great courage and inflicting heavy casualties on the enemy.

Maraventano's column, which had by now been reduced to about 7,000, found their retreat to Debre' Sina cut off by our occupation of the fort at Uoghidi and so deployed and took up a defensive position in the Borena area. Opposing him were some 1,000 patriots with a further 500 patriots and 37 Sudanese in reserve, but Maraventano still refused to surrender.

Finally, on 22nd May, after being told that he would be attacked unceasingly, Maraventano capitulated and his force was escorted back to Ficche and handed over to the 11th (A) Division. So ended what must have been for the whole of his column an exhausting and desperate flight through mountainous country full of hostile Ethiopians.

D. – *Internal Security and Mopping Up Operations in North East Somaliland.* (20th April – 21st May, 1941.)

65. These operations, carried out in north-east Somaliland, resulted in the clearing of that part of the country of all Italian posts, the re-establishment of British control in the Mijertein, and the re-commissioning of the lighthouse of Cape Guardafui, which the Commander-in-Chief, East Indies, required.

66. On 20th April, a column under the command of Major G.R. Musgrave, consisting of a company of Aden G(R) troops and a section of R.A.F. armoured cars, also from Aden, left Burao in hired transport. Accompanying the column was the Senior Political Officer of British Somaliland. Moving by way of Durukhsi and Bohodle, the column reached Garoe on 24th April where the post was handed over by the Italian Residente. The column reached Gardo on the 28th April and found it evacuated by the Italians.

The arrival of the column at Gardo, combined with the movement of a police patrol from Burao to Erigavo and Buran, did little, however, to stop the raiding instigated by dispersed Italian Banda, which was being carried on in the Mijertein and into British territory as far as Adad, and it was not until a detachment of the resuscitated Somaliland Camel Corps engaged a party of raiders at Karamam Plain on 7th May, that the raiders began to show signs of withdrawing from British Somaliland.

67. The column left Gardo on 2nd May and at Laso Dawao, on 4th May, was joined by a flight of Vincent aircraft from Aden.

It was known that there was a small Italian force at Bender Cassim, and opposition was anticipated in a narrow defile at Carin. In order to induce the Italians to surrender a message was dropped from the air over Bender Cassim on 5th May calling for an envoy to be sent to Carin on 6th May. As the aircraft performing this task met no opposition, a second aircraft landed and immediate negotiations were made with the Residente for the surrender of the post. The column reached Bender Cassim on 6th May, and 67 Italians, of whom 50 were naval military or government employees, were collected together with their arms.

68. After Bender Cassim had been taken over by a detachment of police, the column left on 11th May for Dante.

Dante is virtually an island, and to capture it the assistance of the navy was sought; but when the column reached Sousciuban on 13th May, reports were received that the Dante garrison was waiting to surrender. The Residente was met 12 miles from Hordic and, after discussions, the Italians agreed not to destroy the oil-tanks and wireless (which had been prepared for demolition) on the condition that they should not be used for military purposes. Dante was occupied on 16th May, with the assistance of boats provided by the Navy, and the 167 Italians were evacuated by sea.

69. The next objective of the column was Cape Guardafui, which it was decided to take by landing from the sea. On 18th May, the ships arrived off Cape Guardafui and under cover of pom-pom fire the troops were landed. The progress of our troops was slow owing to the extreme heat, high winds and soft sandhills. Any attack on the Tohen wadi, where the enemy was reported to be had to be postponed to the following day. Meanwhile a detachment had been despatched to capture the lighthouse, which it achieved successfully, and the lighthouse was put into use at dusk that day.

On 19th May, the enemy in Tohen Wadi surrendered without opposition, and 19 officers and 61 Italian O.R.s were embarked and evacuated to Aden.

70. On the 21st May, a platoon was sent round by sea to Alula, where 4 Italian officers and 35 O.R.s were evacuated without incident to Aden.

71. The success of these small operations, which entailed a march of 800 miles and the maintenance by hired transport of a small column 630 miles from its base, reflects great credit on all those who carried them out. Close co-operation between the column, the Navy and the Royal Air Force accounted for the fact that no effective resistance was offered by the enemy.

E. Operations for the Occupation of Maji by 25th E.A. Infantry Brigade
(8th April – 20th April, 1941)

72. In accordance with the policy stated in my previous report, I decided to send the 25th E.A. Infantry Brigade north from Kalam to occupy Maji, to get in touch with the Sedan Equatorial Corps which was operating westwards from the Sudan, and to hand over this area to them.

73. The advance from Kalam commenced on 8th April, the 2/3 K.A.R. providing the advanced guard. Washa-Waha, 75 miles to the north, was reached without incident on 9th April. During this period it rained almost continuously and movement of M.T. was only possible through the continuous efforts of the section of the South African engineers attached to the force.

The 2/4 K.A.R. reached Washa Waha on 12th April after further delay owing to floods. The native chief of Maji district reported to our troops at Washa Waha that the Italians were evacuating Maji and burning buildings and that he was anxious that we should occupy the town.

Owing to the administrative limitations imposed by the state of the roads the 2/3 K.A.R. remained at Washa Waha and only the 2/4 K.A.R. proceeded to Maji.

Slow progress was made owing to rain, landmines and road demolitions. In all 134 land mines were removed from five separate minefields and three effective road-blocks were cleared.

74. Maji was entered by our advance troops on 20th April without opposition. The following day contact was made by W/T with the patrol of the Equatorial Corps approaching from the north-west.

Our troops pushed forward to Masci, six miles north of Maji and met the company of the Equatorial Corps there on 28th April.

On the same day a company of the 2/4 K.A.R. with attached troops set out north from Masci to clear the road to Baciuma, 58 miles to the north.

75. Approaching Giamo, 30 miles north of Masci, the force encountered and routed a small enemy patrol. Giamo was occupied without further incident.

Pushing on from Giamo, an enemy force, consisting of some 25 Italians and 200 banda, was found occupying a defensive position on a ridge overlooking the road.

Our patrol attacked the position, inflicting considerable casualties on the enemy with mortar and L.M.G. fire, but was unable before nightfall to clear the whole position.

The following morning, however, reconnaissance revealed that the enemy had withdrawn during the night.

76. Once this district had been handed over to the Equatorial Corps, I had intended to withdraw the brigade to the area Lokitaung – Kalam, but owing to the rains and floods the road Kalam – Maji became almost totally impassable to M.T. and 2/4 K.A.R. was immobilised at Maji for over a month.

There is no doubt that our occupation of this area had a quietening effect on the Merille, but, since the withdrawal back to Lokitaung, there have again been some signs of truculence.

PART III. – GENERAL

Political.

77. It will be recalled that owing to my fears regarding the possibilities of unfortunate incidents on first entry into Addis Ababa, I had impressed on the Italians the necessity of leaving what, in their opinion was a sufficiency of armed men for guarding their civilians during the period my troops were entering the town. On entry into the city it was found that some 10,000 armed men had been left, an indication of their own fear of reprisal for what was proved, on examination of the prison records, to have been a ferociously harsh rule. The greater part of this armed force was police, but two whole Blackshirt battalions were also discovered. Most of the town, which is large and straggling, was surrounded by wire and a ring of blockhouses, and permanent machine-gun posts were sprinkled throughout the area. In addition, on the hills above, covering the main roads into the town, were a ring of forts, all full of armed men. It was quite impossible, without seriously prejudicing military operations, to provide protection on this scale from my troops, nor indeed was it necessary. It was therefore decided to retain two Nigerian battalions in Addis Abeba which in any case would have been the minimum required for the defence of the place, and to pursue a policy of gradual disarmament of the Italian police, replacing them by Ethiopians as and when they could be trained. The Italian civil population had been scattered all over the town, so I also arranged for them to be segregated into three areas.

It was satisfactory to find that my fears of lawless elements amongst the Ethiopians getting out of hand were ungrounded. The Ethiopians behaved with admirable restraint, and except for minor instances of looting, no major incidents on their part took place. Not so with the Italians, who, civilians and police alike, were in a highly nervous condition. Within the first 48 hours of entering the town two shooting incidents on the part of the Italians occurred. The perpetrators were brought to trial before the Military Courts.

78. These incidents convinced the authorities in Addis Abeba that the danger of leaving the Italians their arms was greater than what might be expected from other sources. The disarmament programme was therefore pushed on with all speed, and by the end of April no more Italian police were left in the town, other than a few unarmed wardens in each of the segregated areas. Their place was taken by a number of trusted Abyssinian police employed by the Italians, and a further number drafted in and given three weeks training. A sprinkling of British officers and N.C.O.s had been provided by E.A. Force for this purpose. This work was carried out under Colonel A.A. Hayton, D.A.P.M. of E.A. Force, who had recently arrived from South Africa, where he had had considerable experience in police matters. He accomplished this most difficult task in very delicate circumstances with calm and efficiency.

79. Meanwhile the armed Italians in the outer ring of forts had been replaced by Ethiopian patriots sent in by the Emperor.

It was felt, in spite of previous customs and traditions, that no armed men of any sort should be allowed in the town. Even the troops when walking out left their arms behind. Armed Ethiopians from outlying districts left their arms at the police stations round the perimeter of the town before being permitted to enter.

80. Before the campaign started it was not apparent that Addis Abeba was going to be entered by the "back door." Both the patriot activity under the Emperor in the Gojjam and the operations proceeding against Keren were many hundreds of miles nearer the heart of Abyssinia than E.A. Force, and appeared to offer the most favourable chances of entering the city. As a result, both the Military Mission to organise the Emperor's offensive movement, and the political organisation (Occupied Enemy Territory Administration) to administer Abyssinia or such parts of it as were captured, were based on Khartoum. With the entry of E.A. Force into Addis Abeba and the occupation by the troops of the greater part of Abyssinia, it was clear that some form of re-organisation would be required. The Emperor was at Debra Marcos and touch with him was most easily maintained through Addis Abeba. It was, therefore, decided to transfer the Deputy Chief Political Officer, Abyssinia, and his staff to Addis Abeba, to work under me, with of course direct reference to the Kaid in connection with matters regarding the area in which his forces were operating. This action gave me a direct link with the Emperor and placed the onus of dealing with him on me.

81. The instructions which I had received were to the effect that I was to establish an Administration in those parts of Abyssinia I had occupied, and that I was to deal with the Emperor on the lines of the statement made by the Foreign Office at the time of the Emperor's entry into Abyssinia. The text of this statement is produced here.

> "H.M.G. would welcome the reappearance of an independent Ethiopian State and will recognise the claims of the Emperor Haile Selassie to the throne. The Emperor has intimated to H.M.G. that he will need outside assistance and guidance. H.M.G. agree with this view and consider that any such assistance and guidance in economic and political matters should be the subject of international arrangement at the conclusion of peace. They reaffirm that they have no territorial ambitions in Abyssinia. In the meantime the conduct of military operations by Imperial forces in parts of Abyssinia will require temporary measures of military guidance and control."

The interpretation of this final sentence was a matter of considerable discussion with the Emperor who was always on the look out for any measure which would infringe the Sovereignty which he claimed. The question will be referred to again later.

82. From the moment my troops entered Addis Abeba I was being pressed continually by the Emperor to permit his return to the capital at once. This I was most anxious to accomplish at the earliest possible moment, both to hasten the structure of an Ethiopian State which might eventually stand on its own legs, and to get the fullest use out of the patriot movement in conjunction with my forces which were still engaged with the enemy, thus compensating to a small degree for the loss of troops and equipment being sent up to Middle East.

It was, however, quite impossible to allow the Emperor back until I had settled the various internal security questions in Addis Abeba and disarmed the Italians. I had some difficulty with the Emperor on this question, and he appeared distrustful of our future intentions towards him. I was, however, in a position to let him in on 5th May on which day he ceremoniously entered the city on the anniversary of the entry by the Italians exactly five years before. In view of the complete disarming of the city there were no major incidents. Considerable credit was due to Brigadier M.S. Lush, M.C., the D.C.P.O., who was in charge of the civil administration, for this happy result.

83. Meanwhile political officers were being sent to the main centres and were engaged in administering the country as far as possible through the local Ethiopian officials and chiefs. The Duke of Harrar, Prince Mackonnen, arrived in Harrar to be the Governor of that Province.

84. The political situation at that time as far as E.A. Force was concerned was that I was Military Governor of Italian Somaliland, British Somaliland, and those parts of Abyssinia in which my troops were in occupation, as far north as Dessie and the

Gojjam. D.C.P.Os. were functioning under my orders in Italian Somaliland at Mogadiscio, and as already stated in Addis Abeba for Abyssinia. British Somaliland was placed under a separate Military Governor, Brigadier A.R. Chater, C.B., D.S.O., O.B.E., under my general direction. In order to avoid for the moment any difficulties with the Somalis in connection with the Emperor's return, Italian Somaliland as delimited by the Italians, and not in accordance with the old boundary, was kept under the D.C.P.O. in Mogadiscio, or in other words, the whole of the area including the Ogaden and southwards from it, was kept under the D.C.P.O. Italian Somaliland, and this area was known as Southern Somalia.

85. At this period considerable trouble was still being given over most of the occupied area by the many armed deserters from the Italian Army who had formed themselves into marauding bands. It was clear that my main object was the defeat of the Italian forces, and therefore I was quite unable to provide the large number of troops which would have been required in the vast area under my control, to establish law and order with efficiency and despatch. I explained to my political officers that they would have to do the best they could with the few garrison battalions I could spare and what they could raise in the way of gendarmerie and police from local resources, and that I quite appreciated I would have to accept a degree of lawlessness until such time as I could spare troops to enforce the law. I have to thank them for the loyal way in which they accepted this position, and the efficiency with which they established a considerable degree of law and order with the assistance of the small military resources available.

86. The general question of military political control in E.A. Force was, however, most unsatisfactory. Owing to operations it was necessary for me to have my Headquarters in Harrar. Under these conditions I was separated from my three administrators in Addis Abeba, Mogadiscio and Hargeisa, by many hundreds of miles. I had no political staff myself. The D.C.P.Os. dealt direct with the Chief Political Officer, Middle East, who had meantime left Cairo and had opened his Headquarters in Nairobi. All political action was presented to me as a fait accompli, and hence though I was responsible, I had no means of exerting authority, of knowing what was going on or even of laying down the policy for the area for which I was responsible. For instance, although I was the authority for confirmation of death sentences I had no independent legal adviser. Again, I eventually found that the militarily most important offence of concealing arms was being dealt with by the death sentence in one area, and mere internment in another; I had no machinery by which I could ascertain the details of the administration, or to see that a general policy was being applied throughout.

The situation was considerably eased by the move back of my Advanced H.Q. to Nairobi on 18th June, a move which was made possible by the fact that by the above date military operations in the Galla Sidamo had been reduced to a scale which enabled them to be undertaken wholly by the Commander of 11th (A) Division.

It was, however, recognised that the normal O.E.T.A. organisation could not apply over the large area for which I was responsible, and a scheme is now in hand by which I will be relieved of all purely civil administrative responsibilities.

Evacuation.

87. It had always been my view, and indeed, that of my political advisers, that before any form of Ethiopian control was permitted in Abyssinia it would be necessary to evacuate all Italians, lock, stock and barrel. I expressed this view to the C.-in-C. with the suggestion that by far the best solution would be repatriation to Italy if it could possibly be arranged.

As soon as it was possible to arrive at some estimate of the numbers involved and the accommodation and transport facilities available, the problem was examined in detail. The numbers of civilians to be evacuated were estimated at 55,000 though to this figure some 70,000 prisoners of war had to be added. Women and children were estimated at 11,000 and 7,000 respectively. It was immediately apparent that total evacuation, even if shipping were available, must be a very long process, probably extending over at least six months. It would, moreover, entail the complete stoppage of all essential services in Abyssinia and the many technical institutions and factories introduced by the Italians and entirely supervised by them. I felt, therefore, that I was forced to revise my previous views on the subject of evacuation, and was confirmed in this opinion by the remarkable restraint shown by the Ethiopians up to that time from avenging themselves against the Italians. I decided, therefore, that evacuation should be started as soon as possible, but should be carried out by categories in the following order, Fascist officials and other undesirables, prisoners of war, police, Government officials, Municipal officials, professional and business men, artisans, etc. As the evacuation of the first four groups would take a considerable time there would be ample opportunity to decide in due course whether the process would have to be carried out to the full or could be halted at any particular stage. As an initial step 80 prominent Fascists with their families were evacuated from Addis Abeba to Diredaua on 28th April.

Although the evacuation was mainly a political matter, it had to be carried out through military resources and hence required the closest co-operation between O.E.T.A. and the military authorities. An evacuation branch of O.E.T.A. was set up by the C.P.O. Middle East in Nairobi.

The implications of the use of Jibuti in connection with evacuation are set out in the following section dealing with French Somaliland.

French Somaliland.

88. With the reoccupation of British Somaliland and the taking of Diredaua (thus cutting the Jibuti railway), connections between the Vichy French in French Somaliland and the Italians virtually ceased. The French had been to a great degree dependent on supplies of foodstuffs from Abyssinia which were now wholly cut off. Meanwhile a strict blockade was still being maintained by us of the

French Somali Coast. As far as could be ascertained supplies existed in Jibuti for six weeks to two months only.

89. On 5th April I received instructions from Middle East to the effect that some detachments of Free French under General Le Gentilhomme were proceeding to British Somaliland to make an attempt to win French Somaliland over to the Free French cause, and that I was to give them facilities. I therefore instructed Brigadier Buchanan who was then commanding the troops in British Somaliland that facilities for approach to the frontier should be given to these parties. Nevertheless I told him that no form of direct military aid was to be given, his troops were not to get involved in armed clashes but Free French elements from French Somaliland could be allowed to rally on British soil.

90. About 15th April Colonel Brossett, Major Appert and Captain Majendie arrived at Berbera.

The plan was to drop leaflets from a Free French aeroplane inviting the French troops to cross the frontier and join the British at Zeilah and Daouenle. If and when the troops began to come over, leaflets were to be dropped on Jibuti asking the colony to join General de Gaulle to recover its prosperity by the intensive use of the harbour and railway by the British. Finally to give notice to the population that the Colony would be blockaded until surrender to the Free French forces.

The plan was duly commenced, but only a very few individuals came over. It was reported that the frontiers were strongly defended by pro-Vichy units who had orders to shoot anyone who tried to cross the border from any side. It was also reported that the port facilities were all mined and that the Governor through hatred of the British was quite ready to blow them up, should any offensive action be taken against him. General Le Gentilhomme came to the conclusion that the Free French plan was likely to be ineffective and that reliance could only be placed on the results of the blockade.

91. It should be stated here that the Governor of Jibuti, besides being fanatically anti-British, was reported to be self-opinionated, obstinate and proud to an extent which precluded all reasonable thinking. He had established himself as a complete dictator and used the death penalty ruthlessly against any who showed any pro-Free French leanings or even were seen picking up Free French leaflets. Although it was reported that the railway and commercial elements in the town were at least more moderate in their outlook, there was no one of sufficient weight to stand up to the Governor whose power therefore appeared supreme.

92. On 1st May the Governor at Jibuti telegraphed to the Governor at Aden that he had received official instructions authorising him to deal direct with the Higher British Authorities to arrive at a temporary modus vivendi taking into account the local situation. He asked for names of delegates to attend a meeting on board ship or at the frontier. General Le Gentilhomme was very against such

negotiations taking place, pointing out that if we used the port of Jibuti, he was convinced that the Italians would demand the use of Bizerta.

93. On 7th May, however, I received from Middle East an order to open up negotiations on the lines indicated in a previous wire. It was stated that arguments in regard to Bizerta did not carry weight as if the Italians wanted to go there, they would do so irrespective of what happened at Jibuti.

I was told to open up negotiations and to report the proposals made and received, but to enter into no commitments. Later I received another wire to say that I was only to receive proposals though I was at liberty to sound the Governor on lines of original instructions "without giving definite indications of our views".

The terms referred to were-

(*a*) Use of port and harbour for a partial raising of blockade to allow in necessities such as milk, etc.

(*b*) Blockade would only be lifted completely if Colony became Free French.

(*c*) Any troops wishing to join Free French should be permitted to do so, but we would consider evacuation of remainder to some other French Colony, e.g. Madagascar.

About this time it did not appear to me that we had very strong reasons for maintaining the blockade. The Colony was almost completely cut off from the Italians, except in the north, south of Assab. In this area there were only very unimportant Italian military forces, cut off from the remainder in Abyssinia.

Again there was no doubt that all the important officials in Jibuti were strongly Vichy French and the presence of the Free French on the borders of the country was serving to inflame them.

Therefore I did not then consider the conditions favourable to a satisfactory agreement.

94. I made arrangements for preliminary conversations to take place near Zeilah on 18th May. On 17th May however, the news of the German use of the aerodromes in Syria came through. I therefore postponed the meeting until I had further instructions which were on the way down to me from Middle East. I had no longer any doubts as to our reasons for continuance of the blockade.

95. It now became necessary to consider to what extent Jibuti port and harbour were vital to our needs, so as to recommend to the C-in-C a line of future conduct vis-a-vis French Somaliland.

The port might be required for the evacuation of the Italian civilians from Abyssinia, and again it might be vital to us for military purposes. It will be recalled that I had come to the conclusion that although it was desirable to evacuate the civilians from Abyssinia as soon as possible, limitations of transport, and the necessity of providing accommodation en route would under any conditions render the evacuation a slow process. Moreover there was no real shortage of food for the civilians and I was informed by the political branch that they could be fed until the end of November. The question of the evacuation was not therefore a matter of the highest degree of urgency. On the other hand I had been informed by the Political Evacuation Committee that they considered the use of Jibuti vital for their purpose. They felt that the dangers to health involved in establishing staging-camps on the 300-mile road link between Diredaua and Berbera precluded the use of this route. It was therefore apparent that at some time or other Jibuti would be required for evacuation purposes.

On the military side the use of the port and railway would be most desirable, not only because of the great saving of transport due to the cutting out of the Berbera – Diredaua road link, but also on account of the greatly superior port facilities as compared with Berbera. At the same time I was able to maintain three brigades from Berbera, and there was no need at this stage for a larger force to liquidate the Italians, nor did it appear that I would ever have to maintain more. The port therefore, though desirable was not vital to me from the military point of view.

96. The situation was then that the use of Jibuti though desirable for all purposes was only vital to us for civilian evacuation. Hence it occurred to me that there would be very great advantages in the matter of the evacuation of the civilians being handled on a higher plane with the Italian Government itself. We could deliver the evacuees at the French frontier after which their onward journey would be the responsibility of the Italians.

All arrangements could be made between them and the French direct. There was an Italian Armistice Commission in Jibuti with whom, under a white flag we could arrange local details direct and there would be no need to approach the French at all. The question of the provision of ships, on which I understood tentative feelers had met with some response, and the journey through French Somaliland could be treated as one question on a govermental level as far as the British were concerned.

If this policy were successful we would be left without need to negotiate with the Governor in French Somaliland at all, and there would be no necessity for the somewhat awkward situation of carrying out negotiations with Vichy under the flags of the Free French which were established at all accessible points near the frontier. Furthermore there would now be no reason to make any concession in respect of the blockade and the full policy of only raising the blockade if the Colony became Free French could be enforced.

I wrote to the C-in-C to the above effect on 25th May, and also suggested that if he was in agreement with the policy, all that would now be required would be to inform the Governor of French Somaliland that in view of the situation in Syria he refused to treat with him.

97. In due course I received a letter from General Wavell for delivery to the Governor of French Somaliland. The letter informed him that the blockade would be maintained until the Colony became Free French, that steps would

be taken to see that the population were informed of the true situation, and that a month's supplies of all kinds were ready to be rushed to the Colony as soon as they gave in.

98. This letter was delivered on 8th June, and on 10th June leaflets were dropped on Jibuti giving the gist of the letter. Meanwhile Free French pamphlet dropping, which has been suspended, was resumed, and permission was given to the French sloop to operate in territorial waters and stop the dhow traffic from the Yemen. Furthermore a successful operation for a landing at Assab, from which place there were indications that supplies had been entering French Somaliland, was initiated by Aden with 3/15 Punjabis from Berbera, under Brigadier W.A. Dimoline, O.B.E., M.C., of the 26th E.A. Brigade, and with supporting arms from E.A. Force. 2/2 K.A.R. of 26th E.A. Infantry Brigade (which had replaced 2nd S.A. Brigade on the departure of the latter to Egypt) was moved on to the French frontier on the Zeilah road and at Daouenle. All steps were taken to tighten up the blockade from the landward side, by preventing Somali traffic across the frontier.

The operation against Assab took place with success on 11th June. The enemy were surprised and very little resistance was encountered.

99. On 15th June a reply to General Wavell's letter by the Governor of Jibuti was passed over the frontier. The letter reviewed the steps already taken by the Governor to try and initiate negotiations for the use of the port and railway for "humanitarian purposes." It also drew attention to a communication made by him to the Governor of Aden to the effect that owing to malnutrition some infant mortality had taken place, and it reaffirmed the rigid intention of French Somaliland to remain under Vichy. No reply was sent to this letter.

100. There arose at this time the question of the possibility of the reduction of French Somaliland by force of arms. The defences of the country were mainly centred round Jibuti. These consisted of a strong concrete trench system about 12 miles long with both ends resting on the sea, outside which were three forts on the main communications into the town. Outside Jibuti, forts with small garrisons, but consisting of very strong concrete defences, existed at Hol Hol, Ali Sabiet, Dikkil and Hadji, and other minor positions were scattered about on the main communications. There was a trench system at Loyada on the frontier on the Zeilah – Jibuti road.

At this period my administrative resources were fully stretched in the maintenance of the two brigades of 11th (A) Division which were engaging the Italians in the Galla Sidamo. Administratively I could engage in no more commitments without ceasing operations against the Italians. Furthermore E.A. Force was not equipped for the reduction of strong concrete defences, neither was the Air Force sufficiently strong in bombers. Admittedly there was a doubt whether the six Senegalese battalions which formed the garrison would fight. There was therefore at least uncertainty whether an attack on French Somaliland could be carried out with success. There appeared no doubt that the blockade must eventually be successful in forcing the Governor to give in, furthermore, by trusting to the blockade, there would be no need for cessation of the operations in the Galla Sidamo. I therefore recommended that offensive operations should not be undertaken against the Vichy French, at any rate for the present.

101. About this time a telegram was received from the War Office, presumably in reply to the representations made by the Governor of Jibuti on the subject of infant mortality, suggesting that the blockade might be lifted sufficiently to allow in milk etc. for the children. I felt that strict supervision of any relaxation of the blockade would be most difficult to ensure without contact and negotiations which I felt were most undesirable at that time. More over I was sure that any relaxation of the blockade occurring immediately after the receipt of the Governor's reply to General Wavell's letter would have an unfortunate effect in strengthening the former's position. He obviously would take steps to gain full propaganda value on these lines. I therefore telegraphed to General Wavell an alternative proposal to make an offer of evacuation of all white women and children to Madagascar or other Vichy French place. In due course I was authorised to make this offer.

102. Meanwhile the Governor of Jibuti had addressed letters both to General Wavell and myself to the effect that he had received instructions that should French Somaliland be reduced by either blockade or direct invasion he was to destroy all facilities which might be of value to the invader. General Wavell replied to this letter to the effect that from the purely military point of view Jibuti was of no consequence to him. If the Governor destroyed the port and railway he would merely make it impossible to feed his own nationals and prevent, or at any rate delay, the evacuation of Italian women and children from Abyssinia.

In due course a reply was received from Jibuti in which the Governor indicated that he took General Wavell's letter as an invitation to open negotiations on a wide scale for the evacuation of the Italian women and children and the relief of Jibuti. I was authorised to reply that General Wavell had given no such invitation and that his intentions remained as notified in the letter summarised in para. 97.

PART IV. – CONCLUSION.

103. During the period after the fall of Addis Abeba E.A. Force, besides capturing Dessie and assisting in the fall of Amba Alagi, has now completed its task of securing the capitulation of all enemy forces in the whole area lying south and inclusive of Assab – Dessie – Bethor.

The area over which these final operations took place was 125,000 square miles, and although, due to the weather conditions, the tempo of the early part of the campaign could not be maintained, the time taken to complete the task cannot be regarded as unsatisfactory. The latter part of the operations was carried out entirely by East and West African infantry, though South Africa supplied most of the supporting arms. In spite of the continuous wet and cold weather the morale and dash of all troops remained unabated, though the physical difficulties caused by mud and demolitions demanded great endurance. It may again be stated that according to popular belief the campaigning season in Northern Abyssinia should have terminated at the end of May, and in Southern Abyssinia by the end of March. The fighting was the toughest yet experienced, due to the naturally strong defensive positions which abounded in the area, to the greater number of supporting arms, fields guns, medium guns and tanks which were available to the enemy, and also the tougher fibre of some of the Italian commanders. These had at last learnt that the true form of defence against the type of attack which we made, lay in the counter-attack with mobile troops rather than in their previous methods of withdrawal into wired perimeters. Though the East and West African troops met the enemy medium tank, the Mark II, for the first time, after the first uncertainty they were not dismayed and showed confidence in their defence against these vehicles.

104. Mention must be made of the artillery of which all but the light batteries were South African units. The extreme shortage in this arm (only 24 field guns) entailed frequent moves over long distances so as to give the greatest concentration of fire at the decisive points, yet the guns always arrived on time. Their action in silencing the enemy guns, often from most exposed positions was without doubt instrumental in most cases in enabling the infantry to get forward, and in some of the battles artillery action alone caused the enemy to vacate their positions.

105. The nature of the country, steep, rugged, with deep canyon-like ravines and broad swift flowing rivers, lent itself to extensive and effective demolitions. The work of the R.E. units, the greater portion of which were also South African, in the rapid construction of bridges and repair of roads was beyond praise. Had there been any greater delay imposed on the advance than was in fact the case, there is every doubt whether our troops would have been able to close with the enemy and finally liquidate him before the really heavy rains set in.

106. In the early part of the campaign much success had attended the use of propaganda leaflets scattered from the air. The capture of an excellent printing press, capable of printing in all local languages, in Addis Abeba greatly speeded up the process of getting out "hot" news by leaflet and many thousands of these were dropped almost daily. Of a total of 7,300,000 pamphlets dropped 3,500,000 were printed in Addis Abeba. There is no doubt that these leaflets undermined the morale of the Italians, and resulted in wholesale disintegration of the enemy troops.

107. From the fall of Addis Abeba to the final surrender of Gazzera the total prisoners accounted for by E.A. Force amounted to approximately 30,000 Italians and 30,000 Africans. Owing to the number of enemy who were killed and the number who deserted, this figure however, does not give a complete picture of the destruction wrought. It is estimated that during that period 105,000 enemy of all types were rendered ineffective.[2]

No estimate can yet be given of the war material in our hands, but except in a few commodities, the Italians were well found, and there is every reason to believe that the captures of war stores are very considerable.

A remarkable feature was the great quantity of valuable and up-to-date machinery, much of it new, of all types with which the country was stocked.

108. I must once more emphasise the success with which the Staff and administrative services continued to overcome the many great difficulties of supply and transport, and the manner in which the transport companies maintained their reputation in face of the wretched conditions of rain and mud.

Particular mention must also be made of the staff and personnel of both naval and military at Berbera. Owing to lack of facilities, torrid temperatures, and a high rate of sickness, supply through this port was always precarious. The kharif, a hot wind which commenced blowing in June, increased their difficulties. In spite of these grave conditions the personnel continued to perform their duties with cheerfulness and determination and are still doing so.

109. I can again with great pleasure draw attention to the skill shown by the two Divisional Commanders, Major General Godwin Austen and Major General Wetherall. The greatest credit is due to Major General Godwin Austen for the dogged persistence with which 12th (A) Division undertook and completed their attack northwards under the worst possible conditions of weather and roads against defensive positions which the enemy had deemed impregnable. To Major General Wetherall and 11th (A) Division fell the lot of undertaking the attacks on Dessie, Sciasciamanna, Soddu and the crossings of the Omo, all of which formidable operations were attended with success and brought about the final collapse.

(sd.) A.G. CUNNINGHAM,
22nd July, 1941.   Lieut.-Gen.

APPENDICES.

Appendix "A" – Order of Battle of E.A. Force, 1st January 1941.
Appendix "B" – Own and Enemy Air Forces in E. Africa, 1st January 1941.
Appendix "C" – Order of Battle 11th and 12th (A) Divisions at commencement of operations, 10th February 1941.
Appendix "D" – Order of Battle 11th and 12th (A) Divisions, 23rd February 1941.
Appendix "E" – Order of Battle 11th (A) Division, 11th March 1941.
Appendix "F" – Conditions presented to Italian envoy on 3rd April 1941, and the reply received on 4th April 1941.
Appendix "G" – Troops left in British Somaliland by A.O.C. Aden for use by E.A. Force.
Appendix "H" – Order of Battle 12th (A) Division, 5th April 1941.
Appendix "J" – Allocation of A.C. Squadrons during operations.

APPENDIX "A."
Order of Battle of E.A. Force.
1st January, 1941.

1st South African Division.

H.Q. 1 *(South African) Division.*

1 (South African) Division Signal Company.

H.Q. 2 *(South African) Infantry Brigade.*

3 (South African) Brigade Signal Company.

1 Natal Mounted Rifles.

1 Field Force Battalion.

2 Field Force Battalion.

2 (South African) Armoured Car Company.

12 (South African) Field Company.

12 (South African) Field Ambulance.

2 (South African) Mobile General Workshop.

H.Q. 5 *(South African) Infantry Brigade.*

1 (South African) Brigade Signal Company.

1 (South African) Irish.

2 Regiment Botha.

3 Transvaal Scottish.

1 (South African) Armoured Car Company.

5 (South African) Field Company.

11 (South African) Field Ambulance.

3 (South African) Mobile General Workshop.

H.Q. 25 *(East African) Infantry Brigade.*

25 (East African) Brigade Signal Section.

2/3 King's African Rifles.

2/4 King's African Rifles.

27 Mountain Battery, Royal Artillery.

Detachment Somaliland Camel Corps Armoured Cars.

3 (South African) Field Company.

6 (Uganda) Field Ambulance.

25 (East African) Infantry Brigade Group Company.

Divisional Troops.

3 (South African) Field Brigade (7, 8, 9 South African Field Batteries).

3 (South African) Anti-Tank Battery.

One Section 6 (South African) Anti-Aircraft Battery.

21 (South African) Field Park Company.

One platoon 1/3 King's African Rifles (Machine-Gun).

1 (South African) Divisional Supply Company.

1 (South African) Divisional Ammunition Company.

1 (South African) Divisional Petrol Company.

2 (South African) Provost Company.

1 (South African) Motor Cycle Company.

2 (South African) Motor Cycle Company.

No. 2 Irregular Company.

No. 5 Irregular Company.

11*th (African) Division.*

  H.Q. 11 *(African) Division.*

    11 (African) Divisional Signals.

  H.Q. 21 *(East African) Infantry Brigade.*

    21 (East African) Brigade Signal Section.

    1/2 King's African Rifles.

    1/4 King's African Rifles.

    1 Northern Rhodesia Regiment.

    53 (Gold Coast) Field Company.

    21 (East African) Infantry Brigade Group Company.

    2 (Zanzibar) Field Ambulance.

  H.Q. 23 *(Nigeria) Infantry Brigade.*

    23 (Nigeria) Brigade Signal Section.

    1 Nigeria Regiment.

    2 Nigeria Regiment.

    3 Nigeria Regiment.

    52 (Nigeria) Light Battery.

    51 (Nigeria) Field Company.

    23 (Nigeria) Infantry Brigade Group Company.

    3 (Nigeria) Field Ambulance.

 Divisional Troops.

    "C" Squadron I East African Armoured Car Regiment.

    7 (South African) Field Brigade (5, 17, 18 (South African) Field Batteries).

    I (South African) Anti-Tank Battery.

    One Section 6 (South African) Anti-Aircraft Battery.

    16 (South African) Field Company.

    Platoon 1/3 King's African Rifles (Machine-Gun).

    I (East African) Pioneers.

    3 (East African) Field Hygiene Section.

    11 Divisional Ordnance Field Park.

    Detachment No. 4 Irregular Company.

12 *(African) Division.*

  H.Q. 12 *(African) Division.*

    12 (African) Divisional Signals.

  H.Q. 1 *(South African) Infantry Brigade.*

    10 (South African) Brigade Signal Company.

    1 Royal Natal Carbineers.

    1 Transvaal Scottish.

    1 Duke of Edinburgh's Own Rifles.

    3 (South African) Armoured Car Company.

4 (South African) Field Brigade (10, 11 and 12 (South African) Field Batteries).

1 (South African) Field Company.

1 (South African) Brigade "Q" Services Company.

10 (South African) Field Ambulance.

1 (South African) Mobile General Workshop.

H.Q. 22 (East African) Infantry Brigade.

22 (East African) Brigade Signal Section.

1/1 King's African Rifles.

5 King's African Rifles.

1/6 King's African Rifles.

22 Mountain Battery Royal Artillery.

54 (East African) Field Company.

22 (East African) Infantry Brigade Group Company.

1 (Tanganyika) Field Ambulance.

H.Q. 24 (Gold Coast) Infantry Brigade.

24 (Gold Coast) Brigade Signal Section.

1 Gold Coast Regiment.

2 Gold Coast Regiment.

3 Gold Coast Regiment.

51 (Gold Coast) Light Battery.

52 (Gold Coast) Field Company.

24 (Gold Coast) Infantry Brigade Group Company.

4 (Gold Coast) Field Ambulance.

Divisional Troops.

"B" Squadron I East Africa Armoured Car Regiment.

2 (South African) Anti-Tank Battery.

1 (South African) Field Battery.

One Section 6 (South African) Anti-Aircraft Battery.

3 (South African) Field Company.

19 (South African) Field Park Company.

One company (less one platoon) 1/3 King's African Rifles (Machine-Gun).

2 East Africa Pioneers.

2 East Africa Field Hygiene Section.

12 Divisional Ordnance Field Park.

No. 1 Irregular Company.

Det No. 4 Irregular Company.

Force Troops.

1 East African Armoured Car Regiment (less two squadrons).

I (South African) Light Tank Company.

I (South African) Medium Brigade (I and 2 Medium Batteries).

53 (East African) Light Battery.

4 (Rhodesian). Anti-Tank Battery.

APPENDIX "B."
Location of Air Units East Africa.
1st January 1941.

Headquarters.

Air Headquarters East Africa – Nairobi.

Advance Air H.Q., East Africa (as from 9.1.41) – Nanyuki.

No. 1 Bomber Brigade S.A.A.F. – Nanyuki.

R.A.F. Station – Nairobi.

R.A.F. Station – Eastleigh.

R.A.F. Station – Mombasa.

No. 2 Squadron S.A.A.F.

Headquarters – Nanyuki.

"A" Flight (Mobile) – Nanyuki.

"B" Flight Detachment (1) – Archer's Post.

"B" Flight Detachment (2) – Ndege's Nest.

"C" Flight Detachment (1) – Marsabit.

"C" Flight Detachment (2) – Lokitaung.

Reserve Aircraft – Nanyuki.

No. 3 Squadron S.A.A.F.

"A" Flight Detachment (I) – Garissa.

"A" Flight Detachment (2) – Lamu.

"B" Flight Detachment (I) – Nairobi.

"B" Flight Detachment (2) – Bura.

"C" Flight – Mombasa.

Squadrons.

No. 11 Squadron S.A.A.F.

H.Q. – Archer's Post.

"A," "B" and "C" Flights – Archer's Post.

No. 12 Squadron S.A.A.F.

H.Q. – Nanyuki.

"A" Flight, "B" Flight and Detachment.

"C" Flight – Nanyuki.

"C" Flight Detachment – Mombasa.

No. 34 Flight.

H.Q. – Mombasa.

Detachment – Mombasa.

Detachment – Dar-es-Salaam.

No. 40 Squadron S.A.A.F.

H.Q. – Marsabit.

"A" Flight – Lokitaung.

"B" and "C" Flights – Marsabit.

No. 41 Squadron S.A.A.F.

H.Q. – Garissa.

"A" Flight – Garissa.

"B" Flight – Bura.

"C" Flight – Ndege's Nest.

Estimated number of enemy aircraft within range of our bases as at 1st January, 1941:-

C.A. 133	28
S. 81	15
S. 79	20
C.R. 32	9
C.R. 42	11
R.O. 37	5
Total	88

Note (i). – It is more than likely that these numbers were added to from time to time during the subsequent months.

Note (ii). – Aircraft stationed north of the line Addis Abeba – Dire Daua are not included but were of course available for operations against our front.

APPENDIX "C."

Order of Battle of 11th and 12th (African) Divisions at commencement of operations, 10th, February, 1941.

11*th (African) Division.*

  H.Q. 11 (African) Division.

    11 (African) Divisional Signals.

  H.Q. 21 (East African) Infantry Brigade.

    21 (East African) Brigade Signal Section.

    1/2 King's African Rifles (attached 12 (African) Division at Wajir).

    1/4 King's African Rifles.

    1 Northern Rhodesian Regiment.

    53 (East African) Light Battery.

    53 (Gold Coast) Field Company.

    21 (East African) Infantry Brigade Group Company.

    2 (Zanzibar) Field Ambulance.

  H.Q. 23 (Nigeria) Infantry Brigade.

    23 (Nigeria) Brigade Signal Section.

    1 Nigeria Regiment.

    2 Nigeria Regiment.

    3 Nigeria Regiment.

    52 (Nigeria) Light Battery.

    51 (Nigeria) Field Company.

    23 (Nigeria) Infantry Brigade Group Company.

    3 (Nigeria) Field Ambulance.

  Divisional Troops.

    "C" Squadron I East African Armoured Car Regiment.

2 (South African) Medium Battery (6-inch Howitzers).

7 (South African) Field Brigade (5, 17 & 18 (South African) Field Batteries).

I (South African) Anti-tank Battery.

5 (South African) Anti-Aircraft Battery (less two sections).

16 (South African) Field Company.

18 (South African) Field Park Company.

"C" Company 1/3 King's African Rifles (Machine-gun).

1 East African Pioneers.

3 East African Field Hygiene Section.

11 Divisional Ordnance Field Park.

3 Ordnance Mobile Workshop.

Detachment No. 4 Irregular Company.

12th (African) Division.

H.Q. 12 (African) Division.

12 (African) Divisional Signals.

H.Q. 1 (South African) Infantry Brigade.

10 (South African) Brigade Signal Company.

1 Royal Natal Carbineers.

1 Transvaal Scottish.

1 Duke of Edinburgh's Own Regiment.

4 (South African) Field Brigade (10, 11 and 12 Field Batteries).

1 (South African) Field Company.

1 (South African) Infantry Brigade "Q" Services Company.

10 (South African) Field Ambulance.

H.Q. 22 (East African) Infantry Brigade.

22 (East African) Brigade Signal Section.

1/1 King's African Rifles.

5 King's African Rifles.

1/6 King's African Rifles.

22 Mountain Battery Royal Artillery.

54 (East African) Field Company.

22 (East African) Infantry Brigade Group Company.

1 (Tanganyika) Field Ambulance.

H.Q. 24 (Gold Coast) Infantry Brigade.

24 (Gold Coast) Brigade Signal Section.

1 (Gold Coast) Regiment.

2 (Gold Coast) Regiment.

3 (Gold Coast) Regiment.

51 (Gold Coast) Light Battery.

52 (Gold Coast) Field Company.

24 (Gold Coast) Infantry Brigade Group Company.

4 (Gold Coast) Field Ambulance.

Divisional Troops.

"B" Squadron 1 East African Armoured Car Regiment.

3 (South African) Armoured Car Company.

1 (South African) Light Tank Company.

1 (South African) Medium Battery (60 pounders).

1 (South African) Field Battery.

2 (South African) Anti-tank Battery.

4 (Rhodesian) Anti-tank Battery.

One section 5 (South African) Anti-aircraft Battery.

6 (South African) Anti-aircraft Battery (less three sections).

19 (South African) Field Park Company.

"A" Company 1/3 King's African Rifles (Machine-gun).

2 (East African) Field Hygiene Section.

12 Division Ordnance Field Park.

I (South African) Mobile General Workshop.

No. 1 Irregular Company.

Detachment No. 4 Irregular Company.

Force Troops.

I (East African) Armoured Car Regiment (less two squadrons).

I (South African) Medium Brigade H.Q. (less two batteries).

APPENDIX "D."
Order of Battle of 11th and 12th (African) Divisions.
23rd February, 1941.

11th (African) Division.

H.Q. 11 (African) Division.

11 (African) Divisional Signals.

H.Q. 22 (East African) Infantry Brigade.

22 (East African) Brigade Signal Section,

1/1 King's African Rifles.

5 King's African Rifles.

1/6 King's African Rifles.

22 Mountain Battery Royal Artillery.

54 (East African) Field Company.

22 (East African) Infantry Brigade Group Company.

1 (Tanganyika) Field Ambulance.

H.Q. 23 (Nigeria) Infantry Brigade.

23 (Nigeria) Brigade Signal Section.

1 Nigeria Regiment.

2 Nigeria Regiment.

3 Nigeria Regiment.

52 (Nigeria) Light Battery.

51 (Nigeria) Field Company.

23 (Nigeria) Infantry Brigade Group Company.

3 (Nigeria) Field Ambulance.

Divisional Troops.

1 East African Armoured Car Regiment (less "A" Squadron).

1 (South African) Light Tank Company.

I (South African) Medium Battery (60 pounders).

7 (South African) Field Brigade (5, 17 and 18 (South African) Field Batteries).

1 (South African) Field Battery.

1 (South African) Anti-tank Battery.

One Anti-Aircraft Section.

Two BREDA Anti-Aircraft Sections.

16 (South African) Field Company.

17 (South African) Field Park Company.

"C" Company 1/3 King's African Rifles (Machine-Gun).

5 (Kenya) Field Ambulance (less "A" Company).

3 (East African) Field Hygiene Section.

11 Divisional Ordnance Field Park.

12*th (African) Division.*

H.Q. 12 *(African) Division.*

12 (African) Division Signals.

H.Q. 21 *(East African) Infantry Brigade.*

21 (East African) Brigade Signal Section.

1/4 King's African Rifles.

1/2 King's African Rifles.

1 Northern Rhodesia Regiment.

53 (Gold Coast) Field Company.

21 (East African) Infantry Brigade Group Company.

2 (Zanzibar) Field Ambulance.

H.Q. 24 *(Gold Coast) Infantry Brigade.*

24 (Gold Coast) Brigade Signal Section.

1 Gold Coast Regiment.

2 Gold Coast Regiment.

3 Gold Coast Regiment.

51 (Gold Coast) Light Battery.

52 (Gold Coast) Field Company.

24 (Gold Coast) Infantry Brigade Group Company.

4 (Gold Coast) Field Ambulance.

Divisional Troops.

"A" Squadron I East African Armoured Car Regiment.

4 (South African) Field Brigade (10, 11 and 12 (South African) Field Batteries).

53 (East African) Light Battery.

Three sections Anti-aircraft.

One BREDA Section Anti-aircraft.

19 (South African) Field Park Company.

"A" Company 1/3 King's African Rifles (Machine-Gun).

2 (East African) Field Hygiene Section.

12 Divisional Ordnance Field Park.

Force Troops.

H.Q. 1 (South African) Infantry Brigade.

10 (South African) Brigade Signal Company.

1 Royal Natal Carbineers.

1 Transvaal Scottish.

1 Duke of Edinburgh's Own Regiment.

3 (South African) Armoured Car Company.

2 (South African) Anti-tank Battery.

One section Anti-aircraft.

1 (South African) Field Company.

1 (South African) Infantry Brigade "Q" Services Company.

10 (South African) Field Ambulance.

1 (South African) Medium Brigade (less 1 (South African) Medium Battery).

"A" Company 1 Northern Rhodesia Regiment.

APPENDIX "E."
Order of Battle of 11th (African) Division.
11*th March* 1941.

H.Q. 11 (African) Division.

11 (African) Divisional Signals.

1 *(South African) Infantry Brigade.*

10 (South African) Brigade Signal Company.

1 Royal Natal Carbineers.

1 Transvaal Scottish.

1 Duke of Edinburgh's Own Regiment.

3 (South African) Armoured Car Company.

2 (South African) Anti-tank Battery.

10 (South African) Field Ambulance.

2 (South African) Brigade "Q" Services Company.

22 *(East African) Infantry Brigade.*

22 (East African) Brigade Signal Section.

1/1 King's African Rifles.

5 King's African Rifles.

1/6 King's African Rifles.

22 Mountain Battery Royal Artillery.

1 (Tanganyika) Field Ambulance.

22 (East African) Infantry Brigade Group Company.

23 *(Nigeria) Infantry Brigade.*

23 (Nigeria) Brigade Signal Section.

1 Nigeria Regiment.
2 Nigeria Regiment.
3 Nigeria Regiment.
52 (Nigeria) Light Battery.
51 (Nigeria) Field Company.
3 (Nigeria) Field Ambulance.
23 (Nigeria) Infantry Brigade Group Company.
Divisional Troops.
1 East African Armoured Car Regiment (less one Squadron).
1 (South African) Light Tank Battery.
1 (South African) Medium Brigade.
4 (South African) Field Brigade.
7 (South African) Field Brigade.
1 (South African) Field Battery.
1 (South African) Anti-tank Battery.
5 (South African) Anti-aircraft Battery (less one section).
17 (South African) Field Park Company.
54 (East African) Field Company.
11 (Divisional) Ordnance Field Park.

APPENDIX "F."
TERMS PRESENTED BY THE GENERAL OFFICER COMMANDING EAST AFRICA FORCES TO THE ITALIAN DELEGATE FOR THE PROTECTION OF THE WOMEN AND CHILDREN IN ADDIS ABEBA.

1. It is accepted that the Italians are responsible for the protection of women and children in Addis Abeba until such time as arrangements are completed for guarding them by British forces, and that the personnel provided by the Italians for the protection of women and children in Addis Abeba will remain in the city until relieved of their duties by the British. This personnel will remain in British hands.

2. All Italian troops between the Awash River and Addis Abeba or in the vicinity of the city, *except those particularly posted for protection of women and children and property* in the town, will be engaged, and treated as enemy forces if they are not withdrawn before the arrival of the British forces.

3. To avoid unnecessary suffering to the civil population, essential services will be left intact with sufficient personnel to maintain them in working order, and at least two months supplies of food and fuel will be left in the city.

4. The railway with rolling stock and track from the Awash to Addis Abeba to be handed over to the British forces intact with the necessary personnel to operate it. If this is not carried out it may not be possible to maintain the civil population, thus entailing unnecessary suffering.

5. It is accepted that there will be no pause in military operations which will continue notwithstanding any of the arrangements agreed to in the foregoing paragraphs, with the exception of paragraph 2.

3 Apr. 41.

(ii)
REPLY RECEIVED FROM THE ITALIAN MILITARY COMMAND
4th April 1941.

1. Il Comando Militare Italiano ha gia provveduto per tutelare la sicurezze e il sostentamento della popolazione in Addis Abeba. I provvedimenti presi restano in atto anche dopo l'occupazione inglese.

2. La responsabilita dell'ordine a della sicurezza della popolazione sara assunta in pieno dal comando Inglese dal momento in cui le sue forze entreranno in Addis Abeba.

3. Un incaricato del Governo della Citta di Abeba si trovera ad Acachi, all'arrivo delle truppe inglesi, munito di bandiera bianca per dare tutte le indicazioni necessarie.

4. Il Comando militare Italiano non prende nessun altro impegno oltre quelli sopra detti. Addis Abeba, Aprile 1941.

Translation.

1. The Italian Military Command has already provided for the security and maintenance of the population of Addis Abeba. The measures taken will still remain in force after the British occupation.

2. The responsibility of order and security of the population will be taken over by the British Command *as soon as* the forces enter Addis Abeba.

3. A representative of the Government of Addis Abeba will be found at Acachi, on the arrival of the British troops, with a white flag. He will give the necessary information on matters.

4. The Italian Military Command takes no other duty apart from the above.

APPENDIX "G."
TROOPS LEFT IN BRITISH SOMALILAND BY A.O.C. ADEN FOR USE BY EAST AFRICA FORCE.

18 Mtn. Bty. R.A.
Four R.A.F. Armd. Cars.
G(R) Unit – Two Companies.
3/15 Punjabis – for protection Berbera Base.
A.A. Unit consisting of two 3″ and two Bofors A.A. Guns, for protection Berbera Base and aerodromes.
1 Flight Gladiators for local reconnaissance.

These were later transferred with the remainder of the Gladiator Squadron to East Africa Air Force.

Signals. Sufficient for the Base Sub Area.

Staff. Sub Area H.Q. and Staff pending the provision of personnel from East Africa Force.

APPENDIX "H."

Order of Battle of 12th (African) Division.

5th April 1941.

H.Q. 12 *(African) Division.*

    12 (African) Divisional Signals.

21 *(East African) Infantry Brigade.*

    21 (East African) Brigade Signal Section.

    1/2 King's African Rifles.

    1/4 King's African Rifles.

    1 Northern Rhodesia Regiment (less one company).

    One platoon 1 (South African) Armoured Car Company.

    53 (East African) Light Battery.

    53 (Gold Coast) Field Company.

    2 (Zanzibar) Field Ambulance.

    21 (East African) Infantry Brigade Group Company.

25 *(East African) Infantry Brigade.*

    25 (East African) Brigade Signal Section.

    2/3 King's African Rifles.

    2/4 King's African Rifles.

    One platoon I (South African) Armoured Car Company.

    3 (South African) Field Company.

    6 (Uganda) Field Ambulance.

    25 (East African) Infantry Brigade Group Company.

Divisional Troops.

    "A" Squadron I East African Armoured Car Regiment.

    1 (South African) Armoured Car Company (less two platoons).

    3 (South African) Field Brigade.

    3 (South African) Anti-tank Battery.

    4 (Rhodesian) Anti-tank Battery.

    One section 5 (South African) Anti-aircraft Battery.

    3 Gold Coast Regiment.

    3/4 King's African Rifles.

    1/3 King's African Rifles (Machine-Gun) (Less one company).

    19 (South African) Field Park Company.

    2 (East African) Field Hygiene Section.

    12 Divisional Ordnance Field Park.

    12 Divisional Survey Section.

12 Divisional Provost Company.

One company 4 (Gold Coast) Field Ambulance.

APPENDIX "J."
Allocation of Army Co-Operation Squadrons.
(11*th February* to 5*th April* 1941.)

Feb. 11*th*

11 (African) Division – 41 Squadron less I Flight.

12 (African) Division – One Flight 41 Squadron.

1 (South African) Division – 40 Squadron.

Mar. 3*rd* redistribution:-

11 (African) Division – One Flight 41 Squadron.

12 (African) Division – One Flight 41 Squadron.

Under Force Control – 41 Squadron H.Q. less 2 Flights.

1 (South African) Division – 40 Squadron.

Mar. 13*th* redistribution:-

11 (African) Division – 41 Squadron.

12 (African) Division – 40 Squadron less 2 Flights.

1 (South African) Division – 1 Flight 40 Squadron.

Notes

1. "I" (Infantry) tanks are medium tanks used for co-operation with infantry.

2. The total for the whole campaign waged by E.A. Force is estimated at 170,000.

NOTICE

The following Amendment should be made to the Despatch submitted by General Sir Archibald P. Wavell, G.C.B., C.M.G., M.C., Commander in Chief in the Middle East on Operations in East Africa, November 1940 – July 1941, published on Wednesday, the 10th of July, 1946, as a Supplement to the London Gazette of Tuesday, the 9th of July, 1946.

Part III – General.

Para. 106, Lines 20–21 *for* "impossible" *substitute* "possible".

3

LIEUTENANT GENERAL SIR WILLIAM PLATT'S DESPATCH ON OPERATIONS OF EAST AFRICA COMMAND, 12 JULY 1941 TO 8 JANUARY 1943

The War Office, July, 1946
OPERATIONS OF EAST AFRICA COMMAND,
12TH JULY, 1941 TO 8TH JANUARY, 1943
The following Despatch was submitted on 31st March, 1943, *to the Secretary of State for War by LIEUT.-GENERAL SIR WILLIAM PLATT, G.B.E., K.C.B., D.S.O., General Officer Commanding in Chief, East Africa Command.*

On 15th September, 1941, East Africa Force as part of Middle East Forces was abolished and replaced by East Africa Command directly under the War Office, covering the territories from Eritrea in the North to the Zambesi in the South. My predecessor Lieut.-General Sir Alan Cunningham, K.C.B., D.S.O., M.C., left East Africa on 29th August, 1941, to assume command of the Eighth Army in Middle East. Until my arrival on 5th December, 1941, Major-General H.E. de R. Wetherall, C.B., D.S.O., O.B.E., M.C., acted in command and was responsible for the operations against Gondar.

The Command was divided into four areas. Eritrea as an administrative area in the North:

12th (African) Division under Major-General C.C. Fowkes, C.B.E., D.S.O., M.C., covered Ethiopia and British Somaliland: 11th (African) Division, transformed into Central Area, covered Italian Somaliland, Uganda, Kenya, Zanzibar and Tanganyika: Southern Area comprising Nyasaland and Northern Rhodesia under Major-General G.R. Smallwood, D.S.O., M.C., with Headquarters at Salisbury in Southern Rhodesia, had also an advisory brief in the last named.

West African formations which had taken part in the operations against Italian East Africa from the South, were due to return to their own countries. The 23rd (Nigerian) Infantry Brigade left in August, 1941, and was followed in October by the 24th (Gold Coast) Infantry Brigade. Owing to shortage of artillery and engineer units in East Africa, 51st Battery and 53rd Field Company, both of the Gold Coast, were retained temporarily to take part in the reduction of the last remaining Italian stronghold at Gondar. Except in that area where General Nasi's forces were still holding out, organised resistance in Ethiopia had ceased prior to my predecessor's last despatch which dealt with operations up to the 11th of July, 1941.

Although military opposition by Italian forces had been almost eliminated, the maintenance of law and order over more than half a million square miles of conquered territory presented no small problem. The country was armed from North to South and from East to West, with rifles, ammunition, grenades and many automatics. More than 20,000 rifles, with over 20 million rounds of ammunition had been pumped into Ethiopia from the Sudan alone to aid the Patriots in their revolt against the Italian oppressor. The Italians issued arms in the unfulfilled hope that they would be used against British forces. Many thousands more were gleaned from deserted battlefields, and looted from hidden reserve dumps. None of these have yet been returned to us. None will be. Few have even been collected for use by the Regular Ethiopian Army. They are in the hands of Territorials, Irregulars, and ordinary brigands. Theft of rifles still continues in a manner worthy of the North-West frontier of India.

Many of these arms were in the hands of Patriot bands owing some form of allegiance and obedience to numerous Chiefs, who, in their turn, owed little allegiance or obedience to anyone. After action, on the elementary principle of living on the country, brigandage against local inhabitants was frequent. Despite this, the general desire of the Ethiopian to rid his country of the Italian, ensured a reasonable degree of security to the roads used by our troops as lines of communication. In attaining this our Occupied Territories Administration and the edicts of His Imperial Majesty The Emperor contributed their full share.

The number and variety of responsible administrators, civil and military, with whom Command Headquarters had to deal, often separately, made the task no easier. These included Military Administrators in Eritrea and Somalia, the Military Governor of British Somaliland, His Imperial Majesty, The Emperor as well as British Military authorities in Ethiopia, in addition to five civil Governors and one Resident in the southern half of the Command territory. The last six were to some extent co-ordinated by the East African Governors' Conference, but that co-ordination did not at that time include either the issue or acceptance of instructions. Even with the good will which has been generally accorded to me, this division into territories under independent civil Governors does not, from a military point of view, tend towards ease or rapidity of execution.

The problems of the Command were further complicated by the state of communications.

Except for the short length of railway joining the Copper Belt in Northern Rhodesia to the Union of South Africa, the only other railways between Eritrea and the Zambesi, and there were in fact only four, ran from West to East. There is no North and South railway communication.

Save in Uganda and the small Island of Zanzibar, there was nothing in the British Colonies, Protectorates and Mandated Territory which could be dignified by the name of "road." The so-called Great North road was "great" and "road" in name only, just an earth surface without foundation which the rain put out of action for anything but the lightest traffic for several days at a time. That was our one and only road of communication by land from North to South throughout British territory.

There was a great contrast, both in accomplishment and in future planning, in the countries captured from the Italians. In Ethiopia the bankrupt nation of Italy had, in the space of five years, constructed many hundred miles of tarred and beautifully graded roads rising at points to 9,000 feet above sea level, capable of use by the heaviest of traffic at all seasons and in all weathers.

PART II. – GONDAR OPERATIONS.

Gondar is situated on the Ethiopian plateau at a height of about 6,800 feet. To the North-East and South-East the country rises considerably higher, the highest peak being 14,000 feet. To the south the country falls to the depression containing Lake Tana, over 1,000 feet below the general level of the plateau. Erosion has been considerable, the plateau being cut up by a series of steep-sided valleys, sometimes several thousand feet deep. Communications on the plateau itself and from the surrounding plains to the plateau are difficult.

A series of small hills surrounding the town of Gondar overlook the principal routes of approach. The country is generally open, with scattered clumps of trees and bush. Streams are numerous, and water is plentiful.

There are three main approaches to Gondar. From the North by a good road from Asmara via Axum and the Wolchefit Pass: from the South-East from Dessie by an earth road with rickety bridges: from the West from Gedaref via Gallabat and Chelga by a rough track devoid of bridges over the main waterways. The forces of General Nasi were concentrated about Gondar with strong outlying detachments at Wolchefit, Kulkaber, Feroaber and Chelga.

The enemy troops about Wolchefit and Chelga were contained by troops from the Sudan under the Kaid. Early in September, with a view to concerting operations against Gondar as soon as practicable after cessation of the rains, East Africa Command accepted responsibility for all activities from the direction of Asmara and Dessie. The Sudanese about Chelga were to conform and co-operate, the Kaid, of necessity, retaining administrative control of his troops, 12th (African) Division took over control of all operations. Plans were made for 25th (East African) and 26th (East African) Infantry Brigades to relieve Sudan troops in the Wolchefit area. 25th (E.A.) Infantry Brigade effected this relief by 26th September, 1941.

Towards the end of September, the garrison of the exceptionally strong position of Wolchefit surrendered. This came as a surprise. It was due to pressure by the 25th Brigade and by Patriot Forces, and to bombing by aircraft. The road was now clear for our troops to move forward and make contact with the enemy defences North of Gondar itself. A change of plan was made necessary since the original plan had included a preliminary operation for the capture of Wolchefit.

The new plan was, briefly, to concentrate the main forces about Amba Giyorgis while a column attacked the Kulkaber – Feroaber position from the direction of Dessie, and others operated along the Metemma – Chelga road and round the West side of Lake Tana against the road Azozo – Gorgora.

Operations were held up for a fortnight by bad weather which made transport very difficult. In the second week of November, the 2nd Ethiopian Battalion under Lieut.-Colonel G. Benson, O.B.E., successfully cleared the Italians from their outlying posts between Gorgora and Azozo, after a long and tedious march round the West side of Lake Tana.

The next thrust was against the Kulkaber – Feroaber position, which was held in strength. An attack by 1/6 King's African Rifles and 1st East African Pioneers on 13th November, drove a deep wedge into the enemy's line. Unfortunately, however, our troops were unable to maintain their positions, and fell back under cover of darkness, bringing prisoners with them.

On 21st November a second attack was launched, 25th Brigade coming in from the North and 1/6 King's African Rifles and 1st East African Pioneers from the East. After stiff fighting this attack was successful.

The way was now clear for the final advance on Gondar. This took place at dawn on 27th November. Opposition was strong and our troops suffered a number of casualties, the majority of which were from mines and booby traps. The enemy's rifle and machine gun fire, though heavy, was inaccurate. By 1730 hours in the evening, the town was in our hands, though some of the surrounding garrisons did not get the order to surrender until the following day. A total of 23,000 prisoners was taken.

Spasmodic disorders and looting continued for several days in and around Gondar, but order was finally restored. The Crown Prince of Ethiopia, who had accompanied Advanced Headquarters 12th (African) Division throughout the operations, was installed on 29th November.

Throughout the operations our air forces, under Lieut.-Colonel Mostert, South African Air Force, had provided active and effective support. The enemy resistance in the air was negligible.

The change of plan brought about by the unexpected fall of Wolchefit in September had necessitated a change of line of supply, but the necessary administrative changes had been carried out satisfactorily and worked well.

The positions chosen by the enemy for the defence of Gondar were naturally strong, and he had plenty of time to strengthen them and protect them with wire, booby traps and landmines. Our artillery amounted to only 25 guns, and though we had control of the air, it was never possible to shell or bomb any centre of resistance with a really heavy concentration. Credit is due to the Infantry who fought their way forward to close quarters with their own weapons. The fall of Gondar, the last stronghold in Ethiopia, completed, in ten months, the eclipse of the Italian East African Empire. This final surrender was accomplished by African troops, drawn principally from East Africa, with a proportion from West Africa and the Sudan, 1st Battalion The Argyll and Sutherland Highlanders were the only troops other than those drawn from Africa to take part. The total number of casualties suffered by troops under East Africa Command during

November, 1941, was 369, the heaviest total for any one month since the inception of the campaign from Kenya.

Besides the officers and men who took part in the operations, credit is due to Major-General H.E. de R. Wetherall, C.B., D.S.O., O.B.E., M.C., who was generally responsible for direction, and to Major-General C.C. Fowkes, C.B.E., D.S.O., M.C., who commanded in the field with boldness and decision.

PART III. – MAJOR EVENTS IN ETHIOPIA AND ERITREA AFTER THE GONDAR OPERATIONS.

The fall of Gondar removed any immediate hostile threat to the territories comprising East Africa Command. It was thereby possible to concentrate on certain important internal matters. The most pressing and complex of these problems was the evacuation of Italians from Ethiopia.

Early in November, 1941, the Cabinet gave a formal decision that all Italians were to be evacuated from Ethiopia. This decision was in accordance with the demand which had been expressed loudly and frequently for some months by most Ethiopians from the Emperor himself downwards.

The Italian population of some 34,000 were mainly concentrated in or near the five largest towns – Addis Ababa, Gimma, Dessie, Diredaua and Harrar. The evacuation was not a simple movement of a mass of people from one area to another, but had several complicated features, namely:

(*a*) Compulsory separation from their families of men for evacuation to British East African territories;

(*b*) Repatriation to Italy in Italian ships of the women, children and old and infirm men;

(*c*) Retention in Ethiopia of a number of Italian men (and their families) for work on essential services pending replacement by Allied nationals from elsewhere;

(*d*) Uncertainty regarding the arrival of the Italian ships, and which port, Berbera or Jibouti – was to be used;

(*e*) The need to construct, and staff, staging camps for the evacuation of Italians of both sexes and all ages in territory that was by nature short of shade and water;

(*f*) A last minute desire on the part of the Ethiopian authorities to retain a large number of Italians for non-essential services, thereby engendering a spirit of opposition to evacuation among the Italians.

In December, 1941, the evacuation of Italian subjects from Ethiopia commenced. By February, 1942, despite shortage of shipping, 10,000 males had been transferred to East African territories. In May over 9,000 women, children and infirm males were embarked at Berbera in Italian ships for repatriation, every body and thing being safely moved from shore to ship by lighter. The Italian staffs of these ships expressed surprise at the healthy and well-fed appearance of the repatriates whom they had expected to find in a condition of starvation.

In November, 1942, a further 8,700 were repatriated to Italy from Benbera and Eritrea. Over 4,000 have changed their location within Africa.

The moves of these civilians were in addition to those of prisoners of war.

Retention of Italian technicians for essential services.

As the fall of Gondar was to be quickly followed by the evacuation of our troops from that neighbourhood, and their replacement by Ethiopian control and administration, it was immediately apparent that valuable and modern works installed throughout Ethiopia by the Italians would fall into disuse and ruin unless some competent technicians maintained them. As qualified personnel from Ethiopia or Allied countries were not available, an interim, proposal was made that a total of 500 Italian technicians should remain subject to my Intelligence staff being satisfied as regards each individual on the grounds of security. This proposal was accepted. The general Ethiopian clamour for total evacuation soon gave way to active obstruction to entrainment, to failure to disclose the presence of enemy subjects and even to hiding them. It is a matter for regret that others besides Ethiopians placed difficulties in my path in my endeavour to carry out the specific policy which I had been instructed to perform by His Majesty's Government.

Immediately on the arrival of His Majesty's Minister at Addis Ababa in February, 1942, I informed him verbally of the decision of His Majesty's Government and of my proposal for the temporary retention of 500 Italians for essential services. I explained fully my reasons, on grounds of military security, why I could not agree to that number being increased. Mr. Howe was good enough to say that he appreciated the position and that he considered my views were reasonable.

It was with some surprise that in April, after no previous consultation, I received copies of telegrams from His Majesty's Minister advocating the retention of no less than 2,800 Italians, making with their families a total of 4,000. It was with even greater surprise that I was informed by His Majesty's Minister himself, in July, 1943, that he had left England at the beginning of the year with instructions to review the whole problem of retention of Italians and to make his own recommendations. That was the first intimation I had received from any source of the existence of any such instructions. The orders I had received were never easy to execute. My difficulties were increased by contrary instructions to one person and their non-disclosure to myself as responsible authority.

In August, 1942, approval was given for the figure of 500 retained Italians to be increased to 700. Since then 600 who had been hiding have been rounded up from country districts. It would be too optimistic to suggest that the country even now is clear of "embusqués."

ERITREA.

When the East Africa Command came into being, Eritrea formed part of it chiefly because of a political supposition in some minds that Eritrea and Ethiopia were indivisible.

Before the Command had been in existence for many weeks it became apparent that this arrangement was not workable, due to the military fact that Massawa was to be developed as a Middle East Base and that an American Air Repair and Assembly Plant was to be established at Gura. Both of these projects were being carried out mainly for Middle East requirements. On 1st February, 1942, Eritrea came once more under the command of General Headquarters, Middle East.

ANGLO-ETHIOPIAN Agreement.

Before entering Ethiopia, the Emperor made repeated attempts to obtain from His Majesty's Government a Treaty of Agreement establishing the relations between Great Britain and Ethiopia. Although His Majesty's Government found itself unable at that stage to enter into any such formal agreement, the Secretary of State for Foreign Affairs made a pronouncement in Parliament on 4th February, 1941, which defined the British Government's intentions as regards the Emperor and his country's future. The text of this important pronouncement was as follows:

"His Majesty's Government would welcome the reappearance of an independent Ethiopian State and will recognise the claim of the Emperor Haile Selassie to the throne. The Emperor has intimated to His Majesty's Government that he will need assistance and guidance. His Majesty's Government agree with this view and consider that any such assistance and guidance in economic and political matters should be the subject of international agreement at the conclusion of peace. They re-affirm that they themselves have no territorial ambitions in Abyssinia.

In the meanwhile the conduct of military operations by Imperial Forces in parts of Abyssinia will require temporary measures of military guidance and control. These will be carried out in consultation with the Emperor, and will be brought to an end as soon as the situation permits."

In the letter formally communicating the text of this pronouncement to the Emperor, the Commander-in-Chief Middle East, General Sir Archibald P. Wavell, G.C.B., C.M.G., M.C., enlarged upon the final paragraph of the Secretary of State's pronouncement and explained the administrative machinery which he proposed to set up to enable him to fulfil the obligations imposed upon him as the Commander of the Army in Occupied Enemy Territory.

These obligations entailed the establishment of a Military Administration to administer the country in collaboration with the Emperor during the interval which necessarily elapsed between the return of the Emperor to his Capital on 5th May, 1941, and the signing of the Agreement some nine months later.

In accordance with the promise implied in the final paragraph of Mr. Eden's pronouncement, it was decided as soon as military circumstances permitted, to put an end as far as possible to the measure of administrative control exercised by the Occupied Territories Administration on behalf of the Commander-in-chief Middle East and subsequently on my behalf. The text of the Agreement which was to achieve this object was prepared by the Political Branch, East Africa

Command, after many discussions with the Emperor, and was the subject of two visits to London by the then Chief Political Officer, Major-General Sir Philip Mitchell, K.C.M.G., M.C. As the result of these discussions the Agreement in its final form was presented by Sir Philip Mitchell to the Emperor in December, 1941. The Emperor raised a number of minor points but eventually accepted the text with only unimportant modifications and the Agreement, and its accompanying Military Convention, were signed with due formality on 31st January, 1942.

The ability and patience with which Sir Philip Mitchell conducted these negotiations during many months against continuous difficulties, the principal and most consistent of which was that an ell was demanded for every inch offered, were beyond praise.

As a result of this Agreement, direct British control in Ethiopia became limited to the Reserved Areas comprising a belt of territory 25 miles wide along the border of French Somaliland, an area occupied principally by Somalis adjoining the British Somaliland border; the territory occupied by the Franco-Ethiopian railway; the Ogaden; and a number of cantonments of which Addis Ababa, Harrar and Diredaua were the most important.

In August, 1941, our troops were withdrawn from Addis Ababa, care of the aerodrome there being taken over by the British Military Mission to Ethiopia.

PART IV. – OUTBREAK OF WAR WITH JAPAN AND ITS EFFECT ON EAST AFRICA COMMAND.

Japan's entry into the war and her early successes brought the threat of war to the East African coast. My immediate problems as a result of this were re-orientation of the Command dispositions with the object of strengthening the defence of the coast, with particular reference to the port of Mombasa; and the preparation of East African formations for service overseas. As a corollary to these problems, some withdrawal of troops commenced from Ethiopia and the Northern Frontier District of Kenya where their retention could not be described as essential for the main war effort.

Operations against Ethiopia had naturally caused the Command to face North. It had now to face East. There were few troops along the coast. The few Coast Defence guns were obsolete British ones or captured Italian ones. There was not one anti-aircraft gun in the whole Command. There were practically no British artillery personnel. The training and expansion of African artillery personnel was in its infancy.

The sudden transformation of the relative quiet of Mombasa into an active naval base and a station for sea and land aircraft, increased the defensive potential in that area, but accentuated the urgency for adequate land defences. The demands of the three Services for material, artisans and transport, most of which had to be provided by the Army, rose to unprecedented heights. The allotment of sites for defence, storage, accommodation and other necessities created the conflicting claims to priority within a limited space usual in circumstances of urgency. Although every wish and every need could not be immediately met, the general spirit of co-operation and give-and-take which prevailed reduced major difficulties to a minimum.

In April the arrival of coast defence and anti-aircraft units, guns, personnel and stores commenced, and the Island of Mombasa and its surrounding territory began to assume an aspect of stronger defence. That improvement has been maintained.

In response to a War Office request made in December, 1941, 21st and 25th (East African) Brigades were selected for service overseas. The former Brigade was located in Kenya, and the latter in Ethiopia where it had recently taken part in the Gondar operations. This was the first time during the war that the employment of East African troops outside Africa had been considered, and the usual number of administrative problems arose in connection with establishments, types of transport, scales of rations, and availability or otherwise of food suitable for consumption by Africans. The 25th Brigade was due to embark at Massawa on 21st February, 1942, but early in that month it became apparent that this brigade would not be in a fit state to be sent overseas on that date or even for several months. I was forced regretfully to cancel its departure and nominated 22nd (East African) Infantry Brigade in its place. This Brigade had fought with distinction throughout the East African campaign, but many of its personnel had been away from their homes and amenities for considerable periods. Leave was an essential preliminary to embarkation, but it required time. Such are the distances, the paucity and condition of communications in East Africa, that it may take as much as four months for the personnel of a battalion to enjoy fourteen days' leave in their homes. In consequence the 22nd Brigade could not be ready for embarkation until the middle of May, 1942.

Early in March, 1942, the 21st (East African) Infantry Brigade completed its preparations and embarked at Mombasa for Ceylon.

Events in Malaya and other parts of the Far East led the Governors of the various territories in East Africa to examine with me how co-ordination between civil and military authorities in the event of invasion could be improved. As a result of this examination, the Secretary of State for the Colonies, on 19th April, 1942, increased the executive powers of the Chairman of the East African Governors in matters of common interest when urgent military necessity required. This decision eased many of the difficulties of my task. I am grateful to the Chairman of the Governors' Conference, and to the Governors, for their co-operation in bringing it about.

PART V. – MADAGASCAR, MAURITIUS, RODRIQUEZ AND SEYCHELLES.

In the first week of May, 1942, combined forces from Great Britain, acting under the direction of the Chiefs of Staff, attacked Diego Suarez in Madagascar. At the conclusion of this successful operation, certain of the British formations which had participated were required elsewhere. As relief the 22nd (East African)

Infantry Brigade Group, already prepared to move overseas, sailed from East Africa for Madagascar on 3rd June, 1942.

On 25th May, 1942, I received instructions that, at a later date, I was to take over command of all British troops in Madagascar. On 1st July, 1942, the occupied area of Madagascar came under my command.

Since the initial occupation of Diego Suarez it had become necessary to extend to the South the area occupied by the British forces as the economic life of Antsirane was dependent on the produce obtained from the country around Ambilobe. British patrols occupied Ambilobe without opposition and a British political officer was established in that place.

In Diego Suarez area, conditions rapidly returned to normal, although trade was restricted since the British blockade had effectively prevented the replacement of trade goods. Warehouses and shops were empty. With the active co-operation of the Union of South Africa, £5,000 worth of goods comprising tea, flour, and cotton piece goods were landed at Diego Suarez on 8th July, 1942. The delivery of these goods created a favourable impression among all sections of local inhabitants, being in strong contrast to the conditions prevailing in the unoccupied area of Madagascar.

On 1st September, 1942, the extent of the Command was further increased by the addition of Mauritius, Rodriquez and Seychelles, transferred from Army Headquarters in India. These Islands, together with Madagascar, were formed into an "Islands Area" under Major-General G.R. Smallwood, D.S.O., M.C., with Headquarters at Diego Suarez.

These Islands provide the Command with outposts in the Indian Ocean but their distance from the mainland, and the uncertainty of shipping and aircraft, render their reinforcement in the event of emergency problematical, and their regular visiting by Commanders and Staff Officers undesirably infrequent. Adequate air communications should be an automatic and immediate corollary to any considerable expansion of an extensive military command. On 1st August, 1942, my responsibility regarding Southern Rhodesia was transferred to the Union of South Africa.

PART VI. – OPERATIONS IN MADAGASCAR SUBSEQUENT TO THE OCCUPATION OF DIEGO SUAREZ.

Events leading up to further operations in Madagascar.

After the occupation of Diego Suarez, it was hoped that the attitude of Monsieur Annet, Governor General of Madagascar, would become more reasonable and that some degree of collaboration would supervene which would enable us to secure certain military objectives from the threat of Axis aggression whilst still maintaining the machinery of French Government in the Island. The most important military objectives were Majunga and Tulear on the West Coast from which we could improve air and sea control of the Mozambique Channel; the port of Tamatave on the East Coast, from which most of the produce of the Island is exported; Tananarive, in the centre, the capital and seat of Government, which possessed long range wireless installations communicating direct with Paris and Indo-China.

Various unofficial visitors from Tananarive arrived at Antsirane, and though they were not accredited by the Governor General, they were understood to represent his views. In July it became obvious that M. Annet, whilst toying with the idea of collaboration, was really playing for time until the rains commenced in October, was dancing to Vichy's tune, and that no sincere "rapprochement" could be expected from him. I was, therefore, reluctantly obliged to advise that further operations were essential. Sinkings of our shipping in the Mozambique Channel had increased. The possibility of enemy submarines receiving assistance from French ports had to be eliminated.

On 2nd July, the Island of Mayotte, the most easterly of the Comoro group, was occupied by English and East African Infantry landed by H.M.S. "Dauntless" and H.M.S. "Active." A seaplane base at the Northern end of the Mozambique Channel was thus secured.

On 26th June, after consultations with Field Marshal Smuts, I submitted a plan of operations for the extension of our control over Madagascar. Preparatory work in the detailed planning of this combined operation was started immediately. Major-General R.G. Sturges, C.B., A.D.C. and Brigadier F.W. Festing, D.S.O., were brought over from Madagascar to assist in this.

The plan of operations proposed by Admiral Sir J.F. Somerville, K.C.B., K.B.E., D.S.O. and myself in conjunction with Air Commodore M.L. Taylor, A.F.C., was briefly as follows:

(*a*) 29th Independent Infantry Brigade Group to carry out a surprise landing under cover of darkness at Majunga with a view to seizing the town and harbour, supported, in the event of opposition, by ships of the Royal Navy and aircraft of the Fleet Air Arm.

(*b*) As soon as a sufficient bridgehead had been secured ashore, the 22nd (East African) Infantry Brigade Group to land and advance on Tananarive. A small detachment of 22nd (E.A.) Infantry Brigade Group and South African Armoured Cars to land with 29th Independent Brigade and capture the important series of large bridges some 90–130 miles beyond Majunga.

(*c*) The advance of the East African Brigade on Tananarive was to be supported by an air component which was to move from Antsirane to Majunga as soon as the aerodrome at that place was fit to use.

(*d*) Whilst Majunga was being attacked, a diversionary landing to be made at Nosy Be while columns from the North were to advance along roads on the North-West and North-East of Madagascar with original objectives at Ambanja and Vohemar respectively. A further diversion was subsequently added by landing from warships at Morandava on the West coast.

(*e*) As soon as 22nd (E.A.) Infantry Brigade could start on their advance to Tananarive, the 29th Independent Brigade was to re-embark and be conveyed to Tamatave for a combined assault on that town. This operation was to be so timed that it would take place as the 22nd (E.A.) Brigade was approaching the capital. 29th Independent Brigade was then to advance on Brickaville, and Tananarive. 22nd (E.A.) Brigade was also to advance on Brickaville from Tananarive thus establishing communication across the centre of the Island.

In view of the approaching rainy season these operations were required to start by 8th September.

As in most plans for attack, and in all cases of landing operations, the chances of success depended greatly on surprise. Surprise in its turn depended on secrecy. The collection at Diego Suarez of the number of His Majesty's ships and transports necessary for the operation and the loading of troops, vehicles and stores, would have banished secrecy and limited surprise to the point or points selected for attack. No efforts at Diego Suarez, where both Infantry Brigades were located, could have eliminated this liability.

The ideal would have been to move all troops to be engaged to the mainland of Africa. Provision of shipping within the time available made that impracticable. 29th Independent Brigade was moved to Mombasa in the middle of August. A chance had to be taken with 22nd (E.A.) Brigade Group sailing from Diego Suarez direct to Majunga, but as they had not to be stowed tactically like the British Brigade, the dangers of leakage and intelligent anticipation were reduced.

As cover to the real plan, India was spoken of in confidential whispers as the destination of 29th Brigade. The arrival at Diego Suarez of 7th (South African) Brigade at the end of June and of 27th (Northern Rhodesian) Brigade in early August, gave colour to the rumour that 22nd (E.A.) Infantry Brigade was being relieved. Whatever the effect of this cover on subsequent operations, it certainly diverted the curiosity of the inhabitants of Kenya onto a false scent.

Other difficulties in implementing the plan were apparent; firstly the necessity of securing undamaged the vital bridges on the road Majunga – Tananarive some 90–130 miles from the coast. The total length of the set of bridges over the River Betsiboka was some 1,600 feet with one span of 452 feet. That span was known to be prepared for demolition. If these bridges were destroyed I had no equipment capable of repairing or replacing them and the advance would have to depend on deviation or the slow and laborious use of pontoon ferries. The problem seemed an ideal opportunity for the employment of paratroops. Unfortunately the War Office were unable to accede to my request that these should be made available for the purpose. Secondly, from a naval aspect, the landing at Tamatave was likely to be difficult, as the only sheltered water is inside the harbour and the possibility of using landing craft elsewhere depended on weather which could not be predicted.

In order to provide sufficient motor transport for these operations, five-and-a-half Reserve Mechanical Transport Companies were required from the mainland of East Africa Command. The provision of reserves of supplies, stores, ammunition and petrol, of signal equipment and personnel, and of personnel to man various installations on the lines of communication, was a severe strain on my slender resources. By reduction to the minimum elsewhere, provision was made, but on a scale of signals far below requirements.

At the end of August advantage was taken of the presence of the 29th Brigade at Mombasa to test defensive arrangements by a practice attack. In addition to the Naval, Military and Air operations involved, whch were made as realistic as circumstances permitted, the whole of Kenya, the eastern half of Tanganyika and the Islands of Zanzibar were, by special legislation, placed under a state of emergency for a period of several days. Surprise landings by the Royal Navy and Royal Marines took place at various points between Mombasa and Dar es Salaam. Pseudo-prisoners of war escaped. "Fifth Columnists" interrupted road and signal communications and spread false rumours. Activities of this nature were widespread and kept even remote places alive. The Civil Governments and population, both European and African, entered wholeheartedly into the exercise with beneficial results.

On 11th August, authority was received from the Chiefs of Staff to proceed with the execution of Madagascar operations. Admiral Sir J.F. Somerville, K.C.B., K.B.E., D.S.O., and myself were charged with the joint Direction of the operations. We nominated Rear-Admiral W.G. Tennant, C.B., M.V.O., and. Major-General R.G. Sturges, C.B., A.D.C., as Joint Commanders. The latter in turn appointed Brigadier F.W. Festing, D.S.O., and Captain G.A. Garnons-Williams, D.S.C., as Joint Assault Commanders for the operations against Majunga and Tamatave.

The assault on Majunga was finally settled to take place on 10th September, a delay of two days owing to the slow speed of some of the vessels in the three convoys that started from Mombasa.

Landing at Majunga.

By noon on 9th September the three convoys from Mombasa and the convoy carrying 22nd (E.A.) Brigade Group from Diego Suarez, met at their rendezvous in the Mozambique Channel. By dusk the whole force was just out of sight of land West of Majunga. Neither air nor surface craft had sighted the movement. Secrecy and surprise appeared to have been obtained. The spirit of all ranks and ratings was high. Shortly before midnight the leading ship of the column of 49 moving in single line ahead, dropped anchor. The remainder moved silently to their appointed stations. The moon had not yet risen. The Royal Navy under Admiral Tennant had, with great efficiency, brought every ship, unobserved, to its exact position with a short margin of time in hand, and gave us the chance of effecting a successful landing. Great credit is due to them.

Shortly after 0100 hours the Royal Welch Fusiliers and East Lancashire Regiment landed at a point on an open beach eight miles north of Majunga, quickly followed by Headquarters, 29th Independent Brigade. Their task was to attack the town from the North and North-East at dawn thus getting behind the coast defences.

At first light, the South Lancashire Regiment and 5 Commando landed at selected points on the sea front of the town itself.

Resistance was slight. No firing by naval guns was necessary. By 0800 hours the town was in our hands at a cost of twenty casualties. The reserve battalion and the transport of the Brigade were retained on board.

Soft sand and scrub in the dark caused some delay to the landing, behind the Royal Welch Fusiliers, of the South African Armoured Cars and one portée Company of 1/1 (Nyasaland) King's African Rifles whose task was to make a dash for the bridges over the River Kamoro and River Betsiboka. Despite this delay the first of these bridges, 90 miles inland, was secured intact by 1800 hours on the same day, 10th September, but the centre bridge of the three over the River Betsiboka, 40 miles further on, was found in the early hours of the following morning to have been blown. As the road-way of this bridge, over 400 feet long, had fortunately fallen straight down on to the river bed without turning over, the construction of ramps at each end enabled a continuous, though slow, stream of traffic to be maintained until the first heavy rains in October made it impassable.

Simultaneously with the landing at Majunga, the Island of Nosy Be on the North-West coast was occupied with its important sugar and carborundum factories. A South African Battalion Group of the 1st City Regiment began an advance from Beremanja towards Majunga. Some days later a small column started North from Majunga to meet the South Africans. When junction had been effected, both columns returned to their bases. Other small columns of South African troops went down the North East coast and cleared the road to Vohemar. A party of forty from 5 Commando landed from H.M.S. "Napier" at Morandava, a small town on the West coast of the Island. By advancing some forty miles inland on their push-bicycles, and by intelligent use of the telephone, this party created the desired impression that a column of various arms with mechanised transport was advancing on the capital from this place. After 48 hours on land, the diversion was re-embarked.

As soon as it became apparent that Majunga was safely in our hands, landing of 22nd (E.A.) Infantry Brigade Group commenced and the 29th Brigade returned to their ships preparatory for their voyage round the North of the Island for a fresh landing at Tamatave. Their re-embarkation was completed by the 13th September. They sailed the same day.

22nd (E.A.) Infantry Brigade had been previously organised into three Battalion Groups so that there would be no delay in the despatch of a small self-contained force as far inland as the strength of opposition permitted. At the same time care had to be taken against becoming prematurely involved with a superior force, and the possibility of defeat in detail. From a careful examination of "form" it appeared to me that the advantage of time gained outweighed the risks. When it became a practical fact that four to five days would be required to land each battalion group complete with its transport and supplies, the advantage of an early forward move became more obvious.

Disembarkation at Majunga was disappointing even though it was known before hand that there was no deep water quay against which the ships could unload. Everything had to be moved by landing craft or captured lighter. The landing craft had only arrived at Mombasa in August from India where they had been used for training purposes. There was no time to give them the complete overhaul they badly needed. There were neither spare craft nor spare parts. Some had to be cannibalised. The deficiency in quantity as well as quality was accentuated by the necessity to re-embark a proportion for the landing at Tamatave. It had not been possible to make a repair ship available. In these operations against Madagascar our luck held, but it may not do so a second time. The conditions as regards landing craft against which we toiled should never be repeated against an effective enemy.

The landing of a follow-up formation, and the setting of it on to an axis of advance inland, is a different operation to an assault from the sea with the limited objective of securing a bridgehead. It needs a separate staff, with vision ahead, who are neither immersed in, nor tired out from, the details of assault action and unloading tables. The assault staff and personnel have a full time task after a long night with little sleep, in dealing with the affairs of the moment in their immediate neighbourhood, which they generally, and of necessity, have to overcome in an *ad hoc* manner. They have no time for planning for more future operations. Exploitation of a successful landing requires a survey of the whole front affected; the selection of routes to the major line of advance; the utilisation of all local facilities, workshops, material, and means of transport; the accommodation of troops and siting of stores; the clearing of quays and beaches; the construction of roadways, etc. They must think days, even weeks, ahead. They must come fresh to their task.

French request for Terms.

On 13th September I moved my Headquarters ashore at Majunga and on the 16th received a wireless message from Monsieur Annet, the Governor General, asking me to receive Plenipotentiaries in order "to ask by what means we can, with honour, cease the conflict before the last battle takes place." The Plenipotentiaries were brought by South African aeroplane to Majunga on 17th September, and presented with conditions for the cessation of hostilities. They declared that these were not acceptable and returned to Tananarive the following morning.

During the advance on Tananarive opposition from fighting troops was encountered on a few occasions when Senegalese troops particularly, fought well. The chief obstacle to the advance was the number of road-blocks that the French had erected. Boulders, felled trees, craters and demolished bridges were constantly encountered. Sometimes these obstacles were continuous for a couple of miles. There were only short intervals between one area of obstruction and the next. Fortunately for us they were seldom covered by fire, but they required much time and labour for removal and repair.

As the column approached Tananarive, air reconnaissance and other intelligence made it clear that the French were withdrawing southwards towards Antsirabe, with Ambositra and Fianarantsoa beyond, blocking all roads heavily as they went. To follow them directly would be slow and would give the maximum opportunity for delaying action. I was therefore anxious to land troops on the South-East Coast of the Island and advance on Fianarantsoa from that direction as well as from Tananarive. From the map Mananjary and Manakara seemed particularly suitable. The former is connected with Fianarantsoa and Ambositra by road, while from the latter there is a railway, but no road inland fit for mechanical transport.

I flew to Diego Suarez on 23rd September to discuss the possibility of landing with Rear-Admiral Tennant. After an exhaustive examination, we reluctantly came to the conclusion that such an operation was not feasible. The swell and surf prevalent at that time of the year, and poor beaches, offered no chance of getting ashore, undamaged, even the minimum of mechanical transport. The same conditions obtained at Fort Dauphin. At Tulear in the South-West the situation was slightly better, but it was still not possible, in a reasonable time, to land sufficient mechanical transport. The port had some facilities which, together with the airfield and possibilities of establishing a sea-plane base, would make it of use for patrolling the Mozambique Channel. It was decided to establish a small garrison there. This was effected by H.M.S. "Birmingham," H.M.S. "Inconstant," H.M.A.S. "Napier" and H.M.N.S. "Vangalen" landing two companies of the Pretoria Regiment and a few armoured cars from Diego Suarez on 29th September.

Landing at Tamatave.

It had been my original intention that the assault on Tamatave on the East coast should take place as the leading troops of the 22nd (E.A.) Infantry Brigade were approaching Tananarive from the West, but the delays caused by demolitions and road-blocks made it undesirable for the convoy and escort to wait for exact co-ordination. Landing was accordingly fixed for the early morning of 18th September.

The only means of landing at Tamatave being from inside the harbour, the original plan had required a bombardment to precede the landing. As a result of negligible opposition encountered at Majunga, and in a desire to save life and avoid destruction, Rear-Admiral Tennant and I agreed to endeavour to enforce surrender without recourse to bombardment. When the convoy was off the town in the early hours of 18th September, wireless messages were sent calling for surrender. Later a Naval Officer approached the quay in a landing craft bearing a white flag to present terms. He was greeted by machine-gun fire. Ships' guns, of light calibre only, opened fire. After very few minutes, a white flag was hoisted on land and firing immediately ceased. Troops were landed and the town occupied without opposition. Little damage had been done by the naval bombardment.

Port facilities at Tamatave were better than at Majunga and disembarkation proceeded quickly.

From Tamatave the troops pushed on by rail and road to Brickaville, and thence towards Tananarive, in the face of difficulties from road-blocks and demolitions but with practically no fighting.

Entry into Tananarive.

On the late afternoon of 23rd September, after an engagement at Mahitsy necessitating the employment of the whole of the leading battalion supported by artillery and armoured cars, 22nd (East African) Brigade entered Tananarive, which had been declared an open town. They were received enthusiastically, by all classes of the population who cheered and threw flowers at the passing soldiers.

During the fourteen days since the first British soldier set foot on shore at Majunga to our entry into the capital, 360 miles distant, the same battalion group was in the lead; it comprised 1/1 (Nyasaland) King's African Rifles, 28 Field Battery, 9th Field Regiment R.A., and South African Armoured Cars, and was under Lieut.-Colonel J. McNab.

Patrols were at once sent southwards to maintain contact with the withdrawing French forces, and eastwards to gain touch with 29th Brigade. The latter was effected on 25th September.

Events subsequent to the occupation of Tananarive.

The distances covered in converging on the capital from the West and from the East had been a severe drain on our resources, especially petrol, of which less than fifty miles per vehicle remained; a short pause was necessary to consolidate our administrative arrangements before any further major move could be commenced.

Fortunately, the railway, with the serious exception of two adjacent bridges just north of Brickaville, was undamaged and in good condition, and a large proportion of the rolling-stock had fallen into our hands. This enabled me to transfer my base from Majunga with its poor harbour facilities, long road carry, and broken Betsiboka bridge, to Tamatave. From this new base troops and stores could be moved by rail to Tananarive in a comparatively short time with only the one break over the bridges destroyed near Brickaville. The construction of diversions to circumvent them was estimated at, and accomplished within, six weeks.

In addition to military considerations, the machinery of Government in the capital had to be restarted. Some of the officials, notably the Secretary-General, were unwilling to co-operate and had to be removed. In a few days a successor was found who carried the support of the heads of the Political, Economic and Financial departments, and a form of Government was set up which kept the administrative machine working. The knowledge and tact of my Chief Political Officer, Major-General Lord Rennell of Rodd, were responsible for effecting this solution.

On the 26th September I moved my Headquarters from Majunga to Tananarive and on the 11th October I handed over command to Major-General Smallwood, General Officer Commanding Islands Area, who was responsible on the spot for operations subsequent to that date.

The Advance Southwards.

At the end of September the advance South from Tananarive was resumed. Antsirabe was occupied on 2nd October and Fianarantsoa on the 29th. A few engagements took place but again opposition was mainly from road-blocks and demolitions.

On 18th October what appeared to be serious opposition was encountered at Andriamanalina. 1/6 (Tanganyika) King's African Rifles made a twenty-four hour march, all on foot without any form of transport, to the rear of the enemy. 5th (Kenya) King's African Rifles moved similarly, but a shorter distance, to one flank. At dawn on 19th October these two battalions, with perfect timing and good execution, attacked, supported by fire from 20th Field Battery R.A. of 9th Field Regiment, and by 56th (Uganda) Field Battery, East African Artillery, the whole under command of Brigadier W.A. Dimoline, O.B.E., M.C. Seven hundred prisoners, two 75 mm. guns, one 20 mm. A.A. gun, 7 mortars and 16 heavy machine-guns were captured. Such was the effect of the artillery fire, and the attack from unexpected directions, that we suffered no casualties.

On 4th November, Monsieur Annet again sent a Plenipotentiary to obtain terms for an Armistice. Our terms, the same as had been offered on 17th September, were accepted. Hostilities ceased at 1400 hrs. on 5th November exactly eight weeks from the day, and 660 miles from the place, of landing at Majunga.

The casualties in 22nd (E.A.) Brigade Group were British officers 4 killed and 4 wounded, British other ranks 5 killed and 9 wounded, Africans 21 killed and 77 wounded.

Throughout the operations air support by bombing and reconnaissance was given by the Air Component under Colonel S.A. Melville, O.B.E., S.A.A.F., consisting of:-

Special Squadron Fleet Air Arm.
1433 Flight Royal Air Force.
16 Squadron South African Air Force.

For the landing at Majunga and Tamatave air cover and reconnaissance was provided by H.M.S. Illustrious.

On many days, especially in the second half of October and in November, weather was bad for flying with frequent thick, low cloud. Smoke-haze from countless grass fires hampered observation. The greater part of the Island was "inhospitable," offering few chances for a forced landing. Despite these difficulties the Air Component carried out all tasks asked of them with zeal and efficiency and gave effective support to the advancing troops. I am grateful to Colonel Melville and to the officers and men of the Royal Navy, Royal Air Force and South African Air Force who took part.

PART VII. – CAPITULATION OF JIBOUTI.

At the end of the Italian East Africa campaign, French Somaliland still adhered to the Vichy Government, and the Port of Jibouti, the terminal of the Addis Ababa – Jibouti railway, could not be used by us.

In the Autumn, of 1941, after negotiations had failed to persuade the Government of French Somaliland to give us port and rail facilities, a land and sea blockade was imposed. On the entry of Japan into the war in December the sea blockade was lifted. Jibouti was able to obtain food supplies by dhow from the Yemen, and by submarine and escorted ship from Madagascar. As a land blockade without a sea blockade was useless, that also was lifted.

The capitulation of the Vichy Forces in Madagascar caused much concern in Jibouti, but the attitude of the Government towards us did not change. The Allied landings in North Africa early in November still further disturbed opinion in French Somaliland. Towards the end of the month it became clear that a crisis was approaching, and on the 28th, Colonel Raynal, Commander of the 1st Battalion Tirailleurs Sengalais, with his Battalion and a large percentage of the artillery personnel of the garrison, crossed the frontier at Zeila and announced their adherence to the United Nations. The party, which amounted to nearly one-third of the garrison, brought with it personal arms and equipment.

On my visiting Harrar on 7th December I learnt that the American Consul from Aden had flown to Zeila the previous day, and had gone into Jibouti, on direct instructions from Washington, to examine and report on the situation.

The next few days were occupied by the authorities in Jibouti endeavouring to play off the Fighting French against ourselves, and either or both of us against a hinted commitment to the American Consul. These manoeuvres were dispelled by a visit to Aden where I met the Acting Governor, Senior Naval Officer, Air Officer Commanding, American Consul and Mr. Hopkinson who arrived opportunely, having been kindly sent by the Minister of State to help me in political discussions.

In the middle of December the Acting Governor of Jibouti, General Dupont, invited the British Military Commander to visit him to discuss the situation. Although the Fighting French were excluded from the invitation, I gave instructions, with specific safeguards regarding the Fighting French, to Major-General Fowkes to accept the invitation. On 17th December he and Mr. Hopkinson presented themselves at the Frontier and were conveyed by special train to Jibouti, where they were greeted with enthusiasm by the populace and accommodated at Government House.

No agreement was reached at the meeting, but an alternative proposal was put forward by General Dupont for an economic agreement with the United Nations. This was unacceptable. General Dupont was informed in clear terms that the only means of settlement was for French Somaliland to join the United Nations as part of the Fighting French. Our representatives returned to Harrar.

On 24th December, a further communication was received from General Dupont to the effect that it was impossible for him to negotiate with the Fighting

French and he returned to his previous proposals for an economic agreement with representatives of the British and United States Governments. From this reply it was clear that more drastic steps were needed to resolve the situation. My instructions from the Chiefs of Staff were to the effect that all efforts short of serious bloodshed were to be made to bring the Colony over to the Fighting French. I felt that this could best be done by continuing to present the facts of the case to the populace who had been misled regarding the true state of affairs. To this end leaflets were frequently dropped from the air.

At the same time I had to be prepared to face the possibility of armed resistance by those whose anti-Gaullist attitude in the past made them ready to go to any lengths for their own salvation. A display of overwhelming armed strength would make it clear that fighting was useless.

The two big bridges on the railway between the frontier station at Dauonle and the town of Jibouti were a further care. One was at Hol Hol, 30 miles inside the frontier, and the other at Chebele only 10 miles from the town of Jibouti. If either of these were destroyed, the railway would be out of action for the rest of the war.

Plans were laid for a Fighting French Force under Colonel Raynal to move into French Somaliland along the railway to secure these bridges, and at the same time try and rally the remaining garrison to their side.

Should this have failed to produce the required effect, and after a last appeal by pamphlet from the air, a naval and air demonstration off the town was arranged, concurrent with an advance of British troops into the Colony. All Services had strict instructions not to open fire unless first fired upon themselves by the French.

On 26th December, Colonel Raynal's Force moved in, and successfully seized the bridges, rallying various outlying garrisons on the way. On the 27th and 28th, a large party of the garrison came over to them, and at 1000 hours on the 28th, the Acting Governor sent a message asking for an interview with General Fowkes. The interview was held that night at Chebele in a railway coach, Monsieur Chancel, Free French Delegate in East Africa, being present. General Dupont signed an agreement whereby French Somaliland took her place as part of the Fighting French on the side of the Allied Nations. The anxieties of the last few days were terminated without bloodshed. Credit for this is due to Major-General Fowkes, Mr. Hopkinson and Monsieur Chancel. The resolution, patience and co-operation of Monsieur Chancel were remarkable and made a great contribution to our common cause.

On New Year's Day, 1943, General de Division P. Legentilhomme, immediately on his arrival in East Africa as High Commissioner for the French Possessions in the Indian Ocean, visited Jibouti where he was received by a guard of honour and carried out a formal inspection of the troops. I accompanied him on this visit, and a week later at Tananarive handed over to him responsibility for the administration of Madagascar, less the defended area at and around Diego Suarez, with due ceremony and in an atmosphere of friendship and collaboration.

4

ADMIRAL E.N. SYFRET'S DESPATCH ON OPERATIONS IN MADAGASCAR, MAY 1942

THE CAPTURE OF DIEGO SUAREZ

The following Despatch was submitted to the Lords Commissioners of the Admiralty on the 16th June, 1942, by Rear-Admiral E.N. Syfret, C.B., Flag Officer Commanding, Force "F":-

Office of Flag Officer Commanding,
Force "F."

16th June, 1942.

Be pleased to lay before the Board the accompanying report on the capture of Diego Suarez, which covers the period when the first convoy left Durban until the entry of the Fleet into Diego Suarez on 8th and 9th May, 1942.

2. In view of the detailed nature of the operation orders and observing that the operations were carried out almost exactly as laid down therein, I have purposely phrased my report in broad terms, sufficient to give a connected and general story, and stressing certain salient factors and incidents.

3. I have not made any mention of the operations of the Army, as these will be reported by Major-General R.G. Sturges, C.B., Royal Marines, who was in command of Force 121 under me, but I wish here to place on record the excellent relations that existed throughout the operation between the Royal Navy, the Army and the South African Air Force.

Co-operation at all times between the Services was most cordial, and to this must be attributed a great measure of the success of the enterprise.

4. I also wish to record the excellent manner in which H.M. Ships, Royal Fleet Auxiliaries, and Ships of the Merchant Navy, carried out their tasks. The enthusiasm and efficiency shown by Captains, Officers and Ships' Companies were most gratifying.

Few references will be found in this report to the work performed by the Corvettes since the nature of their duties was not so spectacular as that of other units. But throughout, and subsequent to, the operation, whether providing A/S[1] protection or ferrying troops and stores, they carried out their duties in fine spirit, and most efficiently.

(Signed) E.N. SYFRET,
Rear-Admiral.

SECTION I
DURBAN TO DISPERSAL FOR FINAL APPROACH TO COURRIER BAY.

The slow convoy comprising eight Motor Transport ships, tankers and the tank landing ship sailed from Durban in accordance with programme on 25th April, escorted by DEVONSHIRE (Captain R.D. Oliver), two low endurance destroyers, 14th M/S² Flotilla and 3rd Escort Group. ANTHONY, delayed by defects, sailed later to overtake the convoy, as did CITY OF HONG KONG, who had not arrived in time to sail with the convoy. She sailed the following day escorted by two corvettes.

2. The passage of the convoy proceeded according to plan, but time had to be "wasted" owing to considerable favourable currents being experienced.

3. On 28th April, the fast convoy comprising the five assault ships, and three transports carrying personnel, and escorted by RAMILLIES (wearing my Flag), ILLUSTRIOUS, HERMIONE, and six destroyers, sailed from Durban.

4. The General Officer Commanding, Major-General Sturges, Royal Marines, and three of his Staff, together with Colonel Melville, South African Air Force, and two Staff Officers, embarked in my Flagship.

5. The passage up the Mozambique Channel was made in excellent conditions, and favourable currents experienced necessitated adjustment of speed to ensure not being ahead of time at the rendezvous with the slow convoy on D minus 2.

6. On 1st May, the course of the convoy was altered to the Eastward to keep clear of shipping, a certain amount of which was sighted from time to time.

7. A report received on 2nd May that a submarine had arrived at Majunga together with reports of sightings of U-boats in mid-channel, suggested that our movements were being anticipated and caused me some apprehension. A/S air patrols maintained for the rest of the passage, however, sighted nothing.

8. During the passage a number of intelligence reports were received which, if accepted, required certain modifications to the orders for the assault. After discussion with the General, certain amendments to the plan were decided upon and subsequently distributed to the Assault Commanders and others concerned. In the event some of these intelligence reports proved to be most valuable.

9. In addition, complete sets of orders for the assaults on Tamatave and Majunga were produced and distributed to all ships concerned.

10. During the night 1st/2nd May definite orders were received from the Admiralty that Operation "Ironclad" was to proceed. On 2nd May instructions were received regarding the nature of an "Ultimatum" which was to be delivered by all possible means to the Governor as soon as the attack on Diego Suarez

had started. This required the production of English and French versions for dropping by aircraft and delivery by hand as and when the opportunity should arise. These instructions were distributed to ILLUSTRIOUS, to the Military Assault Commander, and to Officers Commanding the Assault Battalions.

D minus 2.

11. At 0835 on 3rd May, INDOMITABLE, wearing the Flag of Rear-Admiral (Aircraft) (Rear-Admiral D.W. Boyd), and escorted by two destroyers, joined me as previously arranged, and a complete set of operation orders were flown across to Rear-Admiral (Aircraft).

12. Less than forty-eight hours were thus available for the Rear-Admiral and INDOMITABLE to study and absorb and arrange for compliance with the many and complicated air commitments.

   Certain alterations in the number and nature of the tasks allotted to the aircraft were considered desirable by Rear-Admiral (A), and as a result of discussion of the points by signal, I approved certain modifications, which, while retaining the essential requirements, made the operation of the aircraft and the co-operation between the carriers more satisfactory for them.

13. Aircraft sent ahead in the morning facilitated contact with the slow convoy located some 60 miles ahead of me.

14. DEVONSHIRE reported that practically all the destroyers, corvettes, and sloops escorting the convoy had been refuelled during the passage from EASE-DALE, whose work in this respect had been magnificent, and from DEVON-SHIRE herself.

15. During D minus 2 and the following night, the destroyers escorting the fast convoy, and HERMIONE, completed with oil from EASEDALE. DERWENT-DALE, also intended for oiling at sea, had proved unsatisfactory for this purpose.

16. By dusk the fast convoy had closed to about four miles from the slow convoy, and remained in that position until the time came to form up for the final approach the following afternoon.

   An unexpected North-Easterly set showed that the convoys were ahead of schedule, and time had to be "wasted" by large alterations of course.

17. Weather conditions were excellent and visibility extreme. The convoys were in sight of Mayotta Island 40 miles distant, for most of the day, but were probably too far off to be observed.

D minus 1.

18. At 1430 Group 1, comprising RAMILLIES, carriers and destroyer screen, disengaged and at 1500 Groups II to V, comprising DEVONSHIRE, transports and escort, proceeded under the orders of the Commanding Officer, DEVON-SHIRE, in execution of previous orders.

At 1700 HERMIONE was detached to proceed with her diversionary operation to the Eastward of Diego Suarez.

SECTION II
FINAL APPROACH UP TO AND INCLUDING
THE ASSAULT LANDING.

19. Whilst Groups II to V inclusive were making their final approach RAMILLIES and the carriers proceeded to a position to the West of Cape Amber some 30 miles from the land.

At 0300 the carriers and four destroyers were detached under the orders of Rear-Admiral (A), to operate independently as requisite for flying operations, RAMILLIES with her screen remaining in the vicinity.

20. ANTHONY, who had been sent in with LAFOREY and LIGHTNING to accompany them during the buoying of the channel and thence to come out and report progress made, to me, rejoined my Flag at 0255.

She reported conditions for landing were very good, that the channel had been buoyed without difficulty, and that at 0115 WINCHESTER CASTLE was approaching the final turning point before the anchorage, with the remainder of the ships closed up.

This was a great relief to me, and everything up to that moment seemed set fair.

21. Groups II to V made the passage to their anchorages as planned. This was greatly to the credit of all, but particularly so to the Commanding Officer, DEVONSHIRE, on whom lay the main responsibility.

22. It had been anticipated that unpredictable, varying and possibly strong currents would be experienced and, in the event, the unpredictable nature of these currents was confirmed.

However, the night being clear, star sights and the use of R.D.F.[3] echoes from islets and prominent land, together with good visibility, made it possible to allow for these variations.

23. Meanwhile, LAFOREY and LIGHTNING had gone inshore, LAFOREY's task being to buoy the channel roughly, and ascertain the conditions for landing craft, LIGHTNING'S initial task being to act as a navigational fixed light to mark Nosi Fati shoal – the starting point for the approaching ships.

In due course, LAFOREY laid her first lighted dan, and thereafter buoyed the approach channel as planned.

D.1.

24. Unfortunately, the first Main Channel buoy was either laid by LAFOREY in the incorrect position or dragged, with the result that the sweepers went too close to Nosi Fati shoal and all four of them parted their sweeps.

M/S 14 was unaware at the time that the sweeps of all had parted, and believed that the channel was being swept according to plan.

In fact, this was not the case, and the channel so far as the initial anchor berth of the leading ships of the Assault Force, was not swept.

25. At 0124 DEVONSHIRE rounded Nosi Hara and anchored as arranged, the transports and M.T. ships anchoring to seaward in their allotted berths.

26. At 0154 WINCHESTER CASTLE anchored silently in her pre-arranged position, assault landing craft were lowered and by 0214 FREESIA, followed by ROMNEY and CROMARTY, assault landing craft, and LAFOREY, were proceeding up Courrier Bay for the point where the assault craft would be unleashed to attack Red Beach.

27. At 0303 a mine detonated in ROMNEY's sweep and others were seen to have been cut by her. A second mine detonated and parted ROMNEY's sweep at 0315.

The setting off point for the assault craft was reached at 0308 by which time it was estimated that at least 17 mines had been cut or detonated.

The skill, coolness, and accuracy with which these ships and craft were brought safely through a most difficult channel bristling with mines, is above all praise, and is a shining example of devotion to duty.

28. At 0230 the assault craft containing troops of No. 5 Commando and B Company of 2 East Lancashire Regiment, which was under command, set off for Red Beach, in the North part of Courrier Bay. LAFOREY and FREESIA stood by as ordered, to give support.

LIGHTNING and ROYAL ULSTERMAN who had followed up the channel arrived at 0415, and on the return of A.L.C.s[4] from Red Beach at 0515, troops from ROYAL ULSTERMAN embarked in them and set off at 0611 for Blue Beach, at Basse Point.

29. Meanwhile, assault craft containing I Royal Scots Fusiliers and 2 Royal Welsh Fusiliers from KEREN[5] and KARANJA respectively had left their ships at 0227 and 0319 for Green and White Beaches in Ambararata Bay. These beaches were located successfully without the use of the Lorenz beam which was ineffective owing to the line of the ships at anchor coinciding with the approach to White Beach.

Complete surprise was achieved at Red, Green and White Beaches, and only at Blue Beach was opposition experienced. This was successfully overcome by troops which had landed at White Beach, crossed the peninsula, and taken the defenders in the rear.

By 0620 about 2,300 of our troops had been landed.

30. The situation in the main anchorage was that mines were likely to be encountered to the North and East of a line joining Nosi Famaho to Mangoaka Point and the move to Ambararata Bay anchorage could not be made until a clearance sweep had been carried out. This was completed without any mines being cut by 0750, and ships were then ordered to shift billet. This anchorage had been laid

out when it was considered that White would be developed as the main beach, and in consequence the turn round to Blue Beach was long and it was obviously desirable to move the anchorage opposite Blue Beach. Sweepers were instructed to clear a new anchorage, but before it could be completed, 24 mines had been cut, AURICULA mined, and so much gear destroyed as to prejudice subsequent sweeping operations in the main harbour. It was therefore decided to abandon further sweeping and accept the longer turn round and bad loading conditions caused by wind and sea. Difficulty was experienced in finding a suitable beach for BACHAQUERO[6] and she was finally beached on Red centre in the afternoon after being swept in by CROMARTY.

31. To turn to the picture of the situation as seen by the G.O.C., and me in the Flagship to seaward.

At 0314, having then received ANTHONY's report, I informed the Admiralty that the operation had begun, this message being cleared at 0351.

My first intimation of any occurrence inshore was LAFOREY's report at 0318 that mines had been cut off Red Beach.

At about 0440 sighting of starshell showed that HERMIONE was carrying out the prearranged diversion on the East coast.

But communication with ships inshore was poor, and undependable, and indeed so they remained for much of D.1.

The first and positive report of progress was LAFOREY's message received at 0540 stating that there was no sign of opposition ashore and an optimistic suggestion that the Fleet could now enter Courrier Bay.

Messages, some of them very much delayed, showed that the vital No. 7 Battery had been captured, and that our troops everywhere seemed to be advancing, taking prisoners and incurring negligible casualties themselves.

32. I knew that air operations had proceeded according to plan and by 0720 I felt that the assault had made a very good start. Troops advancing, prisoners taken, HERMIONE's diversion had proceeded satisfactorily, and air attacks successful both on the aerodrome and hangar and on ships including an A.M.C. and a submarine, in harbour.

On the debit side, it was clear, however, that the unswept mines in Courrier Bay were causing delays to disembarkation and the rejection of my "ultimatum" by the Military Commander showed that opposition might be expected to stiffen.

In view of the probable presence of French submarines, I was apprehensive for the safety of RAMILLIES and the carriers operating in restricted waters to seaward, and also to some extent for the ships inshore, though the establishment of A/S patrols by the corvettes in the entrances was some comfort.

33. During the forenoon, although news was somewhat scanty, it seemed clear that the disembarkation was proceeding satisfactorily, and our assault troops advancing to their objectives though it was evident that resistance on the Antsirane axis was stiffening.

SECTION III
AFTER THE ASSAULT LANDING TO THE FLEET'S ENTRY INTO DIEGO SUAREZ.

D.1.

34. As soon as the 17th Brigade started to land, the G.O.C. expressed his wish to disembark and accordingly RAMILLIES proceeded down the channel to the Eastward of Nosi Fati and at 1430, G.O.C. and Staff, together with my Chief of Staff, were disembarked into ANTHONY and thence to KEREN and the shore.

35. During the afternoon two Morane fighters machine-gunned the beaches on two occasions without causing any casualties. This was the only time throughout the entire operation when enemy aircraft caused any inconvenience.

36. At 2325 orders were given to sail the fast convoy at 0400/D.2 and the slow at 1600/D.2 for Diego Suarez. At 0245 these orders were cancelled as it had become obvious that the entry into Diego Suarez could not be made on D.2. As DEVONSHIRE was no longer required for bombarding she was ordered to refuel and put to sea; later she was ordered to join HERMIONE in readiness for bombarding Oranjia. Four ships of 14th M/S Flotilla were also sailed to be ready to sweep the entrance channel to Diego Suarez.

37. G.O.C. reported that the attack on the Antsirane position had been held up but that a fresh assault would be made at daylight. He asked for air support and this was arranged.

D.2.

38. As the time when entry into Diego Suarez would be possible was so uncertain, I deemed it advisable to refuel RAMILLIES and screen forthwith. This was commenced at 0800/D.2 in the Ambararata anchorage. Subsequently the aircraft carrier screening destroyers were relieved to enable them to refuel.

39. During the forenoon, no information was forthcoming as to the progress of the assault, and it was not until 1250 that I learnt that it had failed.

40. At about 1400 the General arrived on board. Things were not going well, he said. The 29th Brigade had been held up about 3–5 miles South of Antsirane since the previous afternoon. The enemy held a strong, well-sited defensive, position; they were plentifully equipped with 75 mm. and machine guns. The 29th Brigade in 30 hours had marched 18 miles, and had made two unsuccessful attacks on this well-defended position. Their casualties were, high – 25 per cent. over the whole brigade.[7] The General decided to put in a night attack against the Antsirane position with the 17th Brigade, assisted as necessary by 29 Independent Brigade, with zero hour at 2000 hours. The 17th Brigade were gradually getting up to the front line, mostly on foot, and the majority should be in position by 1800. He considered that after a two hours' rest they should be ready to go into battle.

He was emphatic the attack must be carried out before the moon rose at 2300, as the position was too strong to be captured in moonlight or daylight in the absence of strong artillery support. Any further delay to give the troops longer to rest would be playing into the enemy's hands.

41. I offered any and all assistance the Fleet could give. The enemy's position was outside the range of RAMILLIES' and cruisers' guns. Aircraft bombing up to zero hour was promised. The General asked if I could land a party on Antsirane peninsula to create a diversion in the enemy's rear. I replied that I would try to get 50 Royal Marines there by means of a destroyer. I asked for zero hour to be delayed till 2030 in order to give a little more time (it was then 1430) to put this project into effect, as the party had yet to be collected, a destroyer detailed, and a 100 miles' journey lay before them. Assistance from No. 5 Commando who were in control of Diego Suarez North peninsula would be forthcoming, the General said, if they could find boats to carry them across Port Nievre.

42. H.M.S. ANTHONY was called alongside and the Commanding Officer, Lieutenant-Commander Hodges, given his instructions. Captain Price, R.M., of H.M.S. RAMILLIES, was sent for, given his instructions and told to collect 50 Royal Marines and embark as quickly as possible in ANTHONY. The General then left RAMILLIES in order to organise the night attack by the 17th Brigade. At 1530 ANTHONY sailed with the Royal Marines. I then proceeded to sea in RAMILLIES.

43. The impression left with me after the General's visit was that the intended quick capture of Diego Suarez was already a 90 per cent. failure. The night attack, planned in a hurry, to be carried out by tired troops against very strong positions, had only a 10 per cent. chance of success. Prolonged operations, which we so much wished to avoid, was the unpleasant alternative.

ANTHONY's chance of success I assessed as about 50 per cent., my advisers thought 15 per cent., and of the Royal Marines I did not expect a score to survive the night. The next few hours were not happy ones.

44. The first indication that the unexpected was about to happen came at 2129 when ANTHONY's signal timed 2115 was received reporting she had accomplished her task successfully. This was a fine achievement brilliantly carried out, and, in my opinion, was the principal and direct cause of the enemy's collapse. The attack by 17th and 29th Brigades commenced at 2030 hours. A success signal from the town showed that the Marines had landed. 17th Brigade secured their objective which was about 1,800 yards beyond the main enemy position at 2300 hours and fired their success signals. The two battalions of the 29th Brigade were then ordered forward and pushed right through to the main town of Antsirane with little or no opposition and reached the main harbour. The Commando were unable to find boats so could not assist.

45. I had decided that RAMILLIES and screen would not join the carriers during the night D.2/D.3 as the latter were carrying out night flying operations to support the attack on Antsirane.

D.3.

At 0313/D.3 I received a message from the General telling me he would like all available air and ship support at 0900 when the 29th Brigade would assault Oranjia Peninsula. From this, it was obvious that the night attack had succeeded. I therefore proceeded with RAMILLIES and screen to join DEVONSHIRE and HERMIONE to the Eastward of the Oranjia Peninsula at daylight in readiness to bombard.

At 0400 a situation report was received confirming the capture of Antsirane.

46. During the night a report was received that GENISTA had attacked a contact to the North-West of Nosi Kara and about 0700 signals were received from ILLUSTRIOUS aircraft that she had sunk a submarine. This subsequently proved to be LE HEROS from whom survivors were picked up in position 12° 03′ S. 49° E.

47. At 0723, Headquarters 121 Force asked me to postpone bombardment until 1000. I instructed RAMILLIES, DEVONSHIRE, HERMIONE and LIGHTNING accordingly, and detailed their respective targets.

At 0945 Headquarters 121 Force gave me some details of the intended assault including the furthest on position of our troops at 1200. The main assault would not commence till noon, but I was asked to commence a preliminary bombardment as soon as possible after 1000 unless I heard that the ultimatum had been accepted.

At 0950 I was asked to postpone the bombardment until 1030 and at 1006 I was asked to postpone action until further orders as chances of surrender appeared good.

48. I was tired of these delays which were keeping the Fleet steaming up and down in dangerous waters, consequently I informed the General that I intended to commence a 15 minutes' bombardment to encourage the enemy to surrender.

At 1040 RAMILLIES, HERMIONE and LIGHTNING commenced a bombardment of Oranjia Peninsula, but "Cease Fire" was ordered 10 minutes later on recipt of a message from Headquarters 121 Force that Oranjia Peninsula had surrendered.

49. DEVONSHIRE, PANTHER and ACTIVE were then detached to screen the carriers.

14th M/S Flotilla swept the channel, entered the Bay and searched the harbour.

On receipt of signal that no mines had been found, RAMILLIES, HERMIONE, LIGHTNING and PALADIN proceeded into Diego Suarez Bay, anchoring at 1730.

50. The slow convoy sailed from Courrier Bay at 1600/D.3 and the fast convoy at 0500/D.4.

D.4.
Both convoys entered harbour on D.4 and anchored in Scotch Bay.

51. INDOMITABLE and screen also entered harbour on D.4, INDOMITABLE being attacked off the entrance by a submarine which was afterwards destroyed by ACTIVE. Her destruction was subsequently confirmed by a Vichy report, which gave her name as the MONGE.

ILLUSTRIOUS, DEVONSHIRE and screen remained at sea to provide A/S and fighter protection, entering harbour on D.5.

Surrender Negotiations.
52. At 0920 on Friday, 8th May, in answer to my summons, the following French Officers appeared on board H.M.S. RAMILLIES:-

Colonel Claerebout, Officer Commanding Defences, Diego Suarez, Capitaine de Vaisseau Maerten, Naval Officer-in-Charge, Madagascar, Capitaine de Vaisseau Simon, ex Commanding Officer of French Sloop D'ENTRE-CASTEAUX, and were received by me in my cabin.

I informed them that since they had not accepted my summons to surrender, British forces under my command had been compelled to take Diego Suarez by force. I intended to ensure that it did not fall into the hands of our enemies and I asked for the co-operation of the French authorities in this task. I stated that the terms of British occupation would be communicated later.

The French Officers then left the ship.

53. At 1100 I held a conference in the Residency at Antsirane, with General Sturges and our respective staffs, to convey to the French authorities the terms of surrender.

54. The following were present:-

Rear-Admiral E.N. Syfret, C.B., Commander-in-Chief,
Major-General R.G. Sturges, C.B., R.M., Military Commander,
Brigadier F.W. Festing, Assault Commander,
Brigadier M.S. Lush, Chief Political Officer,
Captain J.M. Howson, R.N., Chief of Staff to Commander-in-Chief,
Colonel Melville, South African Air Force,
Colonel Claerebout, Officer Commanding Defences, Diego Suarez,
Capitaine de Vaisseau Maerten, Naval Officer-in-Charge, Madagascar,
Colonel Rouves, Commanding Infantry Regiment,
M. Bourgine, Administrateur-Maire of Diego Suarez.

55. I opened the conference by stating the general conditions of the occupation of Diego Suarez by British forces. These allowed for the port remaining under French administration, to be handed back to them after the war, for payment of

salaries and pensions to all who would co-operate, and for repatriation of those who would not, excluding wives and families who, however, could be evacuated by private arrangements at their own risk.

56. As evidence of our good faith to regard Diego Suarez as French, subject to temporary control by us, I expressed a wish to see a tricolour ceremony and, though coldly received at the time, this suggestion was complied with a few days later.

57. After considerable discussion over matters of detail, general agreement was reached and the following document embodying the surrender terms was signed by myself and Colonel Claerebout, Officer Commanding the Defences of Diego Suarez:-

Conditions agreed upon regarding the French Naval, Military and Air Force in the Diego Suarez area.
1. Hostilities on Land, Sea and Air between the British Forces and the Forces under the command of the French Officer Commanding the defence area of the Naval Base of Diego Suarez will cease as from the time of signature of this document.

2. The French Forces will be accorded the honours of war. Officers will be treated as prisoners on parole in so far as the Military situation shall allow.

3. All arms will be deposited at a place to be notified later with the exception of officers who will be permitted to retain either one revolver or pistol.

4. The area of the French minefields in the Diego Suarez and neighbouring waters will be described exactly to the British Naval Authorities and all maps.

5. The conditions of repatriation to Metropolitan France as described by Commander-in-Chief of the British Force will apply, viz.:- "If any civil and military employees do not wish to co-operate they will, provided they can claim the right to residence in Metropolitan France, be repatriated as and when shipping becomes available." No objection will be raised to the evacuation of families of the men therein referred to under arrangements to be made by them with the approval of the British Military Authorities.

6. The British Military Authorities will consider particular cases, not exceeding 100 (one hundred), of European members of the French Forces who, after engaging themselves in writing not to take up arms against British Naval, Military and Air Forces or their Allies in Madagascar or surrounding waters, wish to reside in the unoccupied part of the Island.

7. The repatriation of Senegalese native troops up to 400 (four hundred) will be carried out in accordance with instructions to be sought from His Britannic Majesty's Government.

8. Malgash native troops will be demobilised under arrangements to be made by the British Military Authorities and returned to their homes.

9. The French Authorities hereby undertake to do all such things necessary to carry into full effect the provisions of this Agreement.

Signed at Diego Suarez on 8th of May,
1942, at 1625 hours by
E.N. SYFRET, *Rear-Admiral,*
Commander-in-Chief, British Forces.

CLAEREBOUT,
Commandant le Défense du Point d'appui de la Flotte.

TRANSLATION OF THE ULTIMATUM.

Board the British Flagship,
Your Excellency,   *3rd May,* 1942.

The strategic position of Diego Suarez requires that it should not fall into the hands of the Japanese and that the territory should be available for those forces which are fighting to restore freedom in the world and secure the liberation of France and French territory. It cannot be allowed to suffer the fate of Indo China.

I therefore request that in order that bloodshed may be avoided you will surrender the territory under your control to me unconditionally and instruct your officials and Armed Forces to obey the orders which I shall issue.

The action which I am now taking on the instruction of H.M. Government has the full approval of the Government of the United States.

In order to assist you in reaching a favourable decision I have been instructed by H.M. Government to inform you of the following:-

(1) Diego Suarez is French and will remain French, and will be restored to France after the war. H.M. Government have repeatedly made it clear that they do not covet an inch of French territory. I repeat this assurance.

(2) Funds will be made available to meet the salaries and pensions of all personnel, Civil and Military, who elect to co-operate with the United Nations.

(3) If any Civil and Military employees do not wish to co-operate, they will, provided they can claim the right to residence in Metropolitan France, be repatriated as and when shipping becomes available.

(4) The trade of Diego Suarez with the United Nations will be restored. H.M. Government will extend to Diego Suarez all the economic benefits accorded to French territories which have already joined the United Nations.

(5) There must be no destruction of Civil and Military installations, W/T Stations, War Stores, etc. Those responsible for any such sabotage will not benefit by conditions (2) and (3) above.

Your reply to this communication should be sent to me immediately in plain language by radio on 500kc/s (600 metres) using call sign GBXZ.

Alternatively it should be sent by hand of officer under flag of truce to the Officer Commanding Occupying Troops.

I am, Your Excellency
E.N. SYFRET.
Rear-Admiral and
Commander-in-Chief, British Forces.

His Excellency,
The Governor of Diego Suarez.

ENCLOSURE I.

H.M.S. DEVONSHIRE.
13*th May,* 1942.

REPORT OF PROCEEDINGS – OPERATION "IRONCLAD".

The Approach to the Western Anchorage.

During the greater part of the passage from Durban with convoy Y (slow convoy) DEVONSHIRE experienced favourable currents which made the problem of arriving at the right time principally a question of delaying the advance of the convoy by the correct amount. It was essential to keep a certain amount in hand since at any moment a strong South Westerly set from the direction of Cape Amber might be experienced. During the night of Sunday, 3rd May/Monday, 4th May, a set of 0.7 knots in a direction of 090° was experienced. It was decided to hold the convoy back sufficiently for DEVONSHIRE to be within reach of position AA at 8 knots. During the forenoon of Monday, 4th May, convoy Y was manoeuvred on courses at right angles to the line of advance in order to achieve the necessary delay, but in so doing the screen became considerably disorganised.

2. At 1500 the signal "Proceed in execution of previous orders" was received and the whole force formed up. DEVONSHIRE was in station 5 miles ahead of the starboard wing of the convoy steering 058° at 9 knots by 1545.

3. Group II formed up as an A/S screen two miles ahead as shown below:-

FREESIA
CROMER   POOLE
ROMNEY   AURICULA
CROMARTY   NIGELLA
ANTHONY   DEVONSHIRE   LAFOREY
WINCHESTER CASTLE   LIGHTNING
ROYAL ULSTERMAN

4. The estimated 1800 position was passed to LAFOREY at 1603 based on the latest fix obtained at noon. At 1800, which was just before dark, LAFOREY, LIGHTNING and ANTHONY were detached. The remainder of the screen

altered course to 118° to conform with DEVONSHIRE's intended alteration at 1830. It had been anticipated that DEVONSHIRE would pass through position 298° AA two miles at 1830.

5. At 1840, by which time it was quite dark, the evening star sights showed that the North Easterly set had in effect reversed during the afternoon, and DEVON-SHIRE's position at 1830 was 220° AA seven miles. Course was therefore altered without signal at 1900 to 096° in order to regain the correct line of approach and to counteract this set. This alteration was not immediately noticed by the screen who got a long way out of position in consequence. However they did not lose touch and had regained their stations by 2000.

6. This last fix also indicated that the force was early. No immediate adjustment was made because the possibility of an adverse current had still to be allowed for.

7. Land echoes by R.D.F. were obtained between 2030 and 2100, but were of no value at that time. At 2100, just before moonrise, the high land on Cape San Sebastian was sighted and a reasonably good fix obtained by visual bearing and R.D.F. range. More land was sighted after moonrise, and at 2150 Windsor Castle was identified at a distance of 40 miles and a good fix obtained. At this time DEVONSHIRE was in position 298° ZB 18 miles.

8. Course was altered to 118° at 2200 and the speed reduced to 8½ knots without signal. The screen detected this alteration with less difficulty than before and was soon back in station.

9. The set now seemed to work round to the Eastward again, and speed was reduced to 8 knots at 2230 to allow for it. No reliable fixes could be obtained between 2230 and 2300 because the land was in shadow, but at 2312 another good fix was obtained putting DEVONSHIRE in position 330° ZB 6 miles, having been set about 2¼ miles to the Northward. It was evident that the sweepers and FREESIA were short of manoeuvring room, but they had to be left to work it out for themselves.

10. The first dan buoy was sighted at 2306. At 2318 DEVONSHIRE altered to 138° and later to 155°.

11. At 2338 LIGHTNING's three vertical lights were switched on, and there-after the navigation was not difficult. At 2342 ANTHONY passed close along-side and reported that there was no set, also that the outer dan had drifted to the South West.

Tuesday, 5th May.
12. At 0001 course was altered to 109° past the first dan buoy to follow the mine-sweepers which could be clearly seen ahead; LIGHTNING was abeam to star-board 6 cables away at 0008 and signalled "Set 150° ½ knot." The right hand edge of Nosi Hara which had been selected as a leading mark was clearly visible bearing 114°. DEVONSHIRE had thus passed ZB 33 minutes early.

13. The passage along the swept channel was somewhat confused because it was difficult to see which sweepers were sweeping, and several of the dans broke adrift. The first or outer dan (laid by LAFOREY) had been cut and had drifted to the South West, so it was left to starboard.

14. At 0018 an Oropesa float was passed on the starboard hand, presumably CROMER's, as that ship was met at 0022 proceeding towards it.

15. Dan buoys correctly marking the channel were passed at 0023, 0042, 0048, 0057, 0101, 0111, 0131 and 0142. In two cases sweeping dans and the original channel dans laid by LAFOREY were close together and were confusing.

16. At 0026 LAFOREY was met steaming to seaward. She reported "Channel O.K. No cross set."

17. At 0028 CROMARTY was passed standing by a drifting dan buoy.

18. At 0052 LAFOREY and ANTHONY passed at high speed steaming towards Nosi Hara.

19. At 0106 ANTHONY turned round and steamed to seaward.

20. At 0130 course was altered to 136° for the passage between Nosi Hara and Nosi Anjombavola and at 0142 DEVONSHIRE passed Q.1 berth and altered course to the Northward round Nosi Hara, coming to an anchor in position 053° Q.1 berth 1.65 miles at 0057. This berth was 3½ cables from the shore, half way along the island, and was chosen to have the island as a background on the bearings from Nos. 7 and 8 batteries.

21. Two minesweepers were already at anchor off Nosi Hara, and CROMER joined them at about 0205. LAFOREY, FREESIA and probably two more minesweepers were to the South Eastward of Q.1 when DEVONSHIRE passed.

Proceedings in the Western Anchorage.
22. A period of waiting followed. The movements of Groups IV and V were obscured by Nosi Hara, but the passage of WINCHESTER CASTLE and KEREN's landing craft, and that of LAFOREY, LIGHTNING, FREESIA and ROYAL ULSTERMAN could be followed almost up to the beaches.

23. At 0342 LAFOREY's report of mines in the vicinity of JJ was received.

24. DEVONSHIRE's position lying head to wind did not enable her to keep all her guns bearing on No. 7 fort. Arrangements were made to slip cable instantly in case it was necessary to open fire. The pinnace was lowered and a dan buoy was laid off Nosi Hara reefs to facilitate manoeuvring the ship in the narrow space available. The officer who laid this buoy reported that it was almost impossible to see the ship against the background of the island, even in the bright moonlight.

25. At 0440 flares were seen on White Beach signifying local success there. At 0454 LAFOREY's report that "Red landing 0430 believed unopposed" was

received. At 0454 star shell appeared in the sky and was presumed to be HERMIONE at Ambodi-Vahibe. At 0523 the Senior Naval Officer (L)'s order for WINCHESTER CASTLE to weigh and proceed to main anchorage was received. At 0540 the Walrus aircraft was sent off to reconnoitre the batteries and report particularly on No. 8 battery. At 0546 the success signal for No. 7 battery was received.

26. By now it was broad daylight; WINCHESTER CASTLE and BACHA-QUERO were seen advancing down the swept channel towards the main anchorage. Simultaneously a signal was received from ROMNEY to the effect that she had cut and exploded two moored mines in the neighbourhood of Nosi Famaho. I decided to stop these ships immediately until I was certain that the Senior Naval Officer (L) understood the situation. Both ships were told that there were mines in the anchorage and that they were not to proceed until ordered by the Senior Naval Officer (L). ROMNEY's signal indicated that 100 per cent. clearance of the anchorage would be necessary to make it safe. Signals explaining the position were passed to WINCHESTER CASTLE at 0620, the Senior Naval Officer (L) at 0625, BACHAQUERO at 0628 and the Flag Officer Commanding, Force "F" at 0652. The Senior Naval Officer (L) subsequently sent a staff officer on board DEVONSHIRE where the situation was fully explained.

27. DEVONSHIRE and LAFOREY were acting as W/T guards for F.O.O.[8] 2 and F.O.O. 1 respectively. Both got into communication quickly and easily, LAFOREY at 0459 and DEVONSHIRE at 0514, reports being passed by V/S[9] to KEREN as they came in.

28. At 0620 the Walrus returned and landed, reporting that no sign of No. 8 battery was visible.

29. Swordfish, Albacores, Martlets and Hurricanes were all now seen at intervals on their various tasks. No hostile aircraft were sighted at this stage.

30. At 0705 Senior Naval Officer (L) asked if DEVONSHIRE was in communication with the Flag Officer Commanding, Force "F." Difficulty was being experienced as the Flag Officer Commanding, Force "F" only answered occasionally and several reports were broadcast.

31. FREESIA and FRITILLARY began inner A/S patrols.

32. At 0750 KEREN and various ships of Group IV moved to the main anchorage, which the sweepers had now swept. Mines continued to be reported from Courrier Bay.

33. Consideration was now given to the question of shifting berth to my inshore bombarding position (N.1). Senior Naval Officer (L) offered me sweepers but it subsequently transpired that no sweepers could be spared from the more important task of clearing the channel for BACHAQUERO. I decided therefore to

proceed to an intermediate position from which I could enfilade the main road to Antsirane and at the same time keep in good visual communication with ships in both anchorages. The position chosen was 105° Q.1 1.4 miles, where the ship anchored at 0851.

34. During the forenoon ships of Group V came into the anchorage and by 1200 the outer anchorage was clear.

35. At 1126 a general call from the Army on shore asked for bombing of the observation post at Windsor Castle. At 1138 the Walrus was sent off for this duty and carried out ten bombing runs. Later two Albacores and Hurricanes joined in and the Walrus returned at 1219. Nothing had been seen of the enemy on the top of the mountain though subsequent events proved them to have been there all the time.

36. At 1054 F.O.O. 2 asked that DEVONSHIRE should close in in order to extend her command of the area to the South of Antsirane and ensure the continuation of W/T communication. This request was complied with and a new berth in position 134° Q.1 2.1 miles was taken up at 1146 and F.O.O. 2 informed that it would be impossible to move the ship any closer. Unfortunately this position shut DEVONSHIRE out from direct visual communication with KEREN, and the disadvantages of this break in communications soon began to be felt. Eventually, when F.O.O. 2 had advanced beyond our extreme gun range, it was decided that the maintenance of good communication outweighed other considerations and at 1420 the ship again shifted berth 2 cables to the Westward from which position KEREN could be seen.

37. At 1149 the Senior Officer, Minesweepers, reported that AURICULA had struck a mine and asked for assistance for her wounded. It could be seen that she had not sunk and that a number of boats were in attendance. Later she drifted out of sight behind a merchant ship. At 1239, having heard nothing further, I asked the Senior Naval Officer (L) if he required any assistance, and at 1248 asked the Senior Officer, Minesweepers, to report the position regarding AURICULA. No news was received until 1530 when a staff officer from the Senior Naval Officer (L) arrived on board to see me. He seemed in some doubt as to who should have been in charge of the operation of salvaging AURICULA, which was still afloat. I explained to him that DEVONSHIRE would provide any assistance asked for but that the Senior Naval Officer (L) was in charge of the anchorage and would have to make the arrangements for towing AURICULA inshore. Hearing that the ship had a shaky bulkhead I sent a boat at 1545 with a Shipwright Officer, three Shipwrights and a load of wood to undertake the necessary shoring. This officer returned and reported to me about 1830 that the ship would undoubtedly sink before the morning, and should be beached as soon as possible. This was reported to the Flag Officer Commanding, Force "F," the Senior Naval Officer (L) and the Senior Officer, Minesweepers.

38. At 1300 three Potez aircraft were sighted over the target area. The air raid warning "Red" was hoisted and passed by W/T. At 1326 the hostile aircraft had disappeared and orders were given to revert to 15 minutes notice.

39. At 0758 the Senior Naval Officer (L) informed me that Captain (D), 12th Destroyer Flotilla had been asked to send EASEDALE to oil DEVONSHIRE as soon as PAKENHAM had fuelled. At 0852 Captain (D), 12th Destroyer Flotilla informed me that DERWENTDALE, alongside whom he was lying, considered the weather unsuitable for berthing alongside. I replied to the effect that I did not wish to oil in any case until my role as bombarding ship had come to an end. During the afternoon EASEDALE anchored in my vicinity and I asked her whether she could come alongside in the weather conditions then prevailing and was informed that she could. Arrangements were therefore made to get her alongside with the last of the light so that I could complete with oil before the moon rose. These arrangements unfortunately clashed with Captain (D), 12th Destroyer Flotilla's organisation, and subsequently led to EASEDALE being emptied of oil at a time when she was required for fuelling destroyers. EASEDALE is more handy than DERWENTDALE and can come alongside under worse weather conditions.

40. About 1630 your signal timed 1533 was received which suggested that the anchorage could not be considered safe from submarine attack and that I should proceed to join your flag before dark. To comply meant proceeding immediately and the sudden removal of the ship would have broken an important line of army communication without adequate warning. I also considered it important to complete with fuel, for which arrangements were already in train, and proposed in my signal timed 1657 to join you in the morning. This signal was repeated to the Senior Naval Officer (L) and cleared to KEREN at 1738. It was subsequently approved by your signal timed 2057.

41. Before proceeding, arrangements were made for PAKENHAM to take over the line of communication with F.O.O. 2 who had not been heard since 1622 and she was subsequently told to confirm that she had made touch (my signal timed 0610/6th May and PAKENHAM's signal timed 0743/6th May which reported that communications had not been re-established with F.O.O. 2 until 0733/6th May).

42. The LINDZ, a small black yacht, wearing the Red Ensign entered harbour at 1510 and proceeded into Ambararata Bay. After enquiries, FREESIA reported that she had been examined by GENISTA.

43. ANTHONY arrived at 1512 proceeding up the anchorage at high speed. I thought it advisable to warn her that the anchorage was mined.

44. Three French Morane fighters were sighted at 1707 machine gunning Blue Beach. Air raid warning "Red" was initiated immemiately afterwards and repeated by the Flag Officer Commanding, Force "F", at 1728. No attacks on the fleet

developed and the fighters were seen to disappear in a South Easterly direction and the air raid warning "White" was passed at 1731.

45. The moon rose at 2213, oiling was completed by 2300. EASEDALE was anchored and DEVONSHIRE slipped from her and proceeded to sea, passing Nosi Kara at 2341. It was assumed that my departure would be reported to the Senior Naval Officer (L) and as V/S signalling in the anchorage was undesirable no further signal reporting my movements was made. This was regretted later when the Senior Naval Officer (L)'s signal timed 0705 was received off Cape Amber asking me to engage the French warship that was making a nuisance of herself in English Bay.

Bombardment of the Oranjia Peninsula.
46. At 0553 the Flag Officer Commanding, Force "F's" signal timed 0350 was received ordering DEVONSHIRE to be ready to bombard the Oranjia Peninsula by 1200. Course was altered for Cape Amber which was passed at 0845 and DEVONSHIRE proceeded to the South to join HERMIONE off the entrance to the harbour about 1000.

47. Consideration had to be given to the employment and subsequent recovery of the Walrus aircraft. It was most desirable to use my own observer for the bombardment and it was most undesirable to leave the Walrus on the catapult when the ship went into action. After an exchange of signals with the Rear-Admiral Aircraft Carriers and ILLUSTRIOUS it was decided to catapult the Walrus before opening fire and land it in Ambararata Bay where it could run up on the beach and remain until an opportunity offered for its recovery in calm water. The weather on the Eastern side of the island was consistently unfavourable for a recovery at sea. While ashore the crew were joined by other Fleet Air Arm personnel from force landed aircraft and communication was maintained by W/T.

48. DEVONSHIRE arrived in position 10 miles East of Oranjia Point by 1000 to find HERMIONE in action with the coast defences. She informed me that the Headquarters of the 29th Independent Brigade had asked for a general strafe of the peninsula, that No. I battery was not firing but that a new battery had opened up and that the maximum range was 18,000 yards.

49. HERMIONE was getting very short of suitable ammunition for bombardment and DEVONSHIRE had none to waste. I knew that the centre of resistance was South of Antsirane and it seemed probable that the Oranjia Peninsula would capitulate as soon as Antsirane fell. In the circumstances it appeared undesirable to damage the batteries unless they came into action against our own troops advancing towards the Oranjia Peninsula, since we would require these batteries for the defence of the port as soon as it passed into our possession.

50. Arrangements were made therefore for one cruiser to maintain her position within range and in readiness for instant action while the other stood off to seaward. The area of operations was limited and made the ships an easy target for

submarine attack unless a high speed and zigzag were maintained. HERMIONE had already spent over 24 hours in the area so the extent of the "pitch" would be obvious to the submarine. Four ships of the 14th Mine-sweeping Flotilla who were waiting off the entrance to sweep the passage in were instructed to carry out an A/S sweep of the area.

51. DEVONSHIRE carried out registration shoots between 1125 and 1300 on Nos. I and 2 batteries, Mamelon Vert and the new position reported by HER-MIONE. The object was to exercise the gunnery control team in preparation for more serious work later if called for. It was found that accurate indirect fire was impossible in the weather conditions and with the speed and zigzag in use, mainly owing to the wander of the gyro compass. With the sun high in the sky visibility deteriorated in the target area and made direct fire impossible. It was decided that if a call for fire came, the firing would be carried out at slow speed and on as straight a course as enemy opposition would permit. Two conspicuous trees at Mamelon Vert which had been used as aiming marks on this occasion were subsequently cut down by the French.

52. HERMIO.NE took over between 1300 and 1600, after which DEVON-SHIRE took over until dark. The Walrus landed at 1345 after which air observation was maintained by Swordfish, from ILLUSTRIOUS until 1700.

53. During the afternoon dispositions were made for the night, and the Senior Officer, 14th Minesweeping Flotilla, was instructed to remain North of a line 115° from Cape Amber during dark hours in order to avoid any possibility of a clash between friendly forces during the night. At 1720 HERMIONE took station astern and as darkness fell the two cruisers withdrew to the Eastward.

54. At 1754 your signal stating that a destroyer with 50 Marines would be proceeding into Diego Suarez was received from HERMIONE. This signal had been missed in DEVONSHIRE and was only discovered by chance, but fortunately both cruisers were in a position to give support when required. At 1749 your amplifying signal was received ordering cruisers to support ANTHONY in any way possible. An effort to inform ANTHONY of my intentions, without giving anything away or causing her to answer on W/T, failed.

55. ANTHONY was due to enter the pass at 2010. It was planned to be in a position five miles 090° from Oranjia Light House at that time and to bombard the searchlights when they were switched on. A strong Westerly set was experienced, and a turn of 360° had to be made in order not to be early. It was obviously imperative that the cruisers should not be sighted until ANTHONY was in, for otherwise the whole "game" would be given away.

56. At 1957 a position 080° 6½ miles from the lighthouse was reached, and course was altered to starboard to 347°. At 2008 course was altered to 257° and when HERMIONE was round, to 167°. The idea was to have at least one of the cruisers with guns bearing all the time. At 2023, while still on the Southerly

course, a searchlight on Oranjia Point was switched on across the entrance, and an object was seen in the beam which might have been ANTHONY so fire was immediately opened with 4 gun salvos of 8 inch. With the arrival of the second salvo the searchlight went out and was not seen again.

57. DEVONSHIRE and HERMIONE continued to patrol across the entrance until 2050 but nothing more was seen. At this time ANTHONY's future movements were not known and it was thought possible that she might go round into English Bay under cover of Andrakaka which was in our hands. Course was altered to seaward for a short time, but at 2109 gunflashes and tracer were sighted which were presumed to be ANTHONY fighting her way out. Fire could not be opened, for there was not point of aim, and the possibility of damaging ANTHONY could not be accepted. At 2128 ANTHONY's report that she was clear was received, so DEVONSHIRE altered course to the Eastward and later to the South East. At 0130 course was altered to 320° to close the entrance at dawn.

Thursday, 7th May.
58. Your intentions to bombard Oranjia Peninsula were received at 0415. I therefore continued to the North Westward to join your flag, sending HERMIONE to be off the entrance at daybreak. Both cruisers joined company by 0830.

59. In the actual bombardment DEVONSHIRE did not open fire. The signals which were being received from the Army on shore indicated that the bombardment was unnecessary.

60. At 1330 DEVONSHIRE was detached with ACTIVE and PANTHER to join Rear-Admiral Aircraft Carriers to give cover to the carriers. INDOMITABLE was sighted at 1630.

Friday, 8th May, and Saturday, 9th May.
61. DEVONSHIRE remained to the West of the island covering the carriers' movements and also that of the fast convoy, finally entering Diego Suarez Bay at 0810 on Saturday, 9th May, astern of ILLUSTRIOUS.

(Signed) R.D. OLIVER,
Captain, R.N.
Commanding Officer.
The Flag Officer Commanding,
Force "F".

ENCLOSURE 2.

H.M.S. LAFOREY.
8th May, 1942.

I have the honour to forward the following report of proceedings in Operation "Ironclad".

2. LAFOREY fuelled from Oiler EASEDALE a.m. 4th May, 1942, rejoining the slow convoy at 1330, and took station to form up for the final approach.

3. At 1800 parted company with LIGHTNING and ANTHONY on course 125° speed 14 knots, to close Nosi Anambo, adjusting course to 114° following fix by stars at 1839.

4. At 1950 ANTHONY reported a suspicious vessel in sight on the starboard bow. Destroyers reduced to slow speed to try to evade, altering to port and forming single line. It was not until 2021, when the Division were about to attack with torpedoes that the phantom vessel was identified as an island, and course to Anambo was resumed.

5. At 2040 soundings shoaled very rapidly to 4 fathoms. Division was stopped to ascertain our position. This shoal was unexpectedly shallow and raised some doubt as to ships' position. Shortly after 2100 a bright white light was seen on a bearing of 100° range 7,000 yards, and at 2122 the moon very conveniently rose directly behind the tower on the island, to the relief of all concerned.

6. ZA buoy was laid at 2150 and course shaped for Nosi Fati shoal, which was found without difficulty, both land and breakers showing up well in the moon's rays. The 3 white light buoy to mark this shoal was dropped at 2249 but to our consternation capsized. It was, however, quickly relaid by the First Lieutenant's danlaying party.

7. At 2310 No. 1 Main Channel buoy was laid and the positions of these two buoys checked. LIGHTNING was instructed to anchor and show her lights immediately, and ANTHONY to inform the convoy that the buoys were properly laid.

8. LAFOREY then proceeded down the channel laying buoys 2 to 5. This part of the operation was not difficult as the entrance to the bay between Nosi Hara and Nosi Anjombavola was well defined by the moon and no appreciable set was experienced. No. 3 buoy was laid 2 cables to the Northward of the correct position.

9. After dropping the last buoy, weather conditions were obviously so good for boatwork that there was no necessity to investigate further, and at 0003/5th course was altered to 295° turning up channel. At that time it was with some foreboding that the whole convoy was visible without binoculars just entering the channel. At 0030 spoke DEVONSHIRE, and at 0040 KEREN, on her way in, informing them that the channel was correctly laid. Course was then reversed to take station close astern of the minesweepers.

10. At 0100 ANTHONY closed and was given a message for transmission to F.O.C. Force "F" that all was in order.

11. At 0127 passed the entrance and at 0141 stopped engines with two minesweepers and FREESIA close ahead. At 0154 WINCHESTER CASTLE anchored very commendably with a minimum of noise, and by 0203 tows were seen lining up.

12. There was a slight hitch at this time as tows went ahead with the leading minesweeper, and caused both of them to haul in their sweeps. However, the loud hailer proved invaluable, and by 0235 the party was sorted out and proceeding up the bay with LAFOREY and 10 landing craft close astern of FREESIA, CROMARTY and ROMNEY. At 0301 a mine exploded ahead in the vicinity of position HH, and various reports were received from sweepers of mines being encountered and being seen close to the ship. At 0328 when near JJ a mine exploded close ahead and was reported to S.N.O. (L), and we all expected the fireworks to begin. To our surprise the quiet of the night was undisturbed while the tows passed LAFOREY and were informed by loud hailer that their dispersal point marked by FREESIA was 2 cables ahead. At 0330 they were seen moving towards the land.

13. At 0438 received a signal that the Commandos had landed unopposed, and informed F.O.C. Force "F" and S.N.O. (L) accordingly at 0444. By this time LIGHTNING and ROYAL ULSTERMAN were in close company, latter disembarking troops. At 0510 it was clear that no opposition from the batteries ashore was likely, and a signal was sent to suggest that ships should enter the bay, expediting minesweeping.

14. At 0525 I was informed that the Commando was still advancing without opposition, and at 0545 the "Success Colt" signal was received and retransmitted to F.O.C. Force "F" and S.N.O. (L).

15. Meanwhile the first flight of landing craft had been seen returning from shore, and at 0520 were closing ROYAL ULSTERMAN. There appeared to have been some delay in getting away Blue Beach landing, and ROYAL ULSTERMAN was told to expedite this.

16. Following reports from F.O.O. 1, a situation report was made at 0606 informing S.N.O. (L) that Windsor Castle had been captured with negligible opposition,[10] that enemy native troops were surrendering, that the advance was continuing and that own troops were mopping up in this area. This was followed by a further report at 0640 that the Commando was reorganising in Windsor Castle area preparatory to advancing on Diego Suarez North. At about 0615 landing craft from ROYAL ULSTERMAN proceeded towards Blue Beach, and when close off shore machine-gun fire could be heard but no flashes were seen. Shortly afterwards troops were seen landing, and communication was established at 0705 by Aldis, and I was informed that the landing craft had been machine-gunned on the way in, but that Army units were now moving inland. S.N.O. (L) was informed at 0723 that landing had been effected.

17. During this period LAFOREY was anchored ready to give any bombardment support required.

18. DEVONSHIRE's signal reporting ROMNEY cutting mines and that the anchorage could not be safe until 1000 was received at 0653. From my

appreciation of the mine situation, I informed DEVONSHIRE at 0745 that mines were unlikely South West of line Nosi Famaho to Mangoaka, and that the Southern part of the anchorage was clear of mines. This signal was passed to S.N.O. (L) by DEVONSHIRE at 0805.

19. At this time KEREN was seen to be entering harbour astern of minesweepers. When the sweepers reached the area Nosi Famaho to Mangoaka Point a number of mines were cut, and LAFOREY weighed and proceeded to sink mines by machine-gun fire.

20. At 0901 I closed KEREN to the South Westwards of the mined area and reported the situation by loud hailer, informing F.O.C. Force "F" of the existence of the minefield, that at least six mines had been cut in the last sweep, and that operations were continuing. There was, however, a narrow channel through the minefield marked by yellow and black dan buoys which I was confident was clear.

21. At 0817 I had ascertained from Blue Beach Signal Station, which had been set up 7 cables from Basse Point, that the beach was suitable for landing M.T., S.N.O. (L) being informed; and at 0849 I offered to take BACHAQUERO through the minefield to the vicinity of JJ, preparatory to her being swept in to Blue Beach. S.N.O. (L) however replied at 0910 that no beach was yet suitable for her, and told me to anchor, which I did at 0920.

22. About 1030 minesweepers were widening the channel in the minefield, and cut at least 18 mines within a few minutes. As some of these were drifting towards BACHAQUERO and ROYAL ULSTERMAN, LAFOREY weighed and helped to sink them using 2 four-barrelled machine-guns and rifles. Several were sunk but none exploded. At 1138 AURICULA struck a mine and was holed forward.

23. At this time all mines still floating had drifted clear of ships, and LAFOREY was proceeding up channel to a suitable bombardment position close to JJ where I anchored at noon.

24. At 1215 AURICULA was still drifting out of control and down by the bows, with 2 minesweepers standing by. She informed me that her First Lieutenant was in command and her Captain wounded and disembarked.

25. At 1232 I asked AURICULA if she had all the assistance she required, to which her reply was "No, think tow stern first possible". As LIGHTNING had been ordered to complete with fuel at 1315 I instructed her to close AURICULA before oiling and assist, and that if she was saleable she should be towed to a lee anchorage.

26. At 1300 three enemy Potez 63 twin-engined reconnaissance bombers appeared over the anchorage but remained at a respectful distance without attacking any ship, flying off in the direction of Windsor Castle.

27. During the period 1100–1330 the Commando had been advancing steadily with little opposition and at 1335 informed S N.O. (L) that they expected to reach Diego Suarez soon.

28. BACHAQUERO proceeded through the minefield swept channel about 1330 and went inshore to Red Beach with a minesweeper ahead of her.

29. At 1408 and 1424 two large explosions, which were definitely not mines, were seen half a mile North East of the ship. It is now suspected that they were large shell fired from some shore battery using Windsor Castle O.P. as observer.

30. At 1330 I was informed that machine-gun fire from the observation tower on Windsor Castle summit was being a nuisance, and at 1526, 29 rounds were fired at the O.P. which then hoisted the white flag. A signal was sent by light "Descendez ou nous continuerons" and I ask the Beach Station whether the French were coming down, to which the reply was "Yes." However they changed their minds and returned, and at 1658 F.O.O. 3 asked me to re-engage, and a further 36 rounds were fired; a direct hit was made on the living quarters just below the summit. The crew of the tower was seen to come out and disappear over the lee side. LIGHTNING took over the shoot at 1732.

31. LAFOREY then proceeded to the main anchorage and fuelled from EASE-DALE. On completion at 0120/6th, anchored in the South West of the anchorage and set A/S watch.

32. At 0600 returned to the bombardment billet close to JJ, and was informed that a French sloop in English Bay was firing on our troops advancing on Antsirane; F.O.O. 2 could not see this target and F.O.O. I was in Diego Suarez, and it was not until 0804 that he obtained transport to take him to observe.

33. At 0843 he was in position and informed me that the fires caused by INDOMITABLE's air attack were out and the battle ensign still flying. At 0855 LAFOREY opened fire and fired 86 rounds at the sloop. A number of these were reported very close, one hit was seen, and at 0930 F.O.O. 1 was asked for general effect. He reported that the bridge was on fire and the ammunition exploding, but that there were no signs of the crew. This convinced me that the ship had been partially abandoned, probably as a result of INDOMITABLE's air attack, and fire was ceased.

34. At 0857 intercepted F.O.O. 2's signal to PAKENHAM urgently requiring bombarding ship. LIGHTNING was detailed and proceeded to a position close to Red Beach at 0926, opening fire at 0953.

35. As soon as the shoot at the sloop D'ENTRECASTEAUX had been completed, LAFOREY proceeded inshore to bombard to support LIGHTNING, being ready at 1026, 3 cables from the shore off Red Beach.

36. At 1033 F.O.O. 2 indicated the bombarding areas, reported position of own troops and suggested air spotting.

37. From map references own troops appeared very close, and at 1101 LAFOREY opened fire with single-gun salvos to see if F.O.O. 2 could observe fall of shot. 7 rounds were fired but none seen. LIGHTNING was also in action until 1055 when F.O.C Force "F's" signal 1044 ordering her to cease fire was received.

38. At 1124 I asked F.O.O. 2 whether I could go on, and told him that the last series had been fired 1500 yards North of own troops. At 1130 F.O.O. 2 informed me that it was impossible for own troops to approach certain areas owing to strong points of enemy batteries and machine-gun posts. LAFOREY continued bombarding but no fall of shot was reported and it was obvious that F.O.O. 2 could not see the fire but that own troops were not being endangered while the enemy lines of communication were being attacked. During this period 3 series of five 2-gun salvos at 2 minute intervals firing 30 in all were carried out. Fire was checked at 1208.

39. At 1159 F.O.O. 2 asked for duplication by LIGHTNING and was informed that 6-gun salvos could be fired and duplicated, and that either series could be repeated, or rapid unseen fire for effect could be commenced. F.O.O. 2 asked for a repetition of the series and this request confirmed that own troops were all right. LAFOREY continued with 2-gun salvos until 1221 when LIGHTNING was ready to fire broadsides of 4 to 6 guns at target. LAFOREY then increased to 4- to 6-gun salvos at target. 38 rounds were fired by LAFOREY with LIGHTNING joining in until 1233 when fire was checked.

40. None of this fire was observed by F.O.O. 2 but it has since been learnt that it proved most helpful to a company of the 2nd Battalion South Lancashire Regiment who had infiltrated behind the enemy's lines and seized the wireless station, being practically surrounded. This was extremely fortunate.

41. In the meantime I had asked ILLUSTRIOUS for a spotting aircraft, and had sent my B.L.O.[11] and one officer to Windsor Castle O.P. to see if they could distinguish the position of the enemy batteries in action against own troops. At 1327 touch was lost with F.O.O. 2 who informed me that he was changing his battery.

42. Windsor Castle O.P. was manned at 1330 and the observer reported that the battle area was obscured by smoke. 8 single rounds were fired at a safe range but accurate observation was impossible from this position.

43. At 1440 touch was obtained with the spotting aircraft from ILLUSTRIOUS but no target could be identified for some time, but at 1527 the aircraft ordered "Open Fire," and one round was fired, reported as 100 yards over.

44. At 1530 9 bombing aircraft were seen going in to attack, and the spotting aircraft was informed that fire would not be continued until this was completed.

45. At 1618, after the bombers had retired, the spotting aircraft called for fire on a gun battery. This was engaged from 1618 to 1705, firing 58 rounds from A and B turrets, when a signal was received from F.O.O. 2 relayed by PAKENHAM, to

"stop firing – moving." This had been transmitted at 1637. The spotting aircraft was then told to return to the carrier. Spotting had been carried out most efficiently with excellent communication.

46. This aircraft had originally been asked for at 1034, and, while it is fully realised that four hours was not a long time under the circumstances, had a spotting aircraft been kept available for destroyers the Army could have been helped more effectively much earlier.

47. Anchor was weighed at 0210/7th and LAFOREY proceeded through the minefield to hunt for a submarine reported by GENISTA as ordered by F.O.C. Force "F" and Captain (D), 12th Destroyer Flotilla.

48. At 0537 while off Nosi Hara received an aircraft's signal passed by Captain (D), 12th D.F. – "Survivors of submarine struggling in the water." There was some difficulty in establishing the position in which the submarine had been sunk, and when it was seen that PAKENHAM and one corvette were closing the right spot LAFOREY returned to the anchorage to provide A.A. protection.

49. LAFOREY proceeded for A/S patrol off the main entrance at 1800, closing JASMINE aground on Nosi Fati shoal at 2100; finding she had got off, A/S patrol was resumed until 0500/8th.

50. LAFOREY then escorted the fast convoy from the anchorage to Diego Suarez, entering harbour at 1500.

51. The bearing and enthusiasm of the Ship's Company over a long period of Action Stations was most satisfactory, and the fact that only one misfire (in Director) was experienced in a total of 297 rounds fired proved that the material of the ship had been maintained in first class condition. In general, all departments carried out arduous duties without a hitch. In particular, I would mention the Engine-room Department who met the constant calls on the engines in very trying conditions of heat most efficiently.

52. I should like to stress the very useful work and fine co-operation carried out by Captain B. Clark, the Royal Artillery, the Bombardment Liaison Officer attached to LAFOREY.

(Signed) R.M.J. HUTTON,
Captain (D),
Nineteenth Destroyer Flotilla.

ENCLOSURE 3.

H.M.S. KEREN.
15*th May,* 1942.

I have the honour to submit the following report of proceedings, covering the period from the time of assembly of the Force for Operation "Ironclad" at Durban until the arrival at Diego Suarez harbour.

Assembly of Ships at Durban.

2. M/V WINCHESTER CASTLE, having on board my Staff, H.Q. Staff of 121 Force and 29th Independent Brigade, arrived at Durban on 22nd April in convoy accompanied by H.M.S. KEREN, H.M.S. KARANJA, M/V SOBIESKI, S.S. ORONSAY and S.S. DUCHESS OF ATHOLL. This force carried the personnel of 29th and 17th Brigades.

3. The following ships connected with Operation "Ironclad" were already at Durban or arrived during the next 3 days:-

H.M.S. BACHAQUERO, H.M.S. ROYAL ULSTERMAN, R.F.A. DERWENTDALE, R.F.A. EASEDALE, M/V THALATTA, S.S. MAHOUT, S.S. EMPIRE KINGSLEY, S.S. CITY OF HONG KONG, S.S. FRANCONIA, M/V NAIRNBANK and S.S. MARTAND, besides H.M. Ships composing escort, minesweeping and covering forces for the operation.

Preparations at Durban.

4. In view of the short time available, arrangements had been made with C.-in-C., South Atlantic, for as many ships as possible connected with the operation, particularly personnel ships and certain M.T. ships requiring to restow cargo, to berth alongside. These arrangements were made very satisfactorily.

5. During the stay at Durban the following preparations were made:-

(*a*) Cargo of M.T. ships not assault stowed was restowed as far as possible, M.T. being serviced and water-proofed.

(*b*) Landing craft brought out by ships not connected with the operation were allocated to their respective ships for the operation.

(*c*) All landing craft were fuelled, engines tried and compasses adjusted.

(*d*) Chart folios brought from the U.K., orders, photographs, maps, propaganda leaflets and intelligence data were distributed to all ships concerned.

(*e*) Dan buoys, taut wire measuring gear and other special stores brought from the U.K. were distributed to destroyers and minesweepers concerned.

(*f*) Conferences were held on board H.M.S. RAMILLIES, Flagship of S.O.F. and on board M/V WINCHESTER CASTLE, (H.Q. Ship until 23rd April), and final planning was made.

Two demonstrations were held on board M/V WINCHESTER CASTLE in which the operation was fully explained with the aid of models, for the benefit of Commanding Officers of ships, Masters and Naval Liaison Officers concerned, with all Military and South African liaison personnel present.

(*g*) Military personnel carried out route marches ashore and, where possible, Naval personnel required to land during the operation did likewise.

(*h*) Special security measures were taken which included the sailing and routeing of the force for Mombasa by N.C.S.O.[12] Durban in two separate convoys by the ordinary routine procedure. The real orders were issued quite separately and only opened after proceeding to sea.

(*i*) W/T and R/T sets in all ships of the force were netted and tuned. Communication stores and personnel were allocated to ships as necessary.

(*j*)Special communication arrangements were made for S.A.A.F., and arrangements were made for the introduction of special broadcast services to cover the area of operations.

Passage from Durban to William Pitt Bay.
Slow Convoy: Convoy Y.
6. Convoy Y, consisting of, DERWENTDALE, BACHAQUERO, MAHOUT, EMPIRE KINGSLEY, THALATTA, EASEDALE, NAIRNBANK and MARTAND sailed on 25th April escorted by DEVONSHIRE, 3 destroyers, the 14th M/S Flotilla and 4 corvettes.

7. S.S. CITY OF HONG KONG, which arrived at Durban a.m. 26th April was sailed p.m. that day after unloading a deck cargo of aircraft, and proceeded with escort of 2 corvettes to overtake and join the slow convoy.

8. This convoy followed the route ordered by S.O.F. which conformed to the normal shipping route Northwards along the coast to approximately 15 degrees South, then East North Eastwards as if to pass North of Madagascar.

9. The speed of this convoy was 9 knots (through the water) and arrangements were made to fuel destroyers and minesweepers from the two oilers on passage. The weather proved sufficiently favourable to allow this speed to be maintained and for fuelling to be carried out. The principal anxiety was that a head sea might stop BACHAQUERO owing to her bow door, but this fortunately did not eventuate.

Fast Convoy: Convoy Z.
10. The Military Commander, Major-General R.G. Sturges, C.B., R.M., transferred a part of his H.Q. to H.M.S. RAMILLIES, Flagship of the Combined C.-in-C., Rear-Admiral E.N. Syfret, C.B., on 23rd April. On the 28th April, S.N.O. (L), Captain G.A. Garnons-Williams and Staff, with Brigadier F.W. Festing, Commanding 29th Brigade and Staff, and a proportion of General Sturges' Staff transferred from WINCHESTER CASTLE to H.M.S. KEREN, the latter becoming Headquarters Ship of the Assault.

11. Convoy Z, consisting of KEREN, KARANJA, WINCHESTER CASTLE, SOBIESKI, ROYAL ULSTERMAN, DUCHESS OF ATHOLL, ORONSAY and FRANCONIA sailed from Durban on 28th April, escorted by RAMILLIES, ILLUSTRIOUS, HERMIONE and destroyers.

12. The route planned was similar to that of Convoy Y. On 30th April, however, reports were received of a hostile submarine off the Mozambique coast and S.O.F. ordered a change of route, the new route passing some 60 miles to the Eastward of the original track.

Approach to objective.

13. H.M.S. INDOMITABLE joined Flag on 3rd May and contact was made between Convoys Y and Z, the latter slowing down and increasing zig-zag so as to remain in rear.

14. Approval having been received from S.O.F., the object of the expedition was announced to all officers and men, maps were issued and Assault Commanders gave lectures outlining the intended plan.

All officers of landing craft received special instruction to enable them to recognise their respective beaches. This included the study of maps, models, panorama sketches and photographs which had been prepared for the purpose.

15. Convoys Y and Z formed into groups p.m. 4th May and the approach was made in accordance with the pre-arranged orders.

16. The strong Westerly set which had been expected between positions AA and ZB did not materialise. Visibility was good and contact was made with H.M.S. LIGHTNING, anchored off Nosi Fati, as expected. The final approach was carried out as ordered, groups anchoring approximately 10 minutes earlier than planned.

17. Slight inconvenience was caused by the fact that the first dan had been laid too close to Nosi Fati. Warning of this however was received from LAFOREY and ships left this dan on their starboard hand. Remaining dans were laid accurately and were easy to pick up; the successful danning of this channel was a first class bit of work and largely contributed to the result.

18. The successful execution of this approach, which resulted from long and careful planning tends to obscure the great difficulties which were overcome. An extract from a Memoire Militaire captured from Windsor Castle battery reads: "Tir de nuit n'est pas envisagé, l'accès de la Baie étant considéré comme impossible de nuit."

The Assault.

19. The assault proceeded according to plan, zero being at 0430 on Tuesday, 5th May (D.1). WINCHESTER CASTLE's (Captain Sebastian Francis New-digate, Master) (No. 5 Commando and 2 East Lancs. Regt.), KEREN's (1st R.S.F.) and KARANJA's (2 R.W.F.) flotillas left their ships at 0230, 0227 and 0319 for Red, Green and White Beaches respectively. Complete surprise was effected in spite of the explosion of at least one mine, and No. 7 battery (Red Beach), White and Green landings were carried out without loss. Landing craft navigation was as good as that of their parent ships and all made accurate beachings.

In accordance with the tactical plan, Blue Beach was then assaulted and encountered machine-gun fire, but was carried.

20. On receipt of the success signal from No. 5 Commando, KEREN, KARANJA, WINCHESTER CASTLE, SOBIESKI and BACHAQUERO were ordered to anchor in the main anchorage off Ambararata Bay. WINCHESTER CASTLE and BACHAQUERO led whilst remainder loaded their second flight.

A signal reporting mines near position HH at the end of the main anchorage had not been received in KEREN, but DEVONSHIRE, who had got it and who was then anchored East of Nosi Hara, promptly and properly ordered both ships to stop. The departure of the remaining ships was therefore delayed by me, until further minesweeping had been carried out.

21. Up to this time surprise had been achieved and by 0620 about 2,300 of our troops were ashore. On the other hand, the turn round for landing craft was very long, and as LAFOREY, LIGHTNING and ROYAL ULSTERMAN were anchored in or near a minefield, I ordered them to remain at anchor.

My joint Assault Commander, Brigadier F.W. Festing and his Command Post landed at 0710 at White Beach.

22. Reports of successful advance and taking of prisoners began to come in. At 0750 KEREN led Group IV to the main anchorage where minesweeping had just been completed, followed by the remainder of the assault force. About this time, the S.E. wind had increased to about force 8[13] and raised a sea of such size that in any other circumstances I would have ordered boats to be hoisted. Ships dropped second anchors.

The handling and loading of craft under these circumstances was exemplary. None were put out of action, and disembarkation continued at full speed.

23. Sweeping continued and at 1138 I regret to report that H.M.S. AURICULA struck a mine close to position HH (without loss of life), and remained anchored by her sweep. No action could be taken without prejudice to the operation and risk to the other ships and sweepers, and as she had ceased to sink she was left where she was, her back being broken.

By this time, minesweepers were 50 per cent. out of action, 35 mines had been swept and sweepers had done splendidly.

24. White Beach, opposite main anchorage, then became unsuitable after half tide so Blue was developed. This involved a 2 mile further turn round for landing craft, but with the risk of yet more sweeper casualties I ordered sweeping to cease and accepted the longer turn round in order to preserve the minesweepers for sweeping the Fleet into Diego Suarez harbour.

25. The landing continued at full pressure, two or three machine-gun attacks being made on the beaches during the day by enemy fighter aircraft. Fleet Air Arm fighter patrols however provided effective protection and with the initial air blow on the aerodrome, no attacks were made on the transports. Landing

operations were suspended during the period from sunset to moonrise, to avoid damage to craft.

26. About 1354 an enemy post on Windsor Castle became a nuisance and a little later was engaged by LAFOREY. Shortly after, signals of surrender and a white flag were observed and fire was ceased. The following morning LAFOREY and LIGHTNING engaged this post which was found to be empty on our troops taking possession.

27. The Hospital Ship ATLANTIS arrived in the afternoon, being led by a corvette through the swept channel to her anchorage close West of the main anchorage.

28. During the day great efforts had been made to find a suitable beach for BACHAQUERO, whose draught was 6 feet forward and 15 feet aft. A beach was eventually found close North of Red centre at the foot of Windsor Castle. The approach to this beach lay through the minefield. However, BACHAQUERO was swept through by CROMARTY who cut 2 mines, and her cargo landed near Red Beach centre in 14 minutes.

29. Before night fell I ordered AURICULA to be abandoned by her ship's company. Destroyers and A/S corvettes were disposed for A/S patrol.

30. General Sturges arrived from the Flagship in a destroyer and after consultation in KEREN proceeded ashore. Situation reports up to the end of D.1 indicated that No. 5 Commando had captured the whole of the Andrakaka Peninsula, and that the 29th Brigade had reached a line about 3 miles South of Antsirane town, where heavy opposition had been encountered.

May 6th, Day Two.
31. After daylight LIGHTNING and LAFOREY engaged the enemy post still holding out at Windsor Castle. INDOMITABLE was asked to attack a sloop in English Bay, Diego Suarez harbour, whose fire was controlling the road to Diego Suarez North. At 0744 INDOMITABLE reported this ship, which proved to be the D'ENTRECASTEAUX, as being on fire. LAFOREY, LIGHTNING and PAKENHAM took up positions to engage targets indicated by F.O.O.s, LAFOREY bombarding D'ENTRECASTEAUX at extreme range.

32. At daylight AURICULA was observed to be lower in the water and as an emergency measure FREESIA was ordered to tow her to shallow water; the effort however was too great and AURICULA broke in half and sank at 0823.

33. H.M.S. RAMILLIES, wearing the flag of S.O.F. arrived and anchored at ZD and proceeded to fuel.

34. The landing continued at full speed, the 13th Brigade being landed on completion of the 17th Brigade. All personnel numbering approximately 10,000 men were ashore by 1700.

35. About 1600 a mine exploded in POOLE's sweep and severely wounded her First Lieutenant, who, I deeply regret to report, died of his wounds. He was buried at sea from POOLE.

36. General Sturges came on board and out-lined the plan of attack on Antsirane for the night, which included the entry of H.M S. ANTHONY in the port of Diego Suarez and the landing of H.M.S. RAMILLIES' Royal Marines at Antsirane.

Day Three: 7th May.
37. From about midnight various reports were received from GENISTA on A/S patrol, indicating that she had been in contact with a submarine, had attacked and lost contact North West of Nosi Kara. PAKENHAM, LAFOREY and corvettes proceeded to assist in the search. At 0500 an aircraft from ILLUSTROUS sighted the French submarine LE HEROS on the surface outside the reefs North East of Nosi Fati and sank her by torpedo. The first news of this received in KEREN was an aircraft report at 0548 that submarine survivors were struggling in the water.

38. From 0330 onwards reports of the successful occupation of Antsirane and subsequent negotiations for the signing of a Protocol began to come in.

39. At 0930 ANTHONY arrived at the main anchorage escorting S.S. GREY-STOKE CASTLE, who had arrived from Durban with ammunition and other stores. In view of the brilliant operation carried out by ANTHONY the previous night in landing the R.M.s from RAMILLIES at Antsirane, I arranged for her to pass all ships at the anchorage who cleared lower decks and cheered her with great enthusiasm.

40. The landing of vehicles and stores continued. Returning landing craft conveyed casualties to the hospital ship. Arrangements were also made to convey several hundred prisoners from Red and Blue Beaches to ORONSAY, where it had been decided to accommodate all prisoners.

41. Survivors of the submarine LE HEROS were interrogated on board KEREN and a report signalled to S.O.F. No information concerning the minefields at Diego Suarez could be obtained from them. The only item of interest was that LE HEROS had left Diego Suarez on 1st May and had been patrolling ever since.

42. On receipt of a signal from S.O.F. approving my proposals to sail slow and fast convoys for Diego Suarez, preparations were made to sail the slow convoy at 1600/7th, and the fast convoy at 0500/8th. A route passing eight miles North of Cape Amber was selected and anchor berths for all ships in Scotch Bay were allocated.

43. The slow convoy, composed as for Convoy Y on passage from Durban with the addition of GREYSTOKE CASTLE, duly sailed by the swept channel

shortly after 1600, escorted by D.12 and all available corvettes, EMPIRE KINGSLEY acting as Commodore as before.

May 8th. Day Four.

44. All landing craft were ordered to leave the beaches by 0300 and to be hoisted.

At 0500 the fast convoy, composed as for Convoy Z on passage from Durban, sailed by the swept channel, escorted by LAFOREY and JAVELIN. KEREN acted as Commodore.

45. I instructed POOLE, the only remaining ship at the anchorage, to recover the dan buoys marking the channel and to follow the Fleet to Diego Suarez.

46. DEVONSHIRE and additional destroyers joined the escort of the convoy when clear of the swept channel and aircraft from ILLUSTRIOUS carried out A/S reconnaissance. The route of both convoys to Diego Suarez fortunately avoided the submarine which was eventually destroyed by ACTIVE and passage was uneventful though S.E. wind force 8 was experienced from Cape Amber onwards.

47. The slow convoy entered harbour at 1000 and the fast convoy at 1330, all ships picking up their berths in Scotch Bay creditably in spite of the strong wind.

48. With regard to the remarks on H.M. Ships, I understand that their reports are all sent to DEVONSHIRE and so presumably none are called for from me, but this report would be incomplete without them.

Very great responsibility lay in the hands of FREESIA (Acting Commander T.C.P. Crick) who led in through the minefield in unswept water, drawing 16 feet, accurately and steadfastly. The navigational responsibility for the whole force rested largely on DEVONSHIRE (Captain R.D. Oliver) although the initial anxiety was LAFOREY's (Captain R.M.J. Hutton).

The offensive spirit shown by PAKENHAM (Captain E.B.K. Stevens) and LAFOREY ably supported by LIGHTNING (Commander H.G. Walters) was a pleasure to watch although I had many moments of anxiety when they were passing through swept channels. However, I realised they knew more of that immediate local situation than I.

All three post captains mentioned are senior to me and I deeply appreciate their full and generous acceptance of being placed under my orders.

CROMER (Commander R.H. Stephenson) ably supported by CROMARTY (Lieutenant Commander C.G. Palmer, R.N.V.R.) were the outstanding ships in the gallant 14th M/S Flotilla.

The A/S corvettes performed their task in guarding the anchorage from submarine attack, and GENISTA (Lt.-Cdr. R. Pattinson, D.S.C., R.N.R.) may have had a contributory share in the sinking of LE HEROS.

49. The task assigned to the cutter LINDI was carried out successfully and provided that one crucial aid to navigation which Captain D.19, from his report,

was very glad to get at 2040/D.-1. Great credit is due to Lieutenant A.G Booker, R.N.V.R., her Commanding Officer, for his very successful navigation.

50. Of the masters and crews of ships of the Merchant Navy taking part, it is impossible to speak too highly. In every way they gave of their best. Their ship handling was superb: groups were composed of ships varying from 20,000 to 5,000 tons and they anchored in station in the swept channel as if they had done it all their lives.

Unstinted help came from all concerned. Docks Operating Groups were backed up by ships' companies; ships' motor boats were run as landing craft; stewards, cooks and boatswains' parties and all took their full share. When volunteers were called for for special engineering parties, the entire engine room staffs volunteered including one old greaser who fought as a cavalryman in the South African war.

51. There is one lesson, however, which is so important and at the same time so commonplace to us all, that it nearly became overlooked. That is the perfect co-operation and friendship that exists between General Sturges and his Headquarters, Brigadier Festing and the 29th Independent Brigade Group Staff and my own Staff. This was not confined to the Commands and Senior Officers; but went right down through to stewards and batmen, all of whom learnt to forget the word "my" and referred to the Force as "our". This state of affairs became crystallised when we joined the Flag of the Commander-in-Chief who turned the Force into a formidable fighting unit.

(Signed) G.A. GARNONS-WILLIAMS,
Captain, Royal Navy.
Senior Naval Officer, Landing.

APPENDIX.
THE CAPTURE OF DIEGO SUAREZ

The following Report was submitted on 15th June, 1942, to the Secretary of State for War by LIEUTENANT-GENERAL SIR ROBERT G. STURGES, K.B.E., C.B., D.S.O., General Officer Commanding 121 Force.

Sir,
I have the honour to forward herewith an account of Operation "Ironclad" for the capture of Diego Suarez.

PLANNING AND EMBARKATION

Operation "Bonus"
1. I first received information on 23rd December, of the project to capture Diego Suarez, when I was informed that I had been nominated as Joint Commander, with Rear-Admiral T.B. Drew, R.N., for this operation, which was to be known by the code word "Bonus".

The military forces allotted were H.Q. R.M. Division, 102 R.M. Brigade, 36 Infantry Brigade, two commandos, and a normal combined operational allotment of supporting and ancillary units. These included a detachment of the M.N.B.D.O.[14] to erect coast defence and A.A. guns for the consolidation of the naval and air base. Sufficient assault, personnel, and motor transport shipping was allotted to carry the formations and units with their vehicles on a reduced scale, similar to that used on various exercises carried out in the previous year. This Force was reasonably well found. The infantry brigades, 102 R.M. Brigade and 36 Infantry Brigade, had been water trained and had exercised on shore over long distances and with little or no transport. Signals were just adequate. All units were tactically stowed and a minimum of personnel was allowed to enable signals to function after capture of objective. The provision of one squadron of aircraft only, fifteen Lysanders, subsequently reduced to six, appeared to me a little peculiar, but the decision by the Chief of the Air Staff was that this was perfectly adequate for the occupation of the objective.

Planning at once commenced, and, by 31st December, the draft operation order, the maintenance project, the detailed order of battle, the allotment of personnel and vehicles to ships, and the landing tables were complete and had been handed to the Q.M.G. Movements Branch at the War Office for the preparation of loading tables and the issue of movement orders for embarkation. Subject to the final decision of the Chiefs of Staff Committee, the expedition was planned to embark at the end of January, to carry out a rehearsal exercise in Loch Fyne in early February, and sail on 20th February.

2. In planning this operation in conjunction with Rear-Admiral Drew, I made a military plan which was in outline that actually used in Operation "Ironclad", and together we reached certain conclusions which were of great importance in planning the latter operation:-

(*a*) The plan prepared by the Joint Planning Section envisaged a landing on the difficult beaches in Ambararata Bay on the West coast, by one brigade, which was to secure a bridgehead and to cover the landing and forming up of the remainder of the force. It was estimated that the advance on Antsirane could commence on D2 or D3. I formed the opinion that this very orthodox plan gave the enemy far too much time to recover from the hoped for initial surprise, and I decided that, in spite of the difficulties of the beaches and terrain, the first brigade to land should advance on Antsirane immediately after securing the beaches. I considered that speed in the advance of this brigade, with limited armour was more important than the completion of its supporting arms and transport. Further, this advance would give sufficient cover to enable the remainder of the force to land without undue risk.

(*b*) Rear-Admiral Drew and I decided that much fuller information than was then available would be necessary, that air photographs of the beach area ought to be taken, and that the risk of compromising surprise in doing so should be accepted. As a result of our request to the Chiefs of Staff, orders were issued for the air photographs to be taken which were subsequently used in the operation "Ironclad" and for the collection of further intelligence which was of great value in that operation.

(c) We also reached the conclusion that, while a night or dawn assault on the beaches was essential, the final approach could only be made under certain combined conditions of moon and tide. These, in the Spring and early Summer of 1942, occurred in the early part of each calendar month. We calculated the time required for loading ships, the move to Durban, adjustments at Durban, and final approach, deciding that, if the expedition sailed on 20th February, the assault could take place in the favourable period at the beginning of April.

Meanwhile arrangements were put in train for the rehearsal exercise which was to be conducted by H.Q. Expeditionary Force. About 15th January orders were received that operation "Bonus" was to be held in abeyance and that much of the shipping required for it was to be taken for other convoys.

On the cancellation of operation "Bonus" the forces concerned reverted to command of their normal formations. Later "Z" H.Q. Signals, the only combined operation signals in the United Kingdom, were drafted away.

Exercise "Charcoal".
3. In spite of the cancellation of operation "Bonus", I decided that rehearsal exercise for which plans had been prepared would be of value to my command. I therefore asked H.Q. Expeditionary Force to continue with the exercise, on the reduced scale necessitated by the removal of much of the shipping. This exercise, known as exercise "Charcoal", was carried out by 102 R.M. Brigade early in February, and many valuable lessons were learnt. I summarise below two lessons which were of particular importance to operation "Ironclad".

This was the first combined operation exercise carried out since October that gave an opportunity to practise the naval and military staffs, the landing craft crews, the beach parties, the docks operating personnel, and the naval and military signals which took part in operation "Ironclad". Due to postings, it was the only combined operations training that many of the new drafts were able to be given.

The exercise was carried out over difficult beaches and required the rapid advance inland of one brigade. This drew attention to the extreme importance of close scrutiny of the landing tables, so that essential vehicles had priority in landing and that these had a high cross country performance. All units had to be prepared to make long advances with very little transport. Although the facts were well known to all concerned in combined operations, a new standard was set by the difficult beaches and terrain used in this exercise.

On conclusion of exercise "Charcoal", my H.Q. and the troops taking part dispersed to their billeting areas, and continued with their training.

Operation "Ironclad".
4. On the 12th March I received orders from H.Q. Expeditionary Force to report to the War Office on the morning 14th March. When I arrived at the War Office,

I was informed that the Chiefs of Staff Committee had decided at 11 o'clock the previous night, that the operation, subsequently known as "Ironclad", was to be prepared to capture and to hold the naval base and air base at Diego Suarez during the favourable May moon and tide period, that is between the 3rd and 8th May. The expedition was to sail with convoy WS 17 which was to be delayed until the 23rd March.

Rear Admiral E.N. Syfret was nominated as Combined Commander and I was nominated as Military Commander under him. I was informed that a meeting with him was quite impossible until the arrival of the convoy at Freetown. For all planning before that, which of course included the vital planning for loading the assault ships, he would be represented by Capt. G.W.A. Waller, R.N., who was to be Chief of Staff for the operation; Captain G.A. Garnons-Williams, R.N., who had acted as C.O.S. to Rear Admiral Drew in planning operation "Bonus", was nominated as Senior Naval Officer (Landing) and Naval Assault Commander. Brigadier F.W. Festing as commander of 29 Independent Brigade, the only combined operationally-trained formation in this revised expedition, naturally became the Military Assault Commander.

It will be seen that the time available for preparing this expedition was far less than previously considered necessary. It was estimated, based on operation "Bonus", that the period of time for a similar operation to be mounted was 91 days from the issue of the preparatory orders to the assault; in the event, 52 days elapsed between the two. This saving of time was effected first by using the 29th Independent Brigade and 5 Commando to capture the beaches, embarking them with minimum transport in the four assault ships semi-permanently allotted to the Expeditionary Force for training and operational purposes; secondly, by the use of 17 Infantry Brigade Group, already embarked close stowed in convoy WS 17, as the second brigade; thirdly by the immediate acceptance by 29 Independent Brigade of the modified "Bonus" plan for the assault forces. If the operation was postponed after sailing, a brigade group front 2 Division in WS 18 would take the place of 17 Infantry Brigade Group.

This plan had certain serious disadvantages. The first was that Force H.Q, 29 Independent Brigade, 5 Commando, and Force troops were reduced to what could be put in the four assault ships. Examination of the problem showed that this was only possible by making severe reductions in the personnel and even severer reductions in vehicles previously considered essential. The second disadvantage was that 17 Infantry Brigade Group had no experience or training in combined operations, and its personnel and vehicles had been embarked as for a normal WS convoy and not for an assault landing. Neither time nor shipping was available to rectify this.

5. Embarkation of vehicles and stores in the four assault ships was to commence on 18th March, and all planning had to be completed to this schedule. After examination of the new intelligence available, which did not as yet include the air photographs, we decided that our previous plans were sound and could be carried

out with the reduced forces available. On the military side, new topographical information suggested that the beaches were far better than was originally reported. The postponement of the operation from April to May placed it at the beginning of the dry season, which considerably reduced anticipated difficulties of advance along the only very doubtful, road which was available. Thanks to this and "Bonus" Captain Garnons-Williams and myself were able to meet Brigadier Festing and Brigadier G.W.B. Tarleton, commanding 29 Independent Brigade and 17 Infantry Brigade respectively, and my advisers and heads of services, all of whom arrived in London on the morning of 15th March, with a completed outline plan and an outline draft of the Force operation order.

From the 15th March to 19th March, Captain Garnons-Williams, Brigadier Festing and myself with our staffs were engaged in close co-operation in preparing the necessary plans for loading the ships and completing necessary preparations for the Force to leave the United Kingdom.

6. A difficult combined problem was to decide in detail the composition of the naval and military forces to be embarked in the four assault ships; *H.M.S. Keren* and *Karanja*, *M.Vs. Winchester Castle* and *Sobieski*. To these were to be added *H.M.S. Royal Ulsterman* and *Bachaquero*. These two ships could not meet the convoy until arrival at Durban, and any troops and vehicles required to make the assault from them had either to be embarked in the four assault ships or be taken from those units already embarked with 17 Infantry Brigade Group. The four assault ships could take an approximate total of 323 officers, 4,753 O.Rs. and 115 vehicles. Of these 76 officers, 499 O.Rs., were finally allotted to Force H.Q. and Force troops including the Docks Operating Company: 38 officers, 328 O.Rs. to Royal Navy: leaving 209 officers, 3,926 O.Rs. for the fighting troops of the assault force. It must be realised that this small allotment of H.Q. and Force troops had to command and administer not only the assault force, but also 17 Infantry Brigade Group, and later the 13 Infantry Brigade Group which was to be added to the Force. In addition they were to be faced with the problems of the control and consolidation of the captured base.

I had also, in this short planning period, to hand over the command of the Royal Marine Division. It was a great disappointment to the two Royal Marine Brigades that they were not employed on this operation, from which they were excluded by the need for extreme speed in embarkation and by the chance disposition of the brigades when the operation was ordered.

29th Brigade were quite fortuitously embarked in the assault ships for exercises and these assault ships were then actually detailed for the operation.

7. On 17th March I met Major-General H.P.M. Berney-Ficklin, commanding 5 Division from which 17 Infantry Brigade Group was to be taken. On the 18th March, I was interviewed by the Chiefs of Staff on my plans for the operation and on 19th March I met the Prime Minister. On the evening of the same day I left for my H.Q. at Melrose, and on 21st March embarked in *M.V Winchester Castle* which sailed on the 23rd March. On the 22nd March I saw

Lieutenant-General E.C.A. Schreiber, commanding the Expeditionary Force which I was now leaving. I thanked him for the great assistance that his staff had given to Force 121, and handed over 101 and 102 R.M. Brigades to his direct command.

During this brief and very fully occupied planning and embarkation period, very great assistance was given to us all by HQ Expeditionary Force. Without it the expedition could not have sailed, in the time and the state of preparation it did. I was also assisted by those branches of the War Office concerned and by the Adviser of Combined Operations and his staff.

The speed with which the revised operation was mounted was only possible because of the experience that all the staffs, advisers and services concerned had gained in planning previous projects, and carrying out exercises based on them.

THE PASSAGE TO THE THEATRE OF OPERATIONS.

The Completion of the Plan for the Assault.

8. Captain Garnons-Williams, Brigadier Festing and myself with limited staffs had embarked in *M.V Winchester Castle*. We were therefore able to continue our study of the operation in constant consultation. Owing to the short planning period, detailed study of the operation, other than that required for embarkation and loading, had not been possible for Brigadier Festing and his staff. Immediately before sailing the air photographs of the beach area had been received on board *M.V. Winchester Castle* (Unfortunately the photographs stopped a few miles short of Antsirane and thus missed the final prepared defence line, which was only discovered during the operation.) We were, now able to make a full and detailed study of the operation, and the final selection of the beaches, the assault commanders dealing with these problems in great detail. Meanwhile the staff was able to complete the maintenance project, the detailed work on the final preparations to be carried out at Durban, and the study of the employment of 17 Infantry Brigade Group. By the time the convoy reached Freetown on 6th April, written draft instructions, both operational and administrative, had been prepared for the employment of that brigade group and for the final preparations that were to be made at Durban. These included the only re-stowage possible for 17 Infantry Brigade Group.

On arrival at Freetown I met for the first time Rear Admiral Syfret. During the short stay at Freetown from 6th to 9th April he examined the plans for the operation, discussed the naval plans with Captains Waller and Garnons-Williams; and the military plans with myself. He gave his approval for the military plans and made certain alterations to the naval plans which however did not affect the military side of the operations.

I was also able to meet and confer with Major General Berney-Ficklin and Brigadier Tarleton on the detailed arrangements for the withdrawal of 17 Infantry Brigade Group from 5 Division and its employment in operation "Ironclad". I would here like to express my appreciation of the assistance and the generous minded attitude of Major General Berney-Ficklin. The withdrawal of one-third of his division could not have been welcome, and there were many points of detail to be settled between us. In all discussions he gave me every possible assistance and encouragement, even to the extent of supplying a few non-commissioned officers and men from units of his division other than those in my order of battle.

During the passage from Freetown to Durban, commanders and staffs in the *Winchester Castle* were able to continue the study of the operation. On 17th April a signal was received from Rear Admiral Syfret in *H.M.S. Malaya* informing me that the War Office had placed 13 Infantry Brigade Group at my disposal for the operation, but it was not to be committed unless the degree of opposition justified it. By the time the convoy reached Durban the final plan for the assault had become firm to a considerable degree of detail, and the final operation and administrative orders and instructions were ready for issue.

Final Preparations at Durban.

9. It was clear that a large amount of work would be necessary at Durban in preparation for the operation. Naval and military representatives had flown to Durban from Freetown where they had reported to the Imperial Movement Control and harbour authorities in order to make all possible preparations for the reception of the convoy. All ships were thus able to come alongside and work started immediately on arrival. Although the convoy only arrived at about noon on the 22nd April, a tour of the dock area that evening showed that work was in full swing. In general terms the work to be carried out was as follows:-

(*a*) The final plans had to be discussed with Rear Admiral Syfret and his staff. Many alterations had occurred in the composition of the naval force; these in practice made little difference to the military plan, but full discussion was of course necessary to ensure proper co-ordination.

(*b*) Vehicles, guns and equipment of the 29 Independent Brigade although embarked for an assault landing had now to be checked, serviced and water-proofed after a month in the holds of the ships.

(*c*) Vehicles, guns and equipment of the 17 Infantry Brigade Group had not been stowed for a combined operation and everything possible had to be done to make a limited amount of transport and guns available tactically stowed. These vehicles had to be serviced, waterproofed and examined. In particular the electrical batteries of the vehicles and wireless sets required re-charging and connecting up and the vehicles had to be filled with petrol, oil and water. Tank guns had to be fired, new tracks on tanks and carriers to be stretched. Mess Tin and Composite rations had to be got up from the bottoms of holds for 17 Infantry Brigade Group and ammunition and equipment loaded into vehicles. On top of this aircraft petrol and bombs had to be loaded for the South African Air Force (S.A.A.F.). It was only possible in the time available to make these arrangements for a limited scale of transport for this brigade group, and for two out of the three batteries of the 9 Field Regiment.

(*d*) Final orders and instructions had to be issued and discussed with the 17 and 13 Infantry Brigade Groups. It had been possible before leaving England to embark one G.S.O.2 with brigade H.Q. and one Assistant Military Landing Officer (A.M.L.O.) in each ship of 17 Infantry Brigade Group, all experienced in Combined Operations training. These officers had been able to do the valuable work in assisting this brigade group to prepare itself for the operation. In addition to this a few officers from 29 Independent Brigade were exchanged with officers of 17 Infantry Brigade for the voyage from Freetown to Durban and were thus able to pass on their experience gained in combined exercises. I was therefore by now assured that 17 Infantry Brigade Group could land over the beaches and play a valuable part in the operation, especially from D2 onwards, if enemy resistance made this necessary. 13 Infantry Brigade Group was a very different matter. Their personnel ships only arrived at Durban on 26th April when I met Brigadier V.C. Russell, the brigade commander for the first time. I was able to do little beyond issuing them with written operational and administrative orders and instructions, and discussing potential situations and problems with Brigadier Russell.

(e) *H.M.S. Royal Ulsterman* and *Bachaquero* joined the convoy at Durban and were loaded; the former with troops and the latter with vehicles and guns.

Meanwhile all units engaged in daily route marches to harden and get them fit after the voyage out.

An offer of the co-operation of a bomber and reconnaissance squadron of the South African Air Force was received while the force was at Durban. It was clear that the addition of this squadron would greatly increase the strength of my force for the consolidation of the objective, although owing to the distance from the nearest base, the squadron would be unable to take part in the capture of the aerodrome. Colonel S.A. Melville, S.A.A.F., arrived from Pretoria with the offer in his pocket. The S.A.A.F. also offered the complete personnel and ground equipment for a fighter squadron if the Air Ministry could supply the aircraft. The offer of the bomber and reconnaissance squadron was accepted with gratitude. The aerodrome was made serviceable and the whole squadron was operating by 12th May. Thereafter it proved a most valuable component for the fortress. That the squadron was grossly overworked was a truism, but none of the many tasks given to it were refused. They included long distance sea patrols and escorts in co-operation with the Royal Navy, photographic reconnaissance in anticipation of future operations, interception and communications.

All this made a vast amount of detailed work for the administrative staff and the services. All ranks concerned worked extremely well and did not spare themselves. In particular I would here draw attention to the work performed by: the A.A. & Q.M.G., Lieutenant-Colonel A.F.J. Elmslie, A.D.O.S., Lieutenant-Colonel E.J. Savage, and D.A.D.O.S.(E), Major A. Blunt.

The Project for the Capture of Tamatave and Majunga
10. Early on the morning of 26 April, a cable was received from London instructing Rear Admiral Syfret and myself to forward our appreciation of the possibility of operations to capture Tamatave and Majunga either simultaneously

or shortly after Diego Suarez. We at once investigated this problem and came to the conclusion that, if 13 Infantry Brigade Group could be permanently allotted to the force and if the opposition at Diego Suarez was such that it could be overcome by 1800 hrs. on D1, these additional operations could be carried out simultaneously by re-embarking 29 Independent Brigade and 5 Commando four or five days after the initial assault on Diego Suarez. Rear Admiral Syfret and I issued combined directives for these operations to Brigadier Festing and Captain Garnons-Williams. During the remainder of the stay at Durban and the passage to Diego Suarez, they prepared and issued orders for these operations. However, on 4 May, orders were received that in view of the extreme importance of 13 Infantry Brigade Group reaching India as soon as possible, these operations were to be held in abeyance. These projects however appeared again later after the capture of Diego Suarez.

11. The slow convoy sailed from Durban 25 April and the fast convoy, containing all the personnel ships, on 28 April. By this time all re-adjustments of personnel, stores and vehicles for the operation were completed. Accompanied by Colonel Melville, S.A.A.F., Lieutenant-Colonel G.F. Houghton, Royal Corps of Signals, C.S.O. and Major R.O. Nash, M.C., GS02, I embarked in *H.M.S. Ramillies* which was flying the flag of Rear Admiral Syfret, while the majority of my H.Q. were embarked in *H.M.S. Keren* with S.N.O.L. and H.Q. 29 Independent Brigade. This arrangement was necessary in order to enable an early start to be made on the beach maintenance project, and to co-ordinate with S.N.O.L. the landing of the 17 Infantry Brigade Group, after disembarkation of 29 Independent Brigade. A further dispersion of my H.Q. was necessary so that a team in *H.M.S. Karanja* could take on the duties of assault H.Q. ship and S.N.O.L. if *H.M.S. Keren* were sunk.

12. The work at Durban was greatly assisted by the facilities made available by the Government of the Union of South Africa, co-ordinated in Durban by Brigadier J. Daniels, Area Commander and Colonel S.A. Melville S.A.A.F.; by the Military Mission under the command of Brigadier A.G. Salisbury-Jones; and Lieutenant-Colonel A.W. Bryant and the staff of the Imperial Movement Control at Durban. It was a hard struggle. The Union was practically denuded of certain commodities such as bostick and insulating tape for waterproofing vehicles and of aircraft bombs and it seemed that almost the impossible had been achieved.

Passage to the Objective
13. The passage to the objective was made according to the naval plan and is fully described in the naval dispatches. The final opportunity to distribute orders occurred on I May by destroyer. At dusk 4 May the complete convoy, which now consisted of the slow and the fast elements, formed up in its assault formation and I observed with some relief, that, when darkness fell, we did not appear to have been discovered by enemy air reconnaissance or surface vessels.

THE CAPTURE OF THE BEACHES AND ADVANCE INLAND.

14. The general plan for the assault was a main landing by 29 Independent Brigade in Ambararata Bay area at three beaches named from South to North: Green, White and Blue.

This brigade which was on a very light scale of transport, and had under its command among other units, "B" Special Service Squadron (6 Valentines, 6 Tetrarchs) and 455 Light Battery (4 × 3.7 howitzers and 2 × 25-pounders), was, as soon as it had secured the beaches, to advance and capture Antsirane, about 21 miles by road to the East. Simultaneously with this landing, 5 Commando (which was under command 29 Independent Brigade) and one company 2 East Lancashire Regiment from 29 Independent Brigade, were to land in Courrier Bay at beaches named Red; South, Central and North: silence two coast defence batteries reported in that area, and then advance East to secure the Andrakaka Peninsula. This peninsula projects into the main harbour of Diego Suarez but is separated from the town of Antsirane by a strip of water about 1,200 yards across. Zero was at 0430 hours 5 May when the leading troops were to reach the beach, 17 Infantry Brigade Group, followed if necessary on D2 by 13 Infantry Brigade Group, was to land, as soon as landing craft had completed 29 Independent Brigade and 5 Commando, on the best of Green, White, or Blue beaches, and come into action as necessary to complete the capture of Antsirane and the Orangea Peninsula. On the latter stood coast defence batteries covering the narrow entrance to the harbour.

The Approach of the Convoy and the Despatch of Landing Craft.
15. The convoy approached Courrier and Ambararata Bays from the West. The leading assault ship, *M.V. Winchester Castle* anchored outside the range of the coast defence guns in case these were not silenced by daylight. Assault Landing Craft and Motor Landing Craft were lowered from the *Winchester Castle* the *Keren* and *Karanja*, and Motor Landing Craft from the motor transport ships. The assault flotillas left for Red, Green and White beaches at 0230, 0227 and 0319 hours respectively, being led in for some of the way by corvettes and minesweepers; and, in the case of Green and White beaches where the low lying ground offered no good landmarks in the moonlight, using Lorenz beam apparatus.

The approach of the transports and the minesweeping, escorting, and covering warships was a difficult and dangerous operation. It was subsequently discovered that, in the defence appreciation, approach from this direction by night was discounted. There is no doubt that the success of the whole operation and the comparatively low casualties sustained by the Army, were largely due to the acceptance of this risk by the Naval Commanders concerned, and by the skill and seamanship displayed by the Royal Navy and Merchant Navy in executing this part of the plan.

The Landing at Courrier Bay and the Action of 5 Commando
16. 5 Commando with B Company and two carriers of 2 East Lancashire Regiment landed at the Red beaches at 0435 hours unopposed. Commando HQ

and three troops, landing at Red North beach, captured No. 7 Coast Defence battery, consisting of four modern 6.1in. guns, at 0500 hours. The garrison was surprised and offered no resistance. The remaining two troops landed unopposed at Red South beach, but were unable to find the reported No. 8 Battery, which in fact did not exist. The two Commando columns, less one troop left at No. 7 Battery, then advanced inland; meeting at the Col du Courrier at 0945 hours. By 1130 hours the Commando, which now included B Company 2 East Lancashire Regiment commenced its advance over the Andrakaka Peninsula, and at 1430 hours it had reached the village of Diego Suarez on the Eastern-most end of the peninsula. They met slight opposition on the initial advance but rapidly dispersed it. Attempts were made without success to find boats to cross to Antsirane.

In the Red beach area, a machine gun and some snipers came to life at daylight. The troop holding No. 7 Battery spent a large part of the day stalking these enemy parties, but in the difficult and precipitous country, they continued to give trouble until D2, when they were finally mopped up by B Company 2 Royal Scots Fusiliers which had taken over the Red beach area.

The Main Landings – 29 Independent Brigade.
17. I Royal Scots Fusiliers at Green Beach and 2 Royal Welsh Fusiliers at White beach were landed punctually and accurately and met no opposition. Green beach was found unsuitable for vehicles and White difficult even for tracked vehicles. Blue beach was now approached from the rear by C Company 2 Royal Welsh Fusiliers which had landed at White beach. Although an infantry post had been reported on this beach, in the half light it appeared to be unoccupied. A and C Companies 2 East Lancashire Regiment were therefore signalled in, using the landing craft which had returned to the *Royal Ulsterman* from the Red beaches. On the approach of these landing craft, a machine gun post manned by Senegalese opened fire but caused no casualties, but when fired on from the rear and from the landing craft, withdrew and left the beach unguarded. Thus by 0630 hours all beaches were in our hands. Meanwhile at 0615 hours Brigadier Festing had issued the order for the assault floating reserve, 2 South Lancashire Regiment less B Company in unarmoured landing craft, to land at White beach.

Air Action and the Diversion by H.M.S. Hermione.
18. At first light, about 0530 hours, aircraft of the Fleet Air Arm bombed the enemy aerodrome about six miles South of Antsirane, and the shipping in the harbour. This was most successful and appears to have deprived the enemy of any means of air reconnaissance or support, except for a few isolated machine gun attacks by aircraft from the South, which were promptly dealt with by the Fleet Air Arm.

At 0440 hours *H.M.S. Hermione* opened fire with star shells and made smoke in the vicinity of Ambodivahibe Bay, the most probable landing place on the East coast South-East of Antsirane. At first light, Fleet Air Arm aircraft dropped parachutes with dummies in the inaccessible country about Mahagaga, which was on the route from Ambodivahibe Bay. It was subsequently learned that this diversion combined with the lack of air reconnaissance, caused the enemy to despatch troops to Mahagaga some time before other troops were despatched towards Ambararata. It did however awaken the French and it is difficult to assess the real value of this diversion.

The Advance of 29 Independent Brigade.
19. 2 Royal Welsh Fusiliers followed by I Royal Scots Fusiliers now commenced the advance to Antsirane, at first with marching infantry and a few cyclists and motor cyclists only. The carriers overtook the leading elements of the 2 Royal Welsh Fusiliers about 0730 hours at Mangoky, five miles East of the beaches. They had not yet met the enemy but about 0815 hours a French naval officer and three ratings were captured a short distance East of the Ansahapano River. In accordance with instructions, the officer was given a letter demanding the surrender of the base, and sent back to Antsirane in his own car.

About 1100 hours the leading carriers came under fire from the high ground about one mile East of Anamakia. The enemy were holding a well-defined spur which commands the flat area between it and the Anamakia Woods and which the road crosses by a rocky and tortuous col, known as the Col De Bonne Nouvelle. By 1115 hours there were in the Anamakia area, about 15 miles from the beaches, two companies 2 Royal Welsh Fusiliers, two 3.7 howitzers of 455 Light Battery, as well as carriers and motor cycles. The Brigadier, who had also reached Anamakia, ordered the infantry to attack supported by the guns. While they were deploying, two Valentines and one Tetrarch, the first tanks to land, arrived and were ordered forward to assist the carriers and motor cyclists. The tanks moved up the road and engaged and silenced the enemy machine gun and rifle positions on the col.

All fire from the position appeared to be silenced, but the extremely rocky ground prevented the tanks from leaving the road and getting right into the position. They therefore went on down the road for another mile, where they were joined by two more Tetrarchs. They were now within three miles of the centre of Antsirane and continued their advance along the road and destroyed a lorry load of Senegalese infantry. Immediately afterwards they came under fire from 75mm. guns firing down the road and from their right flank. At this point they were unable to leave the road, and four tanks were very quickly disabled. The squadron commander, Major J.E.S. Simon, Royal Tank Regiment, sent his last remaining tank back to Brigade to report, and then brought the survivors from the disabled tanks into dismounted action. They found it impossible to advance, but beat off several enemy attacks until, at 1545 hrs., when only three of the party were left unwounded, and even revolver ammunition was expended, they were taken prisoner. The fifth tank met and destroyed another lorry load of infantry on its way back.

Meanwhile at the Col de Bonne Nouvelle, after the tanks had gone, the enemy defences came to life and held up our infantry. At 1415 hrs. seven more tanks under Captain P.L. Palmer, 10 Royal Hussars, arrived in the area, and the position was finally captured and mopped up by 1500 hrs. Thus, from about 1200 to 1500 hrs., there were two battles taking place on the road. The French were attacking our tank crews a few hundred yards in front of their main position, and at the same time, about 3,000 yards further back, our infantry were attacking the French outpost position.

It was subsequently learned that the Col de Bonne Nouvelle was the last of several prepared positions facing West which had not at first been manned. The French on hearing, from the officer sent back with the letter, that our main threat was along the Ambararata road, had hurried forward lorried infantry to occupy this position. Our attack was made before this occupation had been completed, and the action of our leading tanks prevented further reinforcements.

20. At 1515 hrs. the advance from Col de Bonne Nouvelle was resumed. Captain Palmer's tanks led and were followed by I Royal Scots Fusiliers. The tanks had been ordered to locate the enemy which had stopped Major Simon's tanks. Captain Palmer ordered his tanks to swing off the road to the right and to move through the scrub and mealie plantation to a hull-down position. He then deliberately moved his own tank into the open to draw fire. It was hit and Captain Palmer was killed assisting his wounded driver to cover. The remaining tanks resumed the advance, but came under heavy 75 mm. fire and withdrew at 1800 hrs. in the failing light.

The carriers of I Royal Scots Fusiliers and 2 Royal Welsh Fusiliers followed by the companies of I Royal Scots Fusiliers were advancing along both sides of the road, and came under fire from the main position about 1700 hrs. On the right they got within a few yards of the enemy anti-tank ditch, some two hundred yards in front of the enemy trenches. As dark fell at 1830 hrs., I Royal Scots Fusiliers was in contact with the enemy on a wide front and under heavy fire. This battalion continued energetic patrolling during the night, while the remaining battalions of 29 Independent Brigade under orders of Brigade HQ, moved into perimeter areas, with Brigade HQ established for the night at Conlieux (Robinson's Hotel).

The situation report (see also para. 24) brought back to me by my G.S.O.1 Lieutenant-Colonel J.L. Moulton, R.M., and my own contacts revealed the following:-

29 Independent Brigade had now advanced 18 miles in tropical heat and in wet clothes along a bad and extremely dusty road. The troops had been actively employed since 0130 hrs. when they had manned the landing craft. Transport was still very short, marching infantry had carried all their weapons and pulled handcarts with their ammunition and stores. Some of the later sub-units to land were still marching up the road and continued to do so all night. All along the road the bush and long grass was burning and for the last few miles there was some inaccurate sniping.

The troops though tired, had their tails well up. 29 Independent Brigade was in contact with the main enemy facing North across the isthmus leading to

Antsirane and the brigade commander intended to issue orders for a dawn attack on 6th May, D2, on a three battalion front. Lack of intelligence of enemy positions, combined with the successful advance to date, led us all to expect a good scrap, which would end when we ate our breakfasts in Antsirane on 6th May. The limited transport of 29 Independent Brigade; "R" Group 17 Infantry Brigade and two companies 2 Northamptons minus any transport were on the way; and the air was ours. The field ambulance was moving up and two motor ambulances were ashore.

In confident expectation of success, my main worry was what would happen should the enemy battalion at Joffreville come down on our flank, or across our lines of communication?

Neither of these events happened as expected. On 6th May, at 0700 hrs., we were further away from Antsirane than the areas reached by our leading elements overnight; and later the battalion from Joffreville was surprised and captured almost intact, as it marched from the South into the rear of our battalion areas.

PROGRESS OF THE LANDING ON 5TH MAY – D1.

Completion of 29 Independent Brigade and 5 Commando.

21. After detailing a flotilla of nine Assault Landing Craft and two Motor Landing Craft for the very important landing at Red beaches, the available landing craft were only sufficient to land in the first trip about 580 men of I Royal Scots Fusiliers, 512 of 2 Royal Welsh Fusiliers and a total of 14 carriers on the brigade front on Green and White beaches respectively. To these were added minimum beach parties, beach signals, engineers, and medical detachments. A further 278 men of 2 East Lancashire Regiment had landed on the second trip of landing craft from Red beach, having been brought close to Blue beach in *H.M.S. Royal Ulsterman.* 2 South Lancashire Regiment was in floating service in *M.V. Sobieski,* and about 500 men with no vehicles could be landed from her by using all available R boats (fast naval motor boats carrying about 18 men) and other unarmoured landing craft, which were not used in the initial assault. Any men or vehicles above these numbers had to come in the second and later trips of landing craft, which had to return the eight or ten miles to the anchorage to reload. It had been hoped that the assault ships could close the beaches as soon as the Courrier Bay batteries were in our hands. Unfortunately the large number of enemy mines between the convoy anchorage and the beaches prevented this starting until 0750 hours, although the success signal was received from 5 Commando at 0615 hours. The remaining mines, however, still kept these ships several miles from Blue beach, which by this time was the only practicable beach. During the morning a strong wind rose blowing from N.E., raising a heavy chop, which slowed up the flat bowed landing craft and drenched the occupants with heavy spray. The combination of these circumstances seriously delayed the progress of the landing. It had been hoped to complete the landing of 29 Independent Brigade personnel by about 0900 hrs; in the event this was not achieved until about 1100 hrs.; similarly

their vehicles were not complete until about midnight, instead of 1800 hrs. as had been hoped.

H.M.S. Bachaquero.
22. Difficulty and delay experienced in finding a suitable beach for *Bachaquero* was a severe set back to the progress of landing vehicles. She had been loaded with 19 Field Battery of 9 Field Regiment (17 Infantry Brigade Group) on a reduced scale of transport and with carriers and load carrying vehicles, a total of 54 vehicles and guns. It was hoped to beach her sometime about 0900 hrs. in the vicinity of Blue beach, or at least on some beach whence exit could be made to the main axis of advance. Unfortunately a reef off Blue beach prevented her approach; her movements were seriously hampered by the numerous mines; and a suitable beach for her could not be found in the Ambararata Bay area. She was therefore ordered, in the afternoon, to beach in Courrier Bay.

She made several attempts and in one of them two quads and two guns were manhandled ashore and up a most difficult beach by men of the 19 Field Battery working up to their necks in the water. Finally just before dark, she was brought in on the rising tide at full speed and reached a depth of water in which she could discharge her vehicles rapidly. This was not the end of the disappointments. In spite of vigorous reconnaissance, no practical route could be found the Courrier Bay area to the main axis of advance. The battery was therefore ordered into action on the Andrakaka Peninsula, but carriers of 2 Royal Scots Fusiliers and some of the 15 cwts. eventually during D2 found a way through and rejoined their units on the main axis.

Disembarkation of 17 Infantry Brigade.
23. The personnel of 17 Infantry Brigade Group in *S.S. Oronsay* and *Duchess of Atholl* arrived in the anchorage shortly before 1100 hours and, as the situation then seemed to be going remarkably well, were ordered to land in accordance with the pre-arranged provisional landing table. This commenced at 1115 hours although vehicles did not start until midnight.

2 Royal Scots Fusiliers, the first battalion to land, took over the beach area, and also found one detached company for the Red beach area, thus freeing the last of the 29 Independent Brigade and 5 Commando from the beaches. This battalion was followed by working parties for the beach areas provided from the first reinforcements of 17 Infantry Brigade.

It was agreed with S.N.O.L. that landing should stop between dark and moonlight (1800 hours to 2230 hours), to prevent damage to landing craft and to rest their crews and the docks operating company. The landing of the remainder of 17 Infantry Brigade then continued and companies commenced the march forward as they got ashore and formed up.

Landing and Assumption of Control by Force Commander.
24. I had embarked in *H.M.S. Ramillies* for the passage to Diego Suarez, expecting to be sent by destroyer to *H M.S. Keren*, in which ship were S.N.O.L. and the

majority of my H.Q., by about 0900 hours on D1, when it was expected that the first troops of 17 Infantry Brigade would land. In view of the delay in disembarkation, I decided to remain with the Combined Commander until 1230 hours. Unfortunately, by this time, the sea had risen and made transfer to a destroyer impossible until a lee had been found. The result was that I did not arrive in the *Keren* until 1530 hours. Rear Admiral Syfret was always prepared to put me ashore at any time, and the lateness of my arrival in the *Keren* was entirely my own fault. I failed to appreciate the time lag required for:-

(*a*) Movement of the *Ramillies* to calm water.

(*b*) Transfer to a destroyer in a sea boat.

(*c*) The destroyer trip to the *Keren*.

Once there I examined available information; landed, reaching Blue beach 1700 hours; and started in a carrier for H.Q. 29 Independent Brigade. The carrier however broke down and, although I later boarded another vehicle, with the A.D.M.S., I failed to reach 29 Independent Brigade H.Q. in the dark. The G.S.O.I, however, got through on a motor cycle and returned with a first class situation report. On receipt of this I returned to the Beach Signal Station. There I met Brigadier Tarleton and instructed him to get his brigade as it landed, forward along the road so that he would be able to assist 29 Independent Brigade as early as possible on D2. I finally returned to the *Keren* where I was able to get good signal communication to the *Ramillies* and the aircraft carriers and hoped to get some communication to 29 Independent Brigade. I arranged to land at first light on D2. At this time and indeed throughout the operation, we were suffering for the heavy cuts which had been made in H.Q. and signals to increase the number of fighting troops and vehicles.

ATTACK ON THE MAIN ENEMY POSITION – MORNING OF 6TH MAY – D2

25. The main enemy position faced South across the narrowest portion of the isthmus of Antsirane and is based on two old but solid and well-concealed forts: Fort Caimans on the West, and Fort Bellevue on the East. These are joined by a continuous line of trenches about 2,000 yards long which cover the flat top of the isthmus. On each flank there are steep scrub covered slopes down to mangrove swamps which border the sea. Three roads run through the isthmus. The most Westerly one leading to Ambararata, and the central one, leading to the South, run between the two forts and are covered by concrete pill boxes with 75mm. guns where the roads cross the trench position. The third road leads around French Bay to Ankorika, and passes through the broken ground to the East of Bellevue fort. Although it avoids the main line, it is covered by a few detached defence works. In front of the trench line runs an uncompleted anti-tank ditch. The trench line is well sited and is covered from direct observation at distances greater than about 300 yards by minor irregular features. However, the pill boxes have sufficient height to enable them to fire down the roads for some 1,000 yards;

and the command given by the forts enables one 75 mm. sited on top of each fort with 360 degrees traverse to cover by direct fire the area in front of the line to about the same range. The isthmus is flat with slight undulations. It is fairly open although there are a number of spaced out bushes and trees, and a considerable amount of thin scrub and maize plantations. About 1,200 yards behind the defence line is the native village, through which all the roads lead, and beyond that, 2,000 yards from the defence line, are the outskirts of Antsirane

26. Brigadier Festing met his battalion commanders at Brigade HQ at 2300 hours. He issued orders for an attack on the enemy defence line by three battalions. On the right 2 South Lancashire Regiment were to move out at 0200 hours through the mangroves and broken country along the shore to get behind the enemy line, I Royal Scots Fusiliers in the centre and 2 East Lancashire Regiment on the left were to attack frontally at 0530 hours. 455 Light Battery was to support this attack with the six guns which were now available; and the Fleet Air Arm were asked to bomb and machine gun the enemy defences between 0500 hours and 0530 hours, almost an impossible task in the bad light.

2 South Lancashire Regiment moved off in an Easterly direction at 0200 hours. On reaching the Eastern edge of the isthmus, they advanced North through the broken ground and mangroves. Progress was extremely slow and difficult, but aided by the darkness, and later by the defilade given by the edge of the isthmus, two companies and Battalion HQ penetrated the enemy line, killed or captured detachments watching this flank, and occupied Anobozaka Barracks which is on this side of the isthmus about 1,200 yards behind (North) of Bellevue fort. Thence they attacked Westwards harassing or capturing enemy artillery, machine gun and mortar positions, capturing or stampeding the pack horses and mules of the enemy artillery and occupying positions, whence they could ambush and fire on vehicles moving up to the front line on all roads. They took many prisoners and eventually got detachments into position about 200 yards behind the enemy trenches. Only man-pack wireless sets could accompany the assaulting infantry and these, after a long night cross-country march over very difficult ground were ineffective, and Liaison Officers from Brigade were unable to get further forward than the two rear companies of the Battalion which were held up short of Fort Bellevue. Similarly messengers and parties escorting prisoners to the rear from advanced Battalion HQ and the leading company found themselves unable to get back. Brigade HQ therefore did not know of this success in time to exploit it and in fact thought that the leading half of this battalion had become casualties or prisoners. The action of this battalion, however, resulted in heavy casualties to the enemy and in the capture of nearly four hundred prisoners, the majority of whom were eventually got back to our lines. In addition to this, the effect of this penetration on the morale of the enemy command and troops was later found to have been great. It was not until 1400 hours that Brigadier Festing learned of the true position on this flank from Lieutenant-Colonel M.M. Alston-Roberts-West commanding 2 South Lancashire Regiment, who, with a small escort, had at last

been able to make his way back through the enemy lines. In the course of this affair Lieutenant-Colonel West got over 35 enemy to his own gun.

Meanwhile the frontal attack by I Royal Scots Fusiliers and 2 East Lancashire Regiment had been held up after casualties in men and carriers. The leading troops of these battalions got very close to the enemy trenches and continued in action there for the rest of the day, although cut off by fire from their company and battalion commanders, and they were assumed to be casualties.

Shortly after daylight, the enemy opened fire with 75s and mortars on all troops in the exposed plateau area. Casualties began to mount up and 455 Light Battery was forced to withdraw from its position by shell and mortar fire. About this time there was a slight withdrawal of our leading troops to avoid continuation of casualties.

27. I arrived at Brigade HQ about 0700 hrs. It was quite clear that the attack had failed. It was an unhappy moment. The whole of 29 Independent Brigade was deployed or being deployed, and with the disappearance of many of the leading troops in the dawn attack, assumed to be casualties, units were considerably under strength. A good deal of most irritating enemy sniping and unarmed rifle fire was going on. To this was added shelling from 75s which was a good deal more terrifying than effective. The shelling set fire to the bush, which caused further embarrassment, but the troops, under the personal leadership of the Brigadier and the unit commanders, re-occupied their original positions after the fire had passed. These fierce and rapidly spreading bush fires caused no serious casualties, but resulted in considerable confusion and loss of equipment. Very little artillery had as yet come into action owing to trouble with *Bachaquero*; and what there was in action, had great difficulty in obtaining observation. There were only five serviceable tanks left, the majority of which were Tetrarchs.

With over 18 miles to the beaches by a sandy track, with indifferent bridges, and few passing places, it was most desirable that the force should be in Antsirane by D3. The personnel of 17 Infantry Brigade had completed landing but were still marching up the road. Provided they could stick the heat, dust, and sniping, the majority of the infantry, say two and a half battalions, could reach the forward area about 1800 hours, while the landing of 13 Infantry Brigade Group had just commenced at daybreak. Adequate tank and artillery support were not available for a daylight attack. The enemy position was about 1200 yards away and reconnaissance of the intervening ground was very difficult owing to the bush, the lie of the ground, and the enemy sniping. However it was fairly well confirmed that there was no wire.

I therefore decided that a silent night advance and assault by 17 Infantry Brigade assisted as necessary by 29 Independent Brigade, should be made during the period of darkness between sunset and the rising of the almost full moon at 2300 hours. I ordered Zero for 2000 hrs. (it had later to be postponed to 2030 hrs.) and arranged for the maximum harassing fire from artillery and the air during the remainder of the day. I issued orders for the attack to Brigadiers

Tarleton and Festing and then left to see the Combined Commander. I wished to try to arrange for a destroyer to force the entrance of the harbour and land a party of Royal Marines in the dock area, thus making a direct assault on the town from the rear. This, even if the destroyer was lost, would draw the enemy's fire, create a diversion, and give the main night attack the best possible chance of success. In addition an officer was sent to No. 5 Commando asking them to collect any small boats available at Diego Suarez North and co-operate in this assault. (This was found to be impossible.) As the *Ramillies* was then anchored with the convoy to refuel, I had to leave at once to catch her and the detailed planning was continued by the two Brigadiers.

28. During the day, 19 Field Battery from the *Bachaquero* came into action on the Andrakaka Peninsula and shelled the enemy position from the rear; it was however handicapped by difficulty in knowing where our troops were in the open scrub on the plateau. This Battery had previously been fired upon by a French Sloop, *D'Entrecasteaux*, and had returned the fire until, with the assistance of the Royal Navy and the Fleet Air Arm, who also claim her, she caught fire and sank. 28/76 Field Battery (9 Field Regiment, 17 Infantry Brigade Group) was landed from the *Mahout* on Blue beach and came into action in the forward area at 1400 hrs. giving harassing fire until dark. During the remaining daylight hours of D2, enemy shelling and sniping continued, but air attacks, which were made at frequent intervals by fighter aircraft going off patrol, and our increasing artillery strength gradually diminished enemy activity.

Meanwhile 29 Independent Brigade reorganised and cleared their area which had become infested with snipers. However, owing to the large number of men still isolated close to the enemy positions, their companies remained very weak. 17 Infantry Brigade was moving up the main axis to the forward area. 2 Northamptons which had been ordered overnight to secure the rear of 29 Independent Brigade from an attack along the road from the South, and had captured about 200 prisoners coming in from this direction, was also moved across for the night attack. Late in the afternoon 2 Royal Scots Fusiliers, who had been released from beach defence on the arrival of the leading battalion of 13 Infantry Brigade, and 6 Seaforths who were the last battalion to land, arrived in the area after their 18 mile march. Carriers including signals had been used to lift some of them, but in these battalions few men could have had more than an hour for rest and reorganisation before moving for the start line.

NIGHT ATTACK BY 17 INFANTRY BRIGADE 6 May – D2
29. It became dark at 1800 hours and the moon rose at 2310 hrs. Owing to the late arrival of many of the troops in the area and owing to the difficulties in observation, very little effective reconnaissance had been possible. 17 Infantry Brigade formed up on a start line formed by a track just over the crest and about 1,200–1,400 yards from the enemy trenches. 2 Northamptons were on the right

of the Westernmost road and 6 Seaforths on the left with one company 2 Royal Welsh Fusiliers under their command, as they were still under strength.

In order to coincide with the destroyer's attack, I had had to postpone Zero until 2030 hrs., this information only reached the forward area at about 1900 hrs., but was passed down to the troops in time. At Zero, the two leading battalions went forward astride the road on a front of about 600 yards passing between the two forts. This was a sheer piece of good luck. The positions of the forts were not known, although they were built when Marshal Joffre was Governor of Diego Suarez in 1910. The leading infantry in the dark by-passed the strong points within 200 yards without being aware of their existence. There was a considerable amount of firing but the advance continued steadily although casualties occurred in the trench system and at the pill boxes. These battalions reached their objectives, which were the far side of the Native village 3,000 yards from their start line and about 1,800 yards beyond the main enemy position, at 2300 hrs. and fired their success signals. Brigadier Tarleton then ordered forward his reserve battalions; 2 Royal Scots Fusiliers and 2 Royal Welsh Fusiliers, the latter having been placed under his command for the attack. These two battalions pushed right through to the main town of Antsirane with little or no opposition and reached the main harbour. Brigadier Festing now pushed forward 29 Independent Brigade and the remaining tanks to assist in mopping up the town. He entered the Residency at 0100 hrs. and assisted by Brigadier M.S. Lush, Chief Political Officer, at once commenced to take over the town.

Assault by H.M.S. Anthony and R.M. Detachment from H.M.S. Ramillies.
30. Rear Admiral Syfret had agreed to the direct assault by a destroyer with 50 Royal Marines from the *Ramillies*. Orders reached this detachment at about 1430 hrs. and three-quarters of an hour later they embarked in *H.M.S. Anthony* which then proceeded at high speed around the Cap D'Embre to reach the entrance to the harbour in time for Zero. Sometime about 2000 hrs. *H.M.S Anthony* came under fire from the batteries guarding the entrance of the harbour which she returned with all weapons. By Zero she was alongside the quay and the Royal Marines disembarked under fire from the town, and dockyard. Good luck also attended this venture. Expecting to meet the Commandos, she mistook a blue flashing light for their recognition signal, but saw the error just in time and went alongside stern first. A French 75 mm. manned by a Capitaine Clavel failed to register a hit, a fact that this officer still disbelieves. The dockyard was still burning and it was difficult to do much more to create a diversion there. The detachment therefore advanced into the town, occupied the Artillery HQ and started some fires in the area. Leaving a guard at Artillery HQ, it continued to advance and arrived at the Naval barracks where it was fired upon. After some grenades had been thrown, a large number of prisoners headed by the Commandant of the barracks surrendered and British prisoners found in these barracks were released. The detachment was now fully occupied dealing with the very

numerous prisoners until contact was made with the British troops, 2 Royal Welsh Fusiliers, who had entered the town from the South.

This attack added greatly to the ease with which the final occupation was carried out and assisted in the avoidance of street fighting, in which casualties might have piled up and the town been severely damaged.

COMPLETION OF THE OPERATION – 7TH MAY – D3

31. I entered Antsirane shortly after daylight and took over from Brigadier Festing. All resistance had ceased in the town, but the two forts were still holding out and firing at traffic on the roads between them. My next urgent problem was to capture the Orangea or Ankorika Peninsula, which was still preventing the Navy from entering the harbour. I had originally intended that 29 Independent Brigade should continue with this task when 17 Infantry Brigade had captured the town. As, however, 29 Independent Brigade were fully occupied in the town, I decided that the 17 Infantry Brigade Group should do it. I therefore sent orders to Brigade HQ, which was now just South of the native village, to commence the advance to Orangea as soon as possible, and placed the remaining tanks under its command. Brigadier Tarleton reported that the head of his column could pass Bellevue fort at 1200 hours. I therefore arranged for a preliminary Naval and Air bombardment of enemy positions on the peninsula to take place between 1000 and 1200 hours; and for Naval supporting fire to be controlled by Forward Observation Officers for the advance of the brigade into the peninsula. This advance was also to be assisted by all available air support.

Meanwhile Lieutenant-Colonel H.C. Stockwell commanding 2 Royal Welsh Fusiliers, and Lieutenant-Colonel B.H. Hanaut, had made contact with French officers, who conducted them to the garrison commanders in the Orangea peninsula, with a view to negotiating a surrender. As soon as I heard of this, I asked for the bombardment to be countermanded, but a few rounds were fired before the message got through. It was a tense moment. The Royal Navy and the Fleet Air Arm were straining at the leash to give all they had got to Orangea peninsula, and with the opening of the bombardment by the *Ramillies* I fully expected everybody on both sides to join in.

Fortunately the cease fire signal got through quickly and negotiations continued. At the same time negotiations for the surrender of Caimans fort were opened by the French with the troops in contact with it.

From marked maps which were now in my hands, I was able to see that the French had prepared positions facing South and protecting the Orangea peninsula from land attack. Before reaching these, 17 Infantry Brigade Group, had first to capture Fort Bellevue, and then to overcome an enemy post at Anbatolamba, where the road around French Bay passes through a very narrow bottleneck. The total distance to be marched to Orangea Point was about 12 miles by a very bad road. I was most anxious to arrange a surrender of the garrison of this peninsula, as I foresaw that an operation to capture it might last for several days (and probably entail at least 300 casualties) especially in view of the limited support which was available and the difficulties of supply with limited transport from the now distant Blue beach.

In order to avoid recurrence of fighting while negotiations were in progress, I ordered 17 Infantry Brigade not to advance past fort Bellevue. 13 Infantry Brigade however was moved up from Blue beach, sending a detachment to take over the airport, and the remainder of the brigade concentrating East of Anamakia. By about 1400 hours the surrender of Bellevue and Ambatolambo had been arranged; 17 Infantry Brigade therefore advanced to a position about 2 miles South of the enemy defences in the Orangea Peninsula. It paid honours of war to the garrison of Bellevue and Ambatolambo as they passed. By the evening, I had been able to make arrangements for the final advance to Orangea to take place at 0700 hours the next day, May 8th. *H.M.S. Ramillies* entered harbour just before dark and I went on board to discuss arrangements for final surrender. Arrangements were made for a meeting with the three senior French officers, Colonel Claerebout (Officer Commanding Defences, Diego Suarez), Capitaine de Vaisseau Maerten (Naval Officer in Charge, Madagascar), Capitaine de Vaisseau Simon (ex Commanding Officer of French sloop *D'Entrecasteaux)* all now prisoners of war, on board the flagship at 0915 hours 8th May. This was to be followed by a conference on shore about 1015 hours with certain other French officials.

It was not easy. Claerebout and Maerten had only surrendered in person, and the Garrison Commander with whom the armistice was arranged was Colonel Rouves. Therefore the terms that I had arranged with Colonel Rouves affected only the troops that were still fighting and not those who had already surrendered.

On 8th May I attended a meeting on board the flagship to hear the Combined Commander outline the conditions of surrender. A subsequent meeting took place at the Residency at 1100 hours presided over by:-

Rear-Admiral E.N. Syfret, and attended by
 Major-General R.G. Sturges, R.M. (Military Commander)
 Brigadier F.W. Festing (Assault Commander)
 Brigadier M.S. Lush (Chief Political Officer)
 Captain J.M. Howson, R.N. (C.O.S. to Commander-in-Chief)
 Colonel Melville (O.C., S.A.A.F.)
 Colonel Claerebout (French Officer Commanding Defence Diego Suarez)
 Capitaine de Vaisseau Maerten (N.O.I.C. Madagascar)
 Colonel Rouves (Commanding Infantry Regiment)
 M. Bourgine (Administrateur-Maire of Diego Suarez).
The final terms of surrender were arranged at this conference.

Consolidation

32. On the 8th May I issued orders for immediate consolidation. 17 Infantry Brigade Group were to hold the Orangea Peninsula; 13 Infantry Brigade Group to reconnoitre and man a position facing South on the high ground about 3 miles South of the airport; 29 Independent Brigade to hold the immediate defences of

and control the town of Antsirane. Detached companies were left at Red and Blue beaches, and arrangements were made for anti-aircraft artillery personnel to take over important coast defence batteries with improvised detachments. On the same day I attended Rear-Admiral Syfret's conference with the French Commanders at which the final terms of surrender were arranged.

GENERAL

Casualties

33. Total casualties were:-

	Killed	Died of Wounds	Wounded	Missing
Officers	13	2	22	–
Other Ranks	64	26	262	4
	77	28	284	4

34. In assessing this operation, it must first be observed that it was conducted against opposition whose air power was weak and who was completely lacking in armour for a counter-attack. The French white and Senegalese troops fought with determination and, although their armament and equipment were below first-class standards, they undoubtedly hoped to repeat the story of Dakar. When after 48 hours, it was clear that this was not to be, they remembered that the true cause of their country lay with the United Nations and did not continue a struggle which had become senseless as well as hopeless. Making due allowance for these facts, there is much of interest in this, the first of many probable amphibious assaults which remained to be carried out during the war.

The forces employed, naval, military, and merchant navy, were largely composed of units which had trained together in Scotland for a considerable time. If this had not been so, it would have been quite impossible to embark operationally at such short notice and to operate with such an extremely low scale of motor transport. The employment of the 13th and 17th Infantry Brigades, which had been embarked non-operationally before the operation was mounted, was an interesting expedient, only made possible by the adaptability of the troops concerned, by embarkation at the last moment of a small cadre of officers trained and experienced in this type of work, and by the great assistance given at Durban by the South African Government in limited restowing of Transports.

The number of landing craft available was small, as it was limited to what could be earned in the ships of the assault brigade. The effect of this in limiting the initial assault, was not important under the circumstances of this operation, but its effect in slowing up further landing was a most serious factor, both in planning and in the event. The build-up in vehicles on the first day was slow, yet it was a great improvement on what had been achieved in previous exercises and represented a very fine achievement by all those concerned.

The assault brigade advanced inland without delay, as soon as it had secured the beaches. This was a departure from usual practice and was most effective. The sudden arrival of the 29th Independent Brigade at the neck of Antsirane Peninsula, seized the initiative from the French and effectively prevented any properly co-ordinated defence. At the same time, it gained us 18 miles of road, which, given a few more hours delay, could and would have been stubbornly and effectively defended.

Finally, the use of a difficult, and therefore unexpected, line of approach, although in itself a risk, gained a degree of surprise which was largely responsible for the success of the operation. The ready acceptance of the approach by the Royal Navy and their skill in overcoming its difficulties and dangers, won the admiration and gratitude of all those responsible for the military part of the operation.

> I have the honour to be, Sir,
> Your obedient Servant,
> (Signed) R.G. STURGES,
> *Major-General,*
> *Commanding* 121 *Force.*

Notes
1. A/S = anti-submarine.
2. M/S = minesweeping.
3. R D F = radar.
4. A L C = Assault Landing Craft.
5. KEREN was the Headquarters Ship of the Senior Naval Officer Landing, Captain G.A. Garnons-Williams.
6. BACHAQUERO was an early type of tank landing ship, not constructed but converted for this purpose.
7. The estimate of 25 per cent. casualties in 29 Independent Brigade Group was caused by the complete disappearance behind the lines of about two and a half companies of the 2nd Battalion South Lancashire Regiment. Actually they were doing stout work, killing and taking large numbers of prisoners.
8. F.O.O. = Forward Observation Officer.
9. V/S = visual signal.
10. It ultimately transpired that the complete eviction of the defenders of Windsor Castle was not accomplished until the morning of D.2.
11. B.L.O. = Bombardment Liaison Officer
12. N.C.S.O. = Naval Control Service Officer.
13. Wind force 8 – fresh gale, 34–40 knots.
14. M.N.B.D.O. – Mobile Naval Base Defence Organisation.

Index

(1) Index of Persons

(2) Naval, Military and Air Units